CW00554603

Environmental Law

To My Children

Environmental Law in Scotland

An Introduction and Guide

Francis McManus

EDINBURGH
University Press

Edinburgh University Press is one of the leading university presses in the UK. We publish academic books and journals in our selected subject areas across the humanities and social sciences, combining cutting-edge scholarship with high editorial and production values to produce academic works of lasting importance. For more information visit our website: www.edinburghuniversitypress.com

© Francis McManus, 2016

Edinburgh University Press Ltd
The Tun – Holyrood Road
12 (2f) Jackson's Entry
Edinburgh EH8 8PJ

Typeset in 11/13pt Monotype Baskerville by
Servis Filmsetting Ltd, Stockport, Cheshire,
and printed and bound in Great Britain by
CPI Group (UK) Ltd, Croydon CR0 4YY

A CIP record for this book is available from the British Library

ISBN 978 0 7486 6897 7 (hardback)
ISBN 978 0 7486 6898 4 (paperback)
ISBN 978 0 7486 6899 1 (webready PDF)
ISBN 978 0 7486 6900 4 (epub)

The right of Francis McManus to be identified as author of
this work has been asserted in accordance with the Copyright,
Designs and Patents Act 1988 and the Copyright and Related
Rights Regulations 2003 (SI No. 2498).

Contents

Foreword
by the Right Honourable Lord Gill

For twenty-seven years Professor McManus, in his teaching and in his writings, has advanced the study of environmental law. During that time the subject has grown in importance and complexity. The national and international legislation by which the United Kingdom is bound has set higher environmental standards and more effective means of enforcing them than ever before. Nevertheless deficiencies remain and the need to deal with them is increasingly urgent.

Professor McManus's work gives us a conspectus of the common law and the statutory law by which our society tries to protect present and future generations against the destruction of the earth. It has the particular merit of setting the development of each aspect of the law in its historical context.

This will be an invaluable guide for practitioners and academics and for those in central and local government and in the planning and environmental professions who deal with problems of pollution and waste management in their everyday work. I have read the manuscript of this work with great pleasure and profit. I congratulate Professor McManus on having produced a valuable and timely contribution to Scottish legal literature. I hope that it will become a standard work of reference.

Brian Gill
August 2015

Acknowledgements

I would like to commence by thanking Edinburgh University Press for kindly accommodating me by extending the deadline for the submission of the completed manuscript of this book which has taken much longer than I originally anticipated. I would also like to thank the staff of the following; the National Library of Scotland; the Library of the Institute of Advanced Legal Studies London; the Wellcome Institute for the History of Medicine, London; the British Library, London; the University of Edinburgh Law Library; Edinburgh Napier University Library; the University of Strathclyde Library; and the University of Stirling Library for their help. I must also acknowledge, with no little gratitude, the financial assistance which was provided by the Carnegie Trust.

I would also like to thank the following who kindly agreed to read and comment on certain draft chapters of the work, namely: Emma Bain, Sarah Hendry; Jim Kerr, Gavin Little, Ann McManus, Andrew Taylor and Colin Reid. However, all errors, omissions and other shortcomings in the work rest firmly and solely with the author.

Finally, I would like to thank the Lord President for agreeing to write the foreword to the book.

The law is considered correct as of 20 May 2015. However, it has been possible to take account of some developments since that date at proof stage.

Francis McManus
Livingston
May 2015

Table of Cases

Table of Statutes

Table of Statutory Instruments

Table of European Legislation

CHAPTER 1

Historical Introduction

The history of environmental law stretches much further back than the Victorian era. However, it was during that august period in British history that the modern law, which is discussed in this book, owes its origins. The law really develops in the wake of the Industrial Revolution which propelled those who formerly were employed in the country to seek work in factories which were situated in towns. This caused the rapid expansion of industrial towns. However, there was insufficient housing stock to accommodate the incoming population. The perfunctory response to the problem was that landlords, many of whom were also employers, either subdivided existing housing stock or constructed jerry-built houses to house the labouring classes. The living conditions endured by the occupants of the houses were generally insanitary and on a par with those that exist in the poorest developing countries of the present day. Indeed, it was not uncommon for more than one family to share a poorly lit and ventilated room in a house that also lacked water and a water closet. The pressure exerted on the housing stock was exacerbated by the influx of Irish migrants during the 1840s.[1]

In the absence of the effective regulation of the development of land (town and country planning), the negative impact of the rapid expansion of industrial towns also resulted in factories being constructed in close proximity to houses, the occupants of which would often had to endure a relentless onslaught of smoke and malodorous fumes. Smoke pollution was a perennial problem for urban Britain.[2] However, industry was not the sole culprit of atmospheric pollution. Smoke from domestic chimneys was also a significant problem. As far as the regulation of smoke pollution was concerned, prosecution against those who flouted the law was only used as a last resort. Often local authorities refrained from taking formal proceedings lest such action would offend powerful manufacturers upon whom the prosperity of towns such as Glasgow[3] and Leith[4] depended. Indeed, Briggs has argued that when Victorian legislation was passed which tampered with the rights of private property, it was always contentious and difficult to implement.[5] Another reason commonly advanced for such a 'hands-off' approach on the part of local authorities is that elected members of local authorities were reluctant to prosecute the occupiers of factories which caused pollution because the elected members would often themselves be the owners of the factories.[6] The problem of smoke in urban Britain, coupled with the unwillingness on the part of local authorities to take remedial action, prompted members of the public to set up smoke suppression societies. By 1843 smoke suppression societies had been set up in Manchester and Leeds.[7]

Pollution from chemical works was a notorious source of atmospheric pollution. The commercial manufacture of alkali (sodium carbonate), while of great economic benefit to the country, posed a threat to the general environment in that the by-products of the process, in the form of hydrogen sulphide and hydrogen chloride, were not only malodorous, but had a destructive effect on the environment which surrounded the works.[8]

The Alkali Works Regulation Act 1863 represented a rather bold attempt to deal with this problem. However, the Act was confined to the regulation of alkali works, which were the largest chemical industry. Importantly, the Act allowed central government to appoint an inspectorate to regulate such works in order to avoid a potential conflict of interest on the part of local authorities. Another reason why Parliament decided to entrust the task of the regulation of alkali works to an independent inspectorate was that local authority sanitary inspectors (who had a lowly status in the minds of both the public and the manufacturers) did not possess the technical expertise to provide effective regulation for such works. The Act was a success and was amended in due course to allow other chemical processes to be regulated. The number of works and processes that were regulated expanded rapidly. In 1864, eighty-four alkali works were registered.

The rapid expansion of towns inevitably placed an unbearable strain on public utilities such as water supply and drainage. As far as water supply is concerned, water companies, water trusts or municipal authorities responsible for the public water supply were inclined to provide only enough water in order to meet the immediate needs of their area. Such a myopic approach to the supply of municipal water was commonly referred to as the 'droplet' method of water supply, the upshot of which was a general shortage of water.[9] Edinburgh provides a good example of such a parsimonious approach to water supply. In effect, the Edinburgh Water Company systematically and gradually moved westward across the Pentland Hills and appropriated springs there to serve the immediate needs of the population of Edinburgh and District.[10]

Furthermore, until well into the nineteenth century, the supply of municipal water tended to be intermittent. The shortage of water bore more heavily on the poor who often were required to queue at public wells for their water. The middle-classes tended to fare better, in that their houses were often equipped with cisterns which could store water during the times when the mains supply was cut off. The fact that the water supply was intermittent also rendered the supply more prone to contamination since the water pressure in the mains makes it more difficult for pollutants to enter the mains. The lack of a constant effective water supply had other unfortunate consequences. In 1841 a fire in Leith could not be extinguished because of lack of water in the mains.[11] However, it should be emphasised that a defective water supply was not confined to urban Scotland. As late as the final years of the nineteenth century, as far as Scotland as a whole was concerned, the supply of water was often defective. The Local Government Board for Scotland, which was the precursor of the Scottish Office, reported in 1897 that water supply in many districts was extremely defective. Indeed, Elgin was prosecuted for failing to supply wholesome water in its area.[12]

One of the outstanding, if not defining, features of Victorian Britain was the state of our rivers. The most infamous example of the sorry state of our watercourses during that era is the River Thames which, by the mid-nineteenth century was nothing more than an open sewer. *The Times* of 18 June 1858 referred to the stench which emanated from the Thames as the 'great London nuisance'. The newspaper went on to inform its readers that elected Members and Lords who occupied portions of the Palace of Westminster over looking the Thames had been driven into the library in order to seek refuge from the smell, only to retreat from there, handkerchiefs to faces.[13] Wohl describes rivers in the UK during this period as 'filthy and smelly as the dirtiest industrial towns'.[14]

Whilst industrial effluent played no small part in contributing to the UK's river pollution problem, municipal authorities were also culpable. As towns grew and sewerage networks developed, WCs were replacing the notorious cesspits and middens. Whilst the benefits of such a transition were obvious, the upshot of this was that more effluent would be produced. The most convenient method of disposing of the effluent was simply to conduct it via public sewers to the nearest watercourse and allow it to flow either downstream or downtide. Indeed, Rosenthal argues that for any members of any sanitary authority, eager not to expend their funds and so tax themselves unnecessarily, was to opt for this cheap and convenient method of sewage disposal.[15] However, inherent in such an approach was the likelihood that proprietors through whose land the polluted river flowed would raise an action in nuisance against the relevant municipal authority.[16]

As far as Scotland was concerned, the major watercourses which flowed through the towns were often nothing more than open sewers. *The Scotsman* of 24 June 1861 gives a graphic account of the state of the Water of Leith. Indeed, some claimed that the Water of Leith, which was really a trickle compared with the River Thames, was much more polluted than the latter.[17] The state of the rivers only improved with the construction of intercepting sewers which would receive effluent from the drains and conduct the effluent to the sea. The problem of river pollution was not confined to towns. Rural or landward areas also suffered the consequences of the Industrial Revolution. The mining industry, shale works and paper mills were notorious polluters of streams in rural Scotland.[18] Amongst the filthiest were the Almond, Esk and Gala.[19]

The Parliamentary response to the woeful state of our rivers was to pass the Rivers Pollution Prevention Act in 1876. For almost eighty years this Act remained the principal statute regulating water pollution. Referring generally to the UK, Clapp expresses the view that within a few years the Act was condemned as a failure.[20] In turn, as far as Scotland was concerned, the Act remained a 'non-starter' for twenty years.[21]

Victorian society was afflicted by a variety of diseases such as typhus, typhoid, smallpox, scarlet fever, dysentery and measles which were all endemic and occurred cyclically. Influenza was also a major killer. Pandemics occurred frequently during the nineteenth century. However, it was cholera that was the most feared disease during the nineteenth century. It afflicted all ranks of society, and it visited the United Kingdom in waves. The main outbreaks occurred during 1831-1833, 1847-1849, 1853-1854 and 1865-1866. The disease had a mortality rate of around 50 per cent.[22] We know now that cholera is carried from person to person via the faecal-oral route.[23] However, well into the nineteenth century, it was believed that smell, or miasms, especially odours that emanated from organic material and decomposing human corpses,[24] spread cholera. Those who adhered to this theory were known as miasmatists. There were variations of the theory. For example, there was the so-called 'local miasmatic theory', to the effect that certain individuals were predisposed to succumb to cholera. This explained, in the view of some, why although many people breathed the air that contained miasma, only some became sick.[25] Most miasmatists believed that the cause of cholera lay dormant in heaps of refuse, rotting vegetation and waste matter, and marshy low-lying and stagnant water until liberated by some unknown activating element in the atmosphere, such as temperature, barometric pressure, wind, lightning or thunderstorms.[26]

The opposing theory to the miasmatic theory of transmission of disease was the contagion theory. However, it should be mentioned parenthetically that some argued that the miasmatic theory and the contagion theory were not mutually exclusive, but, rather, complemented each other.[27] The supporters of the contagion theory adhered to the view that disease, including cholera, was passed from person to person by physical contact. The contagion theory was rather old by around 1800.[28] However, until germs were discovered by Pasteur and Lister there was no theoretical foundation to support the contagionists' beliefs. The contagion theory simply did not work. Although the miasmatic theory was not without its critics, the miasmatists were in a majority. Foremost amongst them was Edwin Chadwick.[29] However, while Chadwick's contribution to sanitary reform was outstanding, some commentators have argued that, perhaps, too much prominence has been given to the view that the whole impetus for sanitary reform came from a small group of Londoners filled with zeal for the sanitary idea.[30] Any legislation that had as its purpose to strike at cholera, *per force*, was required to eradicate its cause. Therefore, the government passed a series of statutes[31] that armed local authorities with the power to remove nuisances in their area. The first environmental revolution had begun.

The miasmatic theory of the transmission of disease continued to play a role, albeit in a more muted form, after the germ theory of transmission of disease had become firmly established. For example, the Public Health (Scotland) Act 1867[32] and the Public Health (Scotland) Act 1897[33] employed the concept of nuisance as a remedial device.[34] The theory may have been a myth. However, it established an important link between human health and the external environment.

Whilst the miasmatic theory did have a profound effect in shaping legislation, its influence on the development of the common law appears to have been far less pronounced. Indeed, the author has failed to find any reference to the theory in any judicial decision concerning private nuisance (especially cases that concerned the emanation of odours etc. from the defender's premises) either north or south of the Border.

Local government

While a discussion of the development of local government is outwith the scope of this work,[35] no account of the historical development of environmental law in Scotland would be complete without providing a brief overview of the structure of local government. This is because the enforcement of environmental law was largely in the hands of local authorities during the Victorian period.

Whereas the system of local government in Scotland at present is not utterly different from that in England and Wales, writing in 1904, Atkinson laconically remarked that English ignorance of what went on beyond the Border was proverbial and foreigners appear to have had no conception that Scotland had still its own laws and its own method of administration.[36]

The first major reform of the nineteenth century as far as burghal government was concerned was the reform of the royal burghs in Scotland, which were openly acknowledged for many years to be both corrupt and inefficient. The royal burghs had become self-perpetuating and self-interested. Indeed, they were models of inefficiency and corruption.[37] So inefficient were the burghs that many functions, such as policing, were carried out by police commissions, which had been set up by private Act of Parliament.[38] In sharp contrast to royal burghs, which were self-electing, police commissions were elected. The Burgh Reform (Scotland) Act 1833[39] applied, in the main, only to royal burghs. However, the Parliamentary Burghs (Scotland) Act 1833[40] extended these reforms to a few large towns that were not royal burghs. Thirteen towns, including Leith, Paisley and Falkirk, were specifically named and given the constitution of a royal burgh. Later, the Police of Towns (Scotland) Act 1850[41] also allowed places with a population of more than 1,200 to set up police burghs. The powers of such burghs did not differ markedly from those of royal burghs.

In 1845 Parochial Boards were established under the Poor Law (Scotland) Act 1845. Whereas their *raison d'être* was to administer poor relief, with the passage of time parochial boards were given other functions to discharge. For example, parochial boards were given power under the Nuisance Removal Act 1848 to remove nuisances during cholera outbreaks. Such a power came to an end with the passage of the Nuisance Removal Act 1856. Similarly, when the Vaccinating (Scotland) Act 1863 was passed, parochial boards were made responsible for enforcing the provisions of the Act.

Brief mention should be made, at this juncture, of the existence of *ad hoc* bodies such as water trusts and improvement trusts. These, although quite separate from the local authority which exercised statutory powers over the same area as the trusts, normally largely comprised members who were drawn from the local authority.[42]

The next major development in local government administration came with the passing of the Local Government (Scotland) Act 1889. The entire powers of the various commissioners of supply which had been set up in 1667 in order to collect cess (which was a national land tax)[43] but whose powers had been extended over the years by statute, were transferred to the new county councils, as were the powers and duties of the county road trusts, the responsibility of enforcing the provisions of the Public Health (Scotland) Act 1867[44] in parishes in the counties, the powers and duties of local authorities which related to contagious diseases under the Contagious Diseases (Animals) Acts of 1878 and 1884 and the Destructive Insects Act 1877. Atkinson observes that the general aim of the 1889 Act was to establish municipal government in the counties and to do away with the old class system of administration.[45] Each council was required to divide its area into suitable districts, each managed by its own committee. Indeed, the real powerhouses of the newly established county councils were the district committees which had the power to set up special districts, for example, in respect of drainage and water supply for which a local tax could be levied. The district committee structure of the new elected county councils provided an efficient administrative structure by means of which the provisions of the Public Health (Scotland) Act 1897[46] could be effectively administered. In effect, Scotland's rapid improvement in public health owes a great deal to both the 1889 and 1897 Acts. Indeed, the significance of these statutes cannot be overestimated. It was really only after the passing of the latter Act, which imposed mandatory as opposed to permissive powers on local authorities, that public health took off in Scotland and began to catch up with England. The latter had greatly benefited from the passing of the Public Health Act 1875 which remained the cornerstone of public health law until the passing of the Public Health Act 1936.

The Local Government (Scotland) Act 1889 established thirty-three county councils (which were democratically elected by ratepayers, including women) which were given extensive powers. In the towns and cities most of the powers were given to the burgh councils.[47] McFadden observes that nevertheless, the structure of local government was far from satisfactory.[48] In 1900 there were thirty-three councils, 200 burgh councils, 860 parish councils, more than 1000 school boards and numerous other bodies such as burgh police commissioners, county road boards, and county district committees. However, the structure of local government in Scotland remained unsatisfactory and wholesale reform was required. Such reform came about with the passing of the Local Government (Scotland) Act 1929.

Conclusions

By way of conclusion, by the end of the nineteenth century, the foundations of modern environmental law had been firmly laid. There were no major changes in environmental law until after the Second World War.

However, things would change in the wake of the London Smog disaster of 1952 which constituted a watershed in the development of environmental law in the UK and would bring about the second environmental revolution in the UK.

The remainder of the book discusses how the law has developed from its Victorian roots.

Notes

1. For example, the census enumerator's notes on the 1861 Census indicate that ten Irish people occupied a house that comprised one room. The house was situated at 33 Cables Wynd in Leith. In another house in Laurie's Close, nine Irish people occupied a one-room house.
2. For a general account of smoke pollution and its effects on Victorian towns, see A. Wohl, *Endangered Lives* (Dent Publishing, 1983) ch. 8.
3. See S. Blackden, 'The Development of Public Health Administration in Glasgow 1842-1872', unpublished University of Edinburgh PhD thesis (1976) at 287.
4. The *Leith Pilot*, 15 January 1870, in referring to the Leith Police Commission being willing to drop smoke prosecutions, condoned such an approach on the grounds that, 'We must look towards the prosperity of the town.'
5. A. Briggs, *Victorian Cities* (Odhams Press, 1964) at 21.
6. For example, Councillor Lundy who sat on the Leith Police Commission and owned a factory in Leith which belched out smoke, claimed at a meeting of the Commissioners that smoke was not injurious to health: *Leith Pilot*, 10 February 1866.
7. H. Sandwith, 'Defective arrangement in large towns', *British and Foreign Medical Review* 1943 at 22.
8. R. Burnett-Hall and B. Jones (gen. eds), *Burnett-Hall on Environmental Law*, 3rd edn (Sweet and Maxwell, 2012) at 1.044.
9. In 1842 the Commission on the Sanitary Condition of the Labouring Population of Scotland reported that Dundee, Stirling, Dunfermline, Lanark and Arbroath were all imperfectly supplied with water; PP XXVII (1842) at 62.
10. See, generally, J. MacRae, 'The present water supply – suggestions for its more perfect distribution' (n. p., 1870).
11. Leith Police Commission Minutes, 12 April 1841.
12. PP 1897 XXXVII at 706. See also T. Ferguson, *Scottish Social Welfare* (Livingstone, 1958) at 182.
13. For an interesting discussion of the state of the Thames and the sterling work of the great Victorian engineer, Sir Joseph Bazalgette who designed a system

of intercepting sewers, pumping stations and treatment works which serve London to this day, see S. Halliday, *The Great Stink of London* (Sutton Publishing, 1999).

14. A. Wohl (note 2) at 233.

15. L. Rosenthal, *The River Pollution Dilemma in Victorian England* (Ashgate, 2014) at 24.

16. Rosenthal (note 16)) discusses nuisance actions which were brought by landed proprietors against various municipal authorities in England. The work focuses on how the authorities reacted in the face of injunctions that were made against them.

17. S. Macadam, 'On the contamination of the Water of Leith by the sewage of Edinburgh and Leith', *Transactions of the Proceedings of the National Association for the Promotion of Social Science* (1864) at 575. The Medical Officer for the Health of Edinburgh, described the Water of Leith as a 'great open sewer': Report on the Sanitary Condition of Edinburgh (1865) at 86.

18. For a useful discussion of the major sources of water pollution during the nineteenth century, see S. Macadam, 'Pollution of streams', in *Transactions of the Proceedings of the National Association for the Promotion of Social Science* (1880) at 565.

19. A. Wohl (note 2) at 237.

20. B. Clapp, *An Environmental History of Britain* (Longman, 1994) at 83.

21. T. Ferguson, *Scottish Social Welfare* (Livingstone, 1958) at 199.

22. P. Vinten-Johanson, *Cholera, Chloroform and the Science of Medicine: A Life of John Snow* (Oxford University Press, 2003) at 169.

23. Koch did pioneering work in this field. In 1848 he published his discovery of the cholera vibrio and its transmission by drinking water, food and clothing. See M. Warren, *A Chronology of State Medicine, Public Health and Related Services in Britain 1066-1999* (2000) at '1884' entry.

24. Dr Henry Littlejohn attributed the outbreak of cholera in certain parts of Edinburgh to the overcrowded graveyards in central Edinburgh; Report on the Sanitary Condition of the City of Edinburgh (1865) at 93-9 incl. For an interesting account of the contribution of Littlejohn to Edinburgh's public health during the Victorian era, see P. Laxton and R. Rodger, *Insanitary City* (Carnegie, 2013).

25. See P. Vinten-Johanson (note 23) at 174.

26. N. Longmate, *King Cholera* (Hamish Hamilton, 1996) at 67.

27. W. Bynum, 'Cullen and the study of fevers in Britain', in W. Bynum and V. Nutton (eds), *Theories of Fever from Antiquity to the Enlightenment* (Wellcome Institute, 1981) 135 at 142.

28. E. Ackerknecht, 'Anticontagionism between 1821 and 1864' (1948) 22 *Journal of the History of Medicine* 562 at 564.

29. S. Halliday (note 14) at 127.

30. See B. Keith-Lucas, 'Some influences affecting the development of sanitary legislation in England' (1953-1954) 6 *Economic History Review* 290 at 290.

31. Namely, the Public Health Act 1848 (which did not apply to Scotland) and the Nuisance Removal Acts 1846, 1848, 1849 and 1856.

32. Repealed.

33. Repealed.

34. See also s 57 of the Local Government (Scotland) Act 1889 (repealed) and s 316 of the Burgh Police (Scotland) Act 1892 (repealed) which empowered local authorities to make bylaws for the suppression of nuisances. See, generally, R. Malcolm and J. Pointing, 'Statutory nuisance: the sanitary paradigm and judicial conservatism' (2006) 18 JEL 37.

35. See M. Atkinson, *Local Government in Scotland* (Blackwood and Sons, 1904); M. McLarty (ed.), *A Sourcebook and History of Administrative Law in Scotland* (Hodge, 1956) and J. Bennet-Miller, *An Outline of Administrative Law in Scotland* (W. Green, 1964).

36. M. Atkinson (note 36) at 2.

37. SME 'Local Government' (Re-issue) para 27, quoting G. Pryde, 'Burghal Administration', in M. McLarty (note 36) at 9.

38. For example, the Edinburgh Police Commission was established in 1805 (45 Geo. III Cap. xxi) and the Leith Police Commission was established in 1828 (7 & 8 Geo IV Cap. Cxii).

39. 3 & 4 Wm IV c 76.

40. 3 & 4 Wm IV c 77.

41. 13 & 14 Vict. c 33.

42. The Edinburgh Improvement Trust was established in 1867 in order to demolish insanitary housing in the Old Town and, in the process, widen the streets in order to, 'breath life' into the Capital. Again, in 1869, the Edinburgh and District and Water Trust assumed the responsibility for supplying water in, and around, Edinburgh. Formerly, during 1819-1869, municipal water supply was under the *aegis* of the unpopular Edinburgh Water company.

43. See A. Whetstone, *Scottish County Government in the Eighteenth and Nineteenth Centuries* (John Donald, 1981).

44. Repealed.

45. M. Atkinson (note 36) at 88.

46. Repealed.

47. J. McFadden, *Local Government in Scotland* (Tottel, 2008) at 4.

48. Ibid.

CHAPTER 2

Nuisance

> The law of nuisance concerns itself with resolving the conflicting interests in the use of land. The law of nuisance protects the occupier of land from unreasonable interference which is taking place outwith the land that is affected. Whether any given state of affairs ranks as a nuisance in law is a question of fact and degree. In order to ascertain whether the adverse state which the pursuer complains of ranks as unreasonable and, therefore, a nuisance in law, the courts take a variety of factors into account. As far as the law of Scotland is concerned, the pursuer requires to prove *culpa* (or fault) on the part of the defender. Also discussed in this chapter are the defences which are available in an action in nuisance.

Introduction

The law recognises that the occupier of land has the right (for example, by virtue of being the owner, tenant or subtenant of the land) to enjoy the occupation of that land. However, such a right to use one's land as one pleases is circumscribed by the law imposing an obligation on the occupier of the land not to use it in such a manner as to unreasonably interfere with the enjoyment of my neighbour's occupation of land.[1] In 1933 Burn-Murdoch observed that the law of nuisance was a modern development and was not recognised as such by the institutional writers.[2] In essence, the law of nuisance is concerned with the law of neighbourhood.[3] However, the expression, 'nuisance' is a rather amorphous concept. Indeed, it is fiendishly difficult to define.[4] According to Smith, a nuisance comprises an operation on the part of the defender which, taking into account the natural rights of his neighbours, is unreasonable or extraordinary on account being unnatural, dangerous or offensive; and such operation must have caused material injury.[5] Walker, in turn, taking a more general approach, regards nuisance as a general term which is employed rather loosely, to cover any use of property which causes trouble or annoyance to a person's neighbours.[6] According to Glegg, 'any act which renders the enjoyment of life and property in the neighbourhood, "uncomfortable" or subjects the neighbourhood to material discomfort and annoyance is a nuisance at common law'.[7] In the author's view, these attempts at defining the expression 'nuisance' do nothing more than poignantly underline the fact that 'nuisance' simply defies attempts at definition. Indeed, these definitions really provide little assistance in law in determining whether any state of affairs does rank as a nuisance in law. The difficulty which academics have encountered in defining the expression 'nuisance' is paralleled by the pronounced reticence of the judiciary to define the term. As far as the law of Scotland is concerned, the most frequently cited case on the law of nuisance is the Outer House case of *Watt v Jamieson*[8] where Lord President Cooper, in effect, attempted to define the expression 'nuisance'. The facts of the case were, indeed, simple. The pursuer, who was proprietor of the upper floors in a flatted residence, brought an action in nuisance against the owner of the lower floors. The pursuer claimed that the effluvium from a gas water heater on the lower floors, which discharged into a flue situated on the mutual gable of the building, had caused damage to his property. By way of a defence, the defender contended that the acts which were complained of involved only a normal, natural and familiar use of a dwelling house. However, Lord President Cooper, sitting in the Outer House, refused to accept such a defence. His Lordship stated:

> The balance in all such cases has to be held between the freedom of a proprietor to use his property as he pleases and the duty on a proprietor not inflict material loss or inconvenience on adjoining proprietors on adjoining property and in every case the answer depends on considerations of fact and degree . . . The critical question is whether what he is exposed to was *plus quam tolerabile* when due weight has been given to all the surrounding circumstances of the offensive conduct and its effects. If that is satisfied, I do not consider that our law accepts as a defence that the nature of the user complained of was usual, familiar and normal. Any type of use which in the sense indicated above subjects adjoining proprietors to substantial annoyance, or causes material damage to their property is *prima facie* not a reasonable use.

The Lord President went on to state[9] that in deciding whether a nuisance existed, the proper angle of approach was from the standpoint of the victim as opposed to that of the alleged offender.[10] Some authors have, therefore, argued that there is some doubt as to whether an activity is *plus quam tolerabile* (and, thus, a nuisance) involves a balancing of the respective interests of that of the pursuer and that of the defender.[11] However, in the view of the author this represents a misunderstanding of *Watt v Jamieson*. That is to say, that simply because the law requires one to assess the relevant state of affairs from the standpoint of the victim does not automatically rule out one disregarding the nature of the conduct of the defender. Indeed, the Lord President, in *Watt*, stated that in determining whether the relevant adverse state of affairs is a nuisance: 'The critical question is whether what he was exposed to was *plus quam tolerabile when due weight has been given to all the surrounding circumstances of the offensive conduct and its effects*' (emphasis supplied).

Watt, therefore, underlines the point that in determining whether any adverse state of affairs ranks as a nuisance in law, one requires to assess, at the very outset, the nature and quality of the impact which the relevant state of affairs has on the pursuer (that is, whether the adverse state of affairs manifests itself in terms of physical damage or discomfort to the occupier as would be the case in relation to both noise and smell nuisances). In so doing, one is really addressing the question as to whether the purpose of the law of nuisance is to protect the occupier of the relevant land from external interference. For example, is the function of the law of nuisance to protect the pursuer from interference to television signals by a tall building,[12] or to protect the pursuer and his family from the visual impact of observing prostitutes and their clients entering and leaving a house of ill-repute?[13]

However, one must also take into account the nature of the conduct of the defender in order to ascertain if the adverse state of affairs constitutes a nuisance in law. Indeed, if one did not take into account the nature of the conduct of the defender many activities such as traffic noise and even neighbourhood noise would automatically rank as a nuisance in law. In the last analysis, the concept of *plus quam tolerabile* in the law of nuisance derives its colour from the nature of the conduct of the defender.[14]

Watt also emphasises the fact that whether any given state of affairs ranks as a nuisance is a question of fact and degree.[15]

Unreasonable conduct

It requires to be stressed at this juncture that it is only unreasonable conduct which is capable of being categorised as a nuisance in law.[16] A good illustration of the application of this principle is the House of Lords case of *Baxter v Camden London Borough Council*.[17] In that case the appellants were local authority tenants who occupied flats which had been constructed or adapted for multiple occupation. Unfortunately, the flats were inadequately soundproofed, the result of which was that the tenants could hear literally everything their neighbours were doing. The tenants, therefore, brought proceedings in nuisance against their landlords. The House of

Lords held, however, that the noise in question did not rank as a nuisance in law since the noise emanated from the everyday and normal use of the flats.

Many activities which are capable of causing a nuisance are now regulated by statute. This would include activities which generate noise as well as odours. The simple question which, therefore, falls to be answered is whether the fact that the activity in question complies with the relevant regulatory regime such activity does not rank as unreasonable, and therefore, not a nuisance in law. The Court of Appeal was required to answer this very question in *Barr v Biffa Waste*.[18] The facts of the case could not have been more simple or straightforward. The defendant waste company operated a landfill site which accommodated pre-treated waste. The claimants, who lived in the vicinity of the site, had been affected by odours which emanated from the site for a period of five years. The claimants brought an action in nuisance against the defendant. By way of a defence, the defendant claimed that, first, if in fact the smell from the site did rank as a nuisance, it could avail itself of the defence of statutory authority, and, secondly, by virtue of the fact that the defendant complied with both the terms of its permit which had been issued by the Environment Agency pursuant to the Pollution Prevention and Control (England and Wales) Regulations 2000 and also with the licensing conditions which were attached to the defendant's licence under the Environmental Protection Act 1990, the use of the land whence the nuisance arose was reasonable and, therefore, did not rank as a nuisance in law. At first instance, it was held that by virtue of the fact that the defendant had complied with the terms of its permit and also its licence, the defendant was making reasonable use of its land and, therefore, such use could not rank as a nuisance in law. The claimants appealed successfully. In essence, the Court of Appeal held that the claimants had inalienable common law rights which were not affected by the relevant environmental and landfill legislation, including the terms of its permit. The test which fell to be applied in determining whether an adverse state of affairs ranked as a nuisance was whether a person would find the state of affairs in question unreasonable to have to put up with.

What factors are taken into account?

Now we consider the various factors which the courts take into account when considering whether an adverse state of affairs ranks as a nuisance in law. At the very outset, however, it should be stressed that the various factors discussed below are not mechanically applied by the court to the relevant facts in every nuisance case. Rather, the courts have tended to emphasise several factors, often to the exclusion of others. For example, in *Fleming v Hislop*[19] the court simply focused on the intensity of the smell which emanated from the offending accumulation of mineral refuse which was situated on the defender's premises. It is, therefore, difficult to predict in advance which factors will determine the outcome of a particular case. Furthermore, judges have refrained from constructing a hierarchy of the various factors which fall to be considered, in terms of their relative importance. There is also little academic discussion on this important point. It should also be emphasised that the factors which are discussed below are probably not exhaustive. Whereas the law of nuisance is slow-moving in comparison with other areas of the law of delict (for example, the law of negligence), with judges showing little creativity, judges have not completely closed their minds to taking new factors into account. For example, in *Hunter v Canary Wharf Ltd*[20] where the House of Lords was required to decide whether a tall building which interfered with the reception of television signals ranked as a nuisance, Lord Cooke stated *obiter*:

> [the] lineaments of the law of nuisance were established before the age of television and radio, motor transport and aviation, town planning, a 'crowded island' and a heightened public consciousness of the need to protect the environment. All these are now among the factors falling to be taken into account in the evolving law.

Social utility
The social utility (or usefulness) of the activity that causes the adverse state of affairs which is the subject-matter of the action (for example, odours or noise) is taken into account. In essence, the more socially useful the activity is, the less likely it is that the court would be willing to castigate the nuisance which is complained of as a nuisance in law. The courts have quite readily recognised the social or public utility of factories.[21] However, as far as other forms of activity are concerned, the courts have been less willing to take into account social utility when determining whether a nuisance exists.[22] A somewhat revolutionary approach to the concept of social utility in terms of the law of nuisance was taken by Buckley J in *Dennis v MoD*.[23] In that case, the claimants owned and lived on a large estate which was situated in close proximity to RAF Wittering, home to the Harrier jet. The Harrier jet is a noisy aircraft; indeed, there is no louder jet. The witnesses who gave evidence to the court described the noise from the aircraft as sometimes 'intolerable'. The claimants brought an action in nuisance against the MoD. At first instance, Buckley J had no hesitation in deciding that the noise in question constituted a nuisance in law.[24] However, it was also beyond dispute that the flying of military aircraft in the manner

which was the subject-matter of the action redounded to the benefit of the public.[25] In simple terms, Britain needs its airforce, including aircraft which inevitably cause a great deal of flight noise. However, to weigh this factor in the judicial scales when determining whether the noise in question amounted to a nuisance would, in the view of Buckley J, have deprived the claimants of a judicial remedy under the common law.[26] In His Lordship's view, the growing *corpus* of human rights law dictated that the appropriate remedy under the law of nuisance should be that of damages, as opposed to an injunction or a declaration.[27] This view as to the relationship between human rights law and the private law of nuisance is, to say the least, somewhat revolutionary. His Lordship seemed to be expressing the view that where any activity has a manifest and palpable public benefit, this factor should automatically be excluded from the factors which normally fall to be taken into account when determining whether a nuisance exists, since this approach would automatically deprive the claimant of a remedy in law. Rather, in such a case, the public utility factor should be employed in order to select the appropriate remedy in law. However, in the author's view, the approach which was taken by Buckley J in *Dennis* does not represent the law of Scotland. In the Outer House case of *King v Advocate General for Scotland*[28] Lord Pentland regarded the approach which was taken by Buckley J in *Dennis* as one where his Lordship had recognised, in effect, a public utility defence in the law of nuisance – that is to say, a complete defence in the law of nuisance. However, Lord Pentland refrained from expressing a view as to whether Dennis represented the law of Scotland.[29]

Motive of the defender

If the relevant state of affairs is caused simply in order to punish or annoy the pursuer – that is to say that the defender has acted out of spite – the courts lean heavily towards the view that the state of affairs in question ranks as a nuisance in law. The leading case is *Christie v Davey*.[30] In that case the plaintiff's family were musically inclined and frequently practised their instruments at home. This annoyed the defendant, who retaliated by banging trays on the party wall which separated his house from that of the plaintiff. It was held that the noise generated by the defendant amounted to a nuisance in law. Another example of the relevance of malice in the law of nuisance is seen in *Hollywood Silver Fox Farm v Emmett*.[31] In that case the plaintiff bred foxes on his land. The defendant, who was about to develop land which adjoined that of the plaintiff, objected to the presence of the foxes on the grounds that he feared this would deter people from purchasing houses on the estate. The defendant, therefore, caused guns to be fired

on the boundary which separated his premises from that of the plaintiff.
As a result of this, vixen on the farm devoured their young. It was held that
the defendant's conduct amounted to a nuisance in law.[32]

Locality

In determining whether a given state of affairs ranks as a nuisance in
law the courts take into account the nature of the relevant locality.[33]
Essentially, the more typical of the relevant area is the adverse state of
affairs complained of, the less likely that such a state of affairs will rank as
a nuisance. Such an approach by the courts is based on the rationale that
if the state of affairs is typical of a given locality, a reasonable person who
resides there is less prone to being annoyed by the adverse state of affairs
by reason of having become habituated, at least to some extent, to the state
of affairs in question. The leading case on the application of the locality
factor in terms of the law of nuisance is *Bamford v Turnley*[34] where Pollock
CB stated: 'That may be a nuisance in Grosvenor Square, which would be
none in Smithfield Market.'

Again, in *Inglis v Shotts Iron Co*[35] (which concerned whether fumes from
the defender's iron works ranked as a nuisance) the Lord Justice-Clerk
stated: 'Things which are forbidden in a crowded urban community may
be permitted in the country. What is prohibited in enclosed land may be
tolerated in the open'. Another case which illustrates the same point is
Swinton v Pedie[36] where it was claimed by the pursuer that the erection of a
slaughterhouse in the vicinity of the Edinburgh Academy would constitute
a nuisance in law. Lord Gillies stated:

> and although Pall Mall or Grosvenor Square be equally open for the driv-
> ing of cattle, as the roads in the vicinity to Smithfield Market, it is very
> evident that the establishment of a great slaughterhouse, however it may
> be arranged internally, would be a nuisance in either of the former of these
> places, though not in the last.[37]

Whereas the courts are less inclined to castigate as a nuisance a state of
affairs which is indigenous in the area, the courts are not prepared to
accord the defender *carte blanche* to create a nuisance. This point is well
illustrated in *Rushmer v Polsue and Alfieri Ltd.*[38] In that case the plaintiff
resided in an area which was devoted to printing and allied trades. The
defendants set up machinery which caused serious disturbance to the
plaintiff and his family during night-time hours. At first instance, the court
granted an injunction to restrain the defendants from causing a nuisance.
The House of Lords, on appeal, upheld the injunction. Lord Loreburn
LC[39] stated:

A dweller in towns cannot expect to have as pure air, as free from smoke, smell, and noise as if he lived in the country, and distant from other dwellings, and yet an excess of smoke, smell and noise may give a cause of action, but in each of such cases it becomes a question of degree, and the question is in each case whether it amounts to a nuisance which will give a right of action. This is a question of fact.[40]

However, the nature of the relevant locality is only important if the state of affairs which is complained of affects the personal comfort. That is to say, if sensible (that is, physical damage) is caused by the adverse state of affairs in question, the nature of the locality is redundant. The leading case on this point is *St Helens Smelting v Tipping*.[41] In that case, vapours from the defendant's copper-smelting works, which was situated in a heavily industrialised area, damaged the trees on the plaintiff's estate. However, the House of Lords held that it was immaterial to take into account the fact that the plaintiff's property was situated in an industrial area.

Locality and the effect of planning law
A somewhat controversial area concerning the law of nuisance is the extent, if any, to which planning permission has an effect on the character of the relevant land. A good example of this would be: if a planning authority were to grant planning permission for the development of an industrial estate on land which was formerly agricultural land, and the planning permission was implemented by the construction of several factories, would the nature of the locality now be deemed industrial as opposed to agricultural in nature? An example of such a situation arose in *Gillingham Borough Council v Medway (Chatham) Dock Co Ltd*.[42] In that case a dock company obtained planning permission to operate the former naval dock in Chatham as a commercial port. However, once the port was in operation, the plaintiff received complaints of noise emanating from the port. At first instance, Buckley J[43] held that in determining whether the noise amounted to a nuisance, one had to ascertain the character of the neighbourhood by reference to the present character of the land in terms of the planning permission for use of the dockyard as a commercial port. In his Lordship's view, whereas the grant of planning permission could not authorise a nuisance, a planning authority could, through its development plans and decisions, change the character of a neighbourhood.[44] However, in *Wheeler v Saunders Ltd*[45] planning permission had been granted to allow the intensification of pig farming on a site which was already used for that purpose by the defendants. The smell from the farm began to annoy neighbouring landowners who raised an action in nuisance. It was claimed by the defendants, by way of a defence, that the planning permission

which had been given had the effect of sanctioning the alleged nuisance. However, this proposition was rejected by the Court of Appeal. In short, the court held that the grant of planning permission could not, in the eye of the law, sanction the creation of a nuisance. However, Staughton LJ stated *obiter* that it was possible for a planning authority, by giving planning permission, to change the character of land in terms of the law of nuisance. Again, in the Court of Appeal case of *Watson v Croft Prom-Sport*,[46] the defendants operated a motor-racing circuit on land which had once been an aerodrome. The claimants instituted proceedings against the defendants, alleging that the use of the circuit by the defendants caused excessive noise and, therefore, constituted a nuisance in law. The defendants claimed, however, that while the noise from the circuit might cause some discomfort and inconvenience to the claimants, there was no actionable nuisance because the defendants' use of the circuit was reasonable, having regard to both the nature and character arising from the grant of planning permission. Whereas the court reaffirmed the law to the effect that planning permission cannot sanction a nuisance, the court was prepared to accept the proposition that, 'the implementation of planning permission may alter both the nature and also the character of the locality as to shift the standard of reasonable user which governs the question of nuisance or not'.[47] However, the court doubted whether there was some middle category of planning permission which, without implementation, would be capable of affecting private rights unless such effect was specifically authorised by Parliament.[48]

The most recent case concerning the effect of planning permission on the law of nuisance is the Court of Appeal case of *Coventry v Lawrence*.[49] The facts of the case were simple. Planning permission was granted in 1979 to construct a sports complex and stadium. At first, speedway racing took place. Later banger and stock-car racing were introduced. Planning permission was subsequently granted for other motor-related sports. The claimants, who lived in close proximity to the stadium, became affected by the noise from the stadium. They raised an action against the organisers of the motor sports amongst others. At first instance, it was held that the noise which emanated from the stadium constituted a nuisance in law. On appeal, the Court of Appeal held that both the grant of planning permission, coupled with the implementation of that permission, had the effect of changing the character of the area in terms of the law of nuisance. For the court, the key question was the effect of implementing the planning permission. The trial judge had been wrong in deciding that the character of the land had not been changed by the grant and subsequent implementation of planning permission. The court held that by dint of the motor sports having taken place over the past thirteen years, these noisy activities, whilst regarded by some as recreation and by others as an unwelcome disturbance, were an established feature of the locality.[50] Such noise could not be ignored when considering whether the matters which were complained of ranked as a nuisance in law. In conclusion, the noise in question did not rank as a nuisance. The claimants appealed.

The Supreme Court held[51] that it was possible for the owner of land to acquire, by prescription, an easement (that is, a legal right to allow one to carry out an activity over another parcel of land) to emit noise, provided that the noise had been emitted for twenty years, albeit not continuously. However, it would be open to the defendant to claim that the complaint could only have arisen because of some post-acquisition use of that property by the claimant. The court also held that, in determining whether an activity caused a nuisance by noise, the court had to assess the level of noise which, objectively, a normal person would find it reasonable to put up with, given the established pattern of uses, or character, of the locality in which the activity concerned was carried out. For that purpose, the defendant could rely on his own activity on his land, in so far as it could be shown that such activity was a lawful part (that is to say, it did not rank as a nuisance in law) of the established pattern of uses of the area. In this respect, any implementation of planning permission for the defendant's activity could be relevant to an evaluation of the established pattern of uses in the locality. Similarly, the terms and conditions of planning permission could be taken into account in order to evaluate the acceptability of the complained-of noise. However, the defendant could not rely on a planning permission which permitted the very noise which was alleged to constitute a nuisance as making that noise an established part of the locality. Furthermore, planning permission was not a major determinant of liability, notwithstanding the fact that the grant related to a major development.

The decision of the Supreme Court certainly means that a planning permission and a relevant development plan are not to be accorded as much status, in English law, as was formerly the case in private nuisance actions. However, to what extent planning decisions are relevant in a private nuisance action, unfortunately, remains uncertain. Lord Neuberger's stating[52] that planning permission is of some relevance on occasions is, with respect, confusing, to say the least. Unfortunately, Lord Carnwath did not clarify matters by stating that planning permission could be of relevance in a nuisance action in certain cases if a set of planning conditions struck a balance between competing uses of land.[53]

By way of conclusion, in *Lawrence*, the Supreme Court had a splendid opportunity to clarify the law as to whether planning permission which has been granted by the planning authority can change the character of land in terms of the law of nuisance. Unfortunately, the opportunity was missed, and the relevance of planning permission in a private nuisance action remains a notoriously grey area of law.

Duration and intensity

Both the length of time over which a state of affairs exists and its intensity are taken into account when the court is deciding if a state of affairs ranks as a nuisance. In the leading case of *Bamford v Turnley*[54] Pollock CB stated:

> A clock striking the hour, or a bell ringing for some domestic purpose, may be a nuisance if unreasonably loud and discordant, of which the jury alone must judge; but although not unreasonably loud, if the owner from some whim or caprice made the clock strike the hour every 10 minutes, or the bell ring continually, I think that a jury would be justified in considering it to be a very great nuisance.

As far as noise is concerned, the nature of the noise is a relevant factor in the court deciding whether the noise ranks as a nuisance. That is to say, the more pleasant-sounding the noise is, the less likely it will rank as a nuisance.[55]

Time of day

The time of day the relevant adverse state of affairs exists may be a relevant factor. However, this factor is only relevant in relation to noise pollution and probably light pollution. The courts are more inclined to regard night noise as a nuisance than noise which takes place during the day.[56]

Sensitivity of the pursuer

It is a general rule in law that the courts are disinclined to award a remedy to the oversensitive. This general principle finds expression in the law of nuisance. The leading case which illustrates this principle as far as sensitivity of the person is concerned is *Heath v Brighton Corporation*.[57] In that case a priest complained about the noise and vibrations which emanated from the defendant's premises. However, the plaintiff was denied a remedy by way of the law of nuisance, since it was proved that the only reason why he was discomfited was because he possessed hypersensitive hearing.

The rule that the law will not provide any help to the oversensitive also applies in relation to the enjoyment and use of the property on one's land. For example, in *Armistead v Bowerman*[58] the defender was involved in moving timber. The timber was dragged across a stream, as a consequence of which the bed of the stream became disturbed. The silt flowed downstream and destroyed ova in the salmon hatchery which was owned by the pursuer. It was held that no liability lay in nuisance since the pursuer's use of the stream was, in the eye of the law, too sensitive to attract the protection of the law. Again, in *Bridlington Relay Ltd v Yorkshire Electricity Board*[59] the plaintiff company carried on a business of providing a relay system of sound and television broadcasts. The plaintiff erected a mast on its own land for that purpose. The defendant electricity board commenced to erect an overhead power line, situating two pylons within 250 yards of the mast. On a *quia timet* action for an injunction by the claimant, Buckley J held, *inter alia*, that since the business of the claimant required an exceptional degree of immunity from interference, an action in nuisance failed.[60] More recently, in the House of Lords case of *Hunter v Canary Wharf Ltd*[61] it was held that the interference with the reception of television signals by the mere presence of a tall building did not constitute a nuisance in law. However, the House did not rule out the possibility that the interference with reception of television signals could never constitute a nuisance in law. Indeed, *Hunter* serves as a good example of the difficulty which the courts have experienced in clearly defining the forms of external interference from which an occupier of land can be protected by the law of nuisance.

The above cases were reviewed by the Court of Appeal in *Network Rail Infrastructure Ltd (formerly Railtrack) v CJ Morris*.[62] In that case it was claimed that Railtrack's signalling system had caused electromagnetic interference to the electric guitars which were being played in the claimant's recording studios, which were situated some 80 metres away. The court held[63] that amplified guitars fell into the category of extraordinary sensitive equipment, which did not attract the protection of the law of nuisance.

Social utility of thing interfered with

We have already observed that in deciding whether an adverse state of affairs ranks as a nuisance in law the court takes into account the social utility of the adverse state of affairs.[64] However, to what extent, if any, does the court take into account the social utility of the activity taking place on the land which is being adversely affected by the conduct of the defender? There is little authority on this point. The relevant case law has concerned television reception. In *Bridlington Relay Ltd v Yorkshire Electricity Board*[65] which concerned liability for interference with television signals, Buckley J took into account the fact that, in the main, since television simply served a recreational function in society, television should be accorded a lowly status when deciding if the interference with television signals ranked as a nuisance. However, in the House of Lords case of *Hunter v Canary Wharf Ltd*,[66] concerning the potential liability in nuisance of the owners of a tall building which interfered with the reception of television signals, Lord Goff[67] expressed the view that, given the fact that the function of television transcended the function of mere entertainment, interference with such an amenity might indeed, in appropriate circumstances, warrant the protection of the law of nuisance.

Could the adverse state of affairs have been avoided by the pursuer?
In deciding whether any adverse state of affairs is capable of ranking as a nuisance, can the court take into account the fact that the pursuer has failed to adopt any measures which would have prevented the nuisance in question? For example, if I were to raise an action in nuisance against the occupiers of a factory, on the grounds that excessive light from the premises penetrated my bedroom curtains and prevented me sleeping at night, could the court take into account the fact that the adverse state of affairs about which I complain could have been avoided if I had used thicker curtains? The general rule is that the courts are unwilling to take into account the fact that the pursuer has failed to implement measures which would have either prevented or mitigated the effects of the adverse state of affairs in question. This point is neatly illustrated in the Outer House case of *Webster v Lord Advocate*.[68] The pursuer, who lived in the vicinity of the Edinburgh Castle esplanade, raised an action alleging that both the noise from the performance of the Edinburgh Military Tattoo and the erection of scaffolding to accommodate seating on the Castle esplanade amounted to a nuisance. The Lord Ordinary rejected the contention that the pursuer would be unable to succeed if it could be shown that the provision of double-glazing to the windows of her flat would have reduced the ingress of noise to an acceptable level.[69]

Is the state of affairs typical of modern life?
Is the fact that the state of affairs complained of is typical of society in general (as opposed to typical of a particular locality) of any relevance in determining if the state of affairs ranks as a nuisance? For example, in relation to an action concerning noise from a wind turbine, could it be argued that wind turbines are now typical of modern life in certain parts of Scotland? The leading case on this point is now *Hunter v Canary Wharf Ltd*,[70] referred to above. In that case, the House of Lords held that the presence of a very tall building which interfered with the reception of television signals did not constitute an actionable nuisance. However, in the Court of Appeal, the Court, in deciding that it was not a nuisance, took into account that tall and bulky buildings had become a feature of the urban landscape.[71] However, Pill LJ seemed to suggest that this factor might not be relevant if

the given state of affairs constituted an activity as opposed to a static state of affairs.

Whilst there is no Scottish authority on the relevance of the adverse state of affairs being typical of modern life, in the author's view, such a factor should be taken into account since the law of nuisance requires to be responsive to circumstances which have become accepted by society as being a feature of the modern world. Such an approach allows the law of nuisance to be both dynamic and responsive to the needs of society. Whether the adverse state of affairs in question is typical of modern life also facilitates a fairer balance to be struck between competing and conflicting uses of land, a concept which, of course, underpins the law of nuisance.

Requirement of culpa

Whereas in English law liability in nuisance is strict,[72] in Scots law the pursuer is required to prove *culpa* or fault on the part of the defender in order to succeed in a nuisance claim. The leading case on this point is *RHM Bakeries Ltd v Strathclyde Regional Council*.[73] In that case bakery premises, which belonged to the pursuer, were flooded as a result of the collapse of a sewer which was vested (that is, under the control of) in the defender local authority. The pursuer sued the local authority on the ground, *inter alia*, of nuisance. It was held by the House of Lords that in order to succeed it was necessary for the pursuer to prove *culpa* on the part of the defender. Unfortunately however, the House refrained from discussing both the nature and scope of the concept of *culpa* as it relates to the law of nuisance.

However, the Inner House of the Court of Session had the opportunity to do so in *Kennedy v Glenbelle Ltd*.[74] The facts of the case were both simple and straightforward. The pursuers were the heritable proprietors of tenement properties in Glasgow. The first defenders, who were the tenants of a basement flat, engaged the second defenders, a firm of consulting engineers, to advise on, design, direct and also supervise a scheme for the removal of a section or sections of wall within the premises. The pursuers raised an action against the defenders, claiming that, as a result of the work carried out in the basement, the pursuer's property had subsided. The basis of the action was that the carrying-out of the renovation works in such a way that the pursuer's property was damaged amounted to a nuisance in law as well as negligence. As far as the action in nuisance was concerned, the Inner House held that it was sufficient to prove that, in this case, a deliberate act had been done in the knowledge that damage would result from it. Lord Hope was of the view that *culpa* could be established by demonstrating negligence on the part of the defender, in which case the

ordinary principles of negligence would apply, or *culpa* could be demonstrated by the fact that the defender was at fault in some other respect.[75] As
far as the latter form of liability was concerned, *culpa* could take the form of
malice on the part of the defender, or it could comprise a deliberate act on
the part of the defender on the basis that the defender knew that his action
would result in harm to the pursuer or derive from the consequences of his
act. Here Lord Hope identified a subspecies of recklessness, that is to say, a
situation in which the defender has indulged in conduct which gives rise to
a special risk of abnormal damage. In such a case, fault would be inferred.
However, as far as liability was concerned, the fact that the defenders knew
the deliberate removal of a section of the basement wall would result in
damage to the pursuer's premises was sufficient to constitute the requisite
culpa to ground liability in nuisance.[76]

However, Lord Kirkwood adopted a more 'broad-brush' approach to
the concept of *culpa*. His Lordship endorsed the view of Lord Gifford in
Chalmers v Dickson[77] to the effect that *culpa* is a flexible term and, therefore,
much lighter fault may make a person liable in some circumstances than in
others.[78] Lord Kirkwood concluded by stating that before liability in damages for nuisance can be established, there must be proof of a deliberate
act of negligence or some other conduct from which *culpa* can be inferred.

The concept of *culpa* relating to the law of nuisance can now be summarised by stating that the requirement of *culpa* can be satisfied if it is proved
that the defender has been negligent in some way. Here negligence simply
means negligence in the duty of care sense. Secondly, liability will lie if the
defender has acted with malice towards the pursuer. Thirdly, liability will
lie if the requisite state of affairs which harms the pursuer is brought about
by the deliberate or reckless act of the defender. Fourthly, and most con-
troversially, liability will lie if, through some fault of his own, the defender
brings into existence a state of affairs which ranks as hazardous.

By way of conclusion, the concept of *culpa* is not well articulated as
far as the law of nuisance in Scotland is concerned. *Kennedy v Glenbelle* of
course, concerned liability in respect of the carrying-out of building works.
The vast majority of nuisance cases, however, concern liability for various
forms of pollution such as noise and air pollution. It may be difficult to
apply the learning in *Kennedy* to this type of nuisance.

Liability in nuisance: who may be sued?
A nuisance, which may take a variety of forms, is normally caused by
the occupier of the relevant premises whence the nuisance emanates.
However, this is not always the case. For example, a fire which is started
on a farmer's field and spreads to neighbouring property, doing damage

there, may have been started by trespassers without the farmer's knowledge. Therefore, we now consider on whom liability for nuisance falls.

The author of the nuisance

The person who creates the relevant nuisance – that is to say, the author of the nuisance – is liable in law.[79] He need have no interest in the land from which the nuisance arises.[80] For example, the operators of very noisy construction equipment which is situated on a building site may be liable in nuisance, notwithstanding the fact that the operators of the equipment have no proprietary interest in the land on which the work is taking place.

The occupier of land

The occupier of land from which the nuisance emanates is normally liable in law.[81] The basis of liability is both the possession and the control of the land from which the nuisance proceeds.[82] However, the occupier of land is not liable for an adverse state of affairs which is created by a third party – for example, a trespasser – or by an act of nature, unless the occupier takes insufficient steps to abate the nuisance after he becomes aware of its presence, either actually or constructively, in which case the law will presume that he has adopted the nuisance.

The leading case is *Sedleigh-Denfield v O'Callaghan*.[83] In that case a local authority trespassed on the land of the defendant and proceeded to construct a culvert on a ditch. One of the employees of the defendant knew of the existence of the culvert. Furthermore, the defendants also used the culvert in order to get rid of water from their own property. However, the culvert was not properly constructed, the upshot of which was that it became blocked by detritus. A heavy thunderstorm caused the ditch to flood. The plaintiff's land became flooded as a consequence. The House of Lords held the defendant liable in nuisance by virtue of the defender both continuing and also adopting the nuisance in question. The defendant had continued the nuisance by virtue of failing to take the necessary remedial action after becoming aware (through its servant) of the existence of the nuisance. The nuisance had been adopted by the defendant using the culvert for its own purposes.

However, it should be noted that in *Marcic v Thames Water Utilities Ltd*[84] the House of Lords held that the learning in *Sedleigh-Denfield* was inapplicable to determining the liability of a public utility in terms of whether it was liable to the claimant for the damage caused by his property being inundated by effluent which had escaped from the defendant's sewer. However, in the author's view, *Marcic* does not represent the law of Scotland.[85]

In *Sedleigh-Denfield* the adverse state of affairs which caused damage to the plaintiff's property was created by the actions of individuals. However, what is the position if the adverse state of affairs is brought about by an act of nature? Should the court's approach be the same? The Privy Council had the opportunity to consider the law relating to a nuisance which was created by an act of nature in *Goldman v Hargrave*.[86] In that case, a tall gum tree, which was 100 feet high and situated on the defendant's land, was struck by lightning. The tree caught fire. The defendant cut the tree down the following day. However, he did not take any further steps to stop the fire from spreading, preferring simply to let it burn itself out. Several days later the weather changed. The wind became stronger and the air temperature increased. This caused the fire to revive. It spread to the plaintiff's land which was damaged. The Privy Council held that the defendant was liable for the damage in that he had failed to remove the nuisance from his land. In so deciding, the court held that no distinction fell to be made between liability in terms of the law of nuisance and the law of negligence.[87] However, in deciding whether the defendant had failed to reach the standard of care which the law demanded of him, one was required to take into account the defendant's knowledge of the relevant hazard as well as his ability to foresee the consequences of not checking or removing it and also his ability to abate the nuisance.[88] One was required to adopt a subjective approach in this process. Therefore, one was required to consider the resources of the defendant. One was also required to expect less of an occupier of small premises than that of larger property. In turn, less would be demanded of the infirm than of the able-bodied.

The Court of Appeal had an opportunity to decide whether the learning in *Goldman* was applicable to the law of England in *Leakey v National Trust for Places of Historic or Natural Beauty*.[89] There the plaintiffs owned houses which were situated at the base of a steep conical hill which rejoiced in the name of the 'Burrow Mump'. Part of the hill which adjoined the plaintiff's land had become unstable. The condition of the land had been made known to the defendants by the plaintiffs. However, the defendants took no remedial action. A few weeks later there was a substantial fall of earth and a few tree stumps from the hill to the plaintiff's land. The plaintiffs brought an action in nuisance. The Court of Appeal held the defendants liable in nuisance. In so doing, the court refused to draw a distinction between an adverse state of affairs which had been foisted on the defendant by man-made activities and a state of affairs which arose by operation of nature. The judgment of Megaw LJ[90] is particularly interesting in that his Lordship discussed both the nature and also the scope of the affirmative duty which the law imposes on the occupier of land in relation to nuisances which have been foisted on him. In his Lordship's view, the extent of the harm to the plaintiff's premises should an accident occur, the practicability of preventative action, the cost of relevant works, and the time available to take the necessary remedial action were all relevant in determining liability.

In the law of Scotland, in contrast to the law of England, one obvious question which requires to be answered is whether *Sedleigh-Denfield*, *Goldman* and *Leakey* represent the law of Scotland. Whilst there is little authority on this important point, in the view of the author, these cases would, indeed, be followed in Scotland. However, given the fact that the concept of *culpa* in the Scots law of nuisance as delineated in *Kennedy v Glenbelle*[91] is wider than the degree of fault which is required to ground liability in terms of the law which is set out in the above trilogy, it would seem that in most cases a Scottish court would have no need to avail itself of the learning in these cases in order to determine whether an occupier is liable for failing to remove a nuisance from his land.

The landlord

A landlord is not liable for every nuisance emanating from the property which he has leased.[92] For example, a landlord is not liable in nuisance for the noise which is made by his tenants. However, a landlord is liable for any nuisance which he has authorised the tenant to create or for a nuisance which is the certain or highly probable result of the tenant's occupation of the premises concerned.[93]

The licensor of the nuisance

The person who authorises the creation of a nuisance is liable, especially if he makes no attempt to either abate or remove the nuisance after he becomes aware of its existence. The leading case on this point is *Webster v Lord Advocate*.[94] Here the pursuer claimed that the noise from the performance of the Edinburgh Military Tattoo and the erection of scaffolding to accommodate seating on the Edinburgh Castle esplanade amounted to a nuisance in law. The Lord Ordinary accepted that the Secretary of State for Scotland, as occupier of the esplanade, was liable in nuisance since he had licensed the creation of the nuisance. It was held irrelevant that the contract between the licensees, namely the Tattoo Policy Committee and the Secretary of State, contained a 'no-nuisance' clause, since no attempt had been made by the latter either to monitor or to enforce the clause. Therefore, if a licensor was capable and did, in fact, take steps to enforce such a clause, he could escape liability.

Defences

We now look at certain defences which have specific application in the law of nuisance. However, it must be emphasised that other defences which apply in the law of delict are also relevant.[95]

Statutory authority

Essentially, if Parliament has sanctioned the very state of affairs which constitutes the relevant nuisance, this deprives the pursuer of a remedy. In short, the defence of statutory authority is a complete defence. It must be emphasised that the defence is confined to Acts of Parliament. For example, if the relevant state of affairs which ranks as a nuisance emanates from something which has been granted planning permission, such approval would not have a similar effect of denying the pursuer a remedy.[96] The defence of statutory authority was invoked during the course of the nineteenth century against alleged nuisances (for example, noise and vibration) which arose from the operation of the rail network.[97] Indeed, the bulk of the learning on the subject of the defence of statutory authority derives from the so-called 'railway cases' which represent a particularly untidy area of law. Fortunately, the law which was embodied in the railway cases was reviewed and also clarified by the House of Lords in the leading case of *Allen v Gulf Oil Refining Ltd*.[98] In that case a private Act of Parliament authorised a multinational company to acquire land, which was situated in a rural area, to construct an oil refinery. However, soon after the refinery commenced operations, certain residents who lived in the vicinity of the refinery began to complain about the smell, noise and vibration emanating from the plant. The residents raised an action in nuisance. The House of Lords held that the Act of Parliament, had, by necessary implication, authorised both the construction and the operation of the refinery, the inevitable consequence of which was the creation of the nuisance in question. The plaintiffs, therefore, failed in their action. The defence of statutory authority does not apply if the relevant activities are being carried out negligently.[99]

Finally, if the relevant statute authorises the relevant activity to be carried out without causing a nuisance, the defence of statutory is inapplicable if the activity is carried on in such a manner as to cause a nuisance.[100]

Prescription

The gist of this defence is that the law will not give a remedy to a pursuer who has failed to complain during a period of twenty years or more in the face of a nuisance.[101] For the defence to succeed, the nuisance must have remained substantially constant over the prescriptive period,[102] and also constituted an actionable nuisance over that period.[103] Since, as explained above,[104] liability in nuisance in Scots law is prefaced on *culpa*, it automatically follows that the relevant prescriptive period begins to run only when there is a convergence between fault on the part of the defender and the existence or manifestation of the adverse state of affairs. Furthermore, on the authority of both *Sturges* and *Webster* the nuisance need not have been in perpetual existence over the prescriptive period for the defence to succeed. It is simply sufficient that the nuisance manifests itself on a regular basis.

For the defence to succeed, the pursuer must have had either actual or constructive knowledge of the nuisance.[105] The prescriptive period commences when the pursuer could have raised a successful action against the defender.[106] Finally, if the defender does acquire a prescriptive right to continue a nuisance, he does not thereby acquire the right to create another nuisance nor to increase the intensity of the nuisance in respect of which the prescriptive right has been acquired.[107]

Acquiescence

The pursuer may lose his right to raise an action in nuisance if he acquiesces in the face of a nuisance. The defence of acquiescence is quite separate from the defence of prescription.[108] The defence of acquiescence must be specifically pled.[109] For the defence to succeed there requires to be a clear, unequivocal and positive act on the part of the pursuer which indicates that he has consented to being adversely affected by the nuisance in question. The person who is alleged to have acquiesced in the face of the nuisance is required to have had full knowledge of the nuisance and also to have possessed the power to abate the nuisance.[110] Mere silence or passiveness in the face of the nuisance is insufficient to ground the defence.[111] Therefore, if I become aware that my house is badly affected by odour from a nearby landfill site and I refrain from taking any action, such awareness and inaction would not of itself disqualify me from raising an action. However, the occupation of the land which is affected by the nuisance, coupled with knowledge of the existence of the nuisance, is capable of raising the presumption that the pursuer has acquiesced.[112] The longer the pursuer remains impassive in the face of the nuisance, the stronger is the presumption that the pursuer has acquiesced. However, in *Colville v Middleton* it was held that twenty-two years' passive inaction was insufficient to ground the defence. Since the defence is based on implied consent, the defence of acquiescence is redundant if the pursuer objects timeously to the state of affairs in question.[113] Furthermore, the pursuer can only acquiesce in the face of the effects of a nuisance in contradistinction simply to the creation of the adverse state of affairs from which the nuisance arises.[114] The relevant act or acts of acquiescence on the part of the pursuer can be implied from the facts and circumstances of the case.[115] The defence does not apply if the nuisance in question differs in either nature or intensity from that which has been consented to.[116]

Importantly, the courts are unwilling to infer acceptance of a given state of affairs from the mere fact that the pursuer has 'come to' the nuisance in question. The leading case is now *Webster v Lord Advocate*[117] where the court swept aside the contention on the part of the defender that the pursuer, by choosing to reside in the vicinity of the Edinburgh Castle Esplanade in full knowledge that she would thereby expose herself to the noise which was generated by the Edinburgh Military Tattoo, had consented to the nuisance. Again, in *Miller v Jackson*[118] it was held to be no defence that the plaintiffs had decided to live in close proximity to a cricket pitch, in the knowledge that by so doing they would expose themselves to the risk of being hit by cricket balls.[119]

Remedies

In order to raise an action in nuisance it is necessary that the pursuer has a proprietary interest in the land which is affected by the relevant nuisance. Therefore, someone who simply resides in the premises which are affected by the nuisance cannot successfully raise an action.[120] The remedies of damages, interdict and declaratory which apply generally in Scots law also apply, of course, to the law of nuisance.[121] However, at this juncture, the author would like to discuss the relevance of *culpa* to the law of interdict. It is the view of some authors[122] that, in sharp contrast to the case in which the pursuer sues the defender for damages, where *culpa* requires to be averred and proved, there is no need for the pursuer to do so in relation to an action for interdict.[123] However, in the view of the author it is, indeed, necessary for the pursuer to aver and also prove *culpa* on the part of the defender when an action is raised for interdict.[124] This is simply because an interdict is a preventative proceeding to prevent a *wrong* being done.[125] The grant of an interdict must, therefore, be prefaced on the existence of either a wrong, or a threatened wrong. There can be no separation of the concept of 'wrong' and that of 'fault 'in terms of any state of affairs which constitutes a nuisance. Fault is inextricably enmeshed in the very activity which generates the adverse state of affairs. Therefore, before any state of affairs can rank as a nuisance and, therefore, a wrong, the relevant state of affairs must, of necessity, possess the stamp of *culpa,* or fault, from the very outset. Indeed, the existence of fault on the part of the defender is a general condition of liability *ex delicto*.[126] Liability in the law of nuisance is, perforce, prefaced on fault, quite irrespective of the remedy which the pursuer wishes to invoke.

Summary

- The law of nuisance protects the enjoyment of the occupier of land from unreasonable interference which takes place on the land.
- The courts take a variety of factors into account when determining whether a nuisance exists, namely, the social utility of the defender's conduct, the motive of the defender, the nature of the locality, duration and intensity, time of day, sensitivity of the pursuer, and social utility of the thing which is interfered with.
- Normally, there will require to be some form of emanation from the defender's premises.
- The pursuer requires to prove *culpa* (or fault) on the part of the defender.
- The author of the nuisance is liable.
- The occupier of the land from which the nuisance emanates is liable.
- A landlord is not liable for every nuisance which emanates from the premises which he has leased.
- The licensor of the relevant nuisance may be liable.
- If Parliament has sanctioned the very state of affairs which constitutes the nuisance, that is a complete defence in a nuisance action.
- The law will not give a remedy in favour of a pursuer who has failed to complain for twenty years or more in the face of a nuisance.
- The pursuer may also lose his right to raise an action in nuisance if he acquiesces in the face of it.
- In order to raise an action in nuisance the pursuer requires to have an interest in the land which is affected by the relevant nuisance.
- The remedies of damages, interdict and declarator are applicable in the law of nuisance.

Notes

1. See, e.g., *Hunter v Canary Wharf Ltd* [1997] Env LR 488.
2. H. Burn-Murdoch, *Interdict* (W. Green, 1933) at 202.
3. See *Lord Advocate v The Rio Stakis Organisation Ltd* 1981 SC 104 at 110
4. Cf. the tort of nuisance. Professor Winfield was of the opinion that nuisance as far as the law of England was concerned, was 'incapable of exact definition but it could be described as the unlawful interference with a person's use or enjoyment of land, or of some right over, or in connection with

it': P. Winfield, *Textbook on the Law of Tort* (Sweet and Maxwell, 1937) at 462.

5. T. Smith, *Short Commentary on the Law of Scotland* (W. Green, 1962) at 1132.

6. D. Walker, *Delict*, 2nd edn (W. Green, 1981) at 955.

7. A. Glegg, *The Law of Reparation in Scotland*, 4th edn (W. Green, 1955) at 324.

8. 1954 SC 56 at 58.

9. Ibid. at 57.

10. This approach was endorsed by the First Division in *Lord Advocate v The Rio Stakis Organisation Ltd* 1981 SC 104 at 108 (Lord Emslie).

11. See, e.g., J. Rowan-Robinson and D. McKenzie-Skene, 'Environmental protection and the role of the common law: a Scottish perspective', in *Environmental Protection and the Common Law* (Hart Publishing, 2000) at 243. See also *Fritz v Hobson* (1880) 14 Ch D 542 at 556 where Fry J stated that one should not attempt to ascertain the existence of a nuisance in terms of its duration, but rather by its effect on the plaintiff.

12. See below at p. 23.

13. See *Thomson-Schwab v Costaki* [1956] 1 WLR 335.

14. See G. Cross, 'Does only the careless polluter pay'? (1995) 111 LQR 445 at 450. See also *RHM Bakeries (Scotland) Ltd v Strathclyde Regional Council* 1985 SC (HL) 17 at 43 per Lord Fraser.

15. See also *Mutter v Fyffe* (1848) 11 D 303.

16. *Watt v Jamieson* 1954 SC 56. See also *Western Silver Fox Ranch Ltd v Ross and Cromarty CC* 1940 SLT 144.

17. [1999] 4 All ER 449.

18. [2012] EWCA Civ 312.

19. (1882) 10 R 426.

20. [1997] AC 655 at 711.

21. See, e.g., *Bellew v Cement Ltd* [1948] IR 61.

22. See, e.g., *Watson v Croft Promo Sports Ltd* [2009] 3 All ER 249.

23. [2003] EHLR 297.

24. Ibid. at 311.

25. Ibid. at 315.

26. Ibid. at 316.

27. See, however, *McKenna v British Aluminium Ltd* [2002] Env LR 721, where Neuburger J supported the contention which was advanced by counsel to the effect that it would be inappropriate to extend the common law by way of the law of nuisance in order to give effect to Art 8 of the ECHR.

28. [2009] CSOH 169.

29. Ibid. at [17].

30. [1893] 1 Ch 316.

31. [1936] 2 KB 468.

32. See also the House of Lords case of *Hunter v Canary Wharf Ltd* [1997] Env LR 488 where it was held that the erection of a tall building which interfered with the reception of television signals did not constitute an actionable nuisance. However, Lord Cooke stated *obiter* (at 534) that the malicious erection of a structure for the purposes of interfering with television reception could rank as a nuisance in law.

33. See, e.g., *Trotter v Farnie* (1830) 9S 144.

34. (1862) 31 LJQB 286 at 286.

35. (1881) 8 R 1006 at 1021.

36. (1837) 15 S 775.

37. Ibid. at 779. Lord Corehouse stated at 779 that if the slaughterhouse were erected, no parent would suffer his children to attend a school close by a great slaughterhouse where there would always be an assemblage of the lowest of the population including butchers' boys and their associates. See also *Scott v Leith Police Commissioners* (1830) 8S 845.

38. [1907] AC 121.

39. Citing Lord Halsbury in *Colls v Home and Colonial Stores* [1904] AC 179 at 185.

40. [1907] AC 121 at 123.

41. (1865) 11 HL Cas 642.

42. [1993] QB 343.

43. Ibid. at 360.

44. Ibid. at 359.

45. [1996] Ch 19.

46. [2009] EWCA Civ 15.

47. Per Richards LJ at para 32, with whom his fellow judges agreed.

48. Ibid. at para 33. For a general discussion of the effect of planning permission on the law of nuisance, see F. McManus, 'Planning permission, the law of nuisance and human rights' (2011) 19 *Tort Law Rev* 29. See also F. Moor, 'Planning for nuisance' (2011) 3 JLBE 65.

49. [2012] EWCA Civ 26.

50. Ibid. at para [74].

51. [2014] UKSC 13.

52. Ibid. at [96].

53. Ibid. at [226].

54. (1862) 31 LJQB 286 at 292.

55. *Webster v Lord Advocate* 1984 SLT 13 at 16.

56. *Bamford v Turnley* (1862) 31 LJQB 286; *De Keyser's Royal Hotel Ltd v Spicer Bros. Ltd* (1914) 30 TLR 257.

57. (1908) 24 TLR 414.

58. (1888) 15 R 814.

59. [1965] Ch 436.
60. Ibid. at 448. See, however, the Canadian case of *Nor-Video Services Ltd v Ontario Hydro* (1978) 84 DLR (3rd) 221 where damages were awarded for interference with the transmission of a cable television service.
61. [1997] 2 WLR 684.
62. [2004] Env LR 861.
63. Ibid. at 867.
64. See p. 15-16 incl.
65. [1965] Ch 436 at 447.
66. [1997] Env LR 488.
67. Ibid. at 493.
68. 1984 SLT 13. A successful reclaiming motion on the terms of the interdict which was granted by the Lord Ordinary was made by the defender to the Inner House; see 1985 SLT 361.
69. 1984 SLT 13 at 15.
70. [1997] Env LR 488.
71. [1996] 1 All ER 482 at 487 (per Pill LJ).
72. *Cambridge Water Authority v Eastern Counties Leather Ltd* [1994] 2 AC 264.
73. 1985 SC (HL) 17
74. 1996 SC 95. For a discussion of *culpa* and the law of nuisance, see F. McManus, '*Culpa* and the law of nuisance' 1997 JR 259.
75. 1996 SC 95 at 100.
76. Ibid. at 101.
77. (1876) 3 R 461 at 468.
78. 1996 SC 95 at 102.
79. *Watt v Jamieson* 1954 SC 56.
80. *Slater v McLellan* 1924 SC 854. See also *Marcic v Thames Water Utilities Ltd* [2004] 2 AC 42.
81. *Sedleigh-Denfield v O'Callaghan* [1940] AC 880. See also *Smith v Scott* [1973] Ch 314.
82. *Sedleigh-Denfield v O'Callaghan* [1940] AC 880 at 903 (per Lord Wright).
83. [1940] AC 880.
84. [2004] 2 AC 42.
85. For a discussion of the *Marcic* decision and its relevance to Scotland, see F. McManus, 'Marcic rules OK? Liability in the law of nuisance in Scotland for escapes from overloaded sewers' (2008) 19 *Water Law* 61.
86. [1967] 1 AC 645.
87. In *Delaware Mansions Ltd v Westminster City Council* [2001] 3 WLR 1007 at 1018, Lord Cooke expressed the view that in circumstances similar to those which featured in *Sedleigh-Denfield* and *Goldman*, the label 'nuisance' or 'negligence' was of no real significance.

88. [1967] 1 AC 645 at 663 (per Lord Wilberforce). See also *Bybrook Barn Garden Centre Ltd v Kent County Council* [2001] Env LR 30.
89. [1980] QB 485.
90. Ibid. at 524.
91. 1996 SC 95.
92. *Smith v Scott* [1973] Ch 314.
93. In *Smith v Scott* ibid. at 321, Pennycuik V-C was of the view that the proper test was that of 'virtual certainty', which in his view was 'another way of saying a high degree of probability'. In *Tetley v Chitty* [1986] 1 All ER 663 at 671, McNeil J was of the view that the proper test for establishing liability in nuisance was whether the creation of the nuisance was the ordinary and necessary consequence of the lease or a natural and necessary consequence of the use of the land which was authorised by the landlord. See also *Dunn v Hamilton* (1837) 15 S 853 and *Caledonian Railway Co v Baird* (1876) 3 R 839.
94. 1984 SLT 13.
95. For a general discussion of the defences in the law of delict, see F. McManus and E. Russell, *Delict*, 2nd edn (Dundee University Press, 2011) ch. 21.
96. *Wheeler v JJ Saunders* [1996] Ch 19. See also *Watson v Croft Promo-Sport Ltd*[2009] 3 All ER 249.
97. See, e.g., *Hammersmith and City Railway Co v Brand* (1869-70) LR 4 HL 171.
98. [1981] AC 1001.
99. Ibid. at 1011 (per Lord Wilberforce). See also *Tate and Lyle Industries Ltd v Greater London Council* [1983] 2 AC 509.
100. *Hammersmith and City Railway Co v Brand* (1869-70) LR 4 HL 171.
101. *Duncan v Earl of Moray* 9 June 1809, FC; *Collins v Hamilton* (1837) 15 S 902: and *Robertson v Stewarts and Livingston* (1872) 11 M 189; Prescription and Limitation (Scotland) Act 1973, s 7(1).
102. *Webster v Lord Advocate* 1984 SLT 13.
103. *Sturges v Bridgman* (1879) 11 Ch D 22.
104. See p. 24-5 incl.
105. *Liverpool Corporation v Coghill and Son* [1918] 1 Ch 307.
106. Ibid.
107. *Baxendale v MacMurray* (1867) LR 2 Ch 790.
108. *Collins v Hamilton* (1837) 15 S 902.
109. *Buccleuch v Cowan* (1866) 5 M 214.
110. *Earl of Kintore v Pirie* (1903) 5 F 818.
111. *Cowan v Kinnaird* (1865) 4 M 236.
112. *Colville v Middleton* 27 May 1817.
113. *Hill v Wood* (1863) 1 M 360.
114. *Earl of Kintore v Pirie* (1903) 5 F 214.

115. Hill v Wood (1863) 1 M 360; *Houldsworth v Wishaw Magistrates* (1887) 14 R 920.

116. *Colville v Middleton* 27 May 1817, FC.

117. 1984 SLT 13.

118. [1977] QB 966.

119. [2009] 3 All ER 249.

120. *Hunter v Canary Wharf Ltd* [1997] Env LR 488.

121. For a general discussion of remedies in the law of delict see F. McManus and E. Russell, *Delict* (note 95) ch. 22.

122. See, e.g., J. Thomson, *Delictual Liability*, 5th edn (2014; Bloomsbury, 2009) at 210; see also N. Whitty in 'Nuisance', in SME para 144 and W. Stewart, *Reparation* (Edinburgh: W. Green, 2000) at para 19-6.

123. See *Logan v Wang (UK) Ltd* 1991 SLT 580 where both parties endorsed the view that it was unnecessary for the pursuer to aver and prove *culpa* on the part of the defender in relation to an action for interdict in terms of the law of nuisance. In the Outer House case of *Esso Petroleum Co Ltd v The Scottish Ministers* [2015] CSOH 21 Lord Docherty was prepared to accept, without discussion, E.'s argument to the pursuer's argument to the effect that it was unnecessary to prove *culpa* or blame on the part of the defenders for the former to succeed in an action for interdict. For a discussion of this case see (2015) 169 SPEL 63.

124. J. Rowan-Robinson and D. McKenzie-Skene endorse the approach taken by the author; see 'Environmental protection and the role of the common law', in J. Lowry and R. Edmunds (eds), *Environmental Protection and the Common Law* (Hart, 2000) at 248.

125. H. Burn-Murdoch (note 2) at 1 citing *Earl of Breadalbane v Jamieson* (1877) 4R 667 at 671 (per Lord President Inglis).

126. D. Walker (note 6) at 42.

CHAPTER 3

Statutory Nuisance

The law of statutory nuisance represents the oldest branch of environmental law. The Environmental Protection Act 1990 places a duty on a local authority to abate a variety of environmental nuisances. The Act also empowers a private individual in certain circumstances to take remedial action.

Introduction

We have already discussed how many environmental nuisances can be redressed by an individual who is adversely affected enlisting the aid of common law nuisance. However, as an instrument of environmental control, the common law has some limitations. For example, before one can succeed in an action under the common law, one is required to have a proprietary interest in the land which is affected.[1] At a more practical level, the cost of raising an action in nuisance has the obvious tendency of discouraging many people from taking such action.

In this chapter we look at the subject of statutory nuisance which represents the oldest branch of environmental law.[2] The subject of statutory nuisance has its origins in the mid-nineteenth century when it was widely believed that cholera was spread amongst the population by foul odours or miasms which emanated from foul matter.[3] Cholera was a shocking disease. Victims of the disease suffered from high temperature, severe abdominal pain, vomiting and explosive diarrhoea which left patients severely dehydrated. The upshot of this was that those who had recently died of cholera were skeletal in appearance.

The opposing theory as to the transmission of disease was the contagion theory. However, until germs were discovered by Pasteur and Lister, the contagionists' theory lacked credibility simply because there was no scientific foundation to which their theory could attach.

The miasmatists were in the majority in government. The views of this majority shaped the content of the legislation which was intended to strike against the cholera threat. The statutes which were passed were, therefore, 'nuisance-based', that is to say, the main purport of the legislation was to eradicate the perceived causes of the environmental threat.[4] Notwithstanding the fact that as the nineteenth century progressed, the miasmatic theory of transmission of disease was discredited, the theory had left an indelible mark on the mind of the legislature. Public health legislation, therefore, continued to enlist the aid of the law of nuisance as a remedial device. For example, as far as Scotland was concerned, the Nuisance Removal Act 1846 and 1848 and the Public Health (Scotland) Acts 1867 and 1897 (all of which are now repealed) employed the concept of statutory nuisance to deal with a range of adverse environmental circumstances. The statutory nuisance provisions which were contained in these statutes[5] are now contained, albeit in a more expanded form, in s 79(1) of the Environmental Protection Act, which we now discuss.

Statutory nuisances

Section 79(1) of the Act designates a variety of adverse environmental circumstances a nuisance in terms of the Act. We now deal with each in turn. However, prior to this, the reader should be aware of the fact that much of the case law which is cited here derives from English case law, the bulk of which was decided in terms of the nuisance provisions[6] of the Public Health Acts 1875 (repealed) and 1936 (largely repealed).

Premises

As we have already observed, the origins of the provisions of the Act which we are now about to discuss derive from the mid-Victorian era. And as we have also observed, an outstanding problem during that period was poor insanitary housing conditions both in urban and rural Scotland.[7] Perforce, public health legislation had to strike at this problem by making such premises a statutory nuisance.

Under s 79(1)(a) of the Act, 'any premises in such a state as to be prejudicial to health or a nuisance,' rank as a statutory nuisance and, therefore, fall to be dealt with in terms of the Act. The subsection comprises two quite separate limbs, namely:

(a) premises which are prejudicial to health, and
(b) premises which are a nuisance.[8]

Therefore, in order to rank as a statutory nuisance, the relevant premises must be either prejudicial to health or a nuisance, or both.

'Prejudicial to health'

In order for premises to be described as prejudicial to health, it is the physical state of the premises, in contrast to the use to which the premises are put, which constitutes the statutory nuisance.[9] Furthermore, it is not sufficient that the relevant state of affairs interferes with personal comfort. Rather, the premises must cause injury to health. However, the mischief at which the Act strikes is risk to human health, in contrast to the risk of accident. Therefore, premises which contain a dangerous stair, which poses a risk of falling to occupants or visitors, would not fall within the scope of the Act.[10]

Expert evidence as to the condition of the premises may be sufficient of itself to establish a *prima facie* case that the conditions are prejudicial to health. However, it is not necessary that there also exists evidence of the effect of such conditions on the occupant's health.[11]

Premises can be rendered prejudicial to health by a state of affairs which exists outside the premises.[12] However, in order for the premises to be prejudicial to health, the premises must have some intrinsic feature or attribute which renders them prejudicial to health. It does not suffice that the physical layout of the premises may lead to insanitary or unhygienic practices on the part of the residents of the premises. The leading case on this subject point is *Oakley v Birmingham City Council*.[13] In that case, the ground floor of a house included a bathroom with a washbasin which was situated next to a kitchen which had a sink. On the side of the kitchen which was opposite the bathroom was a door which led into a lavatory. There was no washbasin in the lavatory. Furthermore, there was no room to install a washbasin. Therefore, anyone using the toilet would require to wash their hands in the kitchen sink, or, alternatively, they would have to go through the kitchen into the bathroom. The local authority served an abatement notice on the owner of the premises. However, the House of Lords held that the premises were not prejudicial to health. It was not sufficient that the layout of the premises was conducive to unhygienic practices on the part of those who resided there. In order to come within the scope of the Act, the relevant risk was required to derive from some source of possible infection or disease or illness which derived from dampness, mould, dirt, evil-smelling accumulations or the presence of rats.[14]

Finally, the question whether premises pose a risk to human health requires to be judged objectively.[15] In other words, one is required to decide whether the premises would pose a risk to the health of an ordinary person in contrast to the health of the residents of the premises.

'Nuisance'

We have seen that, at common law, in order to rank as a nuisance, the relevant adverse state of affairs must exist outside the affected premises.[16] However, there is no similar requirement as far as premises which rank as a statutory nuisance is concerned. In short, the relevant premises can be rendered a nuisance in terms of s 79(1)(a) by virtue of adverse circumstances which manifest themselves within the relevant premises.[17] *Robb v Dundee City Council* is also authority for the proposition that in order to rank as a statutory nuisance the impact of the adverse state of affairs must be of a similar nature to that which would rank as a nuisance at common law.[18] Therefore, in order to rank as a nuisance, the use to which the relevant property is put and which, in turn, adversely impacts on the property, requires to be *plus quam tolerabile*, that is to say, something which unreasonably interferes with the enjoyment of that property.[19] One of the many examples of such a form of interference would be water percolating from an upper flat of tenement property into a lower flat, thereby causing physical damage to the ceiling of the latter.

Smoke

Under s 79(1)(b), 'smoke[20] emitted from premises so as to be prejudicial to health or a nuisance' ranks as a statutory nuisance which falls to be dealt with under the provisions of the Act. This paragraph supplements the provisions of the Clean Air Act 1993.[21] However, the prohibition which is imposed by the paragraph is subject to certain exceptions.[22]

Fumes etc.

Under s 79(1)(c) 'fumes[23] or gases[24] emitted from premises so as to be prejudicial to health or a nuisance' rank as a statutory nuisance. However, the subsection does not apply in relation to premises other than private dwellings.[25] Whilst there is no authority on the point, it is suggested that the paragraph would also cover odours and smells.

Dust, steam etc.

Under s 79(1)(d) 'any dust,[26] steam,[27] smell, or other effluvia arising on industrial, trade[28] or business[29] premises[30] and being prejudicial to health or a nuisance' ranks as a statutory nuisance. In *Wivenhoe Port Ltd v Colchester BC*[31] it was held at first instance that dust which fell on the cars of members of the public could not be categorised as a statutory nuisance; in contrast, dust which caused physical discomfort to individuals could rank as a nuisance.

Accumulations, deposits etc.
Under s 79(1)(e) 'any accumulation or deposit which is prejudicial to health or a nuisance' ranks as a statutory nuisance.

Whilst it has been held that the expression 'accumulation' implies some gradual accretion or heaping-up of matter from day to day,[32] the accumulation can come about by reason of deliberate human conduct, for example, by way of dumping.[33] In order to rank as a statutory nuisance the deposit or accumulation must pose the threat of disease or odour etc. However, it is insufficient that people could be injured while walking on the land where the deposit exists.[34]

There is a tendency to construe the terms 'accumulation' and 'deposit' conjunctively.[35]

Water
Under s 79(1)(ea) 'any water covering land or land which is covering water which is in such a state as to be prejudicial to health or a nuisance' ranks as a statutory nuisance in terms of the Act. There is little authority on this paragraph which was introduced by the Public Health (Scotland) Act 2008. However, the paragraph would cover smell nuisance from stagnant water. The paragraph would also cover water which escapes from, say, a pond on adjoining land.

Animals
Under s 79(1)(f) 'any animal kept in such a place or in such a manner as to be prejudicial to health or a nuisance' ranks as a statutory nuisance which falls to be dealt with under the Act.

It requires to be shown that either the place or the manner of keeping the animal in question either prejudices health or is a nuisance. The keeping of the animal may only be for a relatively short time in order to come within the scope of the Act.[36] Animals such as dogs which create a noise nuisance would, in the author's view, come within the scope of the paragraph.[37] The paragraph would also cover a situation in which zoonotic diseases could be transmitted to humans by virtue of either the place or the manner in which the animals are kept.

Insects
Under s 79(1)(faa) 'any insects[38] emanating from premises[39] and being prejudicial to health or a statutory nuisance' ranks as a statutory nuisance in terms of the Act. The paragraph could cover a range of situations including one where insects have bred in stagnant pools.

Artificial light

Under s 79(1)(fba) 'artificial light emitted from premises or any stationary object so as to be prejudicial to health or a nuisance' ranks as a statutory nuisance.

Light pollution has become a problem in recent years. Powerful lamps are increasingly being used to illuminate the exteriors of premises. Furthermore, outdoor all-weather tennis courts and football pitches are often artificially illuminated, sometimes to the annoyance of those who live in the vicinity.

Noise

Under s 79(1)(g) 'noise emitted from premises so as to be prejudicial to health or a nuisance' ranks as a statutory nuisance under the Act. Furthermore, under s 79(1)(ga) noise which is prejudicial to health or a nuisance and is emitted from or caused by a vehicle in a road, also ranks as a statutory nuisance.

The above provisions are discussed below.[40]

Other statutory nuisances

Under s 79 (1)(h) 'any other matter declared by any enactment to be a statutory nuisance' ranks as a statutory nuisance'. Therefore, any nuisance provision in any public general or private Act of Parliament would come within the scope of the paragraph, as would similar nuisance provisions which are contained in local authority byelaws. Generally, this would allow the court to impose a more severe penalty for failure to comply with an abatement notice.

The Scottish Ministers may amend s 79(1) in order to add to the above list of statutory nuisances, or it may vary the description of any matter which constitutes a statutory nuisance. [41]

Statutory nuisance and contaminated land

The Act makes special provision for land which is in a contaminated state.[42] Therefore, in order to avoid any overlap between the statutory nuisance regime which we have just discussed and that which governs contaminated land, the Act specifically excludes contaminated land from the statutory nuisance provisions of the Act.

The Act, therefore, provides that no matter constitutes a statutory nuisance to the extent that it consists of or is caused by any land being in a contaminated state.[43] The expression 'land in a contaminated state' is defined 'as land by reason of substances in, or under the land that:

(a)   significant harm is being caused or there is a possibility of such harm being caused, or

(b)   significant pollution of the water environment is being caused or there is a significant possibility of such pollution being caused'.[44]

Statutory nuisances and the Pollution Prevention and Control Act 1999
A local authority may not institute statutory nuisance proceedings in terms of s 79(1)(b)(d)(e)(g) or (ga) of Part III of the Environmental Protection Act in respect of activities which fall to be regulated in terms of regulations which have been made under the Pollution Prevention and Control Act 1999[45] without the consent of the Scottish Ministers. The rationale for this provision is in order to avoid regulatory duplication, in that the Scottish Environment Protection Agency (SEPA) regulates the range of installations which fall within the scope of these regulations.[46]

Duty of local authority to inspect area
A local authority is under a mandatory duty to inspect its area from time to time in order to detect any statutory nuisances which ought to be dealt with in terms of the Environmental Protection Act 1990 ('the Act').[47] Where a complaint of a statutory nuisance is made to a local authority by a person who lives within its area, it is required to take such steps as are reasonably practicable to investigate the complaint. In actual practice, a local authority does not systematically inspect its area to ascertain the presence of nuisances. Rather, local authorities simply react to complaints from members of the public. In short, the statutory nuisance regime is one that is largely, if not entirely, complaints-driven. In this context it is pertinent to note that the Act does not specify precisely what steps a local authority requires to take to investigate a complaint. There is no obligation on the local authority to either visit the relevant *locus* or communicate in any way with the complainant or the alleged (if any) author of the reputed nuisance. Nor does the Act specify the form which the complaint should take. It would seem, therefore, that a relevant complaint could be by means of email, phone call, fax or letter or verbal.

Summary proceedings for statutory nuisances
The procedure for the abatement of statutory nuisances has hardly changed since the inception of the statutory nuisance regime in the 1840s. We now discuss the procedure under the Environmental Protection Act 1990.

Where a local authority is satisfied that a statutory nuisance exists, or is likely to occur or recur, in the area of the local authority, it is required to serve an abatement notice which imposes all or any of the following requirements:

(a) requiring the abatement of the nuisance or prohibiting or restricting its occurrence or recurrence; and

(b) requiring the execution of such works, and the taking of such other steps, as may be necessary for any of those purposes.[48]

The notice is required to specify the time or times within which there must be compliance with the notice.

Once the local authority has decided that a nuisance exists, the abatement notice must be served. In other words, the local authority has no discretion.[49] Furthermore, there is no requirement that the local authority should consult with the author of the nuisance prior to serving the notice.[50]

Finally, brief mention should be made of the fact that some local authorities adopt the practice of sending out statutory nuisance intimation notices. Such a notice simply draws the attention of the person who is responsible for causing the nuisance to the fact that the nuisance exists. The rationale for serving such notices is to allow the recipient to take the necessary remedial action by voluntary action. However, such notices have no statutory force.

Content of abatement notice

The Act does not prescribe the precise content of the relevant abatement notice. However, the notice is required to contain a statement to the effect that an appeal against the notice lies to the sheriff.[51] The terms of the notice require to be both precise and practicable.[52] The notice can be worded to take immediate effect.[53] The notice must be drafted in such a way as to draw the attention of the relevant person to what requires to be remedied. Here, external factors can be taken into account by the local authority. For example, previous correspondence between the local authority and the recipient of the notice could be taken into account, or simply the undoubted knowledge on the part of the recipient of the relevant adverse state of affairs.[54] Again, the meaning of the notice could be derived from an accompanying letter.[55] The abatement notice need not specify whether the adverse state of affairs which is the subject-matter of the notice is either prejudicial to health or a nuisance. It suffices that the acts which constitute the nuisance are sufficiently specified that the person on whom the notice is served knows what he is required to do in order to abate the nuisance.[56]

The local authority can simply require the recipient of the notice to abate the relevant nuisance, that is to say, the former is not required to specify the measures which are required to abate the nuisance in question.[57] In other words, the local authority can leave the mode of abatement of the nuisance to the author of the nuisance. However, in *Budd v Colchester BC*[58] it was stated *obiter* that in certain circumstances it might be wholly unreasonable for the local authority not to specify the steps which are required to be taken to rectify the nuisance.[59] If the abatement notice requires works or other steps to be carried out, the relevant measures must be specified.[60] The measures which are specified in the notice must be practicable in their terms and also couched in language which is easily understood.[61]

If the abatement notice simply requires the recipient of the notice to take steps to abate the nuisance, the requisite steps need not be specified.[62] For example, an abatement notice could lawfully require someone who is causing a noise nuisance by playing his guitar during the night to take steps to abate the nuisance.

The above case law leads one to the conclusion that an abatement notice should make clear whether the execution of works or other measures is required on the part of the recipient of the notice. Furthermore, in order to avoid confusion on the part of the recipient of the notice, a local authority should simply require the relevant individual to abate the nuisance in question (or to prohibit its recurrence) unless there is some good reason why further measures should be specified.

Much of the case law concerning the content of abatement notices concerns the subject of noise abatement. As far as noise abatement notices are concerned, the local authority is not required to specify a maximum noise level which would be acceptable.[63] However, if the local authority chooses to specify noise levels which must not be exceeded, the method of ascertaining (or measuring) whether such levels are being exceeded must also be specified. For example, a local authority may require to specify at which part of the premises the noise in question requires to be measured.[64]

If the notice relates to a noise nuisance, it is quite legitimate for the notice in question to simply specify a noise level and then leave it to the recipient to determine how he should comply with it.[65] In order to ascertain the validity of the notice, one should look objectively at its substance. That which is of extrinsic or secondary importance to the substance of the notice can be ignored.[66]

Time for compliance
It is quite legitimate for the abatement notice to be framed in such a way that it has immediate effect.[67] Again, if the abatement notice simply pro-

hibits the recurrence of a nuisance, the notice is not required to specify the period of time, at the end of which the notice expires. That is to say, the effect of the notice automatically continues indefinitely.[68]

Person on whom the notice is to be served
The abatement notice is required to be served on the person who is responsible[69] for the nuisance, unless the nuisance arises from a defect of a structural character, in which case the notice requires to be served on the owner of the premises.[70] The abatement notice must also be served on the owner of the premises if either the person responsible cannot be found or the nuisance has not yet occurred. The Act defines the expression 'person responsible' as the person to whose act, default or sufferance the nuisance is attributable.[71] The words 'act', 'default', and 'sufferance' have tended to be construed conjunctively by the courts, that is to say, the courts have given the words the words the same meaning.[72] However, whilst the meaning of these words overlap to some extent, they have separate and distinct meanings to which we now turn our attention.

'DEFAULT'
The word 'default' simply means one not doing what is reasonable to do in the circumstances.[73] One can be in default in terms of the Act, notwithstanding that the nuisance may be caused to some extent by another party's failure to meet relevant statutory obligations.[74]

'SUFFERANCE'
One suffers an adverse state of affairs if one is in a position to put an end to that state of affairs but fails to do so.[75] In order for the relevant person to suffer an adverse state of affairs, one must have either actual or constructive knowledge of its existence.[76]

Finally, in *Robb v Dundee City Council*[77] a majority of the Inner House were of the opinion that a landlord was not responsible for any defect which was brought about by the tenant's failure to use facilities which the former had provided in the relevant premises. Therefore, the landlord was not responsible for the relevant state of affairs.

Defect of a structural character
As we have already noted,[78] if the nuisance arises from a defect of a structural character, the abatement notice requires to be served on the owner of the relevant premises. As far as the meaning of 'structure' is concerned, in *Cardiff Rating Authority and Cardiff Assessment Committee v Guest Keen Baldwin's Iron and Steel Co.*[79] Denning LJ (as he then was) stated:

A structure is something which is constructed, but not everything which is constructed is a structure. A ship, for instance, is constructed, but it is not a structure. A structure is something of substantial size which is built up from component parts and intended to remain permanently on a permanent foundation; but it is still a structure even though some of its parts may be moveable, as, for instance, about a pivot.

As far as Scottish authority is concerned, in *Robb v Dundee City Council*[80] Lord Johnston considered that the lack of thermal insulation in a building which rendered the premises more difficult to heat did not constitute a structural defect in terms of s 82(4)(b) of the Act.[81] In turn, in her dissenting judgment, Lady Paton thought that a distinction should be drawn between a structural defect and a defect of a structural character.[82] Whereas, in her Ladyship's opinion, the phrase, 'structural defect' implied that the premises were structurally unsound, possibly to the extent that there was a risk of some or all of the premises cracking or subsiding or disintegrating in some way, a 'defect of a structural character' could cover situations where there existed a defect which did not threaten the structural integrity of the premises but nevertheless arose from the manner in which, or the materials from which, the premises were built. However, in the author's view, the distinction which her Ladyship draws between the expressions which are in quotations is difficult to endorse.

In the sheriff court case of *Anderson v City of Dundee Council*[83] it was held that the expression 'defect of a structural character' implied that the existing state of the building should be different from what was originally designed. In order to ascertain whether there existed such a defect, one was required to take into account whether or not the building conformed to the relevant building standards, byelaws[84] etc. Furthermore, the fact that the building in its present form did not suit its purpose in the way it did thirty years ago did not *per se* make it structurally defective.

It has been held that defects in sound insulation in a house ranked as defects of a structural character in terms of s 82(4)(b) of the Act.[85]

OWNER

The expression 'owner' is not defined in the Act. In *Camden LBC v Gunby*[86] it was held that the expression 'owner' of the premises in terms of s 80 of the 1990 Act was the person who received the rack rent for the premises, regardless of whether that person was acting as an agent.

Appeals against notice

A person who is served with an abatement notice can appeal against the notice to the sheriff within a period of twenty-one days, beginning from the date on which the notice was served.[87] The Statutory Nuisance (Appeals) (Scotland) Regulations 1996[88] apply in relation to appeals which are brought under s 80 of the Act. The regulations specify the grounds upon which an appeal may be made. Such grounds include: that the abatement notice is not justified by s 80 of the Act; that there has been some informality in the notice; that the requirements in the abatement notice are otherwise unreasonable in extent, or are unnecessary; and, that the time (or times) within which the requirements of the abatement notice are to be complied with is not reasonably sufficient for the purpose.[89]

Failure to comply with notice

It is an offence for the person on whom an abatement notice is served to fail without reasonable excuse, to comply with an abatement notice.[90] In *Wellingborough BC v Gordon*[91] it was held that having a birthday party did not provide a reasonable excuse for the defendant's breach of a noise reduction notice which had been served in terms of the Control of Pollution Act 1974.[92] However, in *Hope Butuyuyu v Hammersmith and Fulham LBC*[93] it was held by the Divisional Court that it was not possible to provide a comprehensive definition of what matters were or were not capable of amounting to a reasonable excuse for failing to comply with an abatement notice. The relevant circumstances would vary from case to case. In this case, the court considered it relevant to take into account the illness of both the defendant and her son. *Hope* is, therefore, authority for the proposition that the court can take subjective factors into account when determining what circumstances constitute a reasonable excuse in terms of the section.

In the English case of *Coventry v Doyle*[94] it was held that the relevant date for determining whether a nuisance abatement notice had been complied with was the date on which the information was laid, as opposed to the date of the relevant hearing. In the absence of authority, it is the view of the author that *Coventry* represents the law of Scotland. Therefore, the relevant date for determining whether an abatement notice has been complied with is the date when the complaint is made. Importantly, the defender cannot challenge the terms of a notice if the notice could have been challenged by way of appeal to the sheriff court.[95]

The Act makes provision for fixed penalty notices. Where a local authority has reason to believe that a person has committed an offence by failing to comply with an abatement notice, the local authority may give the relevant individual the opportunity of discharging any liability in terms of the Act by paying a fixed penalty.[96] Except in relation to offences which relate to either industrial, trade or business premises, a person who commits an offence under s 80(4) is liable on summary conviction to a fine which does not exceed level 5 on the standard scale, together with a further fine of an amount equal to one-tenth of that level for each day on which the offence continues after conviction.[97] A person who commits an offence under s 80(4) on industrial, trade or business premises is liable, on summary conviction, to a fine which does not exceed £40,000.[98] There is no provision for the imposition of daily penalties on such premises.

Defence of best practicable means

The Act makes provision for the defence of best practicable means[99] in relation to proceedings for failure to comply with an abatement notice. Subject to certain exceptions[100] it is a defence to prove that the best practicable means were used to either prevent or counteract the effects of the nuisance.[101] The onus of establishing the defence is on the defender. The standard to which the defender requires to establish the defence is that of a balance of probability.[102] In *Wivenhoe Port v Colchester Borough Council*[103] it was held that incurring increased expenditure or unprofitability was not *per se* sufficient to establish a defence under the Act. The court may not take into account the fact that the defender can relocate elsewhere the business which is the subject-matter of the abatement notice. In short, the concept of practicability in terms of the defence requires to be judged solely in terms of the premises to which the notice elates.

Noise nuisances: special defences

The Environmental Protection Act 1990 makes provision for special defences in relation to noise nuisances which are covered by various notices served under Part III of the Control of Pollution Act 1974 which relates to noise abatement zones.[104] Essentially, it is a defence to proceedings under the 1990 Act for failure to comply with an abatement notice which is served under s 80 of the Act if the relevant state of affairs is the subject of a notice which has been served under the relevant provisions of the 1974 Act.[105]

Proceedings by local authorities

Exceptionally, a local authority may form the view that the statutory nuisance abatement machinery under the Act would be insufficient to secure redress. In such circumstances, the Act provides that if a local authority is of the opinion that the abatement proceedings under the Act would afford an inadequate remedy in the case of any statutory nuisance, the authority may take proceedings to abate the nuisance in any court of competent jurisdiction for the purpose of securing the abatement, prohibition or restriction of the nuisance.[106] The local authority need not have suffered any damage from the nuisance in question. In Scotland the relevant local authority would normally take proceedings for an interdict against the author of a nuisance. In order to invoke court proceedings, the local authority would require to conclude that the statutory nuisance proceedings would afford an inadequate remedy as opposed to a less convenient remedy.[107] In *Barns (NE) Ltd v Newcastle upon Tyne City Council*[108] it was held by the Court of Appeal that the procedure for dealing with a statutory was intended to comprise consecutive steps. First, there was the service of the abatement notice. If there was no compliance with the notice, either prosecution or self-help would be available to the local authority. Only as a last resort could the local authority take action in the High Court to avail itself of injunctive relief.[109]

Powers of enforcement
The Act makes provision for the enforcement of the various nuisance abatement provisions, such as powers of entry.[110]

Summary proceedings by private individuals
We have seen how the Act gives local authorities the power to abate statutory nuisances. However, for a variety of reasons, the relevant local authority may be unwilling to take statutory action against the relevant individual. The Act allows an aggrieved person[111] to take summary action before a sheriff for the abatement of the relevant nuisance. Such a provision is quite rare, if not unique in environmental law generally. Somewhat ironically, the provision has been used by private individuals against local authorities.[112] If the sheriff is satisfied that: (1) the alleged nuisance exists; or (2) although abated it is likely to recur on the same premises, or in the case of a nuisance within s 79(1)(ga) in the same road, the sheriff must make an order for either or both of the following purposes, that is to say: (1) requiring the defender to abate the nuisance within a time which is specified in the order, (2) executing any necessary works for that purpose; (3) prohibiting the recurrence of the nuisance; and (4) requiring the defender within a time which is specified in the order to execute any works which are necessary in order to prevent recurrence of the nuisance.[113] If the sheriff is satisfied that the alleged nuisance renders the premises unfit for human habitation, the sheriff may prohibit the use of the premises for human habitation until the premises are rendered fit for that purpose.[114]
   Generally, proceedings require to be brought against the person who is

responsible for the nuisance.[115] However, in the case of a nuisance which arises from any defect of a structural character,[116] proceedings must be brought against the owner of the premises.[117] Where the person who is responsible for the nuisance cannot be found, proceedings require to be instituted against either the owner or the occupier of the premises.[118] In the case of a nuisance which falls within the scope of s 79(1)(ga) which is caused by noise which is emitted from or caused by an unattended vehicle or unattended machinery or equipment, proceedings must be instituted against the person who is responsible for the vehicle, machinery or equipment.[119] Where more than one person is responsible for a nuisance which falls within the ambit of s 82, liability under the section is both joint and several, irrespective of whether or not the adverse state of affairs which each has created would amount to a nuisance in itself.[120]

Prior to instituting proceedings under s 82(2) the person aggrieved by the nuisance is required to give the person responsible for the nuisance notice in writing of his intention to bring the relevant proceedings.[121] The notice is required to specify the subject-matter of the complaint. It is an offence, without reasonable excuse,[122] to contravene any requirement or prohibition which is imposed by an order made under s 82(2).[123]

The defence of best practicable means[124] is available in summary proceedings which are brought by private individuals.[125] However, the defence is not available in certain circumstances.[126] If a person is convicted of an offence under s 82(8), the sheriff may, after giving the relevant local authority the opportunity of being heard, direct the authority to do anything which the person who was convicted of the offence was required to do by the relevant order.[127] The sheriff also has the power to order the defender to compensate the person who has brought the proceedings.[128] If the person who is responsible[129] for the nuisance cannot be found, the sheriff, after giving the local authority the right to be heard, has the power to direct the authority to do anything which the sheriff would have ordered that person to do.[130]

Conclusions

The law which relates to statutory nuisance arguably represents one of the most arcane areas of environmental law. As is the case with common law nuisance, the law of statutory nuisance is very much anchored in its Victorian past. In the last analysis, the courts interpret the statutory nuisance provisions of the Environmental Protection Act 1990 through the eyes of a Victorian, and an early Victorian at that!

One of the major questions which presents the courts with a formidable challenge is the interrelationship between common law and statutory nuisance. In the author's view, the former should play no role in shaping the latter, since common law nuisance is exclusively concerned with regulating the respective rights of those who have an interest in land, whereas the latter is concerned with the abatement of adverse circumstances for the benefit of the community as a whole. In other words, the body of law which has developed to balance the conflicting rights of landed proprietors has simply no role to play in the development of statutory nuisance. Indeed, the difficulty which judges have experienced by attempting to integrate common law nuisance with statutory nuisance quite pointedly emphasises, in the author's view, that public law concepts present a serrated edge to the common law in general.

Summary

- The Environmental Protection Act 1990 makes provision for the abatement of certain nuisances.
- A local authority can serve an abatement notice on the person responsible for the nuisance to remove the nuisance.
- It is made an offence, subject to certain defences, to fail to comply with the notice.

Notes

1. *Hunter v Canary Wharf Ltd* [1997] AC 655.
2. For a more detailed discussion of statutory nuisance, see F. McManus, 'Statutory nuisance', in F. McManus (ed.), *Environmental Law in Scotland* (W. Green/SULI, 2007) ch. 4.
3. See E. Ackerknecht, 'Anticontagionism between 1821 and 1864' (1948) 22 *Journal of the History of Medicine* 562; N. Longmate, *King Cholera* (Hamish Hamilton, 1966) and R. Morris, *Cholera 1832* (Croom Helm, 1976).
4. See, e.g., the Public Health Act 1848, and the Nuisance Removal Acts 1846-1855.
5. The Public Health (Scotland) Act 1867 simply replicated the list of statutory nuisances which were contained in the nuisance removal Acts. In turn, the 1897 Act repealed and replicated the provisions of the 1867 Act.
6. Repealed.
7. See F. McManus, 'Victorian foundations of environmental law in Scotland', in F. McManus (ed.), *Environmental Law in Scotland* (W. Green, SULI) (looseleaf).
8. *Salford City Council v McNally* [1976] AC 379.

9. See, e.g., *R v Parlby* (1889) 22 QBD 520.

10. See *R v Bristol City Council ex p Everett* [1999] 2 All ER 193.

11. *R v Knowsley MBC ex p O'Toole* (1999) 22 LSGR 36. Expert evidence requires to be provided by someone with appropriate expertise, e.g. an environmental health officer: *London Borough of Southwark v Simpson* [1999] JPL 107.

12. *Pollway Nominees Ltd v Havering LBC* (1989) 88 LGR 192; *Southwark LBC v Ince* (1989) 21 HLR 504.

13. [2001] 1 All ER 385.

14. Ibid. per Lord Slynn of Hadley at 627.

15. *Robb v Dundee City Council* 2002 SLT 853.

16. See p. 11.

17. *Robb v Dundee City Council* 2002 SLT 853.

18. See also *Newham LBC v White* 2015 (Queen's Bench Divisional Court) (unreported).

19. *Watt v Jamieson* 1954 SC 56.

20. 'Smoke' includes the smell of smoke; *Griffiths v Pembrokeshire CC* [2000] Env LR 622.

21. See Chapter 5.

22. Section 79(1)(b) does not apply to various premises which are occupied on behalf of the Crown or premises which are occupied for the purpose of a visiting force for the purpose of defence; ibid. s 79(2). Furthermore, s 79(1)(b) does not apply to smoke which is emitted from a chimney of a private dwelling within a smoke control area, or dark smoke which is emitted from a chimney which serves the furnace of a boiler or industrial plant which is attached to a building or, for the time being, which is fixed to or installed on any land, or dark smoke which is emitted from a railway locomotive steam engine, or dark smoke which is emitted otherwise than as aforementioned, from either industrial or trade premises; ibid. s 79(1)(3).

23. 'Fumes' means any airborne solid matter smaller than dust; ibid. s 79(7).

24. 'Gas' includes vapour and moisture precipitated from vapour; ibid. s 79(7).

25. Ibid. s 79(4).

26. 'Dust' does not include dust emitted from a chimney as an ingredient of smoke; ibid. s 79(7).

27. 'Steam' does not include steam which is emitted from a railway locomotive engine; ibid. s 79(5).

28. In *Skinner v Breach* [1927] 2 KB 220 it was held (Lord Hewart CJ at 225, 226) that the term 'trade' indicated a process of buying and selling and could also mean a calling or industry or class of skilled labour. In *Aviation and Shipping Co v Murray* [1961] 1 WLR 974 Donovan J (as he then was) held that a trade is an organisation with the aid of physical assets seeking after profits as a rule.

29. In *Re a Debtor* (No 490 of 1935) [1936] Ch 237 it was stated that the expression 'business' had a wider meaning than the expression 'trade'. The expression 'trade' would connote any form of commercial activity. In *Rolls v Miller* (1894) 27 Ch D 71 at 88 it was held that the expression 'trade' could mean 'almost anything which is an occupation, as distinguished from a pleasure – anything which is an occupation or duty which requires attention is a business'. In *R v Breeze* [1973] 1 WLR 994 at 997 Lord Widgery was of the view that a business was a continuous activity with a view to gain or profit.

30. The expression 'industrial, trade or business premises' means premises used for any industrial, trade or business purposes, or premises not so used on which matter is burnt in connection with any industrial, trade or business process, and premises are used for industrial purposes where they are used for the purposes of any treatment or process as well as where they are used for the purposes of manufacturing; ibid. s 79(7). In *Hounslow LBC v Thames Water Utilities Ltd* [2004] QB 212 it was held that sewage treatment works comprised premises within the meaning of the paragraph.

31. [1985] JPL 175.

32. *Great Northern Railway v Lurgan Commissioners* [1897] 2 IR 340 at 351.

33. *Coventry City Council v Cartwright* [1975] 1 WLR 845.

34. Ibid.

35. Ibid.

36. *Steers v Manton* (1893) 57 JP 584.

37. However, see *Galer v Morrissey* [1955] 1 WLR 110.

38. Section 79 (1)(faa) does not apply to insects that are wild animals which are included in Schedule 5 to the Wildlife and Countryside Act 1981; ibid. s 79(5AA).

39. For the purposes of s 79(1)(faa) 'premises' does not include -
    (a) a site of special scientific interest (within the meaning of section 3(6) of the Nature Conservation (Scotland) Act 2004
    (b) such other place (or type of place) as may be prescribed in regulations made by the Scottish Ministers; *ibid.* sv79(1)(5AB).

40. See Chapter 4.

41. Section 79(1)(1ZA).

42. See Chapter 7.

43. EPA s 79(1)(1A).

44. Ibid. s 79(1)(1B). The expressions 'harm', 'pollution' (in relation to the water environment), 'substance' and the water environment have the same meanings as those which are used in Part IIA of the EPA (see Chapter 7).

45. See the Pollution Prevention and Control (Scotland) Regulations 2012 (SSI 2012 No 360).

46. See Chapter 9.

47. Environmental Protection Act 1990, s 79(1).

48. Ibid. s 80(1).

49. *R v Carrick DC ex p Shelley* [1996] Env LR 273.

50. *R v Falmouth and Truro Port Health Authority ex p South West Water Services* [2000] 3 All ER 306.

51. Environmental Protection Act 1990, Sched 3.

52. *Strathclyde RC v Tudhope* 1983 SLT 22. See also *Network Housing Association v Westminister City Council, The Times,* 8 November 1994.

53. *Strathclyde Regional Council v Tudhope* 1983 SLT 22.

54. *Myatt v Teignbridge DC* [1995] Env LR 18; see also *Cambridge City Council v Douglas* [2001] Env LR 41.

55. *London Borough of Camden v London Underground Ltd.* [2000] Env LR 369.

56. *Lowe and Watson v South Somerset DC* [1998] Env LR 143.

57. *Budd v Colchester BC* [1999] Env LR 739.

58. Ibid.

59. Ibid. at 747.

60. *R v Falmouth and Truro Port Health Authority ex p South West Water Ltd* [1999] Env LR 833 at 861; see also *Surrey Free Inns Group plc v Gosport BC* [1999] Env LR 750, and *Elvington Park Ltd v City of York Council* [2010] Env LR 10.

61. *R v Fenny Stratford Justices ex p Watney Mann (Midlands) Ltd* [1976] 1 WLR 1101 at 1106.

62. *Sevenoaks DC v Brands Hatch Leisure Group Ltd.* [2001] Env LR 5.

63. *Cambridge City Council v Douglas* [2001] Env LR 639.

64. *R v Fenny Stratford Justices ex p Watney Mann (Midlands) Ltd* (note 61).

65. *R v Crown Court at Canterbury ex p Watney Mann (Midlands) Ltd* [1976] 1 WLR 1101.

66. *McGillivray v Stephenson* [1950] 1 All ER 942.

67. *Strathclyde RC v Tudhope* 1983 SLT (Notes) 22.

68. *R v Birmingham Justices ex p Guppy* (1988) 152 JP 159. See also *R v Tunbridge Wells Justices ex p Tunbridge Wells BC* [1996] Env LR 88.

69. 'Person responsible' is defined as in relation to a statutory nuisance, as (a) the person whose act, default or suffrance the nuisance is attributable, (b) in relation to a vehicle, includes the person in whose the vehicle is for the time being registered under the Vehicle Excise and Registration Act 1994 and any other person who is for the time being the driver of the vehicle and (c) in relation to machinery and equipment, includes any person who is for the time being the operator of the machinery or equipment; ibid. s 79(7). Where more than one person is responsible for a statutory nuisance, the provisions of s 80 apply to each of those persons whether or not what any one of them is responsible for would be itself amount to a nuisance; ibid. s 81(1).

70. Ibid. s 80(2).

71. Ibid. s 79(7).
72. *Robb v Dundee City Council* 2002 SLT 853. See also *Network Housing Association v Westminster City Council* [1995] Env LR 176.
73. *Re Young and Hartson's Contract* (1885) 31 Ch D 168 at 174.
74. *Wincanton RDC v Parsons* [1905] 2 KB 34.
75. *Rochdale v Port of London Authority* [1914] 2 KB 916.
76. *Network Housing Association v Westminster City Council* [1995] Env LR 176.
77. 2002 SLT 853.
78. See p. 47.
79. [1949] 1 KB 385 at 396.
80. 2002 SLT 853.
81. Ibid. at 865.
82. Ibid. at 867.
83. 2000 SLT (Sh Ct) 134.
84. Prior to the advent of the Building Standards (Scotland) Regulations 1964 (repealed) which were made under the Building (Scotland) Act 1959 (repealed) new building work required to conform to the provisions of the byelaws which local authorities could make under the Public Health (Scotland) Act 1897 (repealed).
85. *Pettigrew v Dundee City Council* (1999) HLR 31.
86. [1999] 4 All ER 602.
87. EPA 1990 s 80(3).
88. SI 1996 No 1076.
89. Ibid. reg 2(2).
90. Environmental Protection Act 1990 s 80(4).
91. [1993] 1 Env LR 218.
92. Section 58(4) repealed.
93. [1997] Env LR D 13.
94. [1981] 1 WLR 1325.
95. *Stagecoach v McPhail* 1988 SCCR 289.
96. Environmental Protection Act 1990 s 80(4A).
97. Ibid. s 80(5)
98. Ibid. s 80(6)
99. 'Best practicable means' is defined as: (a) 'practicable' means reasonably practicable having regard, among other things, to local conditions and circumstances, to the current state of technical knowledge and to the financial implications; (b) the means to be employed include the design, installation, maintenance and manner and periods of operation of plant and machinery, and the design, construction and maintenance of buildings and structures; (c) the test is to apply only so far as compatible with safety and safe working conditions, and with the exigencies of any emergency or unforeseeable

circumstances, and in circumstances where a code of practice under s 71 of the Control of Pollution Act 1974 is applicable, regard is also to be had to guidance given by it.

100. The defence of best practicable means does not apply to: (a) a nuisance falling within paras (a), (d), (e) or (g) of s 79(1) except where the nuisance arises on industrial, trade or business premises: (aa) in the case of a nuisance falling within para (ga) of s 79(1) except where the noise is emitted from or caused by a vehicle, machinery or equipment being used for industrial, trade or business purposes; (b) in the case of a nuisance falling within para (b) of s 79(1) except where the smoke is emitted from a chimney, and (c) in the case of a nuisance falling within paras (c) or (h) of s 79(1).

101. Ibid. s 80(7).

102. *Chapman v Gosberton Farm Produce Co Ltd* [1993] Env LR 191.

103. [1985] JPL 175.

104. Environmental Protection Act 1990 s 80(9)

105. The relevant sections of the 1974 Act are: ss 60, 61 or 65 (construction sites), s 66 (noise reduction notices), and s 67 (new buildings).

106. Environmental Protection Act 1990 s 81(5).

107. *Vale of White Horse District Council v Allen* [1997] Env LR 212.

108. [2006] Env LR 25.

109. For a criticism of *Barnes*, see F. McManus, 'Statutory nuisance' (2007) 119 SPEL 21.

110. Environmental Protection Act 1990, Sched 3.

111. In *Att-Gen of Gambia v N'Jie* [1961] 2 All ER 504 at 511, Lord Denning MR stated that the words 'person aggrieved' were of 'wide import and should not be subjected to a restricted interpretation. They did not include a mere busybody who is interfering in things which do not concern him; but included a person who has a genuine grievance'. The expression 'person aggrieved' would include a person who is or whose family is adversely affected by the nuisance in question: *Anderson v Dundee City Council* 1999 SCLR 518; *Robb v Dundee City Council* 2002 SLT 853.

112. *Robb v Dundee City Council* above.

113. Environmental Protection Act 1990 s 82(2).

114. Ibid. s 82(3).

115. Ibid. s 82(4)(a).

116. For a discussion of the expression 'structural character', see p. 47-8 incl.

117. Ibid. s 82(4)(b).

118. Ibid. s 82(4)(c).

119. Ibid. s 82(4)(d).

120. Ibid. s 82(5). In relation to motor vehicle noise for which more than one person is responsible, liability falls on each person responsible for the nui-

sance who can be found: s82(5A). In relation to motor vehicle noise which is either emitted from or caused by an unattended vehicle or unattended machinery or equipment for which more than one person is responsible, liability falls on any person who is responsible for the nuisance in question; ibid. s 82(5A).

121. Ibid. s 82(6).
122. For a discussion of the meaning of the phrase 'reasonable excuse', see p. 49.
123. Ibid. s 82(8).
124. For a discussion of the defence of best practicable means see p. 50.
125. Ibid. s 82(9).
126. Ibid. s 82(10). The exceptions where the defence is unavailable correspond to those which are applicable to s 79(1) with the addition that the defence is not available in relation to a nuisance which renders a house unfit for human habitation; ibid. s 82(10).
127. Ibid. s 82(11).
128. Ibid. s 82(12). The right to compensation exists if it is proved that the alleged nuisance existed at the date on which the summary application was made, irrespective of whether the nuisance still exists or is likely to recur.
129. Or the owner or occupier of the premises, or the person who is responsible for the relevant vehicle, machinery or equipment.
130. Environmental Protection Act 1990 s 82(13).

CHAPTER 4

Noise

Noise has been described as a Cinderella pollutant on account of the traditional lack of attention accorded to it by central government. Local authorities have powers under the Environmental Protection Act 1990 and the Antisocial Behaviour (Scotland) Act 2004 to deal with noise nuisance. The police have power to deal with noise under the Civic Government (Scotland) Act 1982.

A variety of other statutes give various authorities the power to regulate noise from a variety of sources. Human rights law is becoming increasingly important in protecting the individual against noise.

The EU is now playing a more important role in tackling noise pollution.

Noise is a unique pollutant in that it is the only pollutant for which people commit murder.[1] Noise has been a perennial environmental problem in the United Kingdom since the Industrial Revolution. Generally speaking, noise, unlike many other forms of pollution, has tended not to be an emotive subject in the eyes of the general public. Individuals tend only to take an interest in noise if they are personally affected. A study conducted on behalf of the Department for Environment, Food and Rural Affairs (DEFRA) in 2003 revealed that 63 per cent of people – that is, close to two out of three people – heard noise from their neighbours.[2] Amongst those who heard noise, actual annoyance was experienced by fewer than 46 per cent of them – that is to say, almost one in three (29 per cent) of the population as a whole. The report recognised that whereas neighbour noise was not as widespread as some noises such as traffic noise, it constituted one of the most annoying sources of noise when it was heard. Loud music, shouting and banging were the most frequent causes of annoyance.[3]

DEFRA has recognised that not only does noise affect quality of life, but that there is evidence that noise affects health, especially the cardiovascular system.[4] In 2006 a survey conducted by MORI on behalf of the National Society for Clean Air and Environmental Protection[5] revealed that nearly two thirds of people are bothered by noise from neighbours. The noises that most disturb people are those from everyday living such as footsteps, doors slamming and shouting. The report also revealed that around half a million people moved home in 2005 because of noise. Noise affected the quality of life of one in ten people living in the United Kingdom, with Londoners and those in rented council properties suffering most. Furthermore, one in ten were kept awake by noise. In a survey which was carried out in 2011 by *Which*, it was estimated that at least 5 million people in the UK are affected by noise generated by their neighbours.[6] The survey found that noise topped the list of neighbour complaints. Three in five people were annoyed by loud voices or arguing, blaring music and TVs.

However, notwithstanding its importance in the development of environmental law in both Europe and the UK, noise is the Cinderella.[7] Its lowly status is no doubt due to the nature of the pollutant. Noise is, of course, invisible. It leaves no residue and, therefore, does not have the fallout factor associated with other pollutants. There can, of course, never be a noise disaster of a similar nature to that which afflicted Bhopal or Seveso. Noise almost seems to have been tacitly accepted by society as the inevitable consequence of modern life. Indeed, in the Court of Appeal case of *AG v Hastings Corp*[8] Tucker LJ laconically observed that 'we move in an age of noise'.

There was no national legislation dealing with noise until 1960, when effective pressure group action[9] managed to secure the passing by Parliament of the Noise Abatement Act 1960. As far as UK is concerned, noise pollution can be dealt with by action under the common law by way of the law of nuisance, or under statute. The various legal controls which relate to noise are now discussed.

Noise and the common law

Until 1960 the law of nuisance was the main form of control in relation to noise pollution. The law of nuisance still continues to be invoked by those who are affected by noise. However, this occurs to a lesser extent since the advent of the plethora of statutory controls over noise which provide local authorities, in the main, with the power to deal with a variety of forms of noise pollution. A wide range of noise sources have been held to constitute a nuisance at common law. These include noise from printworks,[10] building works,[11] a sawing mill,[12] singing,[13] domestic birds,[14] cattle,[15] horses,[16] an oil refinery,[17] an unruly family,[18] power boats,[19] a children's playground,[20] a military tattoo,[21] the firing of guns,[22] amusements,[23] dancing,[24] church bells,[25] quarrying,[26] recreational activities,[27] an electricity generating station,[28] a go-kart track[29] and pumping operations.[30]

Statutory controls over noise

Whereas individuals in the UK who are affected by noise continue to take action at common law against the author of the relevant noise nuisance, the vast majority of those affected by noise enlist the aid of local authorities in order to redress the problem. The statutory powers which local authorities can employ to deal with noise pollution are now discussed.

Environmental Protection Act 1990

The most important statute in terms of the control of neighbourhood noise is the Environmental Protection Act 1990 (EPA). We have already looked at the statutory nuisance provisions which are contained in s 79 of the EPA which arms local authorities with the power to abate a variety of adverse circumstances which constitute a nuisance.[31] We have also noted that the Act[32] allows private individuals to take summary action in the sheriff court to abate a statutory nuisance including noise nuisance. As far as the subject of noise is concerned, s 79(1)(g) provides that 'noise[33] emitted from premises so as to be prejudicial to health or a nuisance' is a statutory nuisance which falls to be dealt with under the provisions of the EPA. However, the general utility of this provision is circumscribed by the fact that the offending noise is required to emanate from premises. Therefore, noise which emanates from streets and other public places would not, therefore, normally fall within the meaning of the section. The courts give the expression 'nuisance' as used in the subsection its ordinary meaning.[34] On the authority of *Robb v Dundee City Council*,[35] in order to constitute a nuisance under the statute, the noise in question would require to be of such intensity, duration etc. as to constitute a nuisance at common law. By virtue of s 79(6), subsection (1)(g) does not apply to noise which is caused by aircraft other than model aircraft. Nor does the paragraph apply to premises which are occupied on behalf of the Crown for naval, military or air force purposes.

The occupants of flats in tenemental property are, of course, particularly prone to noise which has been created by neighbours. This problem can be compounded by the poor sound insulation of the walls and ceilings of such premises. We have already seen in the House of Lords case of *Baxter v Camden LBC*,[36] which concerned an action for common law nuisance against the landlords of council flats which were so inadequately insulated against the transmission of noise that the tenants of the flats could hear literally everything which their neighbours were doing, the House held that since the noise in question was everyday noise and, therefore, was not unreasonable, it did not rank as a nuisance. In this context *Vella v London Borough of Lambeth*[37] is interesting. In that case, the occupant of a house which was situated in a block of local authority flats brought an action under s 82 of the EPA against the local authority, on the basis that the sound insulation in the premises was so poor that he could hear almost everything which his neighbour, who lived upstairs was doing. The claimant's mental health suffered as a result of being exposed to such noise. It was not claimed that the noise which the claimant was subjected to ranked as a nuisance under the EPA, since the noise was not caused by unreasonable conduct on part of the neighbour. However, it was claimed that the premises in question (that is to say, either the flat above or his own flat) were prejudicial to health in terms of s 79(1)(a) of the EPA. The Queen's Bench Divisional Court held that the premises were not a statutory nuisance in terms of the section on the grounds that the statutory nuisance provisions which were contained in the predecessors to the EPA, namely the various Nuisance Removal Acts and subsequent Public Health Acts, were aimed at suppressing disease from insanitary, filthy or verminous premises. Section 79(1)(a) was not aimed at the state of affairs which was the subject-matter of the action, namely noise pollution caused by premises which was poorly insulated.

Road traffic noise is a major urban problem. We shall look later at how urban traffic noise is being dealt with at EU level.[38] Again, noise from motor-vehicle entertainment systems is a perennial problem for members of the public, especially householders. The problem has been compounded in recent years by the use of very large loudspeakers in motor cars for the entertainment of the vehicle driver and other occupants. Under s 79(1)(ga) 'noise that is prejudicial to health or a nuisance and is emitted from or caused by a vehicle,[39] machinery or equipment in a street or in Scotland a road, ranks as a statutory nuisance'.

Noise and Statutory Nuisance Act 1993

Audible intruder alarms
The use of audible intruder alarms by occupiers of both domestic and commercial premises is becoming increasingly common. However, burglar alarms have the tendency to be activated and, thereby, to cause a disturbance. Section 9 (which, at the time of writing,[40] is not yet in force) of the Noise and Statutory Nuisance Act 1993, makes specific provision for audible intruder alarms. A local authority is given power under the

section, after consulting with the Chief Officer of Police, to pass a resolution to the effect that Schedule 3 to the Act applies to the area. That schedule provides that an audible alarm which is installed in or on any premises must comply with any prescribed requirements,[41] and also that the local authority must be notified within forty-eight hours of the installation of the alarm. It is an offence for a person without reasonable excuse to fail to comply with this provision. A duty is placed on the occupier of any premises where an intruder alarm is installed not to permit the alarm to be operated unless the alarm complies with the prescribed requirements and the local authority is notified within 48 hours of the installation of the alarm. It is an offence for a person without reasonable excuse to fail to comply with this provision.

A duty is placed on the occupier of any premises where an intruder alarm is installed not to permit the alarm to be operated unless the alarm complies with the prescribed requirements,[42] the police have been informed *inter alia* of the names and addresses and telephone numbers of current key holders, and the local authority have been informed of the address of the police station to which the aforementioned notification has been given. Power is given to an officer of the local authority, who is authorised for the purpose, to enter any premises and turn off any intruder alarm which has been operating audibly for more than one hour after it was activated and the audible operation of the alarm is such as to give persons living or working in the vicinity of the premises reasonable cause for annoyance. The officer is empowered to apply to a justice of the peace for a warrant to enter by force, if need be, to deactivate an alarm if the alarm has been operating for more than one hour, and the alarm is giving cause for annoyance, and the officer has taken steps to obtain access to the premises, but has failed to do so.

Control of Pollution Act 1974

Construction site noise
Noise from construction sites presents a potential problem for those living in close proximity to the site in question. The noise from construction sites is normally generated by the carrying-out of building operations (ranging from pile-driving to demolition work) or caused by site traffic. Construction site noise in general may, justifiably, prompt complaints from those living in close proximity to the site for two main reasons. First, those who live in proximity to the site are not habituated to the noise in question by virtue of the fact that the life of a construction site is, normally, comparatively quite short. Second, individuals tend to be more easily annoyed by intermittent

noise, which is associated with building sites, than noise which is of a continuous nature. Noise from construction sites, therefore, warrants special legislative attention.

Section 60 of the Control of Pollution Act 1974 (COPA) gives local authorities extensive power to deal with noise from construction sites. The section applies to:

(a)   the erection, construction, alteration, repair or maintenance of buildings, structures or roads;
(b)   breaking up, opening or boring under any road or adjacent land in connection with the construction, inspection, maintenance or removal of works;
(c)   demolition or dredging work; and
(d)   whether or not comprised in paragraph (a)(b) or (c) above) any work or engineering construction.

Section 60(2) empowers a local authority to serve a notice which imposes requirements as to the way in which the relevant works are either being carried out or are going to be carried out. The terms which the local authority can stipulate require to be practical and also precise.[43] The notice must relate to and also specify works which are being carried out or will be carried out in the future. If the notice simply relates to works which are currently being carried out, the notice is ineffective in relation to noise which emanates from work which is not, at that time, within the contemplation of the local authority.[44] In other words, the notice is only effective in relation to work which is taking place on the date on which the notice is served. However, there is no requirement that the local authority be in possession of definite information as to the precise nature of the relevant operations, before it can lawfully serve notice.[45] It must be clear to the person upon whom the notice is served that it relates to a specific area of land.[46]

Section 60(3) provides that the local authority may, in particular, specify the plant or machinery which is or is not to be used, and also specify the hours during which the works may be carried out, and the level of the noise which may be emitted from the premises in question, or at any specified point on those premises which may be emitted during specified hours. In *Adam (Scotland) Ltd* v *Bearsden and Milngavie District Council*[47] it was held by the sheriff that it was legitimate for a local authority to specify a requirement in the appropriate notice that all works which were audible at a site should be carried out between certain hours. There was no justification for the view that the 'audibility test' was objectionable on the basis that it was subjective. The notice can also provide for any change in circumstances.

Under s 60(4) when a local authority acts under the provisions of s 60, it is required to have regard to both the relevant provisions of any code of practice which is issued under Part III of the Act[48] and the need to ensure that the best practicable means are employed to minimise noise. Before specifying any particular methods or plant or machinery the local authority is required to address its mind to the desirability, in the interests of any recipients of the notice in question, of specifying other methods or plant or machinery which would be substantially as effective in minimising noise and which would be more acceptable to the recipient. Finally, the local authority is required to have regard to the need to protect persons in the locality in which the premises in question are situated from the effects of the noise.

Under s 60(5) the relevant notice requires to be served on the person who appears to the local authority to either be carrying out, or going to carry out, the works, and on other persons who appear to the local authority to be responsible for, or to have control over, the works. Notice could, therefore, be served on the relevant building contractor, as well as the person who has commissioned the works (if they are different persons) such as the owner or occupier of the land concerned. The notice may specify the time within which its terms are to be complied with and may require the person on whom the notice is served to execute works and to take other such steps as may be necessary for the purpose of the notice or as may be specified in the notice. The person served with a notice under s 60 may appeal against the notice to the sheriff, within twenty-one days from the service of the notice.[49] Under s 60(8) if a person on whom a notice is served under s 60 contravenes, without reasonable cause, any requirement of the notice, he commits an offence under the Act.

One can quite readily see that the prospect of the relevant local authority serving notice under s 60 could present a constant threat to a building contractor, who requires to know at the very outset of the construction operations in question how long the building operations will last, as well as the type of machinery and also the plant which will be used on the site. Section 61 therefore allows a person who intends to carry out building works to apply to the local authority for consent. If, as will normally be the case, the building works require a building warrant in terms of the Building (Scotland) Act 2003, the application for consent requires to be made at the same time or later than the request for building warrant approval under the former statute.[50] The application must contain particulars of the works, the method by which they are to be carried out, and also the steps proposed to be taken in order to minimise noise which results from the works.[51] The local authority is required to give its approval to the application if the local authority considers that the application contains sufficient information for the purpose and that if the works are carried out in accordance with the application, the local authority would not serve notice under s 60. When considering whether to grant consent, the local authority must address its mind to the provisions of s 60 of the Act.[52] If the local authority deems it appropriate to grant consent to the application, the potential of the site to create noise can be reduced by the local authority having power to attach relevant conditions to the consent in question, or to limit or qualify the consent in order to allow for any change in circumstances. The local authority can also limit the duration of the consent. It is made an offence for any person to knowingly carry out works or permit the works to be carried out in contravention of any conditions which are attached to a consent.[53]

The local authority is required to inform the applicant of its decision within twenty-eight days of the receipt of the application.[54] The applicant can appeal to the sheriff against the refusal of a local authority to grant consent or against any condition or qualification which is attached to the consent.[55] In any proceedings for an offence under s 60(8) of the Act, it is a defence to prove that the alleged contravention amounted to the carrying-out of works which are in accordance with a consent which was given under s 61.[56] A consent which is given under s 61 is required to contain a statement to the effect that such a consent does not, of itself, constitute any ground of defence against any proceedings which are instituted under s 82 of the EPA.[57] Finally, where a consent has been given under s 61 and the works are carried out by a person (for example, a subcontractor) other than the applicant, a duty is imposed on the applicant to take all reasonable steps to bring the consent to the notice of that other person.[58] A penalty is imposed for failure to comply with this requirement.

Loudspeakers in roads

Loudspeakers in vehicles have been a problem for a number of years. More recently, the problem has worsened by virtue of certain anti-social individuals (almost exclusively, young people) using loudspeakers in their cars, the former being capable of generating great volumes of noise, to the discomfort of members of the public. However, Parliament did not consider the problem sufficiently serious to warrant legislative intervention until 1960 when the Noise Abatement Act 1960[59] made special provision for loudspeaker street noise. This problem is now dealt with by COPA. Section 62(1)(a) makes it an offence to use a loudspeaker in a road[60] between 9.00 in the evening and 8.00 the following morning for any purpose. It is also made an offence to use a loudspeaker in a road at any other time for the purpose of advertising any trade or business. Power is given to the Scottish Ministers to amend the times which are specified in s 62(1)(a) by order.[61] However, any such order may not amend the relevant times so as to permit the operation of a loudspeaker in a road at any time between the hours of 9.00 in the evening and 8.00 the following morning.[62] However, s 62(2) exempts from the provisions of s 62(1) certain types of loudspeaker, including those which are used by the police, fire and ambulance services. Also exempt is the use of a loudspeaker which is used solely to entertain or communicate with the occupant of a vehicle (for example, a loudspeaker which is part of a car radio system), provided that the loudspeaker is not operated so as to give reasonable cause for annoyance to persons in the vicinity. Another important exemption, in practical terms, is that made in respect of the operation of a loudspeaker between noon and 7.00 in the evening of the same day, provided that the loudspeaker is fixed to a vehicle which is used for the purpose of sale of a perishable commodity (for example, ice cream) for human consumption and is operated so as not to give cause for annoyance to persons who are in the vicinity.[63] Under s 62(3A) power is given to the relevant local authority to give consent to the operation of a loudspeaker in terms of Sched 2 to the Noise and Statutory Nuisance Act 1993, in which case the provisions of s 62(1) do not apply. However, the provisions of that schedule only come into effect if the local authority passes a resolution to that effect.[64]

Noise from plant and machinery
Under s 68 of COPA the Scottish Ministers have power to make regulations to require the use, either on or in connection with plant or machinery, of devices or arrangements for reducing the noise which is caused by plant or machinery.[65] Regulations may also limit the level of noise which may be caused by any plant or machinery when used for works to which s 60 of the Act applies[66] or which may be caused outside a factory within the meaning of the Factories Act 1961 by the use of plant or machinery in the factory. It is made an offence to contravene such regulations.[67]

Other statutory controls over noise
We now look at other statutory controls on noise pollution.

Civic Government (Scotland) Act 1982

Noise from musical instruments etc., dogs
Noise from televisions, radios and record players is a perennial problem in the United Kingdom. Excessive noise from such devices can rank as

a nuisance[68] or a statutory nuisance.[69] However, the Civic Government (Scotland) Act 1982 gives the police power to deal with specific types of noise. Under s 54 (1) of the Act any person who sounds or plays a musical instrument, sings or performs or operates any radio or television receiver, record player, tape recorder or other sound-producing device so as to give reasonable cause for annoyance and fails to desist on being required to do so by a constable in uniform commits an offence under the Act. Where a constable reasonably suspects that an offence has been committed in relation to a musical instrument or in relation to a radio, television receiver, record player or other sound-producing device, the constable may enter the premises on which he reasonably suspects that instrument or device to be and seize any such instrument or device which he finds there.[70] The constable may use reasonable force in entering the premises and seizing the equipment.[71]

Anecdotal evidence suggests that the Act operates effectively in practice.

Antisocial Behaviour etc. (Scotland) Act 2004

In its *A Partnership for a Better Scotland*[72] the Scottish Government committed itself to social justice, in particular to ensure that everyone in Scotland can enjoy a decent quality of life. Noise pollution was recognised as something which could have a negative impact on the quality of life. In particular, the creation of excessive neighbourhood noise was to be regarded as anti-social and, therefore, required to be dealt with along with other forms of anti-social conduct. The Antisocial Behaviour etc. (Scotland) Act 2004 (ABSA) makes provision for various forms of antisocial behaviour, amongst which is noise.

Antisocial behaviour orders

Under Part 2 of the Act a sheriff, on the application of a relevant authority,[73] if satisfied that the following conditions are met, can make an antisocial behaviour order.[74] The conditions are:

(a) that the specified person is at least twelve years of age;
(b) that the specified person has engaged in antisocial behaviour towards a relevant person; and,
(c) that an antisocial behaviour order is necessary for the purpose of protecting relevant persons from further antisocial behaviour by the specified person.[75]

The expression 'anti-social behaviour' is defined as such if the relevant person:

(a)   acts in a manner that causes or is likely to cause alarm or distress; or

(b)   pursues a course of conduct[76] that causes or is likely to cause alarm or distress to at least one person who is not of the same household as that person.[77]

Anti-social behaviour can, therefore, include conduct which generates noise. The expression 'distress', as used in the Act, is not defined. It should, therefore, be given its everyday meaning. Any form of noise which causes annoyance or anxiety on the part of the receiver could, therefore, fall within the scope of the Act. It will be a question of fact whether the conduct in question has caused distress etc.

Noise nuisance

Part 5 of the ABSA makes special provision for neighbourhood noise. The provisions of the ABSA which relate to noise are simply adoptive and apply to the area of a local authority only if the authority has so resolved.[78] Adoptive legislation was much more common during the nineteenth century.[79] A local authority which has resolved to adopt the ABSA has some flexibility as to the periods of the week during which the Act should apply.[80] The provisions of the ABSA could, for example, be confined to night-time hours. The ABSA may be made to apply for the whole week.[81] Furthermore, different noise control periods could be made to apply to different areas and also to different times of the year. The Act makes provision for publicity. If a local authority resolves to apply the noise control provisions in its area, the local authority is required to have a notice published in a local newspaper which circulates in the area.[82] At least one month before the commencement date the local authority is required to give a copy of the resolution to the Scottish Ministers and also to each local authority whose area adjoins its area. The relevant notice requires to state that the resolution has been passed.[83] The notice also requires to contain its commencement date, and *inter alia*, set out the general effect of the noise control provisions of the ABSA and also the relevant noise control periods during which the provisions of the ABSA will apply. The ABSA also makes provision for the resolution to be either revoked or amended.[84]

Investigations of excessive noise

Where a local authority receives a complaint from an individual that excessive noise[85] is being emitted from relevant property[86] during a noise control period, the local authority must ensure that an officer of the authority investigates the matter.[87] However, the expression 'investigates' is not defined in the ABSA. There is, therefore, no statutory requirement, for example, that any officer of the local authority should visit the alleged offender's premises or the complainant. The relevant complaint can be by any means.[88] If, in consequence of such an investigation, an officer is satisfied that noise is being emitted from a relevant property (the 'offending property') and the noise, if it was measured from the relevant place,[89] would or might exceed the permitted level,[90] the officer may serve a notice about the noise under s 44.[91] It is a matter for the discretion of the officer concerned to decide, first, whether any noise, if it were measured from a relevant place, would or might exceed the permitted level, and secondly, to decide from what place to assess the noise and whether to use a device for measuring the noise.[92] Where a local authority receives a complaint which concerns offending property which is situated within the area of another local authority, the first authority is empowered to deal with that property under the ABSA as if that property were situated in the area of the former, notwithstanding the fact that the noise control provisions of the ABSA apply to the latter area.[93]

Warning notices

If an officer of the local authority considers that noise is being emitted from the offending property during a noise control period and that the noise exceeds or may exceed the permitted level as measured from the relevant place, the officer may serve a warning notice on the person responsible.[94] The notice must state the fact that the noise exceeds the permitted level in the officer's opinion.[95] The notice is also required to state that any person who is responsible for noise which is emitted from the offending property in the period which is specified in the notice and also exceeds the permitted level of noise as measured from a relevant place, may be guilty of an offence. The period which is specified in a warning notice is the period which begins not earlier than ten minutes after the time when the notice is served and ends at the relevant time.[96] The expression 'relevant time' is defined as the earlier of the end of the noise control period during which the warning notice is served and the point (if any) at which the permitted level at the time the notice is served ceases to be applicable.[97] The warning notice requires to be served by delivering it to any person who is present at, or near, the offending property, such person appearing to the officer of the authority to be responsible for the noise.[98] If it is not reasonably practicable to identify any person who is present either at or near the offending property as being a person responsible[99] for the noise, the notice may be served by leaving it at the offending property.[100] The warning notice is required to state the time at which it is served.[101]

Offences

If a warning notice has been served in respect of noise which is emitted from a relevant property, any person who is responsible for such noise in the period which is specified in the notice and exceeds the permitted level as measured from a relevant place, commits an offence.[102] Liability for the offence is strict. There is no need for the prosecution to establish either intention or fault on the part of the accused. It is a defence for a person who is charged with an offence under the section to prove that there was reasonable excuse for the act, failure by reference to which the person was charged.[103] A measurement of noise by a device is not admissible as evidence of a noise level unless the device is an approved device and any conditions subject to which approval was given are satisfied.[104] The Scottish Ministers have power to approve by regulations any type of device which is used for the measurement of noise.[105] Approval may be given subject to conditions as to the purposes for which or the manner and circumstances in which devices of the type approved are to be used as may be prescribed in the regulations.[106]

Fixed penalty notices

Traditionally, one of the main failings of noise control legislation has been the inability of local authorities to immediately compel an individual who is making excessive noise to refrain from so doing. The ABSA empowers a relevant officer[107] who has reason to believe that a person is either committing, or has just committed, an offence under s 45, to give that person a fixed penalty notice which offers the relevant individual the opportunity of discharging any liability for conviction for that offence by payment of a fixed penalty.[108] If a fixed penalty notice is given to a person in respect of noise which is emitted from relevant property in the period which is specified in a warning notice, then no further fixed penalty notice may be given to that person in respect of the noise emitted from the relevant property during that period.[109] A fixed penalty notice may be given to a person by delivering the notice in person.[110] However, if it is not reasonably practicable to deliver the notice to the person, a fixed penalty notice requires to be given by leaving the notice, addressed to the person at the offending property.[111] The notice requires to contain sufficient particulars of the circumstances which are alleged to constitute the offence.[112] The fixed penalty notice also requires to state the period during which proceedings may not be taken for the offence, the amount of fixed penalty, and the address at which the fixed penalty can be paid.[113] Proceedings may not be instituted during a period of twenty-eight days from the date of the service of the notice.[114] A person may not be convicted if the appropriate penalty is paid before the expiration of that period.

Power of seizure of equipment

In practicable terms, and indeed, in the mind of the public, one of the most important features of the ABSA are the provisions which relate to the seizure of equipment which is used to create noise. An officer of the local authority, or a person who is authorised by the local authority for the purpose, is empowered to seize and remove equipment which appears to be being used or to have been used in the emission of noise.[115] The equipment can be seized and removed if a warning notice has been served in respect of the noise which has been emitted from the relevant property, and an officer of the local authority in whose area the relevant property is situated has reason to believe that at any time in the period which is specified in the notice, noise which was emitted from the relevant property has exceeded the permitted level as measured from the relevant place.[116] If required to do so, a person who is exercising the power of seizure etc. must produce his authority.[117] If a sheriff or justice of the peace is satisfied by evidence on oath that a warning notice has been served in respect of noise emitted from relevant property, and that at any time in the period which has been specified in the notice, noise which is emitted from the relevant property has exceeded the permitted level (as measured from a relevant place), and that entry of an officer of the local authority, or of a person who is authorised by the authority for the purpose, to a relevant property has been refused or refusal is apprehended (or, alternatively, a request by an officer of the authority or of such a person would defeat the object of entry), the sheriff or justice may grant a warrant.[118] The relevant warrant authorises the local authority, by any of its officers, or any person authorised by it for the purpose, to enter the relevant property and seize and remove any equipment which appears to be being used or to have been used in the emission of noise, and in order to do so, to open lockfast places on the relevant property.[119] The person who enters premises by virtue of a warrant which is granted under s 47 may be accompanied by such persons and take such equipment as may be necessary.[120] Where the relevant property is unaccompanied, on the person's departure it must be left as effectively secure against trespassers as it was when the person entered it. It is made an offence for a person to wilfully obstruct a person in the exercise of his powers of seizure and removal of equipment under s 47(2) or in exercising the power which is conferred by warrant under s 47(2).[121]

Power to fund local authorities
A unique feature of the ABSA is that, in order to ensure that the provisions of the Act are properly enforced, the Act empowers the Scottish Ministers make payments to a local authority in respect of the whole or part of the expenditure of the authority in carrying out its noise enforcement functions under the Act.[122]

General overview of the Antisocial Behaviour etc. (Scotland) Act
We see, of course, that the ABSA employs noise standards which are based on fixed noise levels, in contrast to the nuisance-based regime which has traditionally played such a prominent role in noise law in Scotland, and indeed, the United Kingdom, thus far. One of the main practical disadvantages with a regime which is nuisance-based is that it is often difficult to ascertain whether a given state of affairs ranks as a noise nuisance in law. This is the case from the viewpoint of both the creator of the noise and the officer. A regime which employs fixed standards is – in theory at least – simpler and easier to understand from the viewpoints of both the creator of the noise and the general public.[123] Another point which requires to be made at this juncture concerns the accountability of enforcers of the ABSA. Given the rather technical and esoteric nature of noise pollution, enforcing officers are less accountable to elected members of local authorities (who are normally laymen and not well-versed in the technicalities of noise) than in respect of other forms of pollution control.[124] A regime which is based on fixed standards, such as those which are contained in the Act, while nonetheless esoteric in nature, is still more comprehensible to the lay councillor than a nuisance-based regime.

Licensing (Scotland) Act 2005

Licensed premises
In recent years, in order to attract custom, licensed premises have increasingly provided entertainment in the form of live music, karaoke and discotheques for their customers. As far as Scotland is concerned, the Licensing (Scotland) Act 2005 allows a licensing board to impose conditions in the licenses of premises as it considers necessary or expedient for the purposes of any of the licensing objectives which are contained in the Act.[125] The licensing objectives for the purposes of the Act include 'the prevention of public nuisances'.[126] While the choice of phrase 'public nuisance' is unfortunate, given its meaning in English law, the phrase would cover noise from licensed premises. Many licensing boards have imposed conditions

in licenses to the effect that no noise can be discernible at the perimeter of the relevant premises.

Town and country planning

In terms of environmental regulation generally, it is preferable that the law should attempt to prevent any adverse situation coming into existence at the very outset, rather than providing machinery by means of which the relevant adverse state of affairs can be abated afterwards. The law of town and country planning therefore has an important role to play as far as the prophylactic control of noise is concerned. This subject is dealt with later in the book.[127]

Noise and human rights

Human rights jurisprudence has an important role to play as far as the control of noise is concerned, given the limitations of the common law of nuisance to secure redress in some cases. Several examples can be used to illustrate this point. In the House of Lords case of *Baxter v Camden LBC*[128] a tenant who resided in a block of flats which was owned by a local authority raised an action against the authority, *inter alia*, on the grounds that, by reason of poor sound insulation in both the walls and ceilings which separated the various flats, she could hear almost everything which her neighbours were doing. One can, therefore, quite readily appreciate that the plaintiff was being subjected to gross discomfort. However, the House held that the adverse state of affairs which she was being subjected to did not rank as an actionable nuisance in law simply because the noise of which the plaintiff complained ranked as everyday noise – that is to say, noise which emanated from the ordinary (as opposed to the unreasonable) use by her neighbours of their property. Another important limitation in the law of nuisance is that in order to be able to successfully raise an action in terms of the law of nuisance, one is required to have a proprietary interest in the land which is affected by the relevant adverse state of affairs.[129] Given the limitations of the law of nuisance in dealing adequately with a noise problem, it seems likely that Art 8 of the European Convention of Human Rights (ECHR) and Art 1 of Protocol No 1 to the ECHR (which guarantee respect for family life and home as well as the right to peaceful enjoyment of property and possessions) will, in future, be more frequently invoked in relation to noise.

UK cases

Almost all of the UK cases on the subject of noise and human rights have related to noise from aviation. In *Dennis v Ministry of Defence*[130] which has already been discussed in the context of the law of nuisance,[131] Buckley J was prepared to hold that the noise from military aircraft infringed both

Art 8 and Art 1 of Protocol No 1 to the ECHR, and also ranked as a nuisance, first, by virtue of the noise in question being sufficiently loud and, second, by dint of the effect of the noise on the market value of the property.[132] However, the damages which fell to be awarded under each head would be satisfied by damages in terms of the law of nuisance.

Whereas *Dennis* concerned noise from military aircraft, *Hatton v The United Kingdom*[133] concerned noise from civil aircraft. Essentially, an action was brought against the UK government by a group of residents who lived under the flightpath of aircraft which used Heathrow Airport. It was claimed that the noise from the aircraft flouted the residents' rights which were embedded in Art 8 of the ECHR. The Grand Chamber of the European Court of Human Rights recognised that there was no explicit right to a clean and quiet environment.[134] However, the court held that where an individual was both directly and seriously affected by noise, or some other form of pollution, it was possible that Art 8 could be engaged. The court went on to state that Art 8 could be equally contravened either by a positive act on the part of the government or, simply, by its failure to protect its citizens against noise. The court held that, in such a situation, the court enjoys a wide margin of appreciation in determining which steps require to be taken in order to secure compliance with the Convention.[135] Another point of interest in *Hatton* is that, in reaching its decision, the Grand Chamber set store by the fact that the noise, which was the subject of the action, did not derive from a state of affairs in relation to which there was any domestic irregularity.[136] In this context, it should be observed that, normally, noise from civil aircraft is immune from action in terms of the law of nuisance.[137] In the last analysis, the court, in deciding in favour of the UK government, held that it was legitimate for the government to take into account the interests of the country, as a whole, in shaping its policy.

Subsequent human rights case law

The European Court of Human Rights had an opportunity to discuss the issue of pollution, including noise pollution, in terms of human rights law in *Fadayeva v Russia*.[138] Ms Fadeyeva resided in a steel-making town in Russia. She alleged that her health had been affected by the severe pollution, which included noise, emanating from the plant. The court held that, in order to infringe Art 8 of the ECHR, the adverse effects of environmental pollution must attain a minimum level. However, the assessment of that level was relative and also depended upon all the circumstances of the case, such as the intensity and duration of the nuisance, and also the physical and mental effects of the noise. The general environmental context was also to be taken into account. There would be no claim under Art 8 if the detriment which was complained of was negligible in comparison to the environmental hazards which were inherent to life. The court went on to hold that, in order to flout Art 8, one would require to show that there was actual interference with the applicant's private sphere, and, secondly, that a level of severity was attained.[139] Whereas the expressions 'private sphere' and 'level of severity' are infelicitous at best, and vague at worst, they both indicate that the court adopted an anthropomorphic approach to that which constitutes an infringement of Art 8.

Gomez v Spain[140] is another interesting case where noise again was the subject of an action before the European Court of Human Rights. Ms Gomez (G.) lived in a flat which was situated in a residential quarter of Valencia. Since 1974 Valencia City Council (VCC) had allowed licensed premises such as bars, pubs and discotheques to open in the vicinity of her home, making it impossible for people who lived in the area to sleep. G. claimed that this state of affairs amounted to a breach of her rights in terms of Art 8 on the grounds that, whereas the Council was not the direct source of the noise pollution, VCC had caused the adverse state of affairs in question to come into existence by issuing an unlimited number of licenses, without taking the requisite measures to reduce the noise. G. claimed that the level of noise which was caused by some 127 nightclubs infringed the right to health, as indicated by the World Health Organisation (WHO) guidelines. The court was of the view that a breach of Art 8 could take place by virtue of the intrusion of noise into the home.[141] Indeed, a serious breach of Art 8 could take place if the adverse state of affairs in question prevented the individual from enjoying the amenities of his home. The court went on to state that whereas the object of Art 8 is essentially to protect the individual against arbitrary interference by public authorities, the Article may place an affirmative duty on the authorities to secure compliance with Art 8 in terms of relations between individuals themselves.[142] However, in both contexts, one had to have regard to the fair balance which had to be struck between the competing interests of the individual and the community as a whole. As to whether the noise in question actually flouted Art 8, it sufficed that the relevant maximum permitted level of noise had been exceeded in terms of the very byelaws which had been made by VCC and had exceeded such levels for a number of years.[143]

In *Dees v Hungary*[144] the applicant, D., claimed that by virtue of the increase in volume of traffic on the road outside his home, it had become almost uninhabitable by virtue of noise, pollution and smell emanating from traffic. D. claimed that, as a consequence, his rights under Art 8 had been infringed. The court recognised that the individual has a right to respect for his home, meaning not simply the individual's right to the actual physical area, but also to the quiet enjoyment of that area within reasonable limits.[145] Breaches of Art 8 were not confined to concrete breaches such as the unauthorised entry into a person's home, but also included breaches which were diffuse in nature such as noise, emissions or smell. A serious breach may result in the breach of a person's right to respect for his home if such a breach prevents him from enjoying the amenities of his home. The noise, vibration, pollution and odour which had been caused by heavy traffic made D.'s property almost uninhabitable.

The court went on to recognise that the state enjoys a certain margin of appreciation in determining regulatory and other measures which are intended to protect Art 8 rights.[146] This was true not simply in a case where the state interfered directly with such rights but also in circumstances where the state had failed to take action to put a stop to third-party breaches of Art 8. Applying this principle to the facts of the instant case, the state was required to balance the interests of road-users and those of the inhabitants of surrounding areas. The court recognised the complexity of the state's task in handling infrastructural issues such as those in the case on this instance where remedial measures required considerable time and resources. However, the court held that the measures which had been taken by the authorities were insufficient, the upshot of which was that D had been exposed to excessive noise disturbance over a period of time. This created a disproportionate individual burden for the applicant. Furthermore, the noise which D had been subjected to exceeded the relevant statutory level. In the last analysis, there had been a violation of Art 8.

Noise pollution was, again, the subject of discussion in *Oluic v Croatia*.[147] It is necessary to recount the facts of this case in some detail. The applicant, Oluic (O.), owned part of a house in Rijeka in Croatia where she lived with her family. Since December 1999 a bar had been run by a third party who lived in the other part of the house. In 2001 O. wrote to the Sanitary Inspection (SI) (a public authority responsible for noise nuisance abatement in the area in which O. lived) claiming that her flat had been constantly exposed to excessive noise from the bar which was open from 7.00 in the morning until midnight. Soon after her initial contact with the SI, O urged it to take urgent action to abate the nuisance on her request. Measurements were carried out in May 2001 at night by an independent expert firm of acousticians. It found that the level of noise from the premises exceeded the permitted level, in terms of the relevant byelaw which governed noise from neighbours. Later in the year, the SI ordered the company which owned the bar to reduce the level of noise from its equipment for the reproduction of music. That decision was quashed by the Ministry of Health. Further measurements were taken later. These showed that noise from the bar exceeded the permitted levels. In 2002 the SI ordered the owner of the bar to add sound insulation to the walls and floor of the bar. A subsequent inspection established that the order had not been complied with. The SI then ordered an enforcement of the order. Sound insulation was subsequently installed. However, it was ascertained that it was insufficient. Further measurements, which were taken in 2003, showed that the noise from the bar exceeded the permitted level. Later in 2003 proceedings against the bar owner were terminated on the basis that only the ground floor was being used as a bar, and that, furthermore, the noise from the bar was not excessive. O. then lodged an appeal against this decision to the Ministry of Health. O. then brought a claim before the Administrative Court, challenging the findings of the administrative bodies. Further measurements indicated that the level of noise in O.'s flat exceeded the permitted level. O. then lodged a complaint with the Supreme Court about the length of the proceedings before the Administrative Court. The complaint was accepted and the former ordered the latter to come to a decision within three months. In April 2007 the Administrative Court quashed the decisions of the lower bodies and ordered them to establish whether the noise from the bar was still excessive. Later in the same year, a second-instance administrative body annulled the decisions which had been made by the SI in 2003, on the basis that the noise which came from the bar was excessive and also that the insulation between the flat and the bar was insufficient.

Between late December 2007 and December 2008 the SI took more measurements. In January 2009 the SI ordered the owner of the bar to reduce the noise level, but a month later measurements showed that the noise levels from the bar had not exceeded the set standards. O. then brought an action before the European Court of Human Rights on the basis that the state had failed to protect her from the excessive noise which emanated from the bar.

Firstly, the government argued that O. had failed to exhaust domestic remedies in the administrative proceedings.[148] The European Court of Human Rights held that before one could enlist the aid of the Court, one was required to make use of normal domestic remedies which are effective, sufficient and accessible.[149] If there were a number of domestic remedies, an individual could make use of any of such remedies which addressed his or her grievance. In other words, when one remedy had been pursued, there was no need for the applicant to pursue another remedy which had the same objective. In this instance, the remedies which O. had invoked were aimed at securing the same objective as the appropriate civil proceedings, namely abating the noise from the bar. Therefore, the government's argument that the applicant had failed to exhaust domestic remedies by reason of failing to take civil proceedings against the author of the nuisance fell to be rejected.

Secondly, the government argued that the applicant had failed to exhaust domestic remedies, in that the administrative proceedings against the bar owner were still pending.[150] Thirdly, the government claimed that the level of noise to which the applicant was exposed had not reached the necessary level of severity for Article 8 to be engaged.[151] Fourthly, the government claimed that the dispute simply concerned two private individuals in contradistinction to an act of the state against the individual.[152] The court held that that the second, third and fourth issues fell to be decided on the merits of the case.

Prior to deciding the second, third and fourth issues, the Court held that whilst there is no right to a clean and quiet environment under human rights law, where an individual is both directly and seriously affected by noise or other forms of pollution, Art 8 could be engaged.[153] The Court went on to state that whereas Art 8 is essentially aimed at protecting the individual against arbitrary interference by public authorities, it may involve the authorities adopting measures which are designed to secure respect for private life even in the sphere of relations between private individuals themselves.[154] However, in determining whether Art 8 had been breached, the applicable principles were the same, namely, regard had to be paid to the competing interests of the individual and of the community. The instant case concerned an allegation that the relevant public authorities had failed to put a stop to third parties breaching the applicant's rights under Art 8.[155]

The court then went on to determine whether the noise to which the applicant had been subjected contravened Art 8. The Court took into account the fact that the noise levels to which the applicant had been exposed had exceeded the permitted levels over the years which had been set by the appropriate byelaw and, furthermore, had exceeded the international standards which had been set by the WHO and also most European countries.[156] The Court then went on to hold that both the volume of noise and also its duration reached the minimum level of severity which required the relevant authorities to implement measures in order to protect the applicant from such a noise in terms of the Article 8.

In the last analysis, the fact that the noise which was excessive and also the fact that the national authorities had allowed the situation to persist for almost eight years, meant that the State had failed to discharge its positive obligation to guarantee the applicant's right to respect for her home and family life. Therefore, there had been a violation of Art 8.[157]

Oluic follows previous decisions such as *Hatton* and *Gomez* where the European Court of Human Rights have held that noise pollution which impacts on the enjoyment of one's home is capable of flouting Art 8. *Oluic* also emphasises the point that in determining whether Art 8 has been flouted, not only is the Court entitled to take into account the relevant domestic law of the country where the complainant lives, the Court is also entitled to take into account WHO environmental noise standards, and also any acceptable noise levels which other European countries have set. Furthermore, *Oluic* also establishes the principle that one is not required to bring civil proceedings against the author of a noise nuisance before enlisting the aid of the European Court of Human Rights. Finally, it is also of interest that in determining whether Art 8 had been contravened, the Court took into account the length of time O.'s case was before the Administrative Court.

Noise pollution featured again in the interesting case of *Zammit Meampel v Malta*.[158] Every year, on the occasion of certain village feasts, firework displays were set up in the fields which were situated close to the applicants' residence. The applicants (Z.) alleged that each time fireworks were let off from the area, they were exposed to risk and peril to their life, physical health and personal security and, importantly, that the state had failed to take all necessary measures to protect Z. from their rights in terms of Art 8 of the ECHR. In the last analysis, the question which the European Court of Human Rights was required to answer was whether the state had struck a fair balance between the competing interests of the individuals who were affected by the disturbance and the community as a whole.[159] In its attempt to strike such a balance, the Court held that the state was allowed a wide margin of appreciation.[160] The Court noted that whereas the mortality rate relating to the fireworks industry in Malta was alarming, such incidents occurred less frequently during actual firework displays than during the manufacturing of such fireworks.[161] Furthermore, the damage which had occurred to the property of Z. was both minimal and reversible. Z. could take action against the authors of the fireworks nuisance by way of civil proceedings. In the last analysis, the repeated letting-off of fireworks at noise levels which exceeded at least 120 decibels for two weeks each year, even though intermittently, created considerable inconvenience for Z. However, such inconvenience had to be balanced against the interests of the community. Importantly, the authorities were, in identifying distances from where third parties could perform relevant displays, required to take into account 'the geographical situation (i.e. the relatively small and compact nature) of Malta and its population density'.[162] Moreover, the state had addressed its mind to the dangers which were inherent in the use of fireworks and had, in turn, put in place a certain degree of protection.[163] The firework displays which were the subject-matter of the action were monitored by the police and the fire service. Furthermore, the Court set store by the fact that Z. were fully aware of the very state of affairs of which they complained before they moved into the affected property. In the last analysis, the state had not overstepped its margin of appreciation by failing to strike a fair balance between the rights of the individuals who were affected by the noise and those of the community as a whole.[164] There had been no violation of Art 8 by the state.

Conclusions on noise and human rights
In terms of addressing environmental pollution, human rights law is at an incipient stage of development, especially in relation to the Cinderella pollutant which is noise. However, one can say with some confidence that, thus far, in determining whether Art 8 has been infringed by noise pollution, the court requires to take into account a variety of factors, including whether the noise in question is of such a level that such noise flouts relevant domestic law; appropriate WHO standards; whether the claimant has come to the nuisance; and also, whether the source of the adverse state of affairs is typical of modern life. Thus far, it also seems fairly certain that in order to flout Art 8, the level of the relevant noise requires to be as loud, if not louder, than that which is deemed a nuisance at common law. Such jurisprudence is not, therefore, four-square with the principles of the law of nuisance. For example, the latter, in ascertaining whether any given noise ranks as a nuisance, ignores the fact that the pursuer has moved to the nuisance.[165]

European noise law

We now turn our attention to how the European Union has addressed the problem of noise pollution. The development of European noise policy was slow and, indeed, unimaginative. The earliest measures which were used by the EU to deal with noise were harmonisation measures aimed at specific products, such as vehicles, in order to eliminate barriers to trade and also facilitate the free movement of goods within the Community.[166] Ostensibly, at least, there was no EU noise policy as such. However, a change in direction was seen in the EU's Fifth Action Programme[167] which dealt with the problem of urban noise. It was recognised that noise has a negative impact on human health. Under this programme a general environmental objective was established to the effect that no person should be exposed to noise levels which endanger health and also the quality of life.

The next major development in EU noise policy was contained in the EC Green Paper *Future Noise Policy*[168] which was published in 1996. A major driving force as far as such policy was concerned was the impact of noise on human health. The Commission accepted the view that whereas the impact of noise is, essentially, a local responsibility and, therefore, best dealt with by Member States themselves, the sources of noise pollution were best dealt with at EU level. Importantly, the Green Paper recognised that the lack of available data on noise was having a detrimental effect on the formulation of a coherent noise policy. The proposal for a Sixth Environmental Action Programme, which was published in 2001,[169] recognised that noise affected both the health and the quality of life of at least 25 per cent of the EU population. The Action Programme set targets for the systematic reduction of the numbers of those who were affected by noise. The policy, which was embedded in the Action Programme, found expression in the EU Directive relating to the assessment and management of noise[170] which is commonly referred to as the 'END' Directive. In the author's view, the END represents the most important measure the EU has taken thus far in the battle against ambient noise. Indeed, the END represents the flagship of the EU's battle against noise pollution.

The END Directive
One of the main obstacles in the way of the EU being able to formulate a noise policy is that Member States have spoken different 'languages' as it were, as far as the measurement of noise is concerned. From an EU perspective it was difficult to ascertain the extent of the ambient noise problem in relation to the EU as a whole. The END's main objective, therefore, is to establish a common EU framework for the assessment and management of exposure to environmental noise[171] by using common methods of noise measurement and, furthermore – and importantly – ensuring that such information is made available to the public.[172] The END focuses mainly on noise from major sources such as road and railway traffic and also aircraft and industrial noise. However, the END does not set limit values (i.e. noise levels which may not be exceeded) in any area. This is left to the discretion of the Member State. Thus, the principle of subsidiarity, which is engrained in EU law, is upheld.

The scope of the END is wide-ranging and it applies to environmental noise to which humans are exposed, particularly in built-up areas, in public parks or other quiet areas in an agglomeration,[173] in quiet areas in open country, and near schools, hospitals and other noise-sensitive buildings and areas.[174] However, the END does not apply to noise which is caused by the exposed person himself, noise from domestic activities, noise created by neighbours, noise at workplaces, noise inside means of transport, or noise which is caused by military activities in military areas. Overall responsibility for implementing the END lies with Member States.[175] Under the END Member States were required to prepare relevant action plans no later than 18 July 2012. The END lays down minimum requirements as far as action plans are concerned.[176]

A fundamental problem which has been associated with noise pollution, whether it takes the form of ambient noise or neighbourhood noise, is that the public are generally unaware of both the nature and extent of the noise which affects their locality. Such a lack of insight into the problem has profoundly affected the accountability of local authorities who have, as we have already seen,[177] the responsibility of implementing the law relating to noise.[178] The END attempts to address at least some of the problem by requiring Member States to ensure that both strategic noise maps[179] and action plans are made available and disseminated to members of the public.[180] Importantly, the information requires to be clear, comprehensible, and also accessible. After the strategic noise maps and the relevant action plans are prepared, the information must be sent to the EU Commission which requires to set up a data bank of information on noise maps.[181] The Commission is also required to submit to the European Parliament and the Council a report on the implementation of the END.[182] In Scotland, the END is implemented by the Environmental Noise (Scotland) Regulations.[183]

Finally, attention should be drawn to the fact that noise is also integrated in other EU environmental policy such as the Thematic Strategy of the Urban Environment[184] and the EU Sustainable Development Strategy.[185]

Noise from aircraft
Aircraft pose a serious problem as far as noise pollution is concerned. We therefore turn our attention to, first, noise from civil aircraft; second, noise from civil aircraft; and, finally, noise generated by military aircraft.

Civil aircraft
Aircraft can cause noise problems for the community when the aircraft is taking off, when the aircraft is landing at an airport, or when the aircraft is in flight. Therefore, the relevant statutory controls which govern aircraft noise can roughly be divided into controls which relate to noise from the flight (or navigation) of aircraft, and those which specifically relate to noise from aerodromes.

FLIGHT NOISE

Given that the flight paths of aircraft are often directly over houses and other occupied premises, the noise which is generated by aircraft which are either taking off from or landing at airports can cause considerable annoyance to individuals who are living beneath such flight paths. However, the Civil Aviation Act 1982[186] (the Act) provides that no action may lie in respect of either trespass or nuisance by reason only of the flight of an aircraft over any property at a height above the ground which, having regard to wind, weather and all the circumstances of the case, is reasonable, or is the ordinary incident of such flight. This defence is subject to the proviso that the provisions of any orders which have been made under the Act[187] have been duly complied with, and also, that there has been no breach of s81 of the Act which proscribes dangerous flying. Section 60(3) allows Air Navigation Orders to be made, *inter alia*, regulating the conditions under which aircraft either entering or leaving the UK may fly, and, also, the conditions under which aircraft may fly from one part of the UK to another. Under the Air Navigation Order 2009[188] the Secretary of State may make Rules of the Air which regulate the manner in which aircraft may fly over the country. It is an offence to fail to comply with the Rules.[189] The current rules of the air are the Rules of the Air Regulations 2007.[190] The Regulations prohibit low flying.[191] Whereas the main aim of the regulation is to protect those on the ground, the provision also has relevance as far as the impact of noise on communities is concerned. Of further relevance is the fact that aircraft may not take off or land within an aerodrome traffic zone unless the aircraft has obtained the permission of the air traffic control unit.[192] Whilst the aim of the regulation is to ensure flight safety, in practice, the power to regulate both take-off and landing of aircraft is often used to reduce the noise from aircraft to those who live in the vicinity of aerodromes.

Whilst the controls which are outlined above have a significant impact in reducing noise from aircraft, much more important is the necessity to reduce noise from aircraft at source, that is to say, from the aircraft itself. The Chicago Convention on International Civil Aviation Organisation (which deals with aviation in general) was signed in 1944. The UK is party to the Convention, Annex 16 of which deals specifically with noise from aircraft. Furthermore, the EU has made a number of directives which relate to noise from aircraft which are based on agreements made under the *aegis* of the International Civil Aviation Organisation. The provisions of both the Convention and the EU directives are implemented by orders which are made under the Civil Aviation Act 1982.[193] EU Regulation 748 /2012[194] makes provision for the noise certification of aircraft. Essentially, as far as the UK is concerned, before a noise certificate can be granted by the Civil Aviation Authority (CAA), the aircraft must comply with the environmental standards which are contained in EU Regulation 216/2008.[195]

As far as subsonic planes are concerned, noise certification is governed by the Aeroplane Noise Regulations 1999.[196] All civil propeller-driven aeroplanes, which are set out in Volume 1 of Annex 16/1981 of the International Civil Aviation Organisation, are required to be in possession of a noise certificate which is granted by the CAA.[197] Similar requirements apply to civil subsonic jet aeroplanes which are registered in the UK.[198] The CAA must grant a noise certificate if it is satisfied that the aeroplane complies with the standard which is specified in the Regulations.[199]

Airport noise

Noise from aircraft poses a particular problem around aerodromes. Under s 77(1) of the Civil Aviation Act 1982 provision may be made by an Air Navigation Order for regulating the conditions under which noise and vibration may be caused by aircraft on an aerodrome, and the Order may provide that s 77(2) of the Act applies to such noise and vibration. Section 77(2) provides that no action may lie in respect of nuisance by reason only of the noise and vibration by aircraft on an aerodrome provided that the Order are complied with. The Air Navigation Order 2009[200] provides that s 77(2) of the Act applies, *inter alia*, to government aerodromes and also aerodromes which are licensed by the Civil Aviation Authority, in respect of which the Secretary of State has prescribed conditions under which noise and vibration may be caused by aircraft on aerodromes.

Another important control over noise from aerodromes is found in the Aerodromes (Noise Restrictions) (Rules and Procedures) Regulations 2003.[201] As far as Scotland is concerned, the Regulations are only applicable to Edinburgh and Glasgow airports, on the basis that the Regulations only apply to civil airports within the UK which have more than 50,000 take-offs and landings of civil subsonic jet aeroplanes per calendar year.[202] In short, the Regulations allow, as far as Scotland is concerned, the competent authority to operate flight restrictions to reduce noise. In Scotland the competent authority is the airport operator (the British Airport Authority). The competent authority is required to adopt a balanced and proportionate approach when dealing with noise problems. Economic incentives may also be used.[203] When considering whether to apply operating restrictions at a relevant airport, the competent authority is required to take into account the matters which are specified in the Regulations.[204]

Planning controls

Town and country planning has an important role to play in controlling noise from aerodromes This topic is discussed later in the book.[205]

Military airports

Noise from military aircraft, airfields, ground-running and testing of engines presents a particular problem.[206] By virtue of their design, military aircraft have a greater capacity than civil aircraft to generate noise. Furthermore, the legal controls which apply to civil aircraft generally do not apply to noise from military aircraft. However, the Crown can be sued for noise with contravenes Art 8 of the ECHR, and also in terms of the law of nuisance.[207]

As far as noise which is caused by aircraft performing military manoeuvres (as defined in the Military Manoeuvres Act 1958)[208] is concerned, compensation would be payable.[209]

Hovercraft

As is the case with other forms of transport, hovercraft are capable of generating noise. The Hovercraft Act 1968 provides that Orders in Council may be made to regulate both the noise and vibration from hovercraft.[210] Such Orders may also provide that no civil action may be brought in nuisance in respect of noise and vibration which is caused by hovercraft if the provisions of the Order are complied with. At the time of writing,[211] no such Order has been made.

Traffic noise

It seems almost a statement of the obvious to say that traffic noise is a serious environmental problem which, unfortunately, is destined to worsen with the passage of time. Indeed, in 1990, the Noise Review Working Party considered road traffic noise as the most serious of all the transportation noise problems.[212] In such a context it is interesting to observe how Parliament has addressed noise from transport. Whereas Parliament has made noise from civil aircraft largely immune from civil action,[213] it has not been similarly indulgent as far as road traffic noise is concerned. However, whilst road traffic noise is not immune from civil action on the part of those who are affected by such noise, road traffic noise is excluded from constituting a statutory nuisance in terms of s 79(1) of the EPA.

As far as the capacity of road vehicles to generate noise is concerned, s 41(1)(2) of the Road Traffic Act 1988 allows the Secretary of State to make regulations which govern, *inter alia*, the construction and equipment of motor vehicles, and also the conditions under which the equipment can be used. Provision can be made in the regulations relating to noise. Section 42 of the Act makes it an offence for a person to fail to comply with regulations which are made under s 41. The main regulations which presently govern the construction and use etc. of vehicles are the Road Vehicles (Construction and Use) Regulations 1986.[214] Under reg 54 every vehicle which is propelled by an internal combustion engine requires to be fitted with an exhaust system, including a silencer, both of which require to be kept in good working order. Importantly, regulations 55-57 make provision for noise limits which vehicles must not exceed. Furthermore, under reg 97 no motor vehicle may be used in such a manner as to cause any excessive noise which could have been avoided by the exercise of reasonable care on the part of the driver.

The Act[215] gives the Secretary of State power to make regulations which require the type approval of vehicles with regard to their design, construction and equipment. If the Secretary of State approves a vehicle as a type, he must issue a certificate which states that the vehicle complies with the relevant type approval. However, the Motor Vehicles (Type Approval) (Great Britain) Regulations 1984[216] make provision for noise and silencers in respect of vehicles.

Location and design of new roads

It is important that public authorities pay attention to the location and design of roads in order to minimise the impact of noise on those who live nearby. As far as the design of new roads is concerned, roads authorities use the memorandum *Calculation of Road Traffic Noise*[217] to calculate road traffic noise. The memorandum describes the procedures for calculating noise from road traffic and provides guidance, *inter alia,* as to the design of new roads and highways.

Finally, town and country planning has an important role to play in relation to noise from roads. In the preparation of development plans, the relevant planning authority can take into account the effect of noise from road traffic on noise-sensitive developments.[218] Town and country planning is dealt with later in the book.[219]

Railway noise

Noise from trains can cause a significant noise problem to those who live in the vicinity. We have already seen that the END Directive covers noise from major railways.[220] The vast majority of railway lines in Scotland were constructed during the nineteenth century when railway construction assumed fever pitch. The authority to construct railways was conferred by way of a private Act of Parliament. As a consequence, the defence of statutory authority was applicable in a nuisance action.[221] The defence of statutory authority would apply in such circumstances provided that the noise in question was the inevitable consequence of that which was authorised by the relevant Act.[222]

The Transport and Works (Scotland) Act 2007 allows the Scottish Ministers to make provision, by way of an order, which authorises the construction and operation of a railway line which starts, ends and remains in Scotland.[224] New railway lines of such a nature will, therefore, require to be authorised by way of an order. There is no authority on whether the defence of statutory authority would be applicable in respect of noise from trains which used a new railway line which was authorised under such an order. In the last analysis, the court would require to decide whether such an order should be accorded similar sanctity to an Act of Parliament in terms of the defence. Thus far, the English courts have refused to allow decisions which have been taken by planning authorities to be equated with private Acts of Parliament. In other words, the fact that a certain activity has been granted planning permission does not confer statutory immunity in terms of the law of nuisance on the grantee.[224]

Planning authorities can take into account railway noise when granting planning permission. The memorandum *Calculation of Railway Noise*[225] may be used to predict rail traffic noise.

Finally, lines for long-distance railway traffic will require an environmental impact assessment under the Town and Country Planning (Scotland) Environmental Impact Assessment (Scotland) Regulations 2011.[227] The topic is dealt with later in the book.[227]

Soundproofing of premises
The effect of environmental noise on individuals can be reduced if premises are adequately insulated. Under the Land Compensation (Scotland) Act 1973 the Scottish Ministers are empowered to make regulations which either impose a duty or confer a power on responsible authorities (such as roads authorities)[228] to insulate buildings or to make grants in respect of the cost of such insulation, against noise which is either caused by, or expected to be caused by, the construction or use of public works.[229] The Noise Insulation (Scotland) Regulations 1975[230] are made under this provision. The regulations provide that where the use of a highway which was first open to the public after 1972 (or in respect of which an additional carriageway has been constructed since that date or is about to be constructed) causes, or is expected to cause, noise at a level which is specified in the regulations, then the appropriate authority is required to carry out

insulation work itself, or to make the appropriate grant in respect of the carrying-out of the insulation works.[231] The authority has power to make grants in other circumstances.[232]

Building regulations
In order to reduce the impact of external noise, buildings require to be adequately insulated. The construction and conversion of buildings is governed by the Building (Scotland) Regulations 2004.[233] Every building which is divided into more than one area of occupation must be designed and constructed in such a way as to limit the transmission of source noise from domestic-type activities between such areas to a level that will not threaten the health of, or cause inconvenience to, the building occupants.[234] However, the regulations only apply to attached dwellings and residential buildings.

Entertainment premises
Premises which are used for the purposes of entertainment, have, of course, the capacity to generate noise. Noise from such premises can be dealt with in terms of the legal regimes which we have already discussed above, for example, in terms of the Environmental Protection Act 1990.[235]

Under the Theatres Act 1968[236] which applies to the UK as a whole, a licence is required for the performance of any play. Any play must be conducted in terms of the relevant licence. Any music which is played during the introduction, during the interval, or at the conclusion of the play, or the music which is played in the interval between the two plays, is to be treated as forming part of the play, if the total time which is taken by the music so played on any day amounts to less than a quarter of the time which is taken by the performance (or performances) of the play (or plays) which are given at the premises on that day. Therefore, the terms of the licence could be used by the licensing authority to control the noise from the relevant premises.

As far as cinemas are concerned, the Cinemas Act 1985 establishes a special licensing regime for cinemas in the United Kingdom. Under the Act no premises may be used for a film exhibition unless the premises are licensed by the appropriate authority. The relevant authority can grant the licence on such conditions as it thinks fit. The authority could, therefore, impose conditions which relate to noise from the relevant premises.

Commercial amusements have witnessed a dramatic change during recent years. The proliferation of electronic amusement machines which can generate noise presents an obvious environmental problem. The Civic Government (Scotland) Act 1982 allows a local authority to license places of public entertainment. The local authority is allowed to attach conditions to the licence.[237] Such conditions could relate to noise reduction. Furthermore, a licensing authority can refuse a licence if there is a possibility of undue public nuisance.

Conclusions

The substantive law relating to noise is fragmented. Indeed, one could plausibly argue that noise law represents one of the most fragmented areas of environmental law. In sharp contrast to, say, atmospheric pollution and waste, neither the UK nor the Scottish Government has deemed it appropriate, thus far, to formulate a noise strategy. Unfortunately, such a negative and, indeed, unimaginative, approach to noise pollution seems unlikely to change in the foreseeable future. There simply is, and probably never will be, strong political pressure for the government to adopt a more robust stance to noise. However, the growing awareness that noise is not simply an annoyance but also has the capacity to harm human health may prompt the government to take a more robust approach to noise.

Summary

- Noise law represents, arguably, the most fragmented area of environmental law.
- Excessive noise can rank as a nuisance at common law.
- Local authorities have power to deal with noise nuisance under the Environmental Protection Act 1990.
- Local authorities have powers under the Antisocial Behaviour (Scotland) Act 2004 to regulate noise from premises.
- Local authorities have the power to create noise abatement zones the purpose of which is to prevent creeping noise.
- Town and Country Planning law has an important role to play in noise prevention.
- Excessive noise can infringe Art 8 of the European Convention of Human Rights which confers the right to the enjoyment of one's home.
- An outstanding feature of noise pollution is that the extent of the problem is unknown. The EU END Directive seeks to redress this by a process of mapping.
- END deals with ambient noise. Member States are placed under a duty to prepare action plans to deal with noise pollution.

Notes

1. See, e.g., *Mitchell v Glasgow City Council* [2009] 1 AC 874. See also *Glasgow City Council v Ferguson* 2009 SLT (Sh Ct) 47.
2. MORI Social Research Institute, *Neighbour Noise* (2003) at 6.
3. Ibid. at 7.
4. DEFRA also recognised that there is emerging evidence to the effect that long-term exposure to some forms of transport noise can cause an increased risk of direct health effects: Noise Policy Statement for England (DEFRA, 2010) para. 2.14. See, also *The Times*, 4 June 2014 reporting proceedings of *The Times* Cheltenham Science Festival, and The Burden of Disease from Environmental Noise (WHO, 2011).
5. Now named Environmental Protection UK (EPUK).
6. *Which*, 16 June 2011.
7. M. Adams and F. McManus, *Noise and Noise Law* (Wiley, 1994) at 151.
8. (1950) 94 Sol. Jo. 225 at 225
9. In effect, a 'one-man' pressure group, the Noise Abatement Society, in the form of the late John Connell. The Society still exists and is based in Hove, East Sussex, UK. See http://www.noiseabatementsociety.com.
10. *Rushmer v Polsue and Alfieri* [1906] 1 Ch 234. See also *Heather v Pardon* (1877) 37 LT 393.
11. *Andreae v Selfridge and Co Ltd* [1938] Ch 1.
12. *Gilling v Gray* [1910] TLR 427.
13. *Motion v Mills* (1897) 13 TLR 427.
14. *Leeman v Montague* [1936] 2 All ER 167.
15. *London, Brighton and South Coast Railway v Truman* (1886) 11 App Cas 45.
16. *Ball v Ray* (1873) 8 Ch App. 467.
17. *Allen v Gulf Oil Refining Ltd* [1981] AC 1001.
18. *Smith v Scott* [1973] Ch 314.
19. *Kennaway v Thomson* [1981] QB 88.
20. *Dunton v Dover DC* (1978) 76 LGR 87.
21. *Webster v Lord Advocate* 1984 SLT 13.
22. *Hollywood Silver Fox Farm Ltd v Emmett* [1936] 2 KB 468.
23. *Becker v Earl's Court* (1911) 56 Sol. Jo. 73.
24. *Johnston v Clinton* (1943) 4 DLR 572.
25. *Hadden v Lynch* [1911] VLR 5.
26. *Harris v James* (1876) 45 LJQB 545.
27. *Ward v Magna International* (1994) 21 CCLT (2d) 178.
28. *Heath v Mayor of Brighton* (1908) 24 TLR 414.
29. *Tetley v Chitty* [1986] 1 All ER 663.
30. *Harrison v Southwark and Vauxhall Water Co* [1891] 2 Ch 409.

31. See Chapter 3.

32. Section 82.

33. 'Noise' includes vibration; Environmental Protection Act 1990, s 79(7).

34. See *A Lambert Flat Management Ltd v Lomas* [1981] 2 AllER 280. See also *East Northamptonshire DC v Fossett* [1994] Env LR 388 and *Godfrey v Conwy CBC* [2001] Env LR 674.

35. 2002 SLT 853.

36. [1999] 4 All ER 449. See p. 13 and 14 incl.

37. [2006] Env LR 33.

38. See p. 83-4 incl.

39. 'Vehicle' means a mechanically propelled vehicle intended or adapted for use on roads, whether or not it is in a fit state for such use, and includes any trailer intended or adapted for use as an attachment to such a vehicle, any chassis or body, with or without wheels, appearing to have formed part of such a vehicle or trailer and anything attached to such a vehicle or trailer; s 79(7).

40. July 2012.

41. That is, regulations which are made for the purpose by the Scottish Government.

42. A duty is also placed on a person who installs an audible intruder alarm to ensure that the alarm complies with any prescribed requirements.

43. *Strathclyde Regional Council v Tudhope* 1983 SLT 22.

44. *Walter Lilley and Co Ltd v Westminster CC* [1994] Env LR 380.

45. *Wiltshier Construction (London) Ltd v Westminster City Council* [1997] Env LR 321.

46. Ibid. per Schiemann LJ at 325.

47. 1996 SLT (Sh Ct) 21.

48. See the Control of Noise (Code of Practice for Construction and Open Sites) Order 1987 (SI 1987/1730).

49. Control of Pollution Act 1974, s 60(7). See also the Control of Noise (Appeals) (Scotland) Regulations 1983 (SI 1983 No 1455) reg 5.

50. Control of Pollution Act 1974, s 61(2).

51. Ibid. s 61(3).

52. Ibid. s 61(5).

53. Ibid. s 61(5).

54. Ibid. s 61(6).

55. Ibid. s 61(7).

56. Environmental Protection Act 1990, s 61(8).

57. Ibid. s 61(9). For a discussion of proceedings under s82 of the Environmental Protection Act 1990, see p. 51-2 incl.

58. Ibid. s 61(10).

59. Repealed.
60. In *Westminster City Council v French Connection Retail Ltd* [2005] Env LR 42 it was held that the face of a shop window formed part of a street. Therefore, the window which was being used by the defendant to amplify sound could rank as a loudspeaker in the relevant street.
61. Control of Pollution Act 1974, s 62(1A).
62. Ibid. s 62(1B)
63. Ibid. s 62(3).
64. Noise and Statutory Nuisance Act 1993, s 8.
65. COPA s 68(1).
66. See p. 65.
67. Section 68(3).
68. See Chapter 2.
69. See Chapter 3
70. Civic Government (Scotland) Act 1982, s 54(2A).
71. Ibid. s 54(2B).
72. May 2003.
73. 'Relevant authority' means: (a) a local authority; or (b) a registered social landlord; s 18.
74. Antisocial Behaviour etc. (Scotland) Act 2004 s 4(1).
75. Ibid. s 4(2).
76. 'Conduct' includes speech; and a course of conduct on at least two occasions; s 143(2).
77. Ibid. s 143(1).
78. Ibid. s 41(1).
79. See, generally, Chapter 1.
80. Antisocial Behaviour (Scotland) Act 2004 s 41(2).
81. Ibid. s 41(3).
82. Ibid. s 41(5).
83. Ibid. s 41(6).
84. Ibid. s 42.
85. The expression 'excessive noise' is not defined.
86. 'Relevant property' means (a) any accommodation; (b) any land belonging exclusively to; or enjoyed exclusively with any accommodation; (c) any land not falling within paragraph (b) (i) to which at least two people have rights in common; and (ii) which is used by those persons as a private garden; (d) any common passage, close, court, stair, lift or yard pertinent to any tenement or group of separately owned houses; or (e) such other place as may be prescribed; ibid. s 53(1).
87. Ibid. s 43(1).
88. Ibid s 43(2).

89. 'Relevant place' means; (a) any place within accommodation (except, in the case of measurement of noise emitted from relevant property which is accommodation, that accommodation) and (b) such other place as may be prescribed; s 53(1).

90. Under s 48 the Scottish Government is empowered to prescribe the maximum level of noise by regulations. The permitted level of noise is the level of noise as measured from any relevant place by an approved device which is used in accordance with any conditions subject to which approval was given. Different permitted levels may be prescribed for different periods of the week, areas or descriptions of areas, times of the year or other circumstances. The Antisocial Behaviour (Noise Control) Regulations 2005 (SSI 2005 No 43) reg 3 prescribe relevant noise levels for the purposes of the Act.

91. Ibid. s 43(3).

92. Ibid. s 43(4).

93. Ibid. s 43(5).

94. Ibid. s 44.

95. Ibid. s 44(1).

96. Ibid. s 44(2).

97. Ibid. s 44(3).

98. Ibid. s 44(4).

99. A person is responsible for noise which is emitted from relevant property if the emission of the noise is wholly or partly attributable to the person's act, failure or sufferance; s 44(7).

100. Ibid. s 44(5).

101. Ibid. s 44(6).

102. Ibid. s 45(1).

103. Ibid. s 45(3).

104. Ibid. s 45(5).

105. Ibid. s 49(1).

106. Ibid. s 49(2). The Antisocial Behaviour (Noise Control) Regulations 2005 (SSI 2005 No 43) reg 5 prescribes noise measuring devices which are approved in terms of the Act.

107. A relevant officer of the local authority means an officer who is authorised for the purposes of the section (normally this would be an environmental health officer) or a constable; ibid. s 46(2).

108. Ibid. s 46(1).

109. Ibid. s 46(3).

110. Ibid. s 46(4).

111. Ibid. s 46(5).

112. Ibid. s 46(6).

113. Ibid. s 46(7). Under s 46(10), the fixed penalty which is payable under the

section is £100; it is payable to the local authority whose officer issued the warning notice; s 46(11).

114. Ibid. s 51(2).
115. Ibid. s 47(2).
116. Ibid. s 47(1).
117. Ibid. s 47(3).
118. Ibid. s 47(4).
119. Ibid. s 47(5). Schedule 1 to the Act makes further provision in relation to anything which is seized and removed under the section; s 47(9).
120. Ibid. s 47(6).
121. Ibid. s 47(7).
122. Ibid. s 50(1).
123. Rowan-Robinson and Watchman argue that the use of general environmental standards such as nuisance make it difficult for traders etc. to know with any degree of certainty whether or not they are complying with the law. Such standards also make enforcement problematic and lead to disagreement as to whether an offence has been committed; J. Rowan-Robinson and P. Watchman, *Crime and Regulation* (T. and T. Clark, 1990) at 191.
124. F. McManus, 'Noise law in the United Kingdom – a very British solution' (2000) *Legal Studies* 264 at 283.
125. Licensing (Scotland) Act 2005, s 27(6).
126. Ibid. s 4(1).
127. See Chapter 10
128. [1999] 4 All ER 449.
129. *Hunter v Canary Wharf Ltd* [1997] AC 655.
130. [2003] EHLR 297.
131. See p. 15-16 incl.
132. Ibid. at 320.
133. (2003) 37 EHRR 28. See A. Layard, 'Night flights – a surprising victory – Hatton v UK' [2002] Env LR 51. See also K. Cook,' Environmental rights as human rights' (2002) 2 EHRLR 196. For a general account of pressure group action against noise from aircraft using Heathrow, see J. Stewart, 'From defeat to victory' (2010).
134. (2003) 37 EHRR 28 at [96].
135. Ibid. at [98].
136. Ibid. at [120].
137. Civil Aviation Act 1982, s 76(1).
138. App. No 55723/00, judgment 9 June 2005.
139. Ibid. at [69]-[70].
140. (App no 4143/02) judgment of November 16, 2004. See F. McManus, '*Gomez v Spain* (2006) 8 Env LR 225.

141. Ibid. at 11.
142. Ibid. at 12
143. Ibid. at 13.
144. Application no 2345/06, 9 November 2010.
145. Ibid. at para 21.
146. Ibid. at para 23.
147. [2010] ECHR 686.
148. Ibid. at para [33].
149. Ibid. at para [35].
150. Ibid. at para [38].
151. Ibid. at para [39].
152. Ibid. at para [43].
153. Ibid. at para [45].
154. Ibid. at para [46].
155. Ibid. at para [48].
156. Ibid. at paras [55]-[64] incl.
157. Ibid. at para [66].
158. Application no 24203/10, 22 November 2011.
159. Ibid. at para [63].
160. Ibid. at para [66].
161. Ibid. at para [67].
162. Ibid. at para [68].
163. Ibid. at para [69].
164. Ibid. at para [73].
165. See, e.g., *Webster v Lord Advocate*1984 SLT 13.
166. See F. McManus and T. Burns, 'The impact of EC Law on noise law in the United Kingdom', in J. Holder (ed.), *The impact of EC Environmental Law in the United Kingdom* (Wiley, 1997) at 183.
167. Fifth Environmental Action Programme [1993] OJ C138/1.
168. Commission, Green Paper on Future Noise Policy, COM (96) 540 of 4 November 1996. See F. McManus, 'The EC Green Paper on Future Noise Policy and its impact on the United Kingdom' (1999) 5 *European Public Law* 125.
169. European Commission, COM (2001) 31 January 2001.
170. Directive 2002/49.
171. 'Environmental noise' is defined as unwanted or harmful outdoor sound created by human activities including noise emitted by means of transport, road traffic, air traffic and from sites of industrial activity such as those defined in Annex 1 to Council Directive 96/61/EC concerning integrated pollution prevention and control; ibid. Art 3.
172. Ibid. Art 1.

173. An agglomeration is defined as 'part of a territory, delimited by the Member State having a population in excess of 100,000 persons and a population density such that the Member State considers it to be an urbanised area; ibid. Art 3.
174. Ibid. Art 2.
175. Ibid. Art 4.
176. These include traffic planning, technical measures at noise sources, selection of quieter sources, reduction of sound transmission and regulatory or economic measures or incentives; ibid. Annex V.
177. See p. 62-74 incl.
178. See F. McManus, 'Noise law in the United Kingdom – a very British solution' (2000) 20 LS 264 at 282.
179. A strategic noise map means a map which is designed for the global assessment of noise exposure in a given area due to noise sources or for overall predictions of such an area; Directive 2002/49, Art 3.
180. Ibid. Art 9(1).
181. Ibid. Art 10.
182. Ibid. Art 11.
183. SSI 2006 No 465.
184. COM (2005) 718 final which was adopted by the European Commission on 11 January 2006.
185. See the Review of the EU Sustainable Development Strategy (EU SDS) Renewed Strategy, Council of the European Union, Brussels, 26 June 2006. Doc 10917/06.
186. Civil Aviation Act 1982, s 76(1).
187. Ibid. s 62.
188. SI 2009 No 3015, Art 160(1).
189. Ibid. Art 169(2).
190. SI 2007 No 734.
191. Ibid. reg 5.
192. Ibid. reg 45(3).
193. Ibid. s 60(3).
194. Sub-part 1.
195. Art 6.
196. SI 1999 No 1452.
197. Ibid. regs 4 and 5.
198. Ibid. reg 8.
199. Ibid. reg 16(1).
200. SI 2009 No 3015, Art 215.
201. SI 2003 No 1742.
202. Ibid. reg 3.

203. Ibid. reg 5.
204. Ibid. reg 6.
205. See Chapter 10.
206. See, generally, the Aircraft Environmental Noise Report (AEN) 'Wray' (MOD, 2004).
207. *Dennis v MoD* [2003] Env LR 741; see also *King v The Advocate General for Scotland* [2009] CSOH 169.
208. Section 1.
209. Section 7.
210. Section 1(1).
211. January 2013.
212. Report of the Noise Review Working Party (1990) at 13.
213. See p. 85.
214. SI 1986 No 1078 (as amended).
215. Road Traffic Act 1988.
216. SI 1984 no 981.
217. Dept of Transport (1988).
218. See Scottish Government PAN 1/2011. For a summary of this PAN see (2011) 145 SPEL 62.
219. See Chapter 10.
220. See p. 83-4 incl.
221. For a discussion of the defence of statutory authority, see p. 29.
222. *Allen v Gulf Oil Refining Ltd* [1981] AC 1001.
223. Ibid. s 1(1).
224. See, e.g., *Coventry v Lawrence* [2012] EWCA Civ 26. See (2012) 152 SPEL 92.
225. DoT, Welsh Office, 1995.
226. SSI 2011 No 139, sch. 1.
227. See p. 278-95 incl.
228. Section 1(4).
229. Section 18(1).
230. SI 1975 No 460.
231. Ibid. reg 3.
232. Ibid. reg 4.
233. SSI 2004/406.
234. Ibid. Sched 5, Pt 5, 5.1.
235. See p. 62-3 incl.
236. Section 12(1).
237. Ibid. s 41(3).

CHAPTER 5

Air Pollution

The London smog disaster of 1952 cruelly exposed the inadequacy of the law relating to air pollution in the UK which was heavily nuisance-based. The Clean Air Act 1956 which was the Parliamentary response to the disaster moved away from this approach and addressed the problem of pollution mainly in the form of smoke, grit and dust from both domestic and industrial sources.

Currently, the EU is the main driver as far as shaping policy on ambient air pollution control. As far as the UK is concerned, the current air pollution strategy is contained in the Air Quality Strategy for England and Wales.

Climate change presents a global threat. The international community, the EU and the UK have responded to that threat. At international level, greenhouse gas targets have been set. The Climate Change Act 2008 and the Climate Change (Scotland) Act 2009 are the UK's response to meeting such targets.

Introduction

In this chapter we address the subject of air pollution and its regulation. The importance of air pollution cannot be over-estimated. In Scotland more than 2,000 deaths annually are linked to air pollution.[1] Air pollution also has the capacity to stunt the growth of children's lungs, with damage starting to be inflicted in the womb.[2] The modern law has its origins in the nineteenth century. An outstanding feature of the Industrial Revolution was the pollution of the atmosphere by dense smoke which belched out from factories. However, the legislation which local authorities could use to suppress air pollution was heavily, but not exclusively,[3] nuisance-based.[4] However, factories were not the sole cause of atmospheric pollution. Domestic fires played no little part in contributing to atmospheric pollution. In the UK as whole, by the end of the nineteenth century, 110 million tons of coal were being consumed annually by domestic consumers. For most of the nineteenth century, Britain had the strongest industrial economy, the most advanced technology, and the largest factories of any country in the planet, all of which consumed enormous quantities of coal.[5] A city the size of Glasgow could burn up to five million tons a year by the 1870s.[6] Significantly, domestic smoke was largely unregulated during this period. For example, domestic smoke did not fall to be regulated under the law relating to statutory nuisance.[7]

One of the main disadvantages of a nuisance-based regime was that it was often difficult to establish a causal link between any smoke source, such as a smoking chimney, and either physical injury to property or personal discomfort to individuals. Not only was the law defective, during the nineteenth century, the law tended to be under-enforced. One reason for the unwillingness on the part of local authorities to prosecute offenders was that elected members of local authorities often had a vested interest in the factories which were causing pollution. Another important reason for local authorities being unwilling to effectively enforce the law was that factories were recognised as vital to the local economy. One had simply to 'take the rough with the smooth'. Fear of the effect upon local industry thus served as a powerful deterrent to environmental improvement.[8]

It was partly due to the lack of confidence in local authorities to effectively deal with air pollution that the Alkali Act[9] was passed in 1863 in order to regulate alkali works. The alkali industry, while invaluable to the national economy, had the capacity to devastate the surrounding land, transforming it to that which resembled a First World War battlefield. Countryside was laid bare. Trees, sometimes situated as far as five or six miles from the relevant works, were stunted by the emissions from the works. In addition to causing pollution of the air, deposits from alkali works were made in the vicinity of the relevant plant and also the sea.[10] Indeed, Wohl argues that the protection of private property, rather than the protection of the nation's health, was the underlying motive for the government's wish to regulate the alkali industry.[11] An important feature of the Act was that it provided for the appointment of an Alkali Inspectorate, which was quite independent of local government, to enforce the provisions of the Act. The Act which was subsequently amended, and then consolidated in 1906, to include other industries was a pronounced success. In 1864 there were eighty-four alkali works which were registered in terms of the 1863 Act. By the end of the century, when alkali was only one of the industries which fell to be registered, though the largest, there were 1,000 works and 1,500 processes registered.[12]

With the exception of the regime which related to alkali works, the law which related to air pollution from other sources, such as factories, which were not regulated by the Alkali Inspectorate, and domestic premises (which were a major source of air pollution) continued to be nuisance-based. The law remained so until its inadequacy was cruelly exposed by the infamous London smog disaster, which terrorised that city in the winter of 1952.[13] The Beaver Committee was appointed in 1953 to 'examine the nature, causes and effects of air pollution and the efficacy of present preventative measures; and to consider what further preventative measures are practicable'. The Committee reported in 1954.[14] It came to the general conclusion that the law, as it then stood, was defective. The recommendations which the committee made were accepted almost in their entirety by the government. The Clean Air Bill had its second reading in November 1955 and became law the following year in the form of the Clean Air Act. Clapp pertinently observes that few reports into a social evil have led to such swift action.[15] Indeed, both the report and the Act were revolutionary in the manner in which air pollution (mainly in the form of smoke, grit and dust) was to be addressed in the UK. The Clean Air Act 1956, which was amended by the Clean Air Act 1968, was repealed and replaced by the Clean Air Act 1993. We will now discuss the main provisions of the 1993 Act. In the view of the author, the London smog disaster and the resultant Clean Air Act 1956 heralded the start of the second environmental revolution in the UK.

Clean Air Act 1993

Industrial provisions

Smoke was the main atmospheric pollutant to afflict the UK in the post-war years. Indeed, it was a combination of both smoke and fog which caused the London smog disaster. It should also be recalled that smoke from domestic chimneys was the main source of smoke. Therefore, it was of paramount importance that Parliament should address this problem. Section 1(1) of the Clean Air Act 1993 ('the Act') makes it an offence for dark smoke[16] to be emitted from the chimney of any building.[17] Liability is strict. Section 1(2) prohibits the emission of dark smoke from a chimney (not being the chimney of a building) serving the furnace of any fixed boiler or plant. The person having possession of the boiler or plant is liable in the event of the emission of dark smoke. However, it is neither practicable nor possible for all furnaces to operate without emitting dark smoke. The Act,[18] therefore, allows the Scottish Ministers to make regulations to permit the emission of dark smoke for limited periods.[19]

As is the case with many statutes which make provision for offences of strict liability, the Act contains a statutory defence in relation to the emission of dark smoke from chimneys in certain circumstances. The Act provides that it is a defence to prove:

(a) that the alleged emission was solely due to the lighting up of a furnace which was cold, and that all practicable steps had been taken to prevent or minimise the emission of dark smoke;

(b) that the alleged emission was solely due to some failure of a furnace, or of apparatus used in connection with that furnace, and that:
  (i) the failure could not reasonably have been prevented by action taken after the failure occurred; or,

(c) that the alleged failure was solely due to the use of unsuitable fuel and that
  (i) suitable fuel was unobtainable and that the least unsuitable fuel which was available was used; and,
  (ii) all practicable steps had been taken to prevent or minimise the emission of dark smoke as a result of the use of that fuel;
  (iii) or that the alleged emission was due to the combination of two or more of the causes specified in paras (a) to (c) and that the other conditions specified in those paragraphs are satisfied in relation to those causes, respectively.

The emission of dark smoke is, of course, not confined to chimneys. Therefore, the Act[20] makes it an offence for an occupier of any industrial or trade premises[21] to either cause or permit the emission of dark smoke from such premises. A wide meaning was given to the expression 'industrial and trade premises' in *Sheffield City Council v ADH Demolition Ltd.*[22]

However, in order for the offence to be committed, there is no need for the smoke, which is the subject-matter of the action, to cross the boundary of the relevant premises. It simply suffices that the dark smoke is emitted from a source on the defender's premises.[23] The prohibition of the emission of dark smoke from premises does not apply to the emission of dark smoke from a chimney to which s 1 of the Act applies.[24]

The Act provides that in proceedings for an offence under the section there is to be taken to have been an emission of dark smoke from industrial or trade premises, in any case where material is burned on those premises, and in circumstances in which the burning would be likely to give rise to the emission of dark smoke, unless the occupier or any person who caused or permitted the burning, shows that no dark smoke was emitted.[25]

Finally, it is a defence for the accused to prove that the alleged emission was inadvertent and, furthermore, all practicable[26] steps had been taken to prevent or minimise the emission of dark smoke.[27]

A person who commits an offence under the section is liable to a fine.[28]

Furnace smoke
It is obvious that furnaces have the potential to pollute the atmosphere. Given the fact that smoke is the result of incomplete combustion, there is a need to regulate the construction of furnaces in order to ensure that they do not emit smoke. The Act, therefore, provides that no furnace may be installed in a building or in any fixed boiler or industrial plant, unless notice of the proposal to install the furnace has been given to the local authority.[29] The Act goes on to provide that no furnace may be installed in a building, or in any fixed boiler or industrial plant, unless the furnace is, so far as is practicable, capable of being operated continuously without emitting smoke when burning fuel which is of a type for which the furnace was designed.[30] However, any furnace which has been installed in accordance with plans and specifications which have been submitted to and approved for the purposes of the Act by the local authority, is deemed to have complied with that requirement.[31] The Act makes provision for penalties in relation to furnaces which have been installed in contravention of the Act.[32] The Act does not apply to the installation of domestic furnaces.[33]

Grit and dust
In addition to smoke pollution, the presence of grit and dust in the atmosphere presented a grave problem in post-war Britain. The main source of the grit and dust was industrial boilers. The Act allows the Scottish Ministers to make regulations which prescribe limits on the rates of emission of grit and dust from the chimneys of furnaces.[34] The Act does not apply to domestic furnaces.[35] If the emissions from a furnace chimney exceed those limits, the occupier of the building in which the furnace is situated is guilty of an offence.[36] However, the Act makes provision for the defence of the use of best practicable means for minimising the alleged emission.[37] If there is no prescribed limit which is applicable to a furnace served by a chimney, and if the occupier fails to use any practicable means which there may be for minimising the emission of grit or dust from the chimney, he commits an offence.[38]

Grit arrestment plant
Grit arrestment plant can substantially reduce the amount of grit and dust which is emitted from the furnace. Under the Act, a furnace (other than a domestic furnace) may not be used in a building:

(a)   to burn pulverised fuel; or
(b)   to burn at a rate of 45.4 kg or more an hour, any other solid matter; or
(c)   to burn at a rate equivalent to 366.4 kW or more, any liquid or gaseous matter,

unless the furnace is provided with plant for arresting grit and dust which has been approved by the local authority or which has been installed in accordance with plans and specifications approved by the local authority, and the plant is properly maintained and used.[39] It is an offence to contravene the Act.[40]

While the intention of the Act is to ensure that larger boilers and, therefore, those most capable of generating grit and dust are provided with grit arrestment plant, there are some types of furnace which are quite capable of being operated without creating grit and dust to any significant extent. The Act, therefore, empowers Scottish Ministers to make regulations which exempt such furnaces from the requirement to have grit arrestment plant.[41] The Act also gives a local authority, on the application of the occupier of a building, power to exempt a furnace from the requirement to have grit arrestment plant if the local authority is satisfied that the furnace will not be prejudicial to health or a nuisance.[42] The occupier may appeal to the Scottish Ministers against the refusal of a local authority to exempt a furnace under the Act.[43] On appeal, the Scottish Ministers may confirm the decision of the local authority or grant the exemption which was applied for, or vary the purpose for which the furnace to which the application relates may be used without compliance with s 6(1) of the Act.[44] It is made an offence for the occupier of any building to use a furnace, other than for a purpose which is prescribed in the relevant regulations, or for a purpose which has been sanctioned by the local authority under s 7(2) or the Scottish Ministers under s 7(5).

As far as domestic furnaces are concerned, if such a furnace burns pulverised fuel at a rate of 1.02 tonnes an hour or more, it is required to be provided with grit arrestment plant which has been approved by the local authority, or which has been installed in accordance with plans and specifications which have been submitted to and approved by the local authority, and the plant must be properly maintained and used.[45] It is an offence for an occupier to use a furnace in contravention of s 8(1).[46]

Where a local authority determines an application for approval of grit arrestment plant under either s 6 or s 8, the local authority is required to give written notification of its decision.[47] If the local authority decides to refuse to grant approval, reasons require to be given. Appeal lies to the Scottish Ministers who have complete powers of review.[48]

Measurement of grit and dust by occupiers
In order to allow enforcing authorities to accurately ascertain the quantity of grit and dust which is being emitted from industrial plant, the Act provides that if a furnace in a building is used:

(a)   to burn pulverised fuel,
(b)   to burn, at a rate of 45.4kg or more an hour, any other solid matter; or
(c)   to burn, at a rate equivalent to 366.4kW or more, any liquid or gaseous matter, the local authority may serve a notice in writing on the occupier of the building, directing that the provisions of s 10(2) of the Act apply to the furnace.[49]

Such provisions then automatically apply. The occupier must then comply with the requirements of the Clean Air (Measurement of Grit and Dust from Furnaces) (Scotland) Regulations 1971.[50] It is an offence to fail to comply with those requirements.[51] The occupier is required to permit the relevant local authority to be represented during the making and the recording of the measurements.[52]

Measurement of grit and dust by local authorities
If the provisions of s 10(2) of the Act apply to any furnace and the furnace is used:

(a)   to burn, at a rate less than 1.02 tonnes an hour, solid matter other than pulverised fuel; or
(b)   to burn, at a rate less than 8.21 MW, any liquid or gaseous matter,

the occupier may, by notice in writing, request the local authority to make and record measurements of the grit, dust and fumes which are emitted from the furnace.[53] While such a notice is in force, the local authority is required, from time to time, to make and record measurements of the grit, dust and fumes which are emitted from the furnace, and the occupier of the building ceases to be under a duty to comply with the regulations which are made under s 10(2). However, the occupier of the premises retains responsibility for complying with provisions in the regulations which relate to the making of adaptations to the appropriate chimney.[54]

Information about furnaces etc.
In order that local authorities can effectively enforce the provisions of the Act which relate to smoke, grit and dust from industrial premises, a local authority is given the power to serve notice in writing on the occupier of any building, to require the occupier to furnish the authority within four-

teen days (or such longer period which is designated in the notice) such information as to the furnaces in the building and the fuel or waste which is burned in those furnaces as the local authority may reasonably require for that purpose.[55]

It is an offence for any person who has been served with a notice to either fail to comply with the requirements of the notice within the relevant time, or furnish any information which he knows to be false in a material particular.[56]

Outdoor furnaces

In order to provide for the control of pollution from industrial plant in general, the Act provides that ss 5-12 apply in relation to the furnace of any fixed boiler or industrial plant as they apply in relation to a furnace in a building.[57] Thus, 'outdoor plant' is covered by the provisions of the Act. The person who is in possession of the plant is responsible for compliance with the provisions of the Act.[58]

Chimneys

It is important that chimneys are of sufficient height to permit the dispersal in the atmosphere of emissions from the relevant furnace. The Act makes provision for the regulation of chimney heights. It is made an offence for the occupier of a building in which there is a furnace which is served by a chimney to knowingly cause or permit the furnace to be used to burn:

(a)   pulverised fuel;
(b)   at a rate of 45.4kg or more an hour, any other solid matter; or
(c)   at a rate equivalent to 366.4 KW or more, any liquid or gaseous matter, unless the height of the chimney serving the furnace has been approved by the local authority, and any conditions subject to which the approval was granted are complied with.[59]

Fixed boilers and industrial plant are required to meet the same requirements.[60]

A local authority may not approve the height of a chimney unless it is satisfied that it will be sufficient to prevent, so far as practicable, the smoke grit, dust, gases or fumes emitted from the chimney from becoming prejudicial to health or a nuisance having regard to:

(a)   the purpose of the chimney;
(b)   the position and descriptions of buildings near it;
(c)   the levels of the neighbouring ground; and
(d)   any other matters requiring consideration in the circumstances.[61]

The local authority may grant approval, without qualification, or subject to conditions as to the rate or quality, or the rate and quality of emissions from the chimney.[62] If a local authority to which an application is duly made for approval fails to determine the application and fails to give a written notification of its decision to the applicant within four weeks of receiving the application (or such longer period as may be agreed in writing between the applicant and the authority), approval is deemed to have been granted without qualification.[63] If a local authority decides not to approve the height of a chimney, or the local authority decides to attach conditions to its approval, the local authority is required to give the applicant a written notification of its decision.[64] Such notification must contain reasons for the decision of the local authority. If the local authority decides not to approve the height of a chimney, the local authority is required to specify the lowest height (if any) which it is prepared to approve, without qualification, or the lowest height which the local authority is prepared to approve (if approval is granted) subject to any specified conditions (or both if the authority deems fit).

The applicant may appeal to the Scottish Ministers against the decision of the local authority within twenty-eight days of receiving notification of the decision of the local authority.[65] The Scottish Ministers have complete powers of review and can confirm the decision of the local authority or the Scottish Ministers may approve the height of the chimney without qualification or subject to conditions as to the rate or quality, of emissions from the chimney. The Scottish Ministers may also cancel any conditions which have been imposed by the local authority, or they may substitute for any conditions so imposed, any other conditions which the local authority had power to impose.[66]

The Act also makes provision for local authority control of chimneys other than those which serve furnaces.[67] The Act applies where plans are deposited with the local authority for inspection in terms of the building regulations[68] for the erection or the extension of a building, other than one which is to be used wholly for one of the following purposes:

(a)   as a residence or residences;
(b)   as a shop or shops; or
(c)   as an office or offices.[69]

If the plans show that it is proposed to construct such a chimney, the local authority is required to reject such plans, unless it is satisfied that the height of the chimney, as shown, will be sufficient to prevent, so far as practicable, the smoke, grit, dust or gases from becoming prejudicial to health or a nuisance, having regard to:

(a)   the purpose of the chimney;
(b)   the position and descriptions of buildings near it;
(c)   the levels of the neighbouring ground; and
(d)   any other matters requiring consideration in the circumstances.[70]

If the plans are rejected by the local authority, any person who is interested in the building may appeal to the Scottish Ministers.[71] On appeal, the Scottish Ministers may either confirm or cancel the rejection.[72] Where the rejection is cancelled, the Scottish Ministers may, if they consider necessary, direct that the time for rejecting the plans (otherwise than under the authority of s 16) is extended so as to run from the date on which the decision is notified to the local authority. This would cover a situation where the local authority considered it fit to reject the application for other reasons, for example, that other proposals failed to comply with the building regulations.

Domestic provisions

Whereas industry was a major contributor to atmospheric pollution in post-war Britain, a significant quantity of smoke derived from domestic premises. Indeed, the Beaver Committee was of the opinion that half of all the smoke in the UK came from domestic sources.[73] The Committee went on to recommend the setting-up of smoke control areas. We can see, however, that for such a system to operate effectively, householders would require to find alternatives to heating their homes by means of coal fires. In short, Parliament would require to legislate to regulate what the public could do in their own homes. An assault on the Englishman's castle for the public weal, therefore, stood in the way of Parliament. However, formidable this obstacle appeared, Parliament adopted Beaver's proposals in the Clean Air Act 1956.[74] The implementation of the smoke control legislation, which we now discuss, dramatically improved the quality of the atmosphere in the UK.

The Clean Air Act 1993 (the Act) empowers a local authority to declare either the whole or part of its area a smoke control area by way of a smoke control order.[75] The relevant local authority has wide discretion as to the form which the order can take. The order may make different provision for different parts of the smoke control area and the order may also limit the operation of s 20 of the Act (prohibition of emissions of smoke) to specified classes of buildings in the area.[76] The order may also exempt specified buildings or classes of buildings[77] or specified fireplaces or classes of fireplace in the area, from the operation of s 20 upon such condition, as may be specified in the order. A smoke control order can be either revoked or varied by a subsequent order.[78]

The Act gives the Scottish Environment Protection Agency (SEPA) certain powers in respect of smoke control areas. If SEPA is satisfied, after consultation with the relevant local authority, that it is expedient to abate pollution of the air by smoke in the relevant district (or part of the district) of the authority and, furthermore, if SEPA is satisfied that the local authority either has not or has not sufficiently exercised its powers under s 18 to abate air pollution, SEPA may direct the local authority to prepare and submit to it for its approval within such period, not being less than six months from the direction, proposals for making and bringing into operation one or more smoke control orders, as the local authority thinks fit.[79] Any proposals which are submitted by the local authority may be varied by further proposals submitted by the authority within the specified period for making the original proposals.[80] SEPA may reject any proposals which are submitted to it, or it may approve them in whole or in part, with or without modifications.[81] If a local authority to which a direction has been made fails to submit proposals to SEPA within the period specified in the direction, or submits proposals which are rejected either in whole or in part, SEPA, with the consent of the Scottish Ministers, may make an order which declares the local authority to be in default and directs the local authority to exercise its powers under s 18 of the Act.[82] Such an order may be varied or revoked by a subsequent order.[83] While proposals which are submitted by a local authority are still in force, the local authority is under a duty to make such order or orders under s 18 as are necessary to carry out the proposals.[84]

Prohibition of smoke

The Act makes provision for the stringent control of the emission of smoke within a smoke control area. If, on any day, smoke is emitted from a chimney of any building within a smoke control area, the occupier of the building commits an offence.[85] Similarly, if on any day, smoke is emitted from a chimney (not being a chimney of a building) which serves the furnace of any fixed boiler or industrial plant within a smoke control area, the person having possession of the boiler or plant commits an offence.[86] No offence is committed if the smoke emission is covered by an exemption which is in force under the Act.[87] In any case, in proceedings for an offence under s 20 it is a defence to prove that the alleged emission was not caused by the use of any fuel other than an authorised fuel.[88]

The upshot of a smoke control area coming into force is that in order to avoid committing an offence under the Act, an occupier of premises requires to either adopt another means of heating such as gas or electricity, or to adapt an existing fireplace to burn an authorised fuel. However, there are fires which are capable of burning fuels other than authorised fuels without emitting smoke in significant quantities. The Scottish Ministers are, therefore, empowered under s 21 of the Act to exempt any class of fireplace upon such conditions as are specified in the order, if they are satisfied that such fireplaces can be used for burning fuel other than authorised fuels without producing any smoke or a substantial quantity of smoke.[89]

The Scottish Ministers, if it appears necessary and expedient to do so, have the power, by order, to suspend or relax the operation of s 20 of the Act (that is, prohibition of smoke in a smoke control area) in relation to either the whole or part of a smoke control area.[90] Before making such an order, the Scottish Ministers are required to consult with the local authority, unless they are satisfied that, on account of urgency, such consultation is impracticable.[91] As soon as practicable after the making of such an order, the local authority is required to take such steps as appear suitable for bringing the effect of the order to the notice of persons affected.[92]

Acquisition of unauthorised fuels in smoke control area

In order to ensure that the above provisions are complied with, the Act makes it an offence for any person to:

(a)   acquire any solid fuel[93] for use in a building in a smoke control area, otherwise than in a building or fireplace exempted from the operation of s 20 (prohibition of smoke emissions in a smoke control area);

(b)   acquire any solid fuel for use in any fixed boiler or industrial plant in a smoke control area not being a boiler or plant so exempted; or

(c)   sell by retail any solid fuel for delivery by him or on his behalf to a building in a smoke control area in which there is any fixed boiler or plant.[94]

It is not an offence to either acquire or to sell solid fuel in a smoke control area where the effect of such an order has been limited to specified classes of buildings, boilers or plant and the relevant acquisition or sale of solid fuel relates to such buildings etc.[95] The Scottish Ministers have the power to either suspend or relax the operation of s 23(1) in relation to either the whole or part of a smoke control area.[96] In proceedings for an offence under the section which consists of the sale of fuel for delivery to a building or premises, it is a defence for the person who is charged with the offence to prove that he believed, and had reasonable grounds for believing, that the building was exempted from the operation of s 20 or, in a case where the operation of that section is limited to specified classes of building, was not of a specified class; or that the fuel was acquired for use in a fireplace, boiler or plant, so exempted or, in a case where the operation of that section is limited to specified classes of boilers or plant, in a boiler or plant not of a specified class.[97]

Adaptation of fireplaces
Generally speaking, the occupier of the relevant premises will voluntarily adapt fireplaces in his premises, which are situated in a smoke control area. Sometimes, however, it may be necessary for a local authority to compel the carrying-out of remedial works. Section 24 of the Act, therefore, empowers a local authority to serve a notice, in writing, on the owner or occupier of a private dwelling which is, or will be, situated within a smoke control area, requiring the carrying-out of adaptations[98] either in, or in connection with, the dwelling, in order to avoid contraventions of s 20 (prohibition of smoke emissions in smoke control area).[99] A person on whom a notice is served can appeal to the sheriff under s 111 of the Housing (Scotland) Act 1987.[100] If any person on whom a notice is served fails to execute the works which are required by the notice, the local authority may itself execute the works required by the notice, and the authority may recover from the owner or occupier of the premises three tenths, or such smaller fraction as the local authority determines, of the expenses which were reasonably incurred by it in carrying out such works.[101]

Finally, the Act allows a local authority to make grants in relation to churches and places of religious worship and premises which are connected with religious worship (such as church halls) and also in relation to any premises whose objects are charitable, or are otherwise concerned with the advancement of religion, education or social welfare, in relation to expenditure which is carried out in order to avoid contravention of s 20.[102] In relation to such premises, the local authority may repay the relevant owner or occupier either the whole or the part of the expenditure which is incurred.

Control over other forms of pollution

Motor fuel
In 2000 road transport was recognised as one of the major sources of air pollution, especially in towns and cities.[103] The Clean Air Act 1993 makes provision for controlling pollution from vehicles. The Scottish Ministers are given the power to make regulations which impose requirements as to the composition and contents of any fuel of a kind which is used in motor vehicles, and also preventing or restricting the production, treatment, distribution, import, sale or use of any fuel which fails to comply with such requirements and which is for use in the UK.[104] Before such regulations

are made, consultation is required with representatives from manufacturers of motor vehicles, producers and users of motor fuel, as well as those who are conversant with the problems of air pollution.[105]

Cable burning
The Act makes it an offence for a person to burn insulation from a cable with a view to recovering metal from the cable, unless the burning is part of a process which is subject to Part 1 of the Environmental Protection Act 1990 (EPA) or an activity which is subject to Part 1 of the EPA or an activity which is subject to regulations which are made under s 2 of the Pollution Prevention and Control Act 1999.[106]

Research publicity etc.
A local authority is empowered by the Act to either itself undertaken or contribute towards the cost of investigation and research which relates to the problem of air pollution.[107] The research may be published.

The Act allows a local authority to obtain information about the emission of pollutants and other substances into the air, by issuing notices under s 36 of the Act, or measuring and recording the emissions, or entering into arrangements with occupiers of premises under which the occupiers measure and record emissions on behalf of the local authority.[108] However, the power which is given to local authorities to obtain information is subject to certain restrictions, for example, in relation to premises which fall to be regulated under the Pollution Prevention and Control (Scotland) Regulations 2012.[109] The Act makes provision for appeals against such notices.[110]

Special cases

Relationship with the Environmental Protection Act 1990 and the Pollution Prevention and Control Act 1999
In order to avoid an overlap between respective regulatory regimes, the Act provides that from the relevant determination date,[111] Parts I to III of the Clean Air Act do not apply to any process which is a prescribed process in terms of s 1 of the Environmental Protection Act 1990,[112] or to an activity which is subject to regulations which are made under s 2 of the Pollution Prevention and Control Act 1999.[113]

Colliery spoilbanks
It is difficult to travel around certain parts of central Scotland without seeing colliery spoilbanks[114] which constitute an ugly legacy of Scotland's

industrial past.[115] The Clean Air Act 1993 places the owner of a mine or quarry[116] from which coal is being extracted under a duty to employ all practicable means for preventing combustion of refuse which has been deposited from the mine or quarry and for preventing or minimising the emission of smoke and fumes from such refuse.[117] It is made an offence to fail to comply with this provision. Neither the provisions of Part III[118] of the Environmental Protection Act 1990 nor those of Parts I to III of the Clean Air Act 1993 apply in relation to smoke, grit or dust from the combustion of refuse which has been deposited from any mine or quarry to which s 42 applies.[119]

Miscellaneous provisions

The Act also makes provision for the prohibition of dark smoke from railway locomotive engines,[120] vessels;[121] the exemption from the provisions of the Clean Act 1993 and the provisions of Part III (statutory nuisances) of the Environmental Protection Act 1990 for the purposes of research etc.;[122] the application of the Clean Air Act to Crown premises;[123] the power of the Scottish Ministers to make regulations to make provisions of the Act which relate to smoke etc. apply to fumes or prescribed gases;[124] and the unjustified disclosure of information.[125]

Duty to notify offences

The Clean Air Act 1993 makes provision for the notification of offences which have been committed under the Act. If an authorised officer of a local authority is of the opinion that an offence has been committed under ss 1, 2 or 20 (which prohibit certain emissions of smoke) of the Act, the authorised officer is placed under a duty to notify the appropriate person,[126] unless the authorised officer has reason to believe that notification has already been given on behalf of the local authority.[127] If such notification is not in writing, it must be confirmed in writing before the end of the four days which follow the day on which the officer became aware of the offence. In any proceedings for an offence under ss 1, 2 or 20 it is a defence to prove that the provisions of s 51(1) have not been complied with in the case of the offence. In any proceedings for an offence under ss 1, 2 or 20 it is a defence to prove that the provisions of s 51(1) have not been complied with in the case of the offence.[128] If no such notification, as is required by s 51(1), has been given before the end of the four days which follow the day of the offence, that subsection is deemed not to have been complied with unless the contrary is proved.

Offences etc.

Where an offence under the Clean Air Act 1993 has been committed by a corporate body or is proved to have been committed with the consent or connivance of, or to be attributable to any neglect on the part of any director, manager, secretary or other similar officer of the body corporate or any person who was purporting to act in any such capacity, he, as well as the body corporate, are guilty of the relevant offence and are therefore, liable to be proceeded against and punished accordingly.[129]

The Act provides that where the commission by any person of an offence under the Act is due to the act or default of some other person, that other commits an offence.[130]

A local authority is under a duty to enforce the provisions of Parts I-III, s 33 and Part VI and associated provisions of the Act.[131] The Act also makes provision relating to powers of entry for authorised officers of a local authority.

The Act also makes provision for rights of entry and inspection by authorised officers of the local authority.[132] However, lack of space precludes detailed discussion of these provisions.

Powers of Scottish Ministers

The Scottish Ministers are empowered to cause a local inquiry to be held in any case where it is considered appropriate for one to be held, either in connection with a provision of the Clean Air Act 1993, or with a view to preventing or dealing with air pollution at any place.[133]

Since the mid nineteenth century central government has possessed default powers over local authorities. The Act gives the Scottish Ministers, if satisfied that any local authority has failed to perform any function which it ought to have performed, power to make an order which declares that the authority is in default.[134] The order may direct the authority to perform such of its functions as are specified in the order. In the face of the defaulting authority failing to comply with any direction which is contained in an order, the Scottish Ministers may make an order which transfers such functions to the authority itself.[135] Finally, the default powers which are conferred by s 60 do not apply to certain local authority functions which pertain to smoke control areas.[136]

Postscript on the Clean Air Acts

The London smog disaster heralded the second environmental revolution in the modern era in the United Kingdom. The disaster cruelly exposed the weakness of over-reliance on nuisance-based legislation to secure environmental improvement. A notable feature, therefore, of the Act is that it represented a shift away from a nuisance-based approach of environmental control which, in essence, had allowed regulators simply to scratch the surface of air pollution problems. The most innovatory provisions of the Act were those relating to the creation of smoke control areas and these had a profound effect on the condition of the atmosphere, especially in urban areas. The 1956 Act can rightly be regarded as a world 'first'. Indeed, in 1990, the UK government noted, with no little satisfaction, that both the 1956 and 1968 Acts had prevented many thousands of deaths from bronchial illness and had changed our cities for the cleaner and better.[137] The Clean Air Act concept had been adopted by many other countries and had laid the basis for air quality standards which had been set by the European Union.

Ambient air quality

We now examine how ambient air quality is regulated in Scotland. We look, first, at the European Union (EU) which has become the main driver, in terms of the regulation of ambient air pollution, and, second, at Scotland.

The European Union and ambient air pollution

The EU was a relative latecomer in terms of addressing the subject of ambient air pollution.[138] Its first actions to deal with air pollution were limited to specific pollution sources, in particular, to emissions from passenger cars.[139] Kramer argues that the real catalyst for change was the concern of governments in central Europe, especially in Germany, in the early 1980s about the effect of air pollution on rain forests.[140] The Directive on Air Quality Limit Values and Guide Values for Sulphur Dioxide and suspended Particulates[141] was the first piece of legislation to lay down mandatory air quality standards. Haigh observes that the Directive brought about a turning-point in British air pollution policy.[142] Notwithstanding the fact that, whilst the EU was a relative latecomer in the field of regulating ambient air pollution, EU air quality policy is now largely driven by concerns about the effect of poor quality air on human health.[143]

Currently, at EU level, the main components of EU air quality policy comprise:

1. The 2005 EU Thematic Strategy on Air Pollution
2. The 2001 National Emission Ceilings Directive (NECD)
3. The Ambient Air Quality Directive
4. Source specific legislation.

The 2005 EU Thematic Strategy on Air Pollution
The European Commission, in its 2005 Thematic Strategy on Air Pollution, has recognised that air pollution is both a local and a transboundary pollutant which either alone or in conjunction with chemical reactions leads to negative health and environmental impacts.[144] The strategy sets health and environmental objectives and emission reduction targets for the main pollutants, namely, O3 (ground-level ozone), S02 (sulphur dioxide), NOx (nitrogen oxides), VOCs (volatile organic compounds), NH3 (ammonia), and primary PM2.5 (particles which are emitted directly into the air). The Strategy also sets specific long-term objectives for the year 2020.

The European Commission has recently reviewed the policy which was set out in the 2005 Thematic Strategy in its Clean Air Programme for Europe.[145] A new strategy, the EU Clean Air Policy Package, is proposed by the Commission. The strategy sets out new interim objectives for reducing health and environmental impacts up to 2030.

The 2001 National Emission Ceilings Directive (NECD)
The National Emissions Ceilings Directive[146] sets national emission ceilings for four pollutants -sulphur dioxide, nitrogen oxides, VOCs and ammonia – for each Member State, which were to be achieved by 2010. The national ceilings have been set with a view to meeting certain interim environmental objectives for the EU as a whole by that date. These objectives are acidification, health-related ground-level ozone exposure, and vegetation-related ground-level ozone exposure.[147] The Directive required Member States to draw up programmes by 2002 for reducing emissions and to send these to the Commission.[148] Member States are required to submit annual emission inventories to the Commission as well as emission projections to 2010.[149] Emissions from international maritime traffic and from aircraft beyond landing and take-off are excluded from the scope of the Directive.[150] However, the Directive required the Commission to report to the European Parliament on the contribution of these sources to acidification, eutrophication and the formation of ground-level ozone within the Community by the end of 2002 and 2004 respectively.[151]

The Directive is implemented in the UK by the National Emission Ceilings Regulations 2002.[152] The regulations require the Secretary of State to ensure that in 2010 and thereafter, emissions of S02, NOx, VOCs and ammonia do not exceed the specified amount in the UK by 2010.[153] The Secretary of State is also required to prepare a national programme (which requires to be updated and revised, as necessary) for progressively reducing emissions from these pollutants.[154] Public authorities are required to have regard to the plan when exercising any function which affects the level of the relevant pollutants in the UK.

In its recent review of ambient air quality, referred to above, the Commission has proposed a revised National Emission Ceiling Directive: with updated national ceiling caps for six key air pollutants – PM, SO2, NOx, VOCs, NH3 and CH4 (methane) – for 2020 and 2030.[155]

Air Quality Directive

In accordance with the aims of the Thematic Strategy, EU air quality legislation has been streamlined by the 2008 Directive on Ambient Air Quality and Cleaner Air for Europe (the CAFÉ Directive).[156] The CAFÉ Directive consolidates[157] the Directive of 1996 on ambient air quality management[158] and its first three daughter directives, together with a Council Decision.[159] The CAFÉ Directive makes provision for: defining and establishing objectives for ambient air quality which are designed to avoid, prevent or reduce harmful effects on human health and the environment as a whole; assessing the ambient air quality in Member States on the basis of common methods and criteria; obtaining information on ambient air quality in order to help combat air pollution and nuisance, and to monitor long-term trends and improvements resulting from national and Community measures; ensuring that such information on ambient air quality is made available to the public; maintaining air quality where it is good, and improving it in other cases; and promoting increased cooperation between the Member States in reducing air pollution.[160] The CAFÉ Directive also makes provision for the establishment of zones[161] and agglomerations[162] where air quality assessment and air quality management is to be carried out.[163] An assessment regime is established in relation to sulphur dioxide, nitrogen dioxide and oxides of nitrogen, particulate matter (PM10, PM2.5) lead, benzene, or carbon monoxide.[164] Member States are required to assess ambient air quality in relation to the aforementioned pollutants in accordance with the criteria laid down in the Directive.[165] In zones and agglomerations where the levels for these pollutants are below the appropriate limit values[166] which are specified in the CAFÉ Directive,[167] Member States are required to maintain the levels of those pollutants below those limit values in order to preserve the best ambient air quality, which is compatible with sustainable development.[168] Member States are also required to ensure that throughout the relevant zones and agglomerations, the levels of SO2 and PM10, lead and CO in ambient air do not exceed the limit values which are specified in the CAFÉ Directive.[169] The CAFÉ Directive goes on to set critical levels[170] for SO2 and NOxs.[171] In turn, a national exposure reduction target[172] and, also, target values[173] are set for PM2.5.[174] The CAFÉ Directive also places an obligation on Member States to take all necessary measures which do not entail disproportionate cost, that the target values and long-term objectives for ozone are attained.[175] If the target value is exceeded, the Member State is required to institute the relevant remedial measures. In the case of zones and agglomerations where ozone concentrations meet the long-term objectives, Member States are required, in so far as factors including the transboundary nature of ozone pollution and meteorological conditions permit, to maintain these levels below the long-term objectives.[176] The CAFÉ Directive makes provision for the postponement and exemption from the requirement to apply certain limit values.[177] If the levels of pollutants in the ambient air in any given zone or agglomeration exceed the relevant limit or target value, plus any relevant margin of tolerance,[178] a Member State is placed under an obligation to ensure that air quality plans are established for the relevant zones and agglomerations in order to achieve the related limit value which is specified in the CAFÉ Directive.[179] Finally, the CAFÉ Directive makes provision for Member States to draw up action plans if, in a given zone or agglomeration, there is a risk that the levels of pollutants will exceed one or more of the alert thresholds.[180] The CAFÉ Directive is implemented in Scotland by the Air Quality Standards (Scotland) Regulations 2010.[181]

An interesting issue which falls to be discussed is the extent to which members of the public can require the government to comply with the terms of the CAFÉ Directive. In the European Court of Justice case of *ClientEarth v The Secretary for State for the Environment and Rural Affairs*[182] proceedings had been brought by ClientEarth (C.) against the Secretary of State (S) to impugn draft air quality plans, which had been published by S., on the grounds that the plans failed to comply with emission values for nitrogen dioxide (NO2) which were set in the CAFÉ Directive. Article 22 of the Directive provides that where, in a given zone or agglomeration, conformity with the limit values for nitrogen dioxide NO2 cannot be achieved by the deadlines which are specified in the Directive, a Member State can postpone those deadlines by a maximum of five years, for that particular zone or agglomeration, on condition that an air quality plan is established in accordance with Art 23 of the Directive. The issue which had to be determined was whether S. was required by the Directive to prepare an air quality plan which demonstrated compliance by 1 January 2015 for zones and agglomerations where compliance with NO2 limit values could not be achieved by 1 January 2010.

It was clear, from at least February 2009, that there was a risk that the UK would be unable to achieve the limit values for NO2 by 2015, especially in Greater London. In June 2011 S. had published draft air quality plans for public consultation. It was made clear to consultees that time extensions would be put to the Commission, but only in respect of zones where compliance with NO2 limit values by 2015 was projected. Importantly, the plans did not include the London zone where compliance was expected only by 2025. C. argued that Art 22 provided for a maximum extension of five years from 1 January 2010 in relation to any zone where there remained exceedances after 1 January 2015. C. also argued that compliance by the UK, after 1 January 2015, could not be avoided simply by the UK doing nothing and leaving it to the European Commission to take enforcement action in terms of the Treaty of the European Union.[183] However, the Court of Appeal had held[184] that Art 22 simply conferred discretion on a Member State to postpone the deadline by a maximum of five years. A Member State was not obliged to use the machinery which was contained in that Article if it was in breach of the deadlines which were set out in the Directive. The Member State could simply do nothing and leave it to the Commission to take the necessary action by way of enforcement under Art 258 of the Treaty.[185] On appeal to the Supreme Court, proceedings were stayed for a preliminary ruling by the European Court of Justice on: whether in a case where the limit values for NO2 were not achieved by the deadline of 1 January 2010, a Member State was obliged to seek postponement of the deadline in accordance with Art 22, and, if so, in what circumstances could it be relieved of such an obligation; to what extent, if any, where a Member State has exceeded its limit values under Art 13, is that position affected by Art 23 and, finally, in the event of non-compliance with Art 22 which, if any, remedies must a national court provide?

The Court of Justice held that in such circumstances, a Member State was under an obligation to seek such a postponement under Art 22. There were no exceptions to this obligation. Furthermore, simply because an air quality plan had been drawn up which complied with Art 23 of the Directive did not permit the view to be taken that a Member State had complied with Art 13. Finally, the Court held that where a Member State has exceeded its limit values, it is a matter for the court of national jurisdiction to take any necessary measures to ensure that the action plan which is required by the Directive is established.

Proceedings were resumed in the Supreme Court which concluded that by reason of fact that the limit values which were contained in Art 13 had been exceeded, S. was under a duty to seek postponement of the relevant deadline under Art 22. In the last analysis, S. was ordered to prepare a plan with a defined timetable, and submit the plan in accordance with Art

23(1) and submit the plan to the European Commission by 31 December 2015.[186]

Source specific legislation

The EU has addressed air pollution according to the source of the pollutant. Space precludes discussion of the various directives which have adopted such a sectoral approach to air pollution. However, some examples would include the Industrial Emissions Directive,[187] the Large Combustion Plant Directive,[188] the Waste Incineration Directive,[189] the Volatile Organic Compounds (VOC) Directive,[190] and the Directive relating to the quality of petrol and diesel fuels.[191]

The Air Quality Strategy for England, Scotland, Wales and Northern Ireland

The traditional UK approach to tackling air pollution was to adopt a sectoral approach. The Alkali Acts, the Clean Acts and the Environmental Protection Act 1990 are good examples of such an approach. However, during the 1990s it was becoming increasingly apparent that a more holistic approach to regulating the quality of air would require to be adopted. The Environment Act 1995 places the Scottish Ministers under a duty to prepare and publish a statement which contains policies with respect to the assessment or management of air quality.[192] The first United Kingdom Air Quality Strategy[193] was published in 1997. The strategy adopted an effects-based approach to human health and also to the natural and man-made environments.[194] The strategy was revised and replaced in 2000 and renamed the Air Quality Strategy for England, Scotland and Wales to reflect the devolution of air quality policy.[195] The most recent version of the strategy was published in 2007.[196] While the strategy does not have the force of law, SEPA is required to have regard to the strategy in discharging its pollution control functions.[197]

At the time of writing[198] the Scottish Government is consulting on its proposed Low Emissions Strategy.[199]

Local authority review of air quality

A local authority is required to conduct a review of the quality of air in its area for the time being, and also the future.[200] In conducting such a review, the local authority is required to assess whether air quality standards and objectives are being achieved within the relevant period within the local authority's area.[201] It should be mentioned at this juncture that, since the Air Quality Strategy does not have the force of law, the relevant air quality objectives which are contained in the Strategy are prescribed in the Air

Quality (Scotland) Regulations 2000.[202] The Regulations set air quality objectives for seven pollutants: benzene, 1,3 butadiene, carbon monoxide, lead, nitrogen dioxide, PM10 and sulphur dioxide. The regulations also make provision for the relevant period within which the relevant air quality objective is to be achieved.

If, after carrying out a review, a local authority is of the opinion that any air quality objective either is not being achieved, or is not likely to be achieved within the relevant period, the local authority is required to identify parts of its area in which it appears that those objectives are not likely to be achieved within the relevant period.[203] If, after having conducted such a review within its area, it appears to a local authority that any air quality objectives either are not being achieved, or are not likely to be achieved, the local authority is required to designate, by way of an order, an air quality management area.[204] Any order which is made may, as a result of a subsequent review, be varied by a subsequent order, or revoked by such an order, if it appears on such a review that the air quality objectives are being achieved and are likely to be achieved in the designated area throughout the relevant period.[205]

Duties of local authorities in designated areas
When an order which designates an order as an air quality management area comes into force, the local authority is required to prepare an action plan.[206] The action plan may be revised from time to time.[207]

Reserve powers of SEPA
It will be recalled[208] that since the mid nineteenth century central government has possessed default powers over local authorities as far as the discharge of their public health functions is concerned. Currently, as far as the powers which local authorities possess under Part IV of the Act are concerned, it is SEPA (which is not, of course, central government) which enjoys default powers over local authorities.[209] SEPA, acting with the approval of the Scottish Ministers, may either itself conduct or cause to be conducted or made:

(a)   a review of the quality of the air for the time being and the likely future air quality within the relevant period within the area of any local authority;

(b)   an assessment of whether air quality standards and objectives are being achieved or are likely to be achieved within the relevant period within the area of the local authority;

(c)   an identification of any parts of the area of a local authority in which it appears that those standards are not likely to be achieved within the relevant period;

(d) an assessment of the respects (if any) in which it appears that air quality standards are not being achieved within the relevant period, or are not likely to be achieved within the relevant period either within the area of a local authority or within a designated area.[210]

SEPA is empowered to give directions to a local authority if it appears that:

(a) air quality objectives are not being achieved, or are not likely to be achieved, within the relevant period within the area of the local authority;

(b) a local authority has failed to discharge any duty which is imposed on it under Part IV of the Act;

(c) the actions or the proposed actions by a local authority in relation to the proposed discharge of its responsibilities under Part IV of the Act is concerned, are inappropriate; or

(d) developments in science or technology, or material changes in circumstances, have rendered inappropriate either the actions or the proposed actions of a local authority in fulfilment of its responsibilities under Part IV of the Act.[211]

SEPA possesses wide powers as to the giving of such directions to local authorities. For example, SEPA may require a local authority to conduct an air quality review or designate an air quality management area, or to prepare an action plan for such an area.[212] The Scottish Ministers have the power to give directions to local authorities, as is considered appropriate, for the implementation of any obligations of the UK under the EU Treaties or any international agreement to which the UK is for the time being a party, in relation to air quality.[213] In turn, the relevant local authority is required to comply with any direction which is given to it under Part IV of the Act.[214]

Transport

Pollution from road transport is significant. Indeed, in 2013 transport emissions, including international aviation and shipping, made up just under a quarter of Scotland's total emissions, and more than two thirds of these emissions came from road transport.[215] Whereas the most important controls which govern the reduction of pollution from transport relate to the control of emissions from vehicles, town and country planning also has an important role to play in reducing pollution from traffic. The Scottish

Government have recognised that planning can play an important role in improving connectivity and promoting more sustainable patterns of transport and travel as part of the transition to a low-carbon economy.[216] In a White Paper published in 2011, the European Commission, as part of its strategy to cut carbon emissions in transport by 60 per cent by 2050, proposed that: there should be no more conventionally-fuelled cars in cities; 40 per cent use of sustainable low-carbon fuels in aviation; at least a 40 per cent cut in shipping emissions, and a 50 per cent shift of medium-distance intercity passenger and freight journeys from road to rail and waterborne transport.[217]

Road vehicle emissions

Scotland's National Transport Strategy was published in 2006. The Scottish Government drew attention to the fact that road transport was, by far, the biggest source of greenhouse gas (GHG) emissions from the transport sector.[218] As far as vehicle emissions in the UK are concerned, vehicle emissions are controlled mainly by two means. The first is the regulation of both the construction and use of vehicles. The second is by means of the type approval of vehicles.

As far as the first is concerned, under the Road Traffic Act 1988 the Secretary of State is empowered to make regulations as to the use of motor vehicles and trailers on roads, their construction and equipment, and also the conditions under which vehicles may be used.[219] In particular, the regulations may make provision for the emission or consumption of smoke, fumes or vapour, and the emission of sparks, ashes and grit.[220] The Road Vehicles (Construction and Use) Regulations 1986[221] were made under the Act. The main purpose of the regulations is to ensure that vehicles are manufactured to high standards, and also to ensure that such standards are maintained while vehicles are still in use. The Regulations have been substantially amended over the years to implement EU legislation on emissions.

As far as the second form of control is concerned, the Secretary of State is empowered under the Act to make regulations which require the type approval of vehicles, with regard to, *inter alia*, their design, construction and equipment.[222] The Motor Vehicles (Type Approval) (Great Britain) Regulations 1984[223] were made under the Act. Goods vehicles are subject to the Motor Vehicles (Type Approval for Goods Vehicles) (Great Britain) Regulations 1982.[224]

As far as the regulation of air pollution from traffic is concerned, mention should be made of the powers which are given to traffic authorities by the Road Traffic Regulation Act 1984 to make traffic regulation orders in relation to roads.[225] A traffic authority may make such an order where it appears to the authority making the order that it is expedient to make it, *inter alia*, for preserving or improving the amenities of the area through which the road runs, or for any purpose which is specified in s 87[226] of the Environment Act 1995 which deals with air quality. A traffic regulation order may prohibit, restrict or regulate the use of a road by vehicular traffic, or vehicular traffic of any class which is specified in the order, either generally or subject to exceptions, as may be specified in the order, and at all times of the day or during certain specified periods.[227]

Aircraft emissions

The Air Navigation (Environmental Standards for Non-EASA Aircraft) Order 2008[228] sets out environmental standards with which specified categories of UK-registered aircraft which are not subject to the basic EASA[229] Regulation[230] must comply. Such aircraft are state aircraft and those coming within one of the categories which are listed in Annex II to that Regulation.[231] Aircraft and aeroplanes are prohibited from taking off or landing at UK airports unless they comply with the fuel-venting requirements for which the Order makes provision, and they are also fitted with engines which are specified in the emissions certificate to comply with the emissions requirements for smoke, unburned hydrocarbons, carbon monoxide and nitrogen. Emissions certificates for aircraft which are registered in the UK are issued by the Civil Aviation Authority. For aircraft which are registered elsewhere, certificates are issued by the competent authority of the relevant state.

Shipping

Emissions from maritime vessels pose a significant problem as far as atmospheric pollution and GHG are concerned. Emissions of CO_2, NOx, SO_2 and $PM2.5$ from shipping in European waters can contribute up to 10-20 per cent of worldwide shipping emissions.[232] Emissions from shipping can also contribute to local air quality problems. In 2002 the European Commission recognised that emissions from seagoing ships included air pollutants, GHGs and ozone-depleting substances. EU Directive 1999 /32/EC[233] regulates sulphur emissions from ships. The provisions of the Directive were implemented in the UK by the Merchant Shipping (Prevention of Air Pollution from Ships) Regulations 2008.[234]

Ozone depletion

The ozone layer is situated about 15-20 kilometres above the earth's surface. The ozone layer forms part of the stratosphere: it absorbs some of the sun's ultraviolet radiation, and so acts as a protective layer. Increased ultraviolet light, which results from ozone depletion, can have an adverse effect on human health, as well as harming aquatic systems and crops. Since the 1960s there have been losses in the ozone layer over the Antarctic during the Southern Hemisphere spring, often referred to as the 'hole' in the ozone layer.[235] More recently, it was discovered that ozone amounts in the Northern Hemisphere were also falling, thus triggering the need for international cooperation in dealing with the problem. A series of meetings (which were held under the UN Environment Programme) which took place over a five-year period, culminated in the Vienna Convention for the Protection of the Ozone Layer. The Treaty was adopted in March 1985, and was the first treaty to address a global atmospheric issue.[236] Whereas the Convention[237] did not set targets or timetables for action, it required four categories of action, namely:

(a)   cooperation, *inter alia*, on research and information exchange,
(b)   adoption of appropriate legislative and administrative methods in order to control, limit, reduce or prevent activities that either have, or are likely to have, adverse effects resulting from modifications to the ozone layer,
(c)   cooperation in the formulation of measures which are required to implement the Convention, as well as cooperation with appropriate international bodies.

The first, and only, Protocol to the Convention, thus far, is the 1987 Montreal Protocol which has been amended several times. The Protocol imposes specific obligations, including banning the export and import of certain ozone-depleting substances (ODS) – namely, chlorofluorocarbons (CFCs) and halons – and the gradual phasing-out of the production and consumption of all ODS.

The EU ratified the Protocol in 1988.[238] The provisions of the Protocol are currently implemented in the EU by Regulation 1005/2009 on substances which deplete the ozone layer. The main provisions of the Regulations include a general ban on the production, marketing and use of ozone-depleting substances subject to certain exemptions and derogations.[239] As far as the enforcement of the EU regulations in the UK is concerned, the Environmental Protection (Controls on Ozone-Depleting Substances) Regulations 2011[240] make the Secretary of State the competent authority for the EU regulations.[241] The enforcement of the EU regulation in Scotland is divided between SEPA and local authorities.[242] Finally, the UK regulations make provision for offences and penalties.[243]

Climate change

The traditional approach in the UK to air pollution has, as mentioned above,[244] been to adopt a sectoral approach. That is to say, specific forms of air pollution, such as smoke, grit and dust from industry, have been regulated by a command and control regime. The Clean Air Acts serve as a good example of such an approach. In this section of the book we turn our attention to the problem of climate change. Birnie et al. pertinently observe that:

> [T]he sectoral approach, which has traditionally dominated international regulation of the environment, is inappropriate to the interconnected and global character of climate change. Pollution control and the use and conservation of natural resources are both involved within the broader context of sustainable development.[245]

However, before we proceed further, it is necessary to consider what climate change actually is. The expression 'climate change' is not a term of art, or a technical term. Rather, it relates to the warming effect which certain greenhouse gases have on the environment. According to Houghton:

> [T]he green house gases are those gases in the atmosphere which, by absorbing thermal radiation, which is emitted by the Earth's surface, have a blanketing effect on it. The most important of the greenhouse gases is water vapour, but its amount in the atmosphere is not changing directly because of human activities. The important greenhouse gases that are directly influenced by human activities are carbon dioxide, methane, nitrous oxide, the chlorofluorocarbons [CFCs] and ozone.[246] Carbon dioxide is the most important of the greenhouse gases which are increasing in the atmosphere because of human activity.[247]

International law and climate change

The first major development in terms of legal measures to combat climate change took place at the Rio Conference on Environment and Development, which was held in 1992. A Framework Convention on Climate Change was adopted. The Convention entered into force on 21 March 1994. The Convention acknowledged that change in the Earth's climate and its adverse effects are a common concern of humankind. The Convention also acknowledged that change in the Earth's climate[248] calls for the widest possible cooperation by all countries, and requires their participation in an effective and appropriate international response, in accordance with their common but differentiated responsibilities, respective capabilities and social and economic conditions. The ultimate objective of the Convention was to achieve the stabilisation of GHG concentrations in the atmosphere which would prevent dangerous anthropogenic interference with the climate system.[249] In order to achieve this objective, the parties to the Convention were required[250] to be guided by certain principles, the four most important of which were the following:

1. The parties were required to protect the climate system for the benefit of both the present and also the future generations of humankind, on the basis of equity, and in accordance with their common, but differentiated responsibilities and respective capabilities. Accordingly, the developed countries were to take the lead in combating climate change and its adverse effects.

2. The specific needs and special circumstances of developing countries, especially those which were particularly vulnerable to the adverse effects of climate change, and who would have to bear a disproportionate or abnormal burden under the Convention, should be given full consideration.

3. The precautionary principle was espoused, in so far as the parties were required to take precautionary measures in order to prevent or to minimise the causes of climate change and also to mitigate its adverse effects. Where there are threats of serious or irreversible damage, lack of full scientific certainty should not be used as a reason for postponing measures.

4. The parties to the Convention both had a right to, and should also promote, sustainable development. To this end, policies and measures to protect the climate system against human-induced change should be appropriate for the specific conditions of each party, and such policies should also be integrated with national development programmes, the parties taking into account that economic development is essential for adopting measures to address climate change.

The Convention, while recognising the fact that the parties to the Convention have common but differentiated responsibilities, and their specific national and regional development priorities, places an obligation on all parties to the Convention, *inter alia*, to develop and publish national inventories of anthropogenic emissions by sources and removals by sinks[251] of greenhouse gases, and to formulate, implement and publish both national and regional programmes which contain measures to mitigate climate change by addressing anthropogenic emissions by sources and removal by sinks of greenhouse gases.[252]

As far as the developed countries are concerned, the Convention commits them to taking corresponding measures which are aimed at the mitigation of climate change by adopting national policies, limiting its anthropogenic emissions of greenhouse gases, and also protecting and enhancing their greenhouse gas sinks and reservoirs.[253] In order to secure such objectives, the parties are required to communicate, within six months of the entry into force of the Convention and periodically thereafter, information on projected anthropogenic emissions by sources and removals by sinks of greenhouse gases which are not controlled by the Montreal Protocol for the period up to 2000 with the aim of returning such emissions to their 1990 levels.[254]

Following an International Panel on Climate Change (IPCC) report to the effect that even given the stabilisation of greenhouse gas emissions at current levels, atmospheric concentrations would continue to rise for the next two centuries, the first Conference of the Parties, which was held at Berlin in 1995, accepted that these commitments were inadequate, and this provided a strong mandate (known as the Berlin Mandate) for negotiating new, more rigorous obligations.[255] This process led to the adoption of a protocol to the Convention at a third conference of the parties, in Kyoto in 1997.[256] The UK negotiates at the Conference to the parties as part of the European Union. The EU bloc of Member States agree common negotiating positions ahead of meetings.

The Kyoto Protocol
The Kyoto Protocol (which entered into force on 16 February 2005)[257] strengthens the commitments which are enshrined in the 1992 Convention, particularly Art 4(2)(a) and (b) of the Protocol, by setting out a firm schedule for the reduction of GHG emissions by Annex 1 countries (that is, the developed countries), and also by setting firm targets to be met within an agreed commitment period. Indeed, the setting of binding emission targets for developed nations is a key feature of the Protocol.

Article 3(1) of the Protocol provides that Annex 1 parties are required to ensure that their aggregate anthropogenic CO_2 equivalent emissions of greenhouse gases[258] is reduced by at least 5 per cent below 1990 levels in the commitment period 2008 to 2012. Different limits are set out for each party. In the majority of cases, a reduction of 5-8 per cent is specified. However, developing states (that is, states not included in Annex 1) need do no more than meet their existing commitments under Art 4(1) of the Convention.[259]

An important feature of Art 3(1) of the Protocol is that parties to the Convention can meet their requirements either individually or jointly. The right of the parties to meet their Protocol commitments is developed further in Art 4, in response to requests by the EU to allow implementation to be done within the EU group of nations as a whole.[260] The so-called 'EU bubble' provides that Annex 1 parties which are included in any joint agreement to fulfil their commitments in terms of Art 3(1) are deemed to have met such requirements, provided that their total combined aggregate anthropogenic CO_2 equivalent (CO_2 e) emissions of GHGs do not exceed their combined assigned amounts, which are calculated in accordance with Annex B to the Protocol.[261]

Article 2 of the Protocol contains a variety of policies and measures which the parties may use in order to achieve their quantified emission limitation and reduction commitments under Art 3. Importantly, a degree of flexibility is incorporated in Art 2, which allows a party in implementing such policies to take into account its national circumstances. The range of measures which can be employed in order to meet emission reduction targets includes the enhancement of energy efficiency in relevant sectors of the national economy, the protection and enhancement of sinks and reservoirs of GHGs, the promotion of sustainable forms of agriculture, and research on, and the promotion of, new and renewable forms of energy. Furthermore, the parties which are included in Annex 1 are required to pursue limitation or reduction of the emissions of GHGs which are not controlled by the Montreal Protocol,[262] from aviation and marine bunker fuels, working through the International Civil Aviation Organisation and the International Maritime Organisation, respectively.

Article 6 of the Protocol builds directly on Art 4(2) of the Convention, by providing that any Annex 1 party may either transfer to or acquire from any other party, emission reduction units (ERUs) which result from projects which are aimed at the removal by sinks of GHGs, provided that any such project has the approval of the parties which are involved. The Article also provides for a reduction in sources of GHGs (or an enhancement of their removal) by sinks that is in addition to any which would otherwise occur.[263] However, a party may not acquire any ERUs if the party is not in compliance with its obligations under other articles[264] of the Protocol. Furthermore, the acquisition of ERUs is required to be supplemental to domestic actions.

An important – and arguably the most innovative feature of the Protocol – is the Clean Development Mechanism (CDM), provision for which is made in Art 12. The purpose of the CDM is to assist non-Annex 1 parties in achieving sustainable development, and also to assist Annex 1 parties in achieving compliance with their emission targets which are set out in Art 3. The CDM will allow companies in the developed world to enter into cooperative projects such as the construction of high-tech, environmentally sound power plants, wind farms, carbon capture and storage,[265] for the benefit of both parties. Parties which are included in Annex 1 may use the certified emission reductions which accrue from such project activities, to contribute to compliance with part of their emission targets which are contained in Art 3.

Emissions trading

Article 17 of the Protocol allows parties which are included in Annex 1 to the Convention to the participate in emissions trading for the purposes of fulfilling their commitments under Art 3. The principle of emissions trading was strongly supported by the United States, which had domestic experience of such schemes.[266] However, any such trading requires to be supplemental to domestic actions for the purposes of meeting quantified emission limitation and reduction commitments under Art 3.

Supervision and compliance

The Convention makes provision for the supervision and compliance of the Convention and also the legal instruments which are made under the Convention.[267] The Conference of the Parties (COP) serves as the principal supervisory institution for both the Convention and the Protocol. The COP is required to keep under review the implementation of both the Convention and any legal instruments which are made under it. In order to achieve this objective, the COP receives advice from the subsidiary body for scientific and technological advice, and also from the subsidiary body for implementation.[268] Finally, the COP is required to review the Protocol periodically, in the light of the best available scientific information and assessments on climate change and its impacts, as well as relevant technical, social and economic information.[269] Based on such reviews, the COP is required to take appropriate action.

Post Kyoto

In 2007 the COP approved an Action Plan which became known as the 'Bali Roadmap', for future negotiations on the replacement of the Kyoto Protocol when its commitment period expired in 2012.[270] The COP met in Copenhagen in 2009. The aim of the conference was to reach a formal decision on the future and form of a post-2012 regime.[271] However, the parties were unable to agree targets for reducing emissions of GHGs. Instead, the Copenhagen Accord was concluded.[272] The Accord recognised that climate change was one of the greatest challenges of our time, and that an increase in global temperature should be kept below 2 degrees centigrade (C). The parties met again in Cacun in Mexico in 2010. One important outcome of the Cancun Conference was the reiteration of the 2 degrees C target, and also the recognition of the need to consider further strengthening the goal by limiting temperature rise to 1.5 C.

Another COP took place in Durban in 2011. One important outcome of the conference was the establishment of the Durban Platform for Enhanced Action.[273] The purpose of the establishment of the platform is to reach an agreement on a protocol, another legal instrument or an agreed outcome with legal force under the Convention. Such an agreement or protocol would be concluded by 2015 with a view to its being in force by 2020 when the current commitment period expires. However, no such agreement or protocol has been reached thus far. The next meeting of the COP is scheduled to be held in Paris in 2015.

The EU and climate change

The EU ratified the Kyoto Protocol in April 2002.[274] However, prior to ratifying the Protocol, the EU had long been committed to tackle climate change. The 6th Environment Action Programme (EAP), which was published in 2001,[275] recognised that climate change posed the main challenge to the EU during the 2002-2012 period. The 7th EAP is regarded as an important instrument, by means of which the EU will meet its 2020 GHG climate and energy targets, and the EU is working towards reducing, by 2050, GHG emissions by 80-95 per cent, compared to 1990 levels, as part of a global effort to limit the average temperature increase below 2 degrees C compared to pre-industrial levels.[276] The agreement of a climate and energy framework was regarded as key in securing that end.

The first major EU programme which was aimed at tackling climate change, in direct response to Kyoto, was the European Climate Change Programme (ECCP) which was established by the European Commission in 2000 in order to cut GHG emissions. The second ECCP was launched in 2005. These programmes have now been overtaken by the 2020 climate and energy package which aims to ensure that Europe meets its climate and energy targets for 2020.[277] The second ECCP package targets were set by EU leaders in 2007. There are three key targets (known as the 20-20-20 targets) for 2020 in the package: namely, a 20 per cent reduction in EU GHG emissions from 1990 levels; raising the share of EU energy consumption produced from renewable resources to 20 per cent; and a

20 per cent improvement in EU energy efficiency.[278] The second package includes the following legal instruments:

1. Directive on the Promotion of the use of Energy from Renewable Resources.[279] This Directive confirms the target of 20 per cent of the EU's energy to come from renewable sources by 2020. The UK's target is set at 15 per cent.
2. Framework Directive on the Geological Storage of Carbon Dioxide.[280] This Directive establishes a legal framework for the environmental safe storage of carbon dioxide in underground geological formations as a means of preventing the emissions of C02 into the atmosphere. The Directive is implemented in the UK by the Storage of Carbon Dioxide (Licensing etc.) Regulations 2010.[281]

A Directive on emissions trading also forms part of the package. Emissions trading will be discussed later in the chapter.[282]

In 2013 the European Commission published an EU Strategy on Adapting to Climate Change,[283] the overall aim of which is to make Europe more climate-resistant by promoting action by Member States, ensuring better-informed decision-making, and promoting adaptation in key vulnerable sectors.

The UK and climate change

Climate change is a complex problem. It is quite clear, at the outset, that in order to effectively tackle climate change, it requires a dramatic shift from the traditional approach in regulating air pollution. The UK's first climate change programme was launched in 2000.[284] The UK government (and also the devolved administrations) recognised that, notwithstanding the fact that the UK's target, which was set under the Kyoto Protocol (which was ratified by the UK in 2002), to reduce its GHG emissions by 12.5 per cent below 1990 levels during the period 2008-2012, the UK could and also should, go further. Therefore, the UK government set a domestic goal of cutting the UK's emissions of CO2 by 20 per cent below 1990 levels by 2010 and a reduction of 60 per cent by 2050. The programme set out a range of policies and measures which included a climate change levy package, a domestic emissions trading scheme, the establishment of a new Carbon Trust, the use of energy labels, integrated pollution prevention and control, an increase in the proportion of electricity which is provided by renewable sources, and an improvement of energy efficiency requirements of the Building Regulations.

A further climate change programme was published in 2006.[285] This programme built on the first, and also set out the UK government's commitment to tackling climate change by taking appropriate action, both internationally and domestically, with the aim of reducing the UK's emissions of CO2 to 15-18 per cent below 1990 levels and also reducing the emissions of GHGs to 23-25 per cent below 1990 levels in 2010. The programme included a variety of plans which included working with other EU Member States to secure further action in the EU, in particular, by extending and strengthening the Emissions Trading Scheme and the Clean Development Mechanisms, and also the introduction of a Renewable Transport Fuel Obligation from 2008.

The influential Stern Review was published in 2006.[286] Stern concluded that there was overwhelming evidence to the effect that climate change presents very serious global risks and therefore demands a global response. Ignoring climate change would eventually damage economic growth, and would create disruption to both economic and social activity. Indeed, Stern presented a rather dismal conspectus of the effects of climate change. Fortunately, there was still time to avoid the worst impacts of climate change if immediate action was taken on an international basis. That warning was, indeed, heeded by the UK government, and it responded by introducing the United Kingdom Climate Change Bill in 2007 which received Royal assent on 27 November 2008. The Climate Change Act 2008 is now discussed.

The Climate Change Act 2008

By way of a general summary, the Act[287] sets legally binding targets for GHG emissions in the UK. The Act does not (as was the case traditionally with UK legislation) target specific sectors but, rather, establishes a framework for the UK to achieve its GHG emissions. The Act sets both medium and long-term targets. In order to meet such targets, the Act introduces a system of carbon budgeting which covers specific periods. The Act also provides for a system of annual reporting by the Government on the UK's GHG emissions. An independent body, the Committee on Climate Change, is established, the function of which is to advise the government and devolved administrations. The Act gives both the UK government and devolved administrations power to introduce domestic trading schemes.

Carbon target and carbon budget
A duty is placed on the Secretary of State[288] to ensure that the net UK carbon account[289] for the year 2050 is at least 80 per cent lower than the 1990 baseline, which is defined as the aggregate amount of net UK carbon

dioxide for that year and the net UK emissions[290] of each of the other tar-
geted GHGs for the year that is the base year[291] for the gas.[292] The targeted
GHGs are the same as those which are covered by the United Nations
Framework Convention on Climate Change (UNFCCC).[293] However, the
Secretary of State can designate any other GHG after taking advice from
the Committee on Climate Change.

The Secretary of State may amend either the 2050 target or the baseline year.[294] However, that power may only be exercised if it appears to the
Secretary of State that there have been significant developments, either
in scientific knowledge about climate change or in European or international law or policy, that make it appropriate to do so.[295] The Secretary of
State must also take into account the advice of the Committee on Climate
Change and any representations which have been made by the other
national authorities.[296]

Carbon budgets
The Secretary of State is placed under a duty to set for the five-year period
which begins with the period 2008-2012,[297] and for each succeeding five-
year period, a carbon budget, that is, for the net UK carbon account.[298]
The Secretary of State is also placed under a duty to ensure that the net
UK carbon account for a budgetary period does not exceed the carbon
budget. The carbon budget for a budgetary period may be set at any
time and, in any case, must be set for the periods 2008-2012, 2013-2017
and 2018-2022 before 1 June 2009.[299] Subsequent budgets require to be
set not later than 30 June in the twelfth year before the beginning of the
relevant period. This means that the Secretary of State is under a duty to
set a subsequent budget at least eleven and a half years before the start of
the relevant budgetary period. The rationale of such a long-term approach
is to allow the necessary measures to be put in place timeously. The
Secretary of State has power to amend both the length of the budgetary
periods, or the dates on which such periods begin and end.[300] However,
such a power may only be exercised if it is deemed necessary to do so in
order to keep the budgetary periods in line with similar periods under any
agreement, either at EU or international level, to which the UK is party.[301]
In setting carbon budgets, the Secretary of State is required to take into
account a number of factors which include scientific knowledge about
climate change; technology relevant to climate change circumstances at
European and international level; and circumstances at European and
international level.[302] The carbon budget for the budgetary period, which
includes the year 2020, must be such that the annual equivalent of the
carbon budget[303] for the period is at least 34 per cent lower than the 1990

baseline.[304] The carbon budget for the budgetary period, which includes the year 2050, must be such that the annual equivalent of the carbon budget for the period is lower than the 1990 baseline by at least the percentage which is specified in s 1 of the Act (the target for 2050).[305] For the budgetary period including any later year which is specified by order of the Secretary of State, the carbon budget must be such that the annual equivalent of the carbon budget for the period is lower than the 1990 baseline by at least the percentage so specified, or at least the minimum percentage so specified, and not more than the maximum percentage so specified, lower than the 1990 baseline.[306] The Secretary of State can amend s 5(1)(a) and (1)(c).[307] However, the power can only be exercised if it appears to the Secretary of State that there have been significant developments in scientific knowledge about climate change or in European or international law or policy. As is the case with setting the carbon target, the Secretary of State must take into account the advice of the Committee on Climate Change and also any representations which are made by the other national authorities.[308] The carbon budget for any period must be set with a view to meeting the 2050 target,[309] and also the requirements as to the level of carbon budgets,[310] with a view to complying with the European and international obligations of the UK.[311] Before setting a carbon budget, the Secretary of State is required to take into account both the advice of the Committee on Climate Change, and any representations which have been made by the national authorities.[312]

Carbon units

The Secretary of State is required to set a limit on the net amount of carbon units[313] which can be credited to the net UK carbon account for each budgetary period.[314] The 'net amount of carbon units', which is a term of art, means the amount of carbon units credited to the net UK carbon account for the period in accordance with regulations under s 27, less the amount of carbon units debited from the net UK carbon account for the period in accordance with such regulations.[315] Carbon units are tradeable[316] and include units which are represented by reductions in emissions which are generated by CDM projects under Art 12 of the Kyoto Protocol, and emission reduction units under Art 6. of the Protocol.[317]

The limit for the budgetary period must be set, for the period 2008-2012, not later than 1 June 2009 and for any later period, not later than eighteen months before the beginning of the period in question.[318]

Climate Change Committee

The Climate Change Act 2008 establishes the Committee on Climate Change ('the Committee') which is a body corporate.[319] The main duty of the Committee is to advise the Secretary of State as to whether the target[320] for 2050 should be amended, and, if so, what the amended percentage should be.[321] The advice was required to be given no later than 1 December 2008.[322] The Committee is also under a duty to advise the Secretary of State on carbon budgets.[323] Furthermore, the Committee is required to advise the Secretary of State on the consequences of treating emissions of targeted GHGs from both international aviation and international shipping as emissions from sources in the UK for the purposes of the Act.[324] Finally, the Committee is required, at the request of a national authority, to give advice on targets, budgets etc. relating to GHGs which have been adopted by the national authority or to which the authority is otherwise subject.[325] For example, the Committee would be required to give advice on any requirements which relate to GHGs which have been set by the Scottish Parliament.

The Act also makes provision for emissions trading schemes. These will be discussed below.[326]

Climate Change (Scotland) Act 2009

Overview

The Climate Change (Scotland) Act 2009 ('the Act') ranks as one of the most important statutes in terms of the environment and, indeed, generally.[327] The main aim of the Act is to secure greater efforts in reducing Kyoto Protocol greenhouse gas (GHG) emissions in Scotland. The GHGs which are covered by the Act are: carbon dioxide, methane, nitrous oxide, hydrofluorcarbons, perfluorocarbons, sulphur hexafluoride and nitrogen trifluoride. The Act creates mandatory climate change targets in order to reduce GHG emissions in Scotland. A long-term target has been set, to reduce Scotland's GHG emissions by at least 80 per cent, by the year 2050.

The 2050 target

The Scottish Ministers are placed under a duty to ensure that the net Scottish emissions account[328] for the year 2050 (the target) is at least 80 per cent lower than the baseline.[329]

Interim target

The Scottish Ministers are placed under a duty to set an interim target for the year 2020 in order to ensure that the net Scottish emissions for the year 2020 are at least 42 per cent lower than the baseline.[330] However, the Scottish Ministers are empowered to modify this percentage and replace it with either a figure which has been provided by the relevant body (at present, the UK Climate Change Committee) or a higher figure.[331] In determining whether the percentage should be modified, the Scottish Ministers are required to take into account the following criteria:

(a)   scientific knowledge about climate change;
(b)   technology relevant to climate change,
(c)   economic circumstances,
(d)   fiscal circumstances,
(e)   social circumstances,
(f)   the likely key impact of the target on those living in remote rural communities and island communities,
(g)   energy policy,
(h)   environmental considerations, and
(i)   European and international law and policy relating to climate change.[332]

Annual targets

The Scottish Ministers are required to set annual targets for the maximum amount of the net Scottish emissions account for each year in the period 2010-2050.[333] The target for 2010 must be set at an amount which is less than the estimated net Scottish emissions account for 2009.[334] The target for each year in the period 2011-2019 must be set at an amount which is consistent with a reduction over that period of net Scottish emissions accounts which would allow the interim target and also the 2050 target to be met. Furthermore, the target for each year in the period 2011-2019 must be set at an amount which is consistent with a reduction over that period of net Scottish emissions accounts which would allow the 2050 target to be met and is also at least 3 per cent less than the target for the preceding year.[335] The Scottish Ministers can modify the target percentage in respect of the 2020-2050 period, the annual targets, the dates by which the annual targets must be set, and also the target-setting criteria.[336] However, before this is done, the Scottish Ministers are required to obtain the advice of the Climate Change Committee.[337]

Domestic effort target

The Act places a duty on the Scottish Ministers to ensure that reductions in the net Scottish GHG emissions make up at least 80 per cent of the reduction in the net Scottish emissions account in any target year.[338] This is known as the domestic effort target.[339] For the purposes of ascertaining if the domestic effort target has been met, any reduction in the net Scottish emissions account which is the result of European carbon units[340] being credited to that account is to be treated as though it is a reduction in net Scottish emissions.[341] European carbon units are carbon units which are surrendered by participants in the European Union Emissions Trading Scheme or by participants in an equivalent emissions trading scheme,[342] as may be specified by the Scottish Ministers.[343] However, the Scottish Ministers may only credit to the net Scottish emissions account for the period 2013-2017 any carbon units which they have purchased up to a limit of 20 per cent of the reduction in the amount of the net Scottish emissions account which is planned for that year.[344]

The Scottish Ministers are empowered to make provision regarding the emissions from international aviation and international shipping that is attributable to Scotland.[345]

Scottish Committee on Climate Change

The Act allows the Scottish Ministers to establish a Scottish Committee on climate change[346] or such other body as the Scottish Government considers appropriate.[347] At present, the relevant advisory functions are being undertaken by the Climate Change Committee.

Reports on annual targets

The Scottish Ministers are required to lay a report before the Scottish Parliament for each target year, for the period 2010-2050 for which an annual target has been set.[348] The report is required to state whether the annual target for each target year has been met.[349] Reasons are required to be given if the target has not been met.[350] The report is also required to state whether the domestic effort target has been met in the target year to which it relates.[351]

Other provisions of the Act

By way of a brief summary of the remaining provisions of the Act, a duty is placed on the Scottish Ministers to lay a programme before the Scottish Parliament, the report setting out proposals of the former for adaptation to climate change, after the UK Secretary of State has laid a report[352] before the UK Parliament on the impact of climate change.[353]

A duty is also placed on the Scottish Ministers to prepare and publish an energy efficiency[354] plan.[355] The Act also makes provision for regulations and guidance relating to the assessment of the energy performance of existing non-domestic buildings and GHG emissions from such buildings as well as requiring building owners to take steps to improve the energy efficiency of such buildings and reduce GHG emissions.[356]

Emissions trading

The concept of emissions trading finds its origins in the United States where it was introduced under the Clean Air Act.[357] Emissions trading is basically an economic instrument which is used to reduce pollution. In theory, at least, emissions trading is potentially more advantageous in reducing pollution than a pure command and control system of regulation. The advantages of emissions trading are succinctly summarised by Anderson who argues:

> Emissions trading affords plant managers greater choice in deciding how to reduce emissions so that they can take advantage of the fact which is well understood by environmental economists that the marginal costs of reducing emissions vary considerably among different types of installations and plants. If left alone, plant managers would choose to reduce emissions the most in plant components for which marginal emission control costs are the lowest. This strategy allows purchase of emissions reductions at the lowest possible cost, freeing the money saved from less efficient approaches for income producing investment elsewhere.[358]

Emissions trading and the EU
Under the Kyoto Protocol, EU Member States are committed to jointly reducing their GHG emissions during the period 2008-2012 by a total of 8 per cent below 1990 GHG emission levels. This is commonly referred to as the 'EU Bubble'. However, in order to better reflect differing GHG emission reduction potentials among Member States, the EU Member States entered into a Burden Sharing Agreement in 1998.[359]

EU ETS Directive
The EU emissions trading scheme (EUETS) is regarded as the cornerstone of EU policy to tackle the problem of climate change. The EUETS is, by far, the largest international trading scheme in the word and covers more than 11,000 power stations and industrial plants in thirty-one countries. The EUETS also covers airlines. The EUETS works on a 'cap and trade' principle. Essentially, a cap or limit is placed on certain GHG

gases which are emitted from factories, power plants and other installations in the system. The EUETS became operational in 2005.[360] Within the cap, companies can buy or trade allowances[361] with one another. In essence, the scheme is a 'downstream' private entity-based emission trading scheme; that is to say, the point of regulation is the installation which releases the GHG into the atmosphere, in contrast to an 'upstream' emissions trading scheme, which would require upstream sources, such as entities which are involved in fossil fuel production, preparation, delivery and sales, to hold allowances for emissions embedded in the fuels which they sell.[362] The EUETS is now in its third phase, which runs from 2013 to 2020. The EUETS covers emissions of CO2 from power plants, a wide range of energy intensive sectors (for example, steelworks and papermills) and commercial airlines. Nitrous oxide emissions from the production of certain acids and the emission of perfluorocarbons from the production of aluminium are included. The EUETS also covers commercial flights between countries participating in the EUETS, and between such countries and non-participating countries.[363]

By way of a brief overview of the EUETS, permits are allocated to 'operators'.[364] Applications for a GHG emissions permit are required to be made to the competent authority which is required to issue a permit if it is satisfied that the operator is capable of monitoring and reporting emissions.[365] The permit is required to impose an obligation on the operator to surrender to the competent national authority, allowances which are equal to the total emissions of the installation in each calendar year, within four months following the end of the year. Allowances can be transferred between persons[366] within the Community and also between persons in third countries.[367] Member States are required to make provision for penalties in the event of the operator failing to surrender sufficient allowances.[368] Finally, brief mention should be made of the so-called 'linking' Directive.[369] The Directive links the Kyoto Protocol project-based mechanisms to the EUETS. Essentially, credits which are obtained from such project-based mechanisms by means of both joint implementation[370] and the clean development mechanism[371] can be used by companies in order to assist the achievement of compliance under the EUETS.

Emissions trading and the UK

The 2004 Directive is implemented in the UK by the Greenhouse Gas Emissions Trading Scheme Regulations 2012.[372] Under the Regulations, no person may carry out an activity at an installation, except to the extent that it is authorised by a permit which is held by the operator of the installation.[373] In Scotland applications for permits require to be made to SEPA.[374] The application for the permit must be granted if SEPA is satisfied that the applicant will be capable of monitoring and reporting emissions from the installation.[375] Otherwise, the application should be refused. The Regulations make provision for the variation,[376] transfer[377] and surrender[378] of permits. SEPA is also empowered to revoke a permit in certain circumstances.[379] A person who has been refused a permit or whose permit SEPA serves notice to vary or revoke, may appeal to the Scottish Ministers.[380] Finally, the Regulations make provision for offences and civil penalties.

Carbon Reduction Commitment Energy Efficiency Scheme

The Carbon Reduction Commitment Energy Efficiency Scheme (CRCEES) establishes an emissions trading scheme in relation to GHGs in terms of the Climate Change Act 2008.[381] The CRCEES is a UK-wide mandatory cap and trade scheme which embraces large, non-energy-intensive organisations in both the public and private sectors.[382] The scheme, which began in 2010, is aimed at reducing $CO2$ emissions, and also at improving energy efficiency. In general, the scheme covers energy supplies which are not used for domestic or transport purposes. In the public sector, the scheme embraces local authorities, central government departments, universities and local authority-controlled schools. As far as the private sector is concerned, the scheme includes organisations such as supermarkets, hotel chains and large offices. Under the CRCEES Order[383] the trading scheme (the current phase commenced in April 2014) extends for six phases, each of five years' duration, with the final phase of four years' duration commencing in 2039. Organisations which meet the qualifications criteria, which are based on how much electricity was supplied to that organisation in 2008, are required to participate in the CRCEES. However, for the purposes of calculating the total emissions which are covered by the scheme, emissions of both electricity and gas are taken into account. Participants in the scheme are required to monitor and report on their energy use each year. The scheme is administered by the Environment Agency, with certain functions devolved to SEPA.[384]

Climate Change Levy

The Finance Act 2000[385] introduced a climate change levy which is, in effect, an environmental tax. The tax came into force on 1 April 2001.[386] By way of a brief overview,[387] the levy is a tax on the use of energy as opposed to a tax on carbon.[388] The levy is an instrument in the UK government's attempt to meet its GHG obligations in terms of the Kyoto Protocol. The philosophy behind the levy is that by taxing the consumption of certain forms of energy, one will encourage fuel efficiency and, therefore, reduce GHG emissions. The levy is imposed at the time of supply, rather than at the time of consumption by end-users. The levy is charged on the basis of a rate per unit of energy. It is the person who supplies the energy (for example, electricity, gas, oil) who is liable to pay the levy.[389]

Summary

- The legislative response to the London smog disaster of 1952 was the passing of the Clean Air Act 1956 (CAA).
- The CAA makes provision for the control of smoke, grit and dust from both industrial and domestic sources.
- The EU is now the main driver of policy concerning ambient air pollution.
- EU air quality policy comprises the 2005 EU Thematic Strategy on Air Pollution, the 2001 National Emission Ceilings Directive, the Ambient Air Quality Directive and source-specific legislation.
- The UK Air Quality Strategy adopts an effects-based approach to human health and also to the natural and man-made environments
- Climate change poses a threat to the world. The problem has been addressed at international, EU and UK levels.
- The Climate Change Act 2008 and Climate Change (Scotland) Act 2009, *inter alia*, set targets for GHG emissions.

Notes

1. *The Times,* 11 April 2014 citing a report by Public Health England. A breakdown of thirty-two council areas revealed that Glasgow had most deaths, with 306 people killed annually, followed by Edinburgh (205), Aberdeen (eighty-six) and Dundee (sixty-nine). The death rate in urban areas contrasted sharply with rural communities. Recorded deaths from air pollution in the Western Isles totalled 8 and 6 per year in Orkney and Shetland, respectively.
2. *The Times,* 29 June 2014 reporting the findings of a study which was carried out by King's College London.
3. For example, s 230 of the Edinburgh Police Act 1848 (repealed) required certain industrial furnaces to have the capacity to consume their own smoke.
4. For example, s 16(10) of the Public Health (Scotland) Act 1897 (repealed) provided that any chimney not being the chimney of a private dwelling house, sending forth smoke in such quantity as to be a nuisance or injurious or dangerous to health, ranked as a statutory nuisance.

5. P. Thorsheim, *Inventing Pollution: Coal Smoke and Culture in Britain since 1800* (Ohio University Press, 2000) at 193.

6. A. Wohl, *Endangered Lives* (Dent, 1983) at 212-13.

7. See note 3.

8. A. Wohl (note 6) at 217.

9. Repealed.

10. *Burnet-Hall on Environmental Law*, 3rd edn (Sweet and Maxwell, 2012) at 1.044.

11. A. Wohl (note 6) at 228. See also P. Thorsheim (note 5) at 111.

12. B. Clapp, *An Environmental History of Britain* (Longman, 1994) at 37.

13. 4,000 lives were lost: The Great Smog of 1952; metoffice.gov.uk.

14. See the Report of the Committee on Air Pollution, Cmnd 9322, 1954.

15. Clapp (note 12) at 50.

16. The expression 'dark smoke' is defined in s 3(1) as smoke which is as dark or darker than shade 2 on the Ringelman Chart. The section also provides that in proceedings for an offence under ss 1 or 2 (see below) the court is entitled to decide that an offence has taken place, notwithstanding the fact that there has been no actual comparison of the smoke in question with a chart. 'Smoke' is defined in s 64(1) as, 'including soot, ash, grit and gritty particles emitted in smoke'.

17. See also the Environmental Protection Act 1990 s 79(1) (b) which makes smoke emitted from premises so as to be prejudicial to health or a nuisance, a statutory nuisance.

18. Clean Air Act 1993 s 1(3).

19. See the Dark Smoke (Permitted Periods) (Scotland) Regulations 1958 (SI 1958 No 1933) and the Dark Smoke (Permitted Periods) (Vessels) Regulations 1958 (SI 1958 No 1934)

20. Ibid. s 2(1)

21. 'Premises' includes land; s 64.

22. (1983) 82 LGR 177.

23. *O'Fee v Copeland BC* [1996] Env LR 66.

24. Clean Air Act 1993 s 2(2).

25. Ibid. s 2(3).

26. 'Practicable' means reasonably practicable having regard amongst other things, to local conditions and circumstances, to the financial implications and to the current state of technical knowledge; ibid. s 64(1).

27. Ibid. s 2(4).

28. Ibid. s 2(5).

29. Ibid. s 4(1). The Act applies in relation to: (a) the attachment to a building of a boiler or industrial plant which already contains a furnace; or (b) the fixing to or installation on any land of any such boiler or plant; ibid. s 4(6).

30. Ibid. s 4(2).
31. Ibid. s 4(3).
32. Ibid. s 4(4).
33. Ibid. s 4(5).
34. Ibid. s 5(2). See the Clean Air (Emission of Grit and Dust from Furnaces) (Scotland) Regulations 1971 (SI 1971 No 625).
35. Ibid. s 5(1).
36. Ibid. s 5(3).
37. Ibid. s 5(4).
38. Ibid. s 5(5). The Act makes provision for penalties for the contravention of the provisions of s 5; ibid. s 5(6).
39. Ibid. s 6(1).
40. Ibid. s 6(5).
41. Ibid. s 7(1). See the Clean Air (Arrestment Plant) (Exemption) Regulations 1969 (SI 1969 No 1262).
42. Clean Air Act 1993, s 7(2).
43. Ibid. s 7(4).
44. Ibid. s 7(5).
45. Ibid. s 8(1).
46. Ibid. s 8(2).
47. Ibid. s 9(1).
48. Ibid. s 9(2) (3).
49. Ibid. s 10(1).
50. SI 1971 No 626.
51. Clean Air Act 1993, s 10(3).
52. Ibid. s 10(4).
53. Ibid. s 11(1) (2).
54. Ibid. s 11(3).
55. Ibid. s 12(1).
56. Ibid. s 12(2).
57. Ibid. s 13(1).
58. Ibid. s 13(2).
59. Ibid. s 14(1)(2)(3).
60. Ibid. s 14(4). It is made an offence under s 14(5) to fail to comply with s 14(4) unless the relevant plant or boiler is exempted; see the Clean Air (Height of Chimneys) (Exemption) (Scotland) Regulations 1969 (SI 1969 No 465).
61. Clean Air Act 1993, s 15(2).
62. Ibid. s 15(3).
63. Ibid. s 15(4).
64. Ibid. s 15(5).
65. Ibid. s 15(6).

66. Ibid. s 15(7).
67. Ibid. s 16.
68. As far as Scotland is concerned, reference to plans which are deposited in accordance with regulations means plans which have been submitted by way of an application for building warrant under s 9 of the Building (Scotland) Act 2003.
69. Ibid. s 16(1).
70. Ibid. s 16(2).
71. Ibid. s 16(3).
72. Ibid. s 16(4).
73. Cmnd 9322, 1954 at 693.
74. Repealed.
75. Clean Air Act 1993, s 18(1).
76. Ibid. s 18(2).
77. Including fixed boilers or industrial plant.
78. Clean Air Act 1993, s 18(3).
79. Ibid. s 19(1).
80. Ibid. s 19(2).
81. Ibid. s 19(3).
82. Ibid. s 19(4).
83. Ibid. s 19(5).
84. Ibid. s 19(6).
85. Ibid. s 20(1).
86. Ibid. s 20(2).
87. Ibid. s 20(3). For example, that smoke emanates from a fireplace which has been exempted by the local authority under s 18(2)(c).
88. Ibid. s 20(4). The Scottish Government is empowered to make regulations which declare fuels as authorised fuels in terms of Part 3 of the Act, ibid s 20(6). The Smoke Control Areas (Authorised Fuels) (Scotland) Regulations 2010 (SSI 2010 No 271) contains a list of such fuels which are colloquially known as 'smokeless fuels'.
89. Ibid. s 21. See the Smoke Control (Exempt Fireplaces) (Scotland) Order 2010 (SSI 2010 No 272).
90. Ibid. s 22(1).
91. Ibid. s 22(2).
92. Ibid. s 22(3).
93. 'Solid fuel' means any solid fuel other than an authorised fuel; Ibid. s 23(2).
94. Ibid. s 23(1).
95. Ibid. s 23(3).
96. Ibid. s 23(4).
97. Ibid. s 23(5).

98. Section 27 contains a list of adaptations which fall to be included as those which are necessary to avoid contravention of s 20.
99. Ibid. s 24(1).
100. Clean Air Act 1993, s 24(4)(b).
101. Ibid. s 24(4)(c). Section 25(1) of the Act specifies that the provisions of Sched 2 to the Act apply to certain expenditure which is incurred in adapting 'old private dwellings' in smoke control areas. An old private dwelling' means a dwelling which was erected after 15 August 1964 or was produced by the conversion, after that date. A dwelling or premises may not be treated as erected or converted after 15 August 1964 unless the erection or conversion was begun after it; ibid. s 25(2).

Schedule 2 makes provision for the payment of grants by local authorities to either the owner, occupier or any person interested in an old private dwelling which is either in or will be in a smoke control area as a result of the order, incurs 'relevant expenditure' which is defined as expenditure on adaptations in or in connection with an old private dwelling to avoid contraventions of s 20 (prohibition of smoke emissions in a smoke control area). A local authority is permitted to approve the incurring of the expenditure after the expenditure has been incurred. The schedule also specifies that no payment may be made in relation to heating appliances which are classified as unsuitable (as defined in the schedule). The schedule also specifies that no payment be made in relation to heating appliances which are classified as unsuitable (as defined in the schedule) by either the local authority or the Scottish Government. Finally, the schedule allows the Scottish Government to make a financial contribution in relation to expenditure which has been incurred by a local authority, *inter alia*, in making payments to owners or occupiers of old private dwellings.
102. Ibid. s 26
103. The Air Quality Strategy for England, Scotland, Wales and Northern Ireland. Cmd. 4548, 2000. The Strategy indicated that road traffic pollution made a significant contribution to nitrogen dioxide emissions which was likely to be the most difficult pollutant to reduce the level which is set by the Strategy.
104. Clean Air Act 1993, s 30(1). See the Motor Fuel (Composition and Content) Regulations 1999 (SI 1999 No 3107) as amended. See also the Sulphur Content in Liquid Fuels (Scotland) Regulations 2007 (SSI 2007 No 27) which are made under s 2(2) of the European Communities Act 1972.
105. Ibid. s 30(2).
106. Ibid. s 33(1). The section has been prospectively amended by the Pollution Prevention and Control Act 1999, Sched 3. After that Act comes into force the provisions of s 33 of the Clean Air Act 1993 will not apply to

the burning of cable which is subject to a process which is covered by the Pollution Prevention and Control (Scotland) Regulations 2012 (SSI 2012 No 360).

107. Clean Air Act 1993, s 34(1).
108. Ibid. s 35(1)
109. SSI 2012 No 360; Clean Air Act 1993, s 36(2A).
110. Ibid. s 37.
111. Essentially, the determination date in relation to a process is the date on which a relevant application for authorisation is either granted or refused, s 41(2), or the date on which the permit is granted or refused, s 41A(2).
112. Clean Air Act 1993, s 41 (prospectively repealed by the Prevention of Pollution and Control Act 1999, Sched 3)
113. Clean Air Act 1993, s 41A(1). See the Pollution Prevention and Control (Scotland) Regulations 2012 (SSI 2012 No 360).
114. Commonly referred to as 'bings'. The bings are composed either of coal or shale (especially in West Lothian) mineral waste. The colliery spoilbanks are to be found mainly in Fife, the Lothians, Lanarkshire and Ayrshire.
115. The creation of spoilbanks was not the only legacy of the mining industry. The waste water which was pumped from mineshafts into nearby watercourses continued to pollute them for years after the mines had closed.
116. The expressions 'mine' and 'quarry' have the same meaning as in the Mines and Quarries Act 1954.
117. Clean Air Act 1993, s 42(1)(2).
118. Which relates to statutory nuisances and clean air.
119. Ibid. s 42(4).
120. Ibid. s 43.
121. Ibid. s 44.
122. Ibid. s 45.
123. Ibid. s 46.
124. Ibid. s 47.
125. Ibid. s 49.
126. The appropriate person to notify is the occupier of the premises, the person having control of the boiler or plant, the owner of the railway locomotive engine or the owner or master or other officer or person in charge of the vessel concerned, s 51(2).
127. Ibid. s 51(1).
128. Ibid. s 51(3).
129. Ibid. s 52(1). Where the affairs of a body corporate are managed by its members, the acts and defaults of a member are to be treated as if such a member was a director of the corporate body, s 52(2).
130. Ibid. s 53(1). A person may be charged with and convicted of an offence by

virtue of the section whether or not proceedings for the offence are taken against any other person, s 53(2).

131. Ibid. s 55(1).
132. Ibid. ss 56 and 57.
133. Ibid. s 59(1).
134. Ibid. s 60(1).
135. Ibid. s 60(2).
136. Ibid. s 60(7).
137. This Common Inheritance, Cmnd 1200 (HMSO, 1990) at 146.
138. C. Lister, *European Union Environmental Law* (Wiley, 1996) at 203.
139. L. Kramer, *EU Environmental Law*, 7th edn (Sweet and Maxwell, 2012) at 8.01.
140. Ibid. at 8.01.
141. Directive 80/779/EC.
142. N. Haigh, *EEC Environmental Policy and Britain* (Longman, 1987) at 188.
143. The European Commission has drawn attention to the fact that in 2010 more than 400,000 are estimated to have died prematurely from air pollution in the EU; European Commission press release, 18 December 2013.
144. Communication of 21 September 2005 from the Commission to the Council and the European Parliament-Thematic Strategy on Air Pollution, COM (2005) 446 para 2. The Sixth Community Environment Action Programme, Decision no 1600/2002/EC, art. 4 required the development of thematic strategies on, *inter alia*, air quality. The concept of a thematic strategy for air quality was endorsed by the Clean Air for Europe (CAFÉ) Programme: Towards a Thematic Strategy for Air Quality, COM/2001/0245 final.
145. See the Communication from the Commission to the European Parliament, the Council, the European Economic and Social Committee and the Committee of the Regions; COM/2013/0918.
146. Directive 2001/81/EC.
147. Ibid. Art 5.
148. Ibid. Art 6.
149. Ibid. Art 8.
150. Ibid. Art 2.
151. Ibid. Art 12.
152. SI 2002 No 3118.
153. Ibid. reg 3.
154. Ibid. reg 4. See the National Emissions Reduction Plan (2003).
155. COM (2013) 920 final.
156. Directive 2008/50/EC.

157. With the exception of provisions for heavy metals, for which provision is made in Directive 2004/107/EC.
158. Directive 96/62/EC.
159. Which related to the exchange of information and data on air pollution between Member States.
160. Directive 2008/50/EC, Art 3.
161. A 'zone' is defined as part of the territory of a Member State, as determined by that Member State for the purposes of air quality assessment and management; ibid. Art 2.
162. An 'agglomeration' is defined as a zone that is a conurbation with a population with an excess of 250,000 inhabitants or less, with a given population density per km^2 to be established by the Member State; ibid. Art 2.
163. Ibid. Art 4.
164. Ibid. Art 5.
165. Ibid. Annex III.
166. A 'limit value' is defined as a fixed level, on the basis of scientific knowledge, with the aim of avoiding, preventing or reducing harmful effects on human health and/or the environment, as a whole, to be attained within a given period and not to be exceeded, once attained; ibid. Art 2.
167. Ibid. Annexes XI and XIV.
168. Ibid. Art 12.
169. Ibid. Art 13. The relevant limit values are laid out in Annex XI of the Directive.
170. A 'critical level' means a level which is fixed on the basis of scientific knowledge, above which direct adverse effects may occur on some receptors, such as trees, other plants or natural ecosystems but not on humans; ibid. Art 2.
171. Ibid. Art 14.
172. A national exposure reduction target is the percentage reduction of the average exposure of the population of a Member State set for the reference year with the aim of reducing harmful effects on human health, to be attained where possible over a given period; ibid. Art 2.
173. A 'target value' is defined as a level which is fixed with the aim of avoiding, preventing or reducing the harmful effects on human health and/or the environment`t as a whole, to be attained where possible over a given period; ibid. Art 2.
174. Ibid. Arts 15 and 16, respectively.
175. Ibid. Art 17.
176. Ibid. Art 18.
177. Ibid. Art 22.
178. 'Margin of tolerance' means the percentage of the limit value by which that

value may be exceeded subject to the conditions which are laid down in the Directive; ibid. Art 2.

179. Ibid. Art 23.
180. Ibid. Art 24. An 'alert threshold' means a level beyond which there is a risk to human health from brief exposure for the population as a whole and at which immediate steps are to be taken by the Member State; ibid. Art 2.
181. SSI 2010 No 204. The regulations also implement Directive 2004/107/EC which relates to arsenic, cadmium, mercury, nickel and polycyclic aromatic hydrocarbons in ambient air.
182. Case C-404/13, judgment date, 19 November 2014.
183. Art 258.
184. [2013] Env LR 4.
185. The UK has not met its NO2 and oxide of nitrogens targets which were set by the Directive since they were transposed into national legislation in 2010. This failure has been described as the longest-running infringement of EU law in history; (2014) 474 ENDS 34 at 34.
186. [2013] Env LR 33.
187. Directive 2010/75/EU.
188. Directive 2001/80/EC.
189. Directive 2000/76/EC.
190. Directive 94/63/EC.
191. Directive 98/70/EC.
192. Environment Act 1995, s 80(1).
193. Cmnd No 3587 (HMSO, 1997).
194. Ibid. at 8.
195. The Air Quality Strategy for England, Scotland, Wales and Northern Ireland, Cmnd No 4548, SE 2000/3 (HMSO, 2000).
196. The Air Quality Strategy for England, Wales and Northern Ireland, Cmnd 7169 (HMSO, 2007).
197. Environment Act 1995, s 81.
198. May 2015.
199. www.scotland.gov.uk/consultations.
200. Ibid. s 82(1).
201. Ibid. s 82(2).
202. SSI 2000 No 97 (as amended).
203. Environment Act 1995 s 82(3).
204. Ibid. s 83(1).
205. Ibid. s 83(2).
206. Ibid. s 84(1).
207. Ibid. s 84(4).
208. See p. 215.

209. Ibid. s 85(1).
210. Ibid. s 85(2).
211. Ibid. s 85(3).
212. Ibid. s 85(4).
213. Ibid. s 85(5).
214. Ibid. s 85(7).
215. Low Carbon Scotland: Meeting our Emissions Reduction Targets 2013-2027: The Second Report on Proposals and Policies (Scottish Government, 2013) para 7.1.
216. Scottish Planning Policy (Scottish Government, 2014) para 269.
217. White Paper – Roadmap to a Single European Transport Area: towards a competitive and resource efficient transport system (European Commission, 2011).
218. Scotland's National Transport Strategy (2006) at para 47. In 2013 the European Environment Agency stated that road traffic contributes significantly to breaches of air quality standards in many cities and other urban areas; TERM 13 para 4.3.
219. Road Traffic Act 1988, s 41(1).
220. Ibid. s 41(2).
221. SI 1986 No 1078 (as amended).
222. Road Traffic Act 1984 s 54(1).
223. SI 1984 No 981 (as amended).
224. SI 1982 No 1271 (as amended).
225. Road Traffic Regulation Act 1984 s 1(1).
226. Environment Act 1995 s 87(1) (a)-(c).
227. Road Traffic Regulation Act 1984 s 2(1).
228. SI 2008 No 3133.
229. The EASA, the European Aviation Safety Agency, was set up by the European Union in order to promote, *inter alia*, common standards of safety and environmental protection.
230. OJ No L240 of 7.09.2002 p. 1.
231. UK registered aircraft which are subject to the Basic EASA Regulation must, instead, comply with the environmental standards which are provided for in that Regulation and in Commission Regulation (EC) No 1702/2003.
232. European Technical Report No 4/2013 (European Environment Agency, 2013) at 5.
233. As amended.
234. SI 2008 No 2924.
235. P. Sands and J. Peel, *Principles of International Environmental Law*, 3rd edn (Cambridge University Press, 2012) at 262.

236. Ibid. at 264.
237. Vienna Convention for the Protection of the Ozone Layer, Art 2.
238. Council Decision 88/540/EEC.
239. Ibid. Arts 4 and 5.
240. SI 20011 No 1543.
241. Ibid. reg 3.
242. Ibid. reg 7.
243. Ibid. regs 4 and 5
244. See p. 121.
245. P. Birnie, A. Boyle and C. Redgwell, *International Law and the Environment*, 3rd edn (Oxford University Press, 2009) at 356.
246. J. Houghton, *Global Warming*, 4th edn (Cambridge University Press, 2009) at 34.
247. Ibid. at 35.
248. Framework Convention on Climate Change, Art 1, defined the expression, 'climate change' as 'a change of climate which is attributed directly or indirectly to human activity that alters the composition of the global atmJ. osphere and which is, in addition to natural climate variability, observed over comparable time periods.
249. Ibid. Art 2.
250. Ibid. Art 3.
251. A 'sink' is defined as any process, activity or mechanism which removes a greenhouse gas, an aerosol or a precursor of a greenhouse gas from the atmosphere; ibid., Art 1.
252. Ibid. Art 4(1).
253. Ibid. Art 4(2)(a).
254. Ibid. Art 4(2)(b).
255. P. Birnie, A. Boyle and C. Redgwell (note 246) at 360.
256. P. Sands and J. Peel (note 236) at 284.
257. Notwithstanding the fact that the Kyoto Protocol had been finalised in 1997, it took eight years before it came into force because of its complicated ratification requirements; see D. Freestone, 'From Copenhagen to Cancun: train wreck or paradigm shift' (2010) 12 Env LR 87 at 87.
258. The GHGs covered by the Protocol are carbon dioxide, methane, nitrous oxide, hydro-fluorocarbons, perfluorocarbons and sulphur hexafluoride.
259. Kyoto Protocol 1997 Art 10.
260. D. Freestone, 'Legal and institutional framework', in D. Freestone and C. Streck (eds), *Legal Aspects of Carbon Trading* (Oxford University Press, 2009) 3 at 12.
261. Kyoto Protocol 1997 Art 4(1).
262. See p. 126.

263. This is sometimes known as the 'but for test', that is to say, 'but for the project, any such reduction or enhancement would not have occurred'.

264. Arts 5 and 7.

265. The Pollution Prevention and Control (Scotland) Regulations 2012, Sched 1 Part 1 (SSI 2012 No 360) make provision for carbon capture and storage. Also see 'Next steps in Capture Carbon Storage' (DECC, 2014).

266. For a useful discussion of emissions trading in the US, see F. Anderson et al., *Environmental Protection* (Aspen, 1999) at 487-96.

267. Framework Convention on Climate Change Art 7.

268. Ibid. Arts 9 and 10.

269. Kyoto Protocol Art, 9.

270. Decision 1/CP 13.

271. For a detailed discussion of the Copenhagen conference, see P, Sands and J. Peel (note 236) at 294.

272. 2/CP.15.

273. 1/CP.17.

274. Council Decision 2002/358/EU Art 1.

275. COM (2001) 31 Final.

276. Decision no 1386/2013/EU.

277. Decision no 406/2009/EC.

278. A 2030 Framework for Climate and Energy has been proposed by the EU Commission; COM/2013/0169.

279. Directive 2009/28/EC.

280. Directive 2009/31/EC.

281. SI 2010 No 2221.

282. See p. 140-2 incl.

283. COM (2013) 0216 Final.

284. DEFRA (and devolved administrations), Climate Change – The UK Programme (2000).

285. DEFRA (and devolved administrations), Climate Change – The UK Programme (2006) Cmnd 6764.

286. Stern Review: The Economics of Climate Change.

287. For a general summary of the Climate Change Act 2008, see M. Grekos, 'Climate Change Act 2008' [2009] JPEL 454; H. Townsend, 'The Climate Change Act 2008' [2009] JPEL 454; H. Townsend, 'The Climate Change Act 2008: something to be proud of after all?' [2009] JPEL 843, and H. Townsend, 'The Climate Change Act 2008 – will it do the trick?' (2009) 12 Env LR 116.

288. In effect, the Secretary of State for Energy and Climate Change.

289. The net UK carbon account for a period means the amount of UK emissions of targeted GHGs for the period, reduced by the amount of carbon units

which are credited to the UK carbon account for the period, in accordance with regulations which are made under s 27 and increased by the amount of carbon units which fall to be debited from the net UK carbon account for the period; s 27(1). The Carbon Accounting Regulations 2009 (SI 2009 No 1257) make provision about carbon units and carbon accounting.

290. The 'UK emissions', in relation to a greenhouse gas, means emissions of that gas from sources in the United Kingdom. The 'net UK emissions' for a period, in relation to a GHG, means the amount of UK emissions of that gas for the period, reduced by the amount for the period of UK removals of that gas. 'UK removals', in relation to GHG, means removals of that gas from the atmosphere due to land use, land use change or forestry activities in the United Kingdom; s 29(1).

291. The relevant base years are set out in s 25(1).

292. Ibid. s 1(1)(2).

293. Ibid. s 24(1).

294. Ibid. s 2(1),

295. Ibid. s 2(2). The same power may also be exercised in connection with the making of an order under s 24(1) (the designation of further greenhouse gases as targeted greenhouse gases) or regulations which are made under s 30(2) (emissions from international aviation or international shipping).

296. Ibid. s 3(1),

297. The UK met its first budget period beginning in 2008; (2014) 474 ENDS 34 at 34.

298. Ibid. s 4(1)

299. Ibid. s 4(2). The carbon budget for these periods was set by the Carbon Budgets Order 2009 (SI 2009 No 1259). The carbon budget for the 2023-2027 period was set by the Carbon Budgets Order 2011 (SI 2011 No 1603).

300. Climate Change Act 2008 s 23(1).

301. Ibid. s 23(2).

302. Ibid. s 10(1) (2).

303. The 'annual equivalent', in relation to the carbon budget for a period, means the amount of the carbon budget for the period, divided by the number of years in the period; s 5(2).

304. Ibid. s 5(1) (a).

305. Ibid. s 5(1) (b).

306. Ibid. s 5(1) (c).

307. Ibid. s 6(1).

308. Climate Change Act 2008 s 7(1).

309. Ibid. s 1.

310. Ibid. s 5.

311. Ibid. s 8(2).

312. Ibid. s 9(1)(2).
313. A carbon unit is defined as a unit which represents a reduction in amount of GHG emissions, the removal of an amount of GHG from the atmosphere or an amount of GHG emissions allowed under a scheme or arrangement imposing a limit on such emissions; ibid. s 26(1). See also the Carbon Accounting Regulations 2009 (SI 2009 No 1257) (as amended) reg 3.
314. Ibid. s 11(1)
315. Ibid. s 11(2). See the Climate Change Act 2008 (Credit Limit) Order 2011 (SI 2011 No 1602) which sets a limit on the amount of carbon units which may be credited to the UK net carbon account for the 2013-17 period. For a useful graphic illustration of how the net UK carbon account is calculated, see 'Calculating the net UK carbon account' in Annual Statement of Emissions for 2012 (DECC, 2014) at 7-8. Carbon units are calculated according to the Carbon Accounting Regulations 2009 (SI 2009 No 1257) (as amended).
316. Carbon Accounting Regulations 2009 reg, 5.
317. Ibid. reg .3.
318. Climate Change Act 2008 s 11(3).
319. Ibid. s 32(1).
320. Ie the net UK carbon account for the year 2050 which is set in s 1(1) of the Act.
321. Ibid. s 33(1).
322. Ibid. s 33(3).
323. Ibid. s 34.
324. Ibid. s 35(1).
325. Ibid. s 38(3).
326. See p. 140-2 incl.
327. For a brief overview of the Act, see (2009) 134 SPEL 92.
328. The net Scottish emissions account means the aggregate amount of net Scottish emissions of GHGs which are reduced by the amount of carbon units which are credited to the net Scottish emissions account for the period in accordance with regulations which are made under s 13(5) and increased by the amount of carbon units that, in accordance with such regulations, are to be debited from the net Scottish emissions for the period; s 13(1); see the Carbon Accounting Scheme (Scotland) Regulations 2010 (SSI 2010 No 216). The net amount of carbon units which is credited to the net Scottish emissions account for a year for which an annual target has been set (that is, a target year) must not exceed the allowable amount; s 13(2). The 'allowable amount' is the amount which is equal to the limit which is set under s 21(1) (see below) of the Act on the net amount of carbon units that may be credited to the net Scottish emissions account during the period which

includes the target year, s 13(3)(a), or, where a net amount of carbon units has been credited to the net Scottish emissions account for any other target year in that period, the balance (if any) which remains of the amount which is referred to in s 13(3)(a); s 13(3)(b).

The expression 'emissions' in relation to a GHG means emissions of that gas into the atmosphere that are attributable to human activity. 'Scottish emissions', in relation to a GHG, means emissions of that gas which are attributable to Scotland. Scottish removals, in relation to a GHG, means removals of that gas from the atmosphere due to land use, land change or forestry activities in Scotland. The net Scottish emissions for a period, in relation to a GHG, means the amount of Scottish emissions of that gas for the period, reduced by the amount of Scottish removals of that gas for the period, s 17(1). GHGs are attributable to Scotland if they are emitted from sources in Scotland and also the share which is attributed to Scotland by an order made under s 16(1) which relates to the share of emissions from international aviation and shipping; ibid s 15.

329. Climate Change (Scotland) Act 2009, s 1(1). The 'baseline' is defined as the aggregate amount of net Scottish emissions of carbon dioxide for 1990 and the net Scottish emissions of each of the GHGs other than CO2 for the year that is the baseline year for that gas, s 11(1). The baseline years for GHGs other than CO2 are 1990 for methane and nitrous oxide, and 1995 for hydrofluoracarbons, perfluorocarbons, sulphur hexafluorides and for nitrogen trifluoride; s 11(2).

330. Ibid. s 2(1). The Scottish Government, citing a recent report of the Climate Change Committee, announced that Scotland remains on track to meet its 42 per cent target; Scottish Government 10/6/2014.

331. Ibid. s 2(3).

332. Ibid. s 2(5).

333. Ibid. s 3(1).

334. Ibid. s 3(2).

335. The Climate Change (Annual Targets) (Scotland) Order 2010 (SSI 2010 No 359) Art 2 sets out annual targets for the period 2010-2022 in tonnes of carbon equivalent (as defined in s 18(2) of the Act) for the period 2010-2022. The Scottish Government failed to meet its annual target for the year 2012 (4th Report Committee Climate Change (March 2015)).

336. Ibid. s 6(1).

337. Ibid. s 7(1).

338. Ibid. s 8(1).

339. Ibid. s 8(2).

340. A carbon unit is a unit which is of a kind specified in regulations made under s 20(1) and which represents a reduction in an amount of GHG from the

atmosphere and an amount of GHG emissions allowed under a scheme or arrangement imposing a limit on such emissions, s 20(4). See the Carbon Accounting Scheme (Scotland) Regulations 2010 (SSI 2010 No 216).

341. Ibid. s 8(3).

342. For a discussion of trading schemes see below.

343. Climate Change (Scotland) Act 2009, s 8(4).

344. Ibid. s 14(3).

345. Ibid. s 16(1). See the Climate Change (International Aviation and Shipping) (Scotland) Order 2010 (SSI 2010 No 218).

346. Climate Change (Scotland) Act 2009, s 25(1).

347. Ibid. s 24(1).

348. Ibid. s 33(1).

349. Ibid. s 33(2).

350. Ibid. s 33(3).

351. Ibid. s 33(4). In 2011 Scotland's GHG emissions fell by 9.9 per cent which was 3.3 per cent more than the UK average. However, the target for 2011 was missed. UK gas emissions fell 1.9 per cent during 2013; (2014) 471 ENDS 32. The 2012 annual target was also missed; Committee on Climate Change Annual Report 2015 at 6.

352. The report is laid under s 56 of the Climate Change Act 2008.

353. Climate Change (Scotland) Act 2009, s 53(1) (2). The first programme was laid before the Scottish Parliament in May 2014; See Climate Ready Scotland: Scottish Climate Change Adaptation Programme (SG 2014/83).

354. The term 'energy efficiency' is defined in s 60(9) of the Act.

355. Ibid. s 60(1). See Conserve and Save: Energy Efficiency Action Plan (Scottish Government, 2010).

356. Ibid. s 63(1). See the Energy Performance of Buildings (Scotland) Regulations 2008 (SSI 2008 No 309) (as amended).

357. For an interesting account of the various emissions trading schemes and also a discussion of the relative merits of such schemes in the United States see F. Anderson et al., *Environmental Protection Law and Policy*, 3rd edn (Aspen Law and Business) at 487-96.

358. Ibid. at 488.

359. See M. Pohlmann, 'The European Union Emissions Trading Scheme', in D. Freestone, *Legal Aspects of Carbon Trading* (Oxford University Press, 2009) 337 at 337.

360. Directive 2003/87/EC (as amended by Directive 2009/29/EC). For a general overview of the Directive, see A. Ellerman et al., *Carbon Pricing* (Cambridge University Press, 2010).

361. An 'allowance' means allowance to emit one tonne of CO_2 equivalent during a specified period; Directive 2003/87/EC Art 3.

362. M. Pohlmann (note 360) at 339.
363. The scope of the EUETS is limited to flights within Europe until 2016.
364. 'Operator' means any person who either operates or controls an installation or, where this is provided for in national legislation, to whom decisive economic power over the technical functioning of the installation has been delegated, Directive 2003/87/EC Art 3.
365. Ibid. Art 6
366. 'Person' means any natural or legal person, ibid. Art 3.
367. Ibid. Art 12.
368. Ibid. Art 16.
369. Directive 2004/101/EC.
370. Kyoto Protocol Art 6.
371. Ibid. Art 12.
372. SI 2012 No 3038 (as amended).
373. Ibid. reg 9.
374. Ibid. reg 10(1).
375. Ibid. reg 10(4).
376. Ibid. reg 11.
377. Ibid. reg 12.
378. Ibid. reg 13.
379. Ibid. reg 14.
380. Ibid. reg 75(1).
381. Climate Change Act 2008 ss 44 and 46.
382. See the CRC Energy Efficiency Scheme Guidance for Participants in Phase 1 (2010/11-2013/14) (2012) published jointly by the Environment Agency, the Northern Ireland Environment Agency and SEPA.
383. SI 2013 No 1119 (as amended).
384. See the CRC Energy Efficiency Scheme (Allocation of Allowances for Payment) Regulations 2013 (SI 2013 No 3103) which make provision for the allocation of allowances etc. by the Environment Agency.
385. Finance Act 2000 s 30, Scheds 6 and 7.
386. See, generally, A General Guide to Climate Change Levy (HM Revenue and Customs, 2014).
387. For a useful brief overview of the climate change levy, see J. Aitken, 'The climate change levy' (2010) 109 Prop. L.B. 5.
388. The rates are based on the energy content of each commodity.
389. Finance Act 2000 Sched 6 para 40.

CHAPTER 6

Waste

The traditional approach to waste has been to regulate its disposal in order to ensure that neither human health nor the environment suffers harm. A licensing or permitting system allows regulatory authorities to supervise landfill sites etc. This is supplemented by legislation which makes provision for penalties for the unlawful disposal of waste. The Environmental Protection Act 1990 introduced the concept of duty of care in relation to those who produce waste. In essence, those who produce waste bear legal responsibility for its lawful disposal.

European Union policy has had a significant impact on waste policy. Greater emphasis is now being placed on the prevention of waste, its re-use and its recycling.

Introduction

In this chapter, we turn our attention to the subject of the regulation of waste. The origins of waste law, and, indeed, environmental law in general, lie in the mid-nineteenth century.[1] We now know that cholera is spread by a *vibrio* (the vibrio cholera) which passes from person to person through the faecal/oral route, most commonly by individuals consuming contaminated water. However, during the mid-nineteenth century, it was widely believed that smell, or miasms, from organic matter such as putrescible waste and excrement caused the much-feared cholera which afflicted the United Kingdom in waves between 1831 and 1866.[2] The obvious way, of course, to deal with the problem was simply to remove waste before it could affect the general public. Parliament, therefore, conferred powers on local authorities in the form of the Nuisance Removal Acts which were passed between 1846 and 1856, to remove waste from their areas when cholera approached the UK. The waste removal provisions of these Acts were repealed and also re-enacted by the Public Health (Scotland) Act 1867[3] and, subsequently, by the Public Health (Scotland) Act 1897.[4] We shall see that, over the years, waste law has become much more complex. The EU has played no insignificant role in this process. By way of a general overview, whereas waste was originally seen simply as an environmental problem for local authorities to deal with after waste had been created, the current approach is to treat waste as a potential resource which is to be used for the general public weal. Whereas currently the disposal of waste is regulated by the state in the form of the Scottish Environment Protection Agency (SEPA), greater responsibility is being placed on those who produce waste to ensure its effective disposal. We shall also see that manufacturers of certain products, such as cars and electrical equipment, are placed under certain duties to ensure that the product is satisfactorily disposed of when it is no longer fit for use.

National waste policy

One of the main indicia of the general store which the Scottish Government attaches to any pollutant can be gauged in terms of whether that pollutant is worthy of being the subject of a national strategy. We have already seen[5] that an air quality strategy has been prepared for the UK, whereas noise is a pollutant which, unfortunately, thus far is not perceived as sufficiently important to warrant a national strategy. As far as waste is concerned, SEPA is placed under a duty to prepare a waste strategy which sets out SEPA's policies for the recovery and disposal of waste in Scotland.[6] The National Waste Strategy was launched by SEPA in 1999.[7] A number of key principles were identified as establishing a sustainable future for waste management. These principals, which derive from EU waste policy,[8] are proximity and self-sufficiency, the precautionary principle, the polluter pays principle, and the waste hierarchy. It is necessary to explain what each principle means.

The proximity principle means that waste should be either treated or disposed of as near as possible to the point where it arises. The precautionary principle involves taking precautions at present, in order to avoid possible environmental damage or harm to human health even although the scientific basis for taking such precautions may be inconclusive. Lastly, the polluter pays principle means that the person who is responsible for pollution should bear the cost of the consequences of his action.

The waste hierarchy provides a general framework for waste disposal practices within which the most desirable waste management practices are set out.[9] The most effective option is the reduction of the generation of waste and also the use of natural resources. The second option consists of items being used again either for the same or for different purposes. The third consists of the recycling of waste, composting or energy recovery by means of incineration or other technologies. Finally, the disposal of waste by means of landfill constitutes the least desirable option, along with the incineration of waste without energy recovery.

National Waste Plan

The First National Waste Plan for Scotland was published in 2003, and it set objectives for the sustainable management of Scotland's waste. The Plan makes provision, *inter alia*, for the widespread segregation of kerbside waste collections across Scotland; stopping the growth of the amount of waste which is produced by 2010; achieving 25 per cent recycling and composting of municipal waste by 2010; achieving 25 per cent recycling and composting of municipal waste by 2006[10] and 55 per cent by 2020 (35 per cent recycling and 20 per cent composting); recovering energy from 14 per cent of municipal waste by 2020; and reducing landfilling of municipal waste from around 90 per cent to 30 per cent by 2020.

This was replaced by the Zero Waste Plan for Scotland which was published in 2010.[11] The Zero Waste Plan, arguably, represents the most ambitious attempt by the Scottish Government to tackle the problem of waste. The Plan places emphasis on the avoidance of the creation of waste, rather than dealing with waste after it has been created. It also espouses the now well-recognised waste hierarchy, namely, waste prevention, re-use, recycling and waste recovery. Waste prevention is seen as a top priority in the 2010 plan.[12] However, the Plan is not to be regarded as an end in itself. Rather, it is to be seen as the first step in the development of a programme to tackle all waste.

The regulation of waste

The Environmental Protection Act 1990 (the EPA) makes provision, *inter alia*, for the unlawful deposit of waste, and places individuals under a duty of care in relation to waste. However, before we discuss the provisions of the Act, we must discuss the meaning of the expression 'waste'.

Meaning of waste[13]

The EPA defines the expression, 'waste' as:

(a)   anything that is waste within the meaning of the Art 3(1) of the Waste Directive[14] as read with Arts 5 and 6 of the Directive, and which is not excluded from the scope of that Directive by Art 2(1)(2) or (3),

(b)   radioactive waste within the meaning of s 1A of the Radioactive Substances Act 1993 which is exempt from the requirement for authorisation under ss 13 or 14 of that Act by virtue of an order made or having effect as made, under s 15(2) of that Act:

(c)   where land is undergoing on-site remediation, that land including unexcavated contaminated soil and any contaminated buildings permanently connected with that land.[15]

'Controlled waste' is defined as household, industrial or commercial waste or any such waste.[16]

The expression 'waste,' to all intents and purposes, derives its meaning from the Waste Directive. The meaning of waste was considered in the Outer House case of *Scottish Power Generation Ltd v Scottish Environment Protection Agency*.[17] In that case, the pursuers, Scottish Power (SP), used certain waste derived fuels (WDF) to produce electricity in a power station which they operated. The fuel was produced from sewage sludge by SMW Ltd (SMW) the sludge having been taken from a waste water treatment works. The power station originally operated under an integrated pollution control authorisation under the EPA, and subsequently under the Pollution Prevention and Control Act 1999 regime. SEPA sought to apply the provisions of the Waste Incineration (Scotland) Regulations 2003[18] (which set more rigorous controls over waste plants, compared with the controls which were applied to the normal operation of a power station) by means of a variation notice. Scottish Power challenged the notice by means of judicial review, and argued that sludge did not rank as waste, *inter alia*, in terms of the Waste Framework Directive (WFD).[19] However, in the opinion of Lord Reed, the sludge remained waste. In short, the processing of the sludge did not constitute a complete recovery operation whereby a substance which was originally waste ceases to be waste, in terms of the Directive. In reaching his decision His Lordship expressed the view that the word 'waste' derived its meaning from the word 'discard' as used in the Waste Framework Directive, the word 'discard' bearing a special meaning. In effect, the word 'discard' was a term of art.[20] Furthermore, the fact that that the processor of a substance derived economic benefit from processing the substance did not prevent the substance from being characterised as waste. In the opinion of His Lordship, indicators of the fact that either a substance is being discarded, or that the holder of the substance has an intention to discard the substance included the following:

(a)   was the substance undergoing, or intended to undergo, a disposal operation or a recovery operation set out in the Directive;

(b)   was the use of the substance as fuel a common method of recovering waste; and,

(c)   was the substance commonly regarded as waste.

Lord Reed went on to state that whereas the Waste Framework Directive did not provide any decisive criteria for determining whether the holder of a substance intends to discard a substance within the meaning of the Directive, decisions as to whether a substance ranked as waste were required to be taken on the basis of the circumstances of the individual cases, and, also, in the light of the aims of the Waste Framework Directive, foremost amongst which was the protection of human health and the environment.[21] In circumstances where there was no doubt that a material was once waste and the question which fell to be considered was whether the substance had ceased to be waste, one still required to ascertain if the material had been discarded. Such an evaluation required to be taken on the basis of the individual case in the light of the aims of the Waste Framework Directive. The danger which is typical of waste is a danger of harm to human health or the environment which is caused by the manner of the disposal of waste. In the instant case, the sewage sludge which was received by SMW was waste in terms of the Waste Framework Directive. Scottish Power claimed that the operation which was carried out by SMW at the sludge treatment centre ranked as a complete recovery operation, the upshot of which was that the sludge thereupon ceased to be waste, on the basis that, to all intents and purposes, the WDF could be used in the same way as coal.[22] However, in His Lordship's view, the WDF could not be used under the same conditions of environmental protection as coal which would otherwise be used by Scottish Power at its power station, or without any greater danger of harm to human health or the environment.[23] His Lordship drew attention to the fact that the WDF itself, and also its emissions on being burnt, contained a higher concentration of heavy metals than the coal which would otherwise have been burnt at the power station.

Lord Reed then went on to discuss the meaning of 'discard' in terms of whether the WDF has ranked as waste in terms of the Directive.[24] In His Lordship's opinion the fact that whilst it was quite clear that SP did not have any intention to discard the WDF in the ordinary sense of the word, on the basis that SP had both paid for the WDF and used it for commercial purposes in order to generate electricity, the word 'discard' bore a special meaning in terms of the Directive.[25] The fact that the WDF had economic value to SP was not inconsistent with the WDF being classed as being discarded in terms of the Directive. Importantly, Lord Reed discussed the important issue of whether, if one were to classify the WDF as waste, this would flout an important principle which was ingrained in the Directive, namely, that of encouraging the recovery of waste material rather than its disposal.[26] Lord Reed emphasised the fact that whereas the Directive upheld this important principle, the Directive also regulated the process by means of which recovery was achieved to the extent which was necessary to protect the environment. The effect of classifying WDF as waste was not to prevent it from being recovered by being used as fuel in order to generate electricity. Rather, such an approach prevented that operation from taking place without the necessary precautions being employed in order to protect the environment.

The meaning of waste in terms of s 33(1) of the EPA was considered again in the Divisional court case of *Environment Agency v Inglenorth*.[27] Here, the defendant company was involved in the transportation, disposal and recycling of waste. The defendant had been contracted to collect materials which had been created by the demolition of a greenhouse at one garden centre and then take the materials to another garden centre. The owner of both the garden centres told the defendant that he wanted to use the materials for the purposes of the construction of a car park. The defendant collected some of the material from the first garden centre and left the material at the second site. The defendant was charged by the Environment Agency with the unlawful deposit of controlled waste contrary to s 33(1) of the EPA. However, the magistrates dismissed the information on the basis that on the date when the waste was delivered at the second site, the defendant knew that the owner of the garden centre intended to use the material as part of the construction of a carpark. Accordingly, there was no necessary intention to discard the material and it was not, therefore, waste in terms of the Directive. On appeal, the Court upheld the decision of the magistrates. In the opinion of Sir Anthony May, the sole question which required to be answered was the status of the material at the time of its deposit at the second garden centre.[28] In short, it was irrelevant where the material came from. In reaching his conclusion that the material which had been deposited did not rank as waste, Sir Anthony drew a distinction between depositing the material for storage pending re-use and, on the other hand, depositing it for use, more or less, straightaway without the material being, in any sensible use of the word, stored. His Lordship stated that depending always on the facts, hardcore which is going to be used the following week for current building operations is not being stored in terms of the Act. However, as far as the charge against the defendant was concerned, at the time of its deposit at the second site, the material in question was not waste.[29]

The question as to whether excavated material ranked as waste was considered again in the Court of Appeal case of *R. v W.*[30] In that case, the first respondent (W.) was the manager of a site upon which a new hotel was to be constructed. The second and third respondents (C.) were owners of a farm which adjoined the construction site. The farm was situated in a Special Area of Conservation as designated under the Habitat Directive.[31] W. agreed to deposit large quantities of materials which had been excavated from the site on C.'s land for the purpose of creating an area of hardstanding. All three respondents were charged with knowingly permitting the deposit of controlled waste and also with keeping controlled waste contrary to s 33(1) of the EPA. However, the trial judge acquitted the defendants. On appeal, the Court held that the question of immediate re-use of the material could not be entirely determinative of its status regardless of other considerations. The trial judge had erred in concentrating entirely on the intentions of the respondents to put the material to immediate re-use. Excavated soil which had to be discarded would be capable of being waste and ordinarily would be waste. Having become waste it remained so until something happened to alter that. Whether such a thing had happened was a question for the jury. The possibility of some re-use at some future time did not alter the status of the material. Actual re-use might do so but only if consistent with the aims and objectives of both the Act and the Directive which was principally the avoidance of harm to either persons or the environment. The trial judge had been in error in assessing the status of the materials entirely by reference to the respondents as holders. It was open to the jury to find that the material had been waste from the moment of their excavation at the neighbouring farm before C. and W. became holders. The additional question of whether the materials ceased to be waste, either because of the intended or actual use by the respondents as new holders of the material, was also a question of fact for the jury.

The meaning of waste was considered again in by the High Court in terms of the Directive in R. (on the application of the OSS Group Ltd) v Environment Agency.[32] In that case two companies sold waste derived products which were marketed on the basis that they had been recovered and, therefore, had ceased to be waste. The first claimant (SRM) operated a solvent recovery process whereby contaminated solvents were collected and recovered to produce Product Grade Distillates (PGD). Following the implementation of Directive 2000/76/EC on waste incineration (the WID), the respondent, the Environment Agency (the EA), classified the material the PGD as waste, the consequence of which was that the burning of the waste was subject to the WID. The second claimants, OSS, operated a business of collecting, recycling and processing used oils and selling the product as recycled fuel oil. Following the implementation of the WID, OSS invested in new and improved processes in order to facilitate the production of higher quality Clean Fuel Oil (CFO). The Environment Agency took the view that the CFO ranked as waste, which meant that any purchaser of it who wished to burn that product would require to comply with the WID. The practical effect of this was that waste, so characterised would be that the market for CFO would be lost. Both SRM and OSS, therefore, sought judicial review of the EA's decision to classify both the Product Grade Distillate and the CFO as waste. The main questions which fell to be answered by the Court were, first, in what circumstances did waste cease to be waste if it was to be burned as fuel? Secondly, the Court was required to determine whether waste ceased to be such, when a prior process was carried out for rendering it safe to be burnt as fuel, or, whether it could only cease to be waste when it was actually burnt? Both companies sought judicial review of the EA's classification of the material in the High Court. The application was rejected. OSS appealed to the Court of Appeal, solely on the issue as to whether a lubricating oil which was not originally used as fuel that subsequently became waste, could, thereafter, be burnt as anything other than waste. The Court allowed the appeal.

Carnwath LJ (as he then was), drawing heavily on EU law, provided a useful summary of how one should define waste:[33]

1.   The concept of waste could not be interpreted restrictively.
2.   According to its ordinary meaning, waste is what falls away when one processes a material or object and is not the end product which the manufacturing process directly seeks to produce.
3.   The term 'discard' includes both the disposal and also the recovery of waste within the terms of Annex IIA of the Waste Directive. However, the fact that an article is treated by one of the methods which is described in the Annexes does not lead to the necessary inference that it is waste.
4.   The term 'discard' must be interpreted in the light of the Directive and also Art 174(2) of the Treaty, respectively, that is to say, the protection of human health and the environment against the harmful effects caused by the collection, transport, treatment storage and tipping of waste; and Community policy on the environment aims at a high level of protection and is based on the precautionary principle and the principle that preventative action should be taken.
5.   Waste includes a substance which has been discarded by its owner even if the waste is capable of economic re-utilisation or has a commercial value and is collected on a commercial basis for recycling, reclamation or re-use.
6.   In deciding whether the use of a substance for burning is to be regarded as 'discarding', it is irrelevant that it may be recovered as fuel

in an environmentally responsible manner and without substantial treatment.

However, importantly, His Lordship stated that a comprehensive definition of waste was probably doomed to failure.[34]

Prohibition of flytipping etc. of waste

One of the most important provisions of the EPA as far as the regulation of waste is concerned is the prohibition of the flytipping of waste, that is to say the disposal of waste in any manner other that which is authorised by the Act. Section 33(1) of the EPA provides that a person may not:

(a)   deposit controlled waste, or knowingly[35] cause or knowingly permit controlled waste to be deposited in or on land unless a waste management licence authorising the deposit licence is in force and the deposit is in accordance with the licence;

(b)   treat, keep, or dispose of controlled waste, or knowingly cause or knowingly permit controlled waste to be treated, kept or disposed of -
    (i)   in or on any land, or
    (ii)   by means of any mobile plant, except under, and in accordance with a waste management licence[36]

(c)   keep or manage controlled waste in a manner likely to cause pollution of the environment or harm to human health.[37]

Waste can be deposited in contravention of the EPA, notwithstanding the fact that the person who deposited the waste did not intend the waste to remain in the place which it was deposited.[38]

The Act provides that where controlled waste is carried in and deposited from a motor vehicle, the person who controls, or is in a position to control, the use of the vehicle, is required, for the purposes of subsection 1(a) to be treated as knowingly causing the waste to be deposited whether or not he gave any instructions for this to be done.[39] It is an offence for a person to contravene s 33(1), or any condition of a waste management licence.[40] An offence under the section may be committed either by the relevant landfill site operator or the licence holder (or both) or, indeed, anyone else. This point was decided in the High Court of Justiciary case of *WRG Waste Management Ltd v Donaldson*.[41] In that case, the appellant company was the operator of a landfill site. The company operated the site in accordance with the conditions of a waste management licence which was held by a related company. One of the conditions of the licence required operations to be conducted in such a manner as not to give rise to offensive odours beyond the site boundary. Both companies were charged in identical terms with the breaches of the condition on numerous occasions. The Court held that the section was concerned with a prohibition on the unauthorised or harmful deposit of waste, which clearly referred to the operation of the site. The section, therefore, imposed an obligation on both the landfill operator and the relevant licence holder.[42]

However, the EPA makes provision for a defence in relation to a person who is charged with an offence under s 33:

(a)   to prove that he took all reasonable precautions and exercised all due diligence to avoid the commission of the offence; or

(b)   that he acted under instructions from his employer and that he neither knew nor had reason to suppose that the acts done by him constituted a contravention of subsection (1) above; or

(c)   that the acts alleged to constitute the contravention were done in an emergency in order to avoid danger to human health in a case where -

  (i)   he took all such steps as were reasonably practicable in the circumstances for minimising pollution of the environment and harm to human health; and

  (ii) particulars of the acts were furnished to the waste regulation authority as soon as reasonably practicable after they were done.[43]

In *Environment Agency v Melland*,[44] Melland (M.) was prosecuted for knowingly causing controlled waste to be deposited on land without a licence, contrary to s 33(1)(a) of the EPA. On various occasions, a vehicle, which was owned but not driven by M., was driven on to an industrial estate, on which the driver deposited controlled waste. The magistrates held that by virtue of the fact that M. was not in a position to control the use of the vehicle, the information fell to be dismissed. The Environment Agency appealed. The Queen's Bench, in allowing the appeal, held that evidence of ownership of a vehicle was capable of amounting to *prima facie* evidence that the owner of the vehicle either controlled or was in a position to control the use of the vehicle.

The EPA makes provision for fixed penalties in relation to contraventions of s 33(1)(a) and (c).[45] However, the Waste Management Licensing (Scotland) Regulations 2011,[46] in order to avoid duplication, exempt certain activities which fall to be regulated under other regimes, from the scope of the Act. The regulations also exempt certain other activities from the scope of the EPA.[47]

The duty of care

Traditionally, legislation has attempted to control waste simply by regulating its unlawful deposit on land by individuals. Until the advent of the
EPA, a person who produced waste ceased to have any legal responsibility
for the manner in which the waste was dealt with after the waste left his
possession. The EPA introduces an entirely new concept in the regulation
of waste where legal responsibility is placed on those who create waste. In
short, the EPA imposes an ongoing obligation on those who have any control over waste to ensure that the waste is disposed of lawfully. Really, the
intention of the EPA is to encourage self-regulation. Those who produce
waste now have a strong incentive to monitor the activities of those who
are commissioned to dispose of waste.[48] Section 34 of the EPA provides
that:

(1)   Subject to subsection (2) below, it shall be the duty of any person who
       imports, produces, carries, keeps treats or disposes of controlled waste
       or, as a broker or dealer, has control of such waste, to take all such
       measures applicable to him in that capacity as are reasonable in the
       circumstances -
       (a)   to prevent any contravention by any other person of s 33 above;
             (aa)   to prevent any contravention by any other person of regu-
                    lation 6 of the Pollution Prevention and Control (Scotland)
                    Regulations 2012 or of a condition of a permit granted
                    under regulation 7 of those regulations;
       (b)   to prevent the escape from his control or that of any other person,
             (ba)   on the transfer of any waste oil, to ensure that this is sepa-
                    rately collected where technically feasible; and
       (c)   that on the transfer of the waste, to secure -
             (i)   that the transfer is only to an authorised person[49] or to a
                    person for authorised transport purposes[50], and
             (ii)   that there is transferred such a written description of the
                    waste as will enable other persons to avoid a contravention
                    of that section or any condition of a permit under regula-
                    tion 7 of those Regulations and to comply with the duty
                    under this subsection as respects the escape of waste.[51]

A person who produces waste for the purposes of the section need not
physically produce the relevant waste himself. For example, the waste in
question can be physically produced by an individual who has been commissioned by another person to execute works on premises which belong
to the former, while the work is carried out by the latter, who, in turn,
produces waste.[52]

The Act places the occupier of domestic property under the sole duty as far as household waste which is produced on the premises is concerned, to take reasonable steps to secure that any transfer of waste is only to an authorised person or to a person for authorised purposes.[53]

As far as liability in terms of s 34(1)(b) is concerned, it suffices that the defender simply failed to take the requisite prophylactic measures to prevent the escape of waste from the control of the other person. In other words, it is unnecessary to prove that any escape actually took place.[54] Furthermore, the word 'escape' does not include the deliberate deposit of waste by the defender.[55]

A duty is placed on any person who produces, keeps or manages controlled waste, or as a broker or dealer of controlled waste, to take all such measures as are reasonable in the circumstances to apply the waste hierarchy set out in Art 4(1) of the Waste Directive.[56] Such a duty may be departed from where this is justified, having regard to the overall impacts of the generation and management of such waste; and does not apply to an occupier of domestic property in respect of the household waste produced on the property.[57] The Scottish Ministers may give guidance on the discharge of such duty, including the circumstances in which the duty may be departed from.[58] Any person who seeks to discharge such a duty must have regard to such guidance.[59]

From 1 January 2014 a duty is placed on any person who produces controlled waste (other than an occupier of domestic premises as respects household waste produced on that property) to take all reasonable steps to ensure the separate collection of dry recyclable waste.[60] From the same date, and subject to certain exceptions, a duty is imposed on any person who controls or manages a food business that produces controlled waste to take all reasonable steps to ensure the separate collection of food waste produced by the business.[61]

Waste management licences

It is obvious that unless premises which treat waste are regulated, problems can arise. The first legislative attempt to introduce a licensing system for landfill sites was the Control of Pollution Act 1974 (COPA).[62] Therefore, in order to operate a waste landfill site, one was required to obtain a licence from the relevant local authority which could attach conditions to the licence to ensure that its operation was satisfactory from, *inter alia*, an environmental viewpoint. The COPA regime was replaced by the regime which was instituted under Part II of the Environmental Protection Act 1990 (EPA) which is now discussed. As far as landfill sites are concerned, they currently fall to be regulated in terms of the Landfill (Scotland) Regulations 2003[63] which will be discussed later.[64]

The regulation of waste treatment facilities

Essentially, the EPA allows SEPA to regulate waste treatment facilities by means of a licensing system. The EPA defines a waste management licence as:

> a licence granted by a waste regulation authorising the treatment, keeping or disposal of any specified description of controlled waste in or on specified land or the treatment or disposal of any specified description of controlled waste by means of specified mobile plant.[65]

SEPA has wide powers as to the nature of the conditions which it can attach to a waste management licence. Under the EPA a licence is required to be granted on such terms and also subject to such conditions as appear to SEPA to be appropriate.[66] The relevant conditions may relate both to the activities which the licence authorises and also to the precautions which require to be carried out either in connection with or in consequence of those activities. Conditions may require the holder of a licence to carry out works or do other things notwithstanding that he is not entitled to carry out the works or do the thing in question.[67] For example, a condition could provide for access to the relevant site over land which is not owned by the licence holder. Any person whose consent would be required is placed under a duty to grant or join in granting the holder of the licence such rights in relation to the land as will enable the holder of the licence to comply with any requirements which are imposed on him by the relevant licence. Conditions may relate to where waste, other than controlled waste, is to be treated, kept or disposed of, and to the treatment, keeping or disposal of that other waste.[68] The Scottish Ministers are empowered to make regulations governing the conditions which are or are not to be included in a licence.[69]

A licence may not be surrendered by the holder except in accordance with the provisions of the Act.[70] Furthermore, a licence is not transferable by the holder of the licence.[71] However, SEPA may transfer the licence to another person in accordance with the provisions of the Act. Any licence which has been granted under the Act ceases to have effect both if and also to the extent that the treatment, keeping or disposal of the relevant waste is authorised by a permit which has been granted under regulations which have been made under the Pollution Prevention and Control Act 1999.[72]

Grant of waste management licence

An application for a site licence requires to be made to SEPA.[73] An application for a mobile plant licence requires to be made to the waste regulation authority in whose area the operator of the plant has his principal place of business. A licence may not be issued for the use of land for which planning permission is required unless planning permission is in force in relation to the land.[74] Subject to this condition, SEPA may not reject an application for a licence if SEPA is satisfied that the applicant is a fit and proper person unless it is satisfied that the rejection of the licence is necessary for the purpose of preventing:

(a) pollution of the environment;
(b) harm to human health; or
(c) serious detriment to the amenities of the locality.[75]

However, (c) is inapplicable where planning permission is in force in relation to the use to which the land will be put under the licence.

The expression 'fit and proper person' is a term of art in terms of the Act. Whether or not a person is a fit and proper person to hold a licence requires to be determined by reference to the carrying-on by him of the activities which are to be authorised by the licence and the fulfilment of the requirements of the licence.[76] A person is to be deemed not a fit and proper person if it appears to SEPA that:

(a) he or another relevant person has been convicted of the relevant offence,[77]
(b) the management of the activities which are to be authorised by the licence are not or will not be in the hands of a technically competent person; or
(c) the person who holds or is to hold the licence has not made and has no intention of making or is in no position to make financial provision adequate to discharge the obligations arising from the licence.[78]

However, SEPA may, if it considers it proper to do so in a particular case, treat a person as a fit and proper person, notwithstanding that either he or another relevant person[79] has been convicted of a relevant offence.[80]

Variation of licences

The Act makes provision for the variation of a licence which has been granted. While a licence which SEPA has granted is in force, SEPA may, on its own initiative, modify the conditions of the licence to any extent which, in the opinion of SEPA, is desirable and is unlikely to require unreasonable expense on the part of the holder.[81] Furthermore, SEPA, on the application of the licence holder, accompanied by the requisite charge which is prescribed for the purpose by a charging scheme under the Act,[82] may also modify the conditions of the licence to the extent which is requested in the application.[83]

Revocation and suspension of licences

In common with other environmental licensing regimes, the Act makes provision for both the revocation and the suspension of licences. Power is given to SEPA to revoke a licence, either entirely or partially, if it appears that the licence holder has ceased to be a fit and proper person, by reason of having been convicted of a relevant offence, or that the continuation of the activities which are authorised by the licence would cause pollution of the environment or harm to human health, or would be seriously detrimental to the amenities of the locality affected, and that the pollution, harm or detriment cannot be avoided by modifying the conditions of the licence.[84] Furthermore, SEPA has power to revoke a licence (either entirely or partially) if it appears to SEPA that the holder of the licence has ceased to be a fit and proper person by reason of the management of the activities which are authorised by the licence having ceased to be in the hands of a technically competent person.[85]

SEPA may also suspend a licence, either in whole or in part, if it appears that the holder of the licence has ceased to be a fit and proper person by reason of the management of the activities which are authorised by the licence having ceased to be in the hands of a technically competent person. The licence can also be suspended in whole or part it if appears that serious pollution of the environment or serious harm to human health has resulted from, or is about to be caused by, the activities to which the licence relates or the happening or threatened happening of an event affecting those activities, and that the continuation of all, or any, of those activities may cause serious pollution of the environment or harm to human health.[86]

An appeal lies to the Scottish Ministers against both the revocation and suspension of a licence.[87]

Surrender and transfer of licences

A licence may be surrendered by its holder to SEPA, but in the case of site licence only if SEPA accepts the surrender.[88] An appeal lies to the Scottish Ministers against the decision of SEPA to reject an application for the surrender of a licence.[89]

Any waste management licence may be transferred to another person, whether or not the licence is either partly revoked or suspended under the

Act.[90] Where the holder of a site licence wishes the licence to be transferred to another person – that is, the transferee – both the licence holder and the proposed transferee require to jointly make an application to SEPA.[91] An appeal lies to the Scottish Ministers against the decision of SEPA to reject an application for the transfer of a licence.[92]

Landfill sites

The disposal of waste to landfill comprises the oldest as well as the most widely practised method of disposing of solid waste.[93] However, this form of disposal of waste is the least acceptable in terms of the EU's waste hierarchy.[94] More specifically, this policy is expressed in the Landfill Directive.[95] The Directive is implemented in Scotland by the Landfill (Scotland) Regulations 2003 ('the Regulations').[96] A landfill is defined as a waste[97] disposal site for the deposit of the waste onto or into land.[98]

Classification of landfills

Before granting a landfill permit SEPA is required to classify the relevant landfill as:

(a)   a landfill for hazardous waste,[99] or
(b)   a landfill for non-hazardous waste[100] or
(c)   a landfill for inert waste.[101]

The classification requires to be stated in the relevant permit.

Conditions to be included in landfill permits, and prohibitions of certain wastes

SEPA can effectively regulate the day-to-day operation of a landfill site by including appropriate conditions in the relevant permit. A landfill permit requires to include appropriate conditions which specify the list of defined types and also the total quantity of waste which is authorised to be deposited in the landfill.[102] The permit also requires to include certain conditions, including those which specify requirements for preparations for the landfill, and carrying-out of landfilling operations, and which specify monitoring and control procedures, including contingency plans.[103]

The Regulations also prohibit the acceptance of certain types of wastes at landfills by the operator of a landfill.[104] For example, the acceptance of any waste in liquid form (including waste but excluding sludge) is prohibited. Furthermore, as from 1 January 2021 biodegradable municipal waste is also prohibited.

Waste which may be accepted in the different classes of landfill
An important feature of the Landfill Directive is that only waste which
has been subject to treatment may be landfilled.[105] The intention here is
to minimise the harmful effects of waste before it is sent to landfill. The
Regulations require the operator of a landfill to ensure that the landfill is
only used for landfilling waste which is subject to prior treatment, unless

(a)   it is inert waste for which treatment is not technically feasible, or
(b)   it is waste other than inert waste and treatment would not reduce
      its quantity or the hazards which it poses to human health or the
      environment.[106]

In turn, the operator of a landfill for hazardous waste[107] is required to
ensure that only waste which fulfils the waste acceptance criteria which are
contained in the Regulations[108] is accepted at the landfill.[109]
      The operator of a landfill for non-hazardous waste[110] is required to
ensure that the landfill is only used for landfilling

(a)   municipal waste,[111]
(b)   non-hazardous waste of any other origin which fulfils the waste
      acceptance criteria which is contained in the Regulations,[112]
(c)   stable non-reactive hazardous waste (such as that which is solidi-
      fied with leaching behaviour which is equivalent to that of the non-
      hazardous waste which is referred to in sub-paragraph (b)) above, and
      which fulfils the waste acceptance criteria which are contained in the
      Regulations.[113]

Offences
The Regulations make it an offence for a landfill operator to contravene
provisions of the Regulations which relate to the acceptance of waste on
a landfill.[114] Where an offence is committed by a body corporate and the
offence is committed with the consent or connivance of, or the offence is
attributable to any neglect on the part of, a person who

(a)   is a director, manager or secretary of the body corporate; or
(b)   the person purports to act in any such capacity; or
(c)   the offence is committed by a Scottish partnership and the offence is
      committed with the consent or connivance of or is attributable to any
      neglect on the part of a person who is a partner or purports to act in
      that capacity,

that person as well as the body corporate or Scottish partnership is guilty of
an offence and is liable to be proceeded against and punished accordingly.[115]

Landfill Allowance Trading Scheme

One of the main aims of the Landfill Directive[116] ('the Directive') is to limit the amount of biodegradable waste which is disposed to landfill.[117] Part 1 of the Waste and Emissions Trading Act 2003 gives legal effect to the general obligations which are imposed by the Directive. Under the Directive each Member State of the EU must reduce the amount of biodegradable waste[118] which is sent to landfills to 75 per cent of the amount produced by that state in 1995 by 2006, to 50 per cent by 2009, and to 35 per cent by 2016.[119] The Secretary of State is empowered to make regulations which specify the maximum amounts of biodegradable waste which may be sent to landfills from each country of the UK for every scheme year which is a target year.[120] The Secretary of State is required to consult the Scottish Ministers before setting limits for Scotland.[121] The Scottish Ministers are required to ensure that the total amount of waste which is authorised to be sent to landfills does not exceed the amount of waste which is allowed for Scotland.[122]

The provisions which are contained in the Act are given effect in Scotland by the Landfill Allowances Scheme (Scotland) Regulations 2005.[123]

Collection of controlled waste

For centuries local authorities have been responsible for the collection of waste in their areas. Currently, the Environmental Protection Act 1990 (EPA) places a duty on each waste collection authority (which, as far as Scotland is concerned, is the relevant local authority)[124] to arrange for the collection of household waste[125] in its area.[126] An exception is made in relation to waste which is situated at a place which, in the opinion of the authority, is so isolated or inaccessible that the cost of collecting it would be unreasonably high, and as to which such waste, the authority is satisfied that adequate arrangements either have been, or can reasonably be expected to be, made by a person who controls the waste. The authority has a duty to arrange for the collection of commercial waste[127] from premises if requested by the occupier of premises in its area to collect such waste. Furthermore, the authority has a duty to arrange for the collection of dry recyclable waste[128] or food waste[129] if so requested by the occupier of premises in its area. However, this duty does not extend to the collection of either dry recyclable waste or food waste which is either household waste or food waste from premises in a rural area.[130]

Separate collection of dry recyclable waste and food waste

The recycling of materials involves subjecting that material to a process which converts it to a usable form of the same material. From 1 January 2014 a local authority must arrange for there to be provided to the occupier of every domestic property in its area such receptacles as will enable the separate collection of dry recyclable waste from the property.[131] From 1 January 2016 an authority must arrange for there to be provided to the occupier of every property in its area (apart from in a rural area) a receptacle which enables the separate collection of food waste from the property; or where an authority is satisfied that the amount of food waste that will be collected is not significantly less than would be collected in such a receptacle, a receptacle which enables the occupier to present food waste and other biodegradable waste for collection.[132] Finally, from 1 January 2014, an authority must take such steps as the authority considers reasonable to both promote the separate collection (including the making of arrangements for the provision of a food waste receptacle) and promote recycling in any other manner.[133]

Duties in relation to disposal of waste

A local authority, in its capacity as a waste disposal authority,[134] is under a duty to arrange for the disposal of any waste which it collects.[135] Furthermore, the authority is placed under a duty to provide, either within or outside its area, places at which to deposit waste (that is, waste transfer stations) and also to provide places at which to dispose of or recycle waste and plant or equipment for processing, recycling or otherwise disposing of the waste.

Power for removal of waste which has been unlawfully deposited

A perennial problem which is associated with waste is that it is often disposed of unlawfully. The EPA makes provision for waste which has been deposited illegally. If any controlled waste is deposited on any land, either SEPA or the relevant local authority may, by a notice which may be served on the occupier of the land, require him to do either or both of the following, namely:

(a)   to remove the waste from the land within a specified period which is not less than twenty-one days commencing from the date of the service of the notice;

(b)   to take within such a period specified steps with a view to eliminating or reducing the consequences of the deposit of the waste.[136]

A person upon whom any requirements are imposed may, within the twenty-one-day period which is mentioned above, appeal to the sheriff by way of summary application.[137] On appeal, the sheriff is required to quash the requirement if he is satisfied that either the appellant neither deposited nor knowingly permitted the deposit of the waste, or that there has been a material defect in the notice.[138] In any other case, the sheriff may either modify the requirement or dismiss the appeal. Where the court modifies the requirement or dismisses the appeal, the court may extend the period which is specified in the notice.[139] If the person on whom a requirement has been imposed fails, without reasonable excuse, to comply with a requirement, that person commits an offence and is liable to pay a fine.[140] If the person on whom a requirement has been imposed fails to comply with a requirement, the authority may do that which the person was required to do and recover from him any expences which have been reasonably incurred by the authority so doing.[141]

If it appears to either SEPA or a local authority that waste has been deposited on or in land in contravention of s 33(1) of the EPA and that:

(a) in order to remove or prevent pollution of land, waste or air or harm to human health it is necessary that the waste be forthwith removed or other steps taken to eliminate or reduce the consequences of the deposit or both; or
(b) there is no occupier of the land; or
(c) the occupier neither made nor knowingly permitted the deposit of the waste,

the authority may remove the waste from the land or take other steps to eliminate or reduce the consequences of the deposit, as the case may require, to remove the waste and also take the necessary steps.[142] Subject to certain exceptions, the authority is entitled to recover costs from the relevant person.[143] Finally, any waste which has been removed by an authority becomes vested in the authority and can be dealt with accordingly.[144]

Civil liability

Normally, environmental legislation simply confers a variety of powers on a regulatory body such as SEPA power to control activities, such as landfill operations, for the general benefit of the public. Seldom does such legislation confer private rights on individuals. However, under s 73(6) of the EPA provision is made in respect of harm which has been caused by the unlawful deposit of waste. The EPA provides that any person who deposited such waste or knowingly permitted it to be deposited in such a manner as to commit an offence under s 33(1) or s 63(2) is liable for the damage which has been caused. For example, damage which has been caused by unlawfully deposited waste oil which ignites, causing flames to spread to the land of an adjoining occupier, could fall within the scope of the section.

In this context, brief mention should be made of the rules which govern remoteness of damage. Whilst one could argue that the rule in *Re Polemis*[145] would apply in relation to such damage, that is to say that liability would lie is the relevant harm which had been sustained by the pursuer was the direct result of the act of the pursuer, it is the view of the author that the rule in the *Wagon Mound*[146] would be applicable.[147]

Finally, the EPA replicates the defences which are found in the common law of delict.[148] The EPA provides that liability lies except where the damage was due wholly to the fault of the person who suffered it, or that the damage was suffered by a person who voluntarily accepted the risk of the damage being caused.[149]

Powers to recycle waste

The EPA gives a local authority power to do such things as the authority considers appropriate for the purposes of enabling waste which belongs to the authority, or waste which belongs to another person who requests the authority to deal with the waste, to be recycled or to enable the waste to be used for the purpose of producing heat or electricity or both from such waste.[150] The EPA also allows an authority to either buy or acquire waste with a view to its being recycled, and the power to either use, sell or otherwise dispose of waste which belongs to the authority or anything which is produced from such waste.

Waste carriers and waste brokers

It is all too easy for waste to be illegally disposed of by those who transport it. We have already seen that those who transport waste are subject to a duty of care in terms of the EPA.[151] Waste carriers are further regulated under the Control of Pollution Act 1989 which makes provision for the registration of waste carriers. As far as Scotland is concerned, SEPA is the regulatory authority. It is made an offence, subject to certain exceptions, for any person who is not a registered carrier of controlled waste to transport to or from any place in Great Britain controlled waste in the course of any business of his or otherwise, with a view to profit.[152]

Waste brokers and dealers are regulated by SEPA in terms of the Waste Management Licensing (Scotland) Regulations 2011.[153] A waste broker is defined as any undertaking arranging the recovery or disposal of waste on behalf of others, whether or not such arrangements involve the broker taking physical possession of the waste.[154] A waste dealer is defined as any undertaking which acts in the role of principal to purchase and subsequently sell waste, whether or not this involves the dealer taking physical possession of the waste.[155] It is made an offence, subject to certain exceptions, for an establishment or undertaking to arrange (as broker or dealer) for the recovery or disposal of controlled waste on behalf of another person, or to purchase and sell controlled waste as a principle unless it is a registered broker or dealer in controlled waste.[156]

Powers to minimise waste

The EPA gives a local authority the power either to carry out itself or to contribute towards the expenses of doing anything which, in its opinion, is necessary or expedient for minimising the quantities of controlled waste or minimising the description of controlled waste which is generated in its area.[157]

Provision of civic amenity sites

The fly-tipping of waste by members of the public is well-known. Often, certain members of the public fly-tip waste because the waste cannot be accommodated in domestic refuse bins. In order to encourage the public to dispose of waste in an environmentally-friendly manner, the Refuse Disposal (Amenity) Act 1978[158] imposes a duty on a local authority to provide places (known as civic amenity sites) where refuse,[159] other than commercial waste, is able to be deposited at all reasonable times, free of charge, by persons who are resident in the area of the local authority.[160] The local authority may impose a charge in relation to the deposit of waste on such sites by other persons.

Special waste

Certain forms of waste may pose a risk to both human health and also to the environment. The EPA allows the Scottish Ministers to make provision, by way of regulations, for controlled waste which is of a kind that is considered dangerous or difficult to treat, keep or dispose of.[161] The Special Waste Regulations 1996[162] were made under the EPA in order to deal with such waste. The Regulations make provision for both the transport and disposal of such waste.

Waste recovery: producer responsibility

By the early 1990s there was growing concern in Europe about the sheer amount of packaging waste and also the environmental problems which it causes. Council Directive 94/62/EC[163] sets both recovery and recycling targets on packaging and packaging waste. The Producer Responsibility

Obligations Regulations (Packaging Waste) Regulations 2007,[164] which apply to the UK as a whole, currently impose obligations on producers in order that the UK can meet these targets. The responsibility to comply with the obligations which are imposed by these regulations in order to meet such EU targets is spread between producers of packaging waste. The targets are confined to specific recyclable materials, namely, glass, aluminium, steel, paper board, plastic and wood.[165] Producer responsibility obligations fall only on the larger producers.

We can see here that this approach to packaging waste serves as a neat example of general EU environmental policy to reduce waste at source.

End-of-life vehicles

It seems a statement of the obvious that vehicles which are no longer fit for purpose can present an environmental problem. The End-of-Life Vehicles Directive[166] (ELV Directive) addresses this problem. The ELV Directive makes provision for the collection, treatment, recycling and other forms of recovery of end-of-life vehicles, as well as the their components, and also the reduction of such waste. Member States are placed under an obligation to ensure that those who are involved in the manufacture of cars limit the use of hazardous substances in cars in order to protect the environment, facilitate easier recycling, and avoid the need to dispose of hazardous waste.[167] Member States are also required to ensure that collection systems are introduced for end of life vehicles and that such vehicles are transferred to authorised treatment facilities.[168] The ELV Directive sets re-use and recovery targets for end of life vehicles.[169] The ELV is transposed into UK law by the End of Life Vehicles Regulations 2003[170] (ELV Regulations) and also by the End of Life Vehicles (Storage and Treatment) (Scotland) Regulations 2003 which are discussed briefly below.

The ELV regulations apply to all vehicles and end of life vehicles, including their components and materials.[171] Any person who puts on the market materials and components of vehicles is required to ensure that the vehicle does not contain heavy metals such as lead, mercury or cadmium, subject to certain exceptions.[172] A producer is required to use material and component coding standards in order to facilitate the identification of those materials and components which are suitable for re-use and recovery.[173] A producer is also required to provide dismantling information in respect of each new vehicle which is put on the market within six months from that date.[174]

The storage and treatment of end of life vehicles is governed by the End of Life Vehicles (Storage and Treatment) (Scotland) Regulations 2003.[175] In short, SEPA is required to include in any site licence which it grants for the keeping or treatment of waste motor vehicles a condition to the effect that the keeping or treatment which is authorised is in conformity with the obligations, and also the minimum technical requirements which are contained in the 2003 Scottish Regulations.[176]

Waste electrical and electronic equipment

Waste from electrical equipment has become an increasing problem. Such waste can not only pose a potential risk to the environment but also harm human health by virtue of its composition. The Waste Electrical and Electronic Equipment Directive 2002[177] makes provision for such waste. The WEEE Directive is implemented in the UK by the Waste and Electrical Equipment Regulations 2006.[178] The Regulations apply to a range of electrical and electronic equipment including large and small household appliances, IT and telecommunications equipment, consumer equipment and lighting equipment. A producer of electrical and electronic equipment (EEE) is placed under an obligation to bear a proportion of the costs of the collection, treatment, recovery and sound disposal of waste electrical and electronic equipment (WEEE) from private households which is deposited at a designated collection facility or is returned during the relevant compliance period.[179] As far as WEEE from users other than private households is concerned, a producer is placed under an obligation to finance the costs of the collection, treatment and recovery and sound disposal of WEEE which is placed on the market after 13 August 2005 by that producer.[180] A producer to whom the WEEE Regulations apply is required to join an approved compliance scheme in respect of any compliance period, or any part of such period, during which the producer puts EEE on the market in the UK.[181] If a producer is a member of a compliance scheme, the producer is exempt from complying with his obligations under the WEEE Regulations in respect of the relevant compliance period during which his membership of the scheme subsists.[182]

Litter

The unlawful deposit of litter in public places is an obvious environmental problem. The vast bulk of the substantive law which governs the unlawful deposit of litter is contained in Part IV of the EPA, which is now discussed.

It is made an offence under the EPA for any person to throw down, drop or otherwise deposit in, into or from any specified place and leave,[183] anything whatsoever in such circumstances as to cause or contribute to the defacement by litter[184] of any such place, subject to certain exceptions.[185] The EPA applies to any open public place[186] and also to certain other places.[187] However, no offence is committed where the depositing and leaving of the litter was either authorised by law, or was done with the consent of the owner, occupier or other person or authority having control of the place in or into which that thing was deposited.[188]

Fixed penalties for litter

The EPA makes provision for fixed penalties in relation to litter. Where an authorised officer[189] of a litter authority has reason to believe that a person has committed an offence under s 87 in the area of that authority, or a constable has reason to believe that a person has committed an offence under that section, either the officer or the constable may give that person a notice which offers him the opportunity of discharging liability to conviction for that offence by the payment of a fixed penalty.[190] The relevant person cannot be convicted for the offence if he pays the fixed penalty within the requisite period.[191]

Duty to keep land and roads clear of litter

The EPA imposes a duty on various administrative authorities to keep land and roads clear of litter and refuse. Amongst those authorities on whom a duty is imposed is each local authority as respects any relevant road for which it is responsible, the Scottish Ministers in respect of certain trunk roads, and a local authority in respect of its relevant land.[192]

Litter control areas

The Scottish Ministers may prescribe descriptions of land which may be designated as a litter control area.[193] Any principal litter authority other than a joint board, may, by order, designate any land, or part thereof, as a litter control area.[194] No order may be made unless the authority is of the opinion that, by reason of the presence of litter or refuse, the condition of the land is, and unless the authority makes a designation order, likely to continue to be, such as to be detrimental to the amenities of the locality.[195]

Summary proceedings by individuals and litter authorities

The EPA allows private individuals to enlist the aid of the court to enforce compliance with the provisions of the EPA. A sheriff is empowered to act on summary application which is made by any person on the ground that he is aggrieved by the defacement by litter of certain places, including roads and any relevant land within the area of a local authority.[196]

The EPA also makes provision for summary proceedings by both litter authorities and joint boards in respect of the defacement of certain areas by litter or refuse. Where a principal litter authority or a joint board are satisfied that certain places, including Crown land and land which belongs to certain educational establishments, is defaced by litter or refuse, or that defacement of such land by litter or refuse is likely to recur, the authority is required to serve a notice (a litter abatement notice) which imposes either or both of the following:

(a) a requirement that the litter or the refuse be cleared within a time which is specified in the notice,

(b) a prohibition of permitting the land to become defaced by litter or refuse.[197]

The litter abatement notice requires to be served on the relevant authority or in any other case, the occupier of land or, if the land is unoccupied, the owner of the land.[198] The person who is served with the notice may appeal to the sheriff by way of summary application within twenty-one days of the notice being served.[199] If the person who appeals proves that he has complied with his duty under s 89(1) of the EPA, the appeal must be allowed.[200] It is an offence, which is subject to a penalty, for a person on whom a litter abatement notice is served, without reasonable excuse, to either fail to comply with or to contravene the requirement or prohibition which is imposed by the notice.[201] In any proceedings for an offence, it is a defence for the person charged to prove that he has complied with his duty under s 89(1).[202] If a person on whom a litter notice is served fails to comply with the relevant notice, the authority is empowered to enter the land and clear the litter or refuse and then recover costs from that person.[203]

Street litter control notices
The EPA empowers a principal litter authority other than a joint board, to issue a street litter control notice on occupiers of premises with a view to the prevention of accumulations of such litter in and around any street or open land which is adjacent to such a street.[204] If the authority is satisfied in relation to premises which are prescribed in terms of s 94(1)(a) of the EPA[205] and have a frontage on a street in its area, that:

(a) there is a recurrent defacement by litter or refuse of any land, being part of the street or open land adjacent to the street, which is in the vicinity of the premises, or

(b) the condition of any part of the premises which is open land in the vicinity of the frontage is, and if no notice is served is likely to continue to be, detrimental to the amenities of the locality by reason of the presence of litter or refuse, or

(c)   there is produced, as a result of the activities which are carried out on the premises, quantities of litter or refuse which is of such a nature or of such amounts that are likely to cause the defacement of any part of the street, or of open land which is adjacent to the street, which is in the vicinity of the premises,

the authority may serve a street litter control notice on the occupier of the premises, or, if the premises are unoccupied, on the owner of the premises.[206] The notice must, *inter alia*, identify the relevant premises and also specify the relevant adjoining land which either adjoins or is in the vicinity of the frontage of the premises on the street.[207] The notice, which must impose requirements which relate to the clearing of litter or refuse from the specified area,[208] may require the provision or the emptying of receptacles for litter or refuse.[209] The person on whom the notice is served may appeal to the sheriff by way of summary application.[210] The sheriff has complete powers of review in relation to the notice, and he can either quash, vary or add to any requirement which is imposed by the notice.

Finally, if it appears to the authority that a person has either failed, or is failing, to comply with any requirement which is imposed by a notice, the authority may apply to the sheriff by way of summary application for an order which requires the person to comply with the requirement within a specified time.[211] It is an offence to fail to comply with the order.[212]

Abandoned motor vehicles

The Refuse Disposal (Amenity) Act 1978[213] makes special provision for the unauthorised dumping of cars. It is made an offence for any person, without lawful authority:

(a)   to abandon on any land in the open air, or any other land forming part of a road, a motor vehicle, or anything which formed part of a motor vehicle, and was removed from it in the course of dismantling the vehicle on the land, or

(b)   to abandon on any such land anything other than a motor vehicle, being a thing which he has brought to the land for the purpose of abandoning it there.[214]

A local authority is placed under a duty to remove a motor vehicle if it appears that the vehicle has been abandoned without lawful authority on any land in the open air or on any land which forms part of a road.[215] The Act also makes provision for the disposal of removed vehicles and the recovery of associated expenses.[216] Finally, the Act makes provision for the removal and disposal of refuse other than motor vehicles which has been abandoned without lawful authority on any land in the open air or on any other land which forms part of a road.[217]

Summary

- In terms of EU and national waste policy the key principles are proximity and self-sufficiency, the precautionary principle, and the polluter pays principle.
- Waste should be prevented, or re-used or recycled or, finally, recovered, in that order.
- The Environmental Protection Act 1990 prohibits the unlawful deposit of waste
- Individuals are placed under a duty of care in relation to the transport and disposal of waste.
- Waste treatment facilities and landfill sites require to be licensed by SEPA.
- Local authorities are under a duty to collect controlled waste.

Notes

1. See Chapter 1.
2. For a general discussion of the miasmatic theory of transmission of disease, see F. McManus, 'Victorian foundations of environmental law in Scotland', paras 1.05-1.07 in F. McManus (ed.). *Environmental Law in Scotland* (W. Green/SULI).
3. Section 16 (repealed)
4. Repealed. Currently, the Environmental Protection Act 1990, ss 79-82 make provision for the removal of statutory nuisances.
5. See p. 121.
6. Environmental Protection Act 1990 s 44B(1).
7. National Waste Strategy: Scotland (SEPA, 1999).
8. See the 6th Environment Action Programme (COM) 2001 Final.
9. National Waste Strategy (SEPA, 1999) at 14-15.
10. The target for 2006 was met. Waste Data Digest 8: Key Facts and Trends (SEPA, 2008) at 16.
11. Zero Waste Plan for Scotland (Scottish Government, 2010).
12. Ibid. at 5.
13. For a useful discussion of the meaning of waste, see S. Choong and M. Grekos, 'Finding a workable definition of waste: is it a waste of time?' [2006] JPL 463.

14. Directive 2008/98/EC.
15. Environmental Protection Act 1990, s 75(2).
16. Ibid. s 75(4).
17. [2005] Env LR 38.
18. SSI 2003 No 170.
19. Directive 75/442/EC. See now Directive 2008/98/EC.
20. [2005] Env LR 38 at [66].
21. Ibid. para [136].
22. Ibid. at [138].
23. Ibid. at [139].
24. Ibid. at [142].
25. For a useful discussion of the concept of 'discard' in relation to waste, see the ECJ case of *Brady v Environmental Protection Agency* [2014] Env LR 13.
26. Ibid. at [143].
27. [2009] Env LR 684.
28. Ibid. at 690.
29. Ibid. at 697.
30. [2010] Env LR 743. See also *R. v Jones* [2011] Env LR D2 and *R. v Jagger* [2015] Env LR 25.
31. Directive 92/43/EC.
32. [2008] Env LR 139. For a discussion of *Oss* see (2007) 122 SPEL 92.
33. [2008] Env LR 139 at 145.
34. Ibid. at 155.
35. The court can infer the requisite knowledge on the part of the defender from the facts of the case; see *Kent County Council v Beaney* [1993] 1 Env LR 225.
36. The Act makes special provision for land which is occupied by disposal authorities; ibid. s 54.
37. Environmental Protection Act 1990, s 33(1). Household waste, subject to limited exceptions, is excluded from the provisions of s 33(1); ibid. s 33(2).
38. *R. v Metropolitan Stipendary Magistrates ex p. London Waste Regulatory Authority* [1993] 3 All ER 113.
39. Environmental Protection Act, s 33(5).
40. Ibid. s 33(6). See below for a discussion of waste management licences.
41. 2009 JC 253.
42. See also *Shanks and McEwan (Teeside) Ltd v Environment Agency* [1997] 2 All ER 332. In that case a tanker which contained controlled waste arrived at a waste management facility which was operated by the defendant company to offload the material into a purpose built tank. The waste was deposited on the land in contravention of the relevant site licence. It was held that the defendant company could be guilty of an offence under s 33(1)(a) if the company simply had knowledge of the controlled waste being deposited in

or on its land. It was not additionally necessary to prove that the defendant had knowingly permitted the relevant breach of the conditions of its waste licence. See also *Ashcroft v Cambro Waste Products Ltd* [1981] 3 All ER 699.

43. Ibid. s 33(7). The Act goes on to make provision for offences which are committed under the section; ibid. s 33(8)-(10).

44. [2002] Env LR 29.

45. Environmental Protection Act 1990 s 33A.

46. SSI 2011 No 228, reg 16.

47. Ibid. reg 17.

48. See M. Poustie, 'A load of rubbish? The duty of care for waste re-visited (1997) 60 SPEL 28 at 28. For a general discussion of s 34 of the EPA, see M. Poustie, 'The duty of care for waste' (1994) 43 SPEL 36.

49. Under s 34(3) of the EPA the following are authorised persons for the purposes of s 34(1)(c):

    (a)   any authority which is a waste collection authority for the purposes of Part 2 of the Act;

    (b)   any person who is the holder of a waste management licence under s 35 of the Act;

    (c)   any person to whom s 33(1) of the Act does not apply by virtue of regulations made under subsection (3) of that section;

    (d)   any person registered as a carrier of controlled waste under s 2 of the Control of Pollution (Amendment) Act 1989;

    (e)   any person who is not required to be so registered by virtue of regulations made under s 1(3) of that Act; and

    (f)   a waste disposal authority in Scotland.

The Scottish Ministers may by regulations, amend the above subsection as to add to the persons who are authorised persons for the purposes of s 34(1)(c).

50. Under s 34(4) the following are authorised transport purposes for the purposes of s 34(1)(c):

    (a)   the transport of controlled waste within the same premises between different places in those premises;

    (b)   the transport to a place in Great Britain of controlled waste which has been brought from a country or territory outside Great Britain not having been landed in Great Britain until it arrives at that place; and

    (c)   the transport by air or sea of controlled waste from a place in Great Britain to a place outside Great Britain.

    (d)   'Transport' is given the same meaning as in the Control of Pollution (Amendment)Act 1989.

51. EPA s 34(1). A reference to a written description includes a written description of the waste that is (a) transmitted by electronic means; (b)

received in legible form; and (c) capable of being used for subsequent reference; ibid. s 34(4AB). The Scottish Government has published guidance as to how the duties which are imposed on individuals by s 34 should be discharged; see Scottish Government, 'Guidance on applying the waste hierachy' (2013).

52. *Mountpace Ltd v Haringey LBC* [2012] EWHC 698.

53. EPA s 34(2).

54. *Camden LBC v Mortgage Times Group Ltd.* [2007] Env LR 4.

55. *Gateway Professional Services Ltd (Management) Ltd v Kingston upon Hull CC* [2004] Env LR 874.

56. EPA s 34(2A). Directive 2008/98/EC Art 4(1) makes provision for a hierarchy in terms of waste prevention and management. The preferred option is (a) prevention (b) preparing for re-use (c) recycling and, (d) recovery.

57. EPA s 34(2B).

58. Ibid. s 34(2C).

59. Ibid. s 34(2D).

60. Ibid. s 34(2E). 'Dry recyclable waste' is defined in s 75(7A) as glass, metals, plastics, paper or card (including cardboard).

61. Ibid. s 34(2F).

62. COPA s 3 (repealed).

63. SSI 2003 No 235 which implements Directive 99/31/EC.

64. See p. 175-9 incl.

65. Environmental Protection Act 1990 s 35(1).

66. Ibid. s 35(3).

67. Ibid. s 35(4).

68. Ibid. s 35(5).

69. Ibid. s 35(6). See the Waste Management Licensing (Scotland) Regulations 2011 (SSI 2011 No 228) (as amended) regs 11-13B as to specific licence conditions which have been prescribed.

70. Ibid. s 35(9).

71. Ibid. s 35(10).

72. Ibid. s 35(11A).

73. Ibid. s 36(1).

74. Ibid. s 36(2).

75. Ibid. s 36(3).

76. Ibid. s 74(2).

77. The Waste Management Licensing (Scotland) Regulations 2011 (SSI 2011 No 228) (as amended) reg 3 lists the relevant offences for the purposes of s 74(3).

78. Ibid. s 74(3).

79. Section 74(7) defines a variety of circumstances where another relevant

person is to be treated in relation to the licence holder or proposed licence holder as having been convicted of the relevant offence.

80. Ibid. s 74(4).
81. Ibid. s 37(1)(a).
82. Ie under s 41 of the Act.
83. Ibid. s 37(1)(b).
84. Ibid. ss 38(1)(3)(4).
85. Ibid. s 38(2).
86. Ibid. s 38(6).
87. Ibid. s 43(1).
88. Ibid. s 39(1).
89. Ibid. s 43(1).
90. Ibid. s 40(1).
91. Ibid. s 40(2).
92. Ibid. s 43(1).
93. WHO Regional Office for Europe, *Landfill* (1995) at 1.
94. Directive 2008/98/EC (Waste Directive), Art 4.
95. Directive 1999/31/EC.
96. SSI 2003 No 235.
97. 'Waste' is defined as waste which falls within the scope of the Waste Framework Directive (Directive 2008/98/EC). SSI 2003 No 235, reg 2.
98. Landfill (Scotland) Regulations 2003 reg 3(2).
99. 'Hazardous waste' means any waste which is to considered as hazardous waste under Arts 3(2) and 7 of the Waste Framework Directive; ibid. reg 2(1).
100. 'Non-hazardous waste' is waste which is not hazardous waste; ibid. reg 2(1).
101. Ibid. reg 9. 'Inert waste' means waste which:
    (i)   does not undergo any significant physical, chemical or biological transformations;
    (ii) does not dissolve, burn or otherwise physically or chemically react, biodegrade or adversely affect other matter with which it comes into contact in a way likely to give rise to environmental pollution or harm to human health; and
    (iii) has insignificant total leachability and does not endanger the quality of any surface water or groundwater; ibid. reg 2(1).
102. Ibid. reg 10(1).
103. Ibid. reg 10(2).
104. Ibid. reg 11(1).
105. Directive 99/31/EC, Art 6.
106. Landfill (Scotland) Regs reg 12(1).
107. 'Hazardous waste' is defined as waste which is described as such under Arts 3(2) and 7 of the Waste Directive; Landfill (Scotland) Regs 2003 reg 2.

108. Landfill (Scotland) Regs, Sched 2.
109. Ibid. reg 12(2).
110. 'Non-hazardous waste' is defined as waste which is not hazardous waste; ibid. reg 2.
111. 'Municipal waste' is defined as waste from households as well as other waste which, because of its nature or other composition is similar to waste from households; Ibid. reg 2.
112. Ibid. Sched 2.
113. Ibid. reg 12(3).
114. Ibid. reg 19(1).
115. Ibid. reg 19(3).
116. Directive 1999/31/EC.
117. Ibid. Art 5.
118. 'Biodegradable waste' means any waste that is capable of undergoing aerobic or anaerobic decomposition such as food and garden waste and paperboard; Waste and Emissions Trading Act 2003, s 21(1).
119. Directive 1999/31/EC, Art 5.
120. Waste and Emissions Trading Act 2003, s 1(1). A 'scheme year' is a year which begins with 1 April between 2005 and 2019. A 'target year' is a year ending with 31 March in 2010, 2013 or 2020; ibid. s 23(1).
121. Ibid. s 1(3).
122. Ibid. s 4(2).
123. SSI 2005 No 157.
124. Environmental Protection Act 1990, s 30(3).
125. 'Household waste' means waste from (a) domestic property, that is to say, a building which is used wholly for the purposes of living accommodation or (b) waste from a caravan (as defined in s 29(1) of the Caravan Sites and Control of Development Act 1960) which usually and for the time being is situated on a caravan site within the meaning of the Act, or (c) a residential home (d) premises forming part of a hospital or which are used to provide a care home service as defined by s 2(3) of the Regulation of Care (Scotland) Act 2001; EPA s 75(5).
126. Ibid. s 45(1).
127. 'Commercial waste' means waste from premises (including premises for agriculture within the meaning of Agriculture (Scotland) Act 1948 used wholly or mainly for the purposes of sport, recreation or entertainment excluding (a) household waste (b) industrial waste (c) waste of any other description prescribed by regulations which have been made by the Secretary of State for the purposes of the EPA; ibid. s 75(7).
'Industrial waste' means waste from any of the following premises:
(a)   any factory (within the meaning of the Factories Act 1961)

(b)   any premises used for the purposes of, or in connection with, the supply to the public of gas, water or electricity or the provision of sewerage services;

(c)   any premises used for the purposes of, or in connection with, the supply to the public of gas, water or electricity or the provision of sewerage services;

(d)   any premises used for the purposes of, or in connection with, the provision to the public of postal or telecommunication services; EPA s 75(7).

128. 'Dry recyclable waste' means controlled waste that is:

(a)   glass,

(b)   metals,

(c)   plastics,

(d)   paper, or

(e)   card (including cardboard, and dry recyclable waste of the same type (such as glass) is referred to as a 'dry waste stream'; ibid. s 75(7A).

129. 'Food waste' means controlled waste that was at any time food intended for human consumption (even of no nutritional value) and includes biodegradable waste produced as a consequence of the processing or preparation of food, but does not include drink; ibid. s 75(7B).

130. Ibid. s 45(1A).

131. Ibid. s 45C(2).

132. Ibid. s 45C(5).

133. Ibid. s 45C(6).

134. A local authority in Scotland is constituted a waste disposal authority for the purposes of the EPA by virtue of s 30(2).

135. Ibid. s 53(1).

136. Ibid. s 59(1).

137. Ibid. s 59(2).

138. Ibid. s 59(3).

139. Ibid. s 59(4).

140. Ibid. s 59(5).

141. Ibid. s 59(6).

142. Ibid. s 59(7).

143. Ibid. s 59(8).

144. Ibid. s 59(9).

145. [1921] 3 KB 560.

146. [1961] AC 388.

147. For a general discussion of remoteness of damage in the law of delict. see F. McManus and E. Russell, *Delict*, 2nd edn (Dundee University Press, 2011) ch. 8.

148. For a general discussion of these defences see F. McManus and E. Russell (note 147) ch. 21.

149. EPA s 73(6)
150. Ibid. s 56.
151. See p. 170-1 incl.
152. Control of Pollution Act 1989 s 1(1).
153. SSI 2011 No 228.
154. Ibid. reg 2(1).
155. Ibid. reg 2(1).
156. Ibid. reg 30(1).
157. Environmental Protection Act 1990 s 63A.
158. As amended.
159. 'Refuse' includes any matter whatsoever, whether inorganic or organic; Refuse Disposal (Amenity) Act 1978, s 1(7).
160. Ibid. s 1.
161. Ibid. s 62.
162. SI 1996 No 972 (as amended).
163. Art 6(1) (as amended). For a general discussion of the Directive, see C. London and M. Lamas, 'EC Packaging Directive' [1995] NLJ 221.
164. SI 2007 No 871.
165. Ibid. reg 2(2).
166. Directive 2000/53/EC.
167. Ibid. Art 4.
168. Ibid. Art 5.
169. Ibid. Art 7.
170. SI 2003 No 2635.
171. Ibid. reg 3.
172. Ibid. reg 6.
173. Ibid. reg 14.
174. Ibid. reg 18(1).
175. SI 2003 No 593.
176. Ibid. reg 5.
177. Directive 2002/96/EC (re-cast by Directive 2012/19/EC).
178. SI 2006 No 3289.
179. Ibid. reg 8(1)(2). The actual amount for which a producer is liable to pay is determined by means of a formula which is contained in reg 8(3). 'Compliance period' means any period of any year which follows that period; ibid. reg 2(1). The first compliance period means the period which commences on 1 July 2007 and ends with 31 December 2007.
180. Ibid. reg 9(1).
181. Ibid. reg 10(1).
182. Ibid. reg 10(5). The Regulations make provision for the procedure for the approval of a proposed compliance scheme; ibid. reg 41.

183. Whether the litter in question has been left is a question of fact and degree in each case; *Westminster City Council v Riding* [1996] Env LR 95.
184. The expression 'litter' is not defined in the EPA. However, in *Westminster City Council v Riding* (note 183), it was held that the word 'litter' should be given its natural meaning of miscellaneous rubbish left lying about. Such rubbish could consist of domestic household waste, commercial waste, street waste and other forms of waste.
185. EPA s 87(1).
186. 'Public open place' is defined as a place in the open air to which the public are entitled or permitted to have access without payment; and any covered place open to the air on at least one side and available for public use; ibid s 87(4). In *Felix v DPP* [1998] Crim LR 657 it was held that an enclosed telephone kiosk which had three fixed sides and a door which was provided with a gap at the bottom did not constitute a public open space within the meaning of the section.
187. EPA s 87(3).
188. Ibid s 87(2).
189. 'Authorised officer' means an officer of a litter authority who is authorised in writing by the authority for the purpose of issuing notices under s 88 of the EPA; ibid. s 88(10).
190. Ibid. s 88(1).
191. Ibid. s 88(2).
192. Ibid. s 89(1).
193. Ibid. s 90(1). See the Litter Control Areas Order 1991 (SI 1991 No 1325) (as amended).
194. Ibid. s 90(3).
195. Ibid. s 90(4).
196. Ibid. s 91(1).
197. Ibid. s 92(1)(2).
198. Ibid. s 92(3).
199. Ibid. s 92(4).
200. Ibid. s 92(5).
201. Ibid. s 92(6).
202. Ibid. s 92(7).
203. Ibid. s 92(9).
204. Ibid. s 93(1).
205. See the Street Litter Notice Order 1991 (SI 1991 No 1324).
206. EPA s 93(2).
207. Ibid. s 93(3).
208. The Scottish Government may prescribe the descriptions of land which

may be included in a specified area-see the Street Litter Notice Order 1991 (SI 1991 No 1324).

209. EPA s 94(4).
210. Ibid. s 94(7).
211. Ibid. s 94(8).
212. Ibid. s 94(9).
213. As amended.
214. Refuse Disposal (Amenity) Act 1978, s 2.
215. Ibid. s 3(1).
216. Ibid. ss 4 and 5.
217. Ibid. s 6(1).

CHAPTER 7

Contaminated Land

The current regime which deals with contaminated land in Scotland is contained in Part IIA of the Environmental Protection Act 19909 (EPA). The responsibility to deal with contaminated land falls on both local authorities and the Scottish Environment Protection Agency (SEPA). The latter regulates special sites. Both enforcing authorities may serve a remediation notice on the appropriate person. The EPA makes provision for appeals against a notice. It is made an offence not to comply with a remedial notice.

Introduction

In this chapter we look at the subject of contaminated land. Land may become contaminated in a number of different ways. For example, it may have been used as a dumping ground for waste from chemical works or incinerators. Land may also have become contaminated in the course of industrial activity, for example, by spillages and leaks from storage tanks and drums, escapes of materials such as dust and liquids, in the course of the activity itself, and contamination which has resulted from the deposition of airborne particulate matter.[1] Whereas much contamination of land has occurred since the beginning of the Industrial Revolution,[2] some contamination took place long before this period. For example, contamination of land has been caused by copper and lead workings during Roman times. The existence of contaminated sites is partly the result of decades of ineffective regulation by the state.[3] In 1990 the House of Commons Environment Committee listed some nineteen categories of use which purported to represent the most common contaminating uses of land, namely, waste disposal sites, gas works, oil refineries and petrol stations, iron and steel works, metal products, fabrication and finishing, chemical works, textile plants, leather tanning works, timber treatment works, non-ferrous metals processing, manufacture of integrated circuits and semi-conductors, sewage works, asbestos works, docks and railway land, paper and printing works, heavy engineering installations and processing radio-active materials.[4] However, as far as Scotland is concerned, the extent of the problem of contaminated land is uncertain. Indeed, unlike some other countries in Europe, there has been no systematic national survey of contaminated land. Significantly, unlike other forms of pollution, there has been no disaster which is associated with contaminated land and has required an immediate legislative response.

However, before we look at the legislative regime in terms of the Environmental Protection Act 1990 (EPA) we will consider the position of contaminated land under the common law and also in terms of statutory nuisance.

Contaminated land and the common law

Contaminated land can rank as a nuisance at common law. For example, harmful chemicals which leach through the soil in the defender's land into the land of the pursuer, thereby causing harm to the latter, could rank as a nuisance in law.[5]

As far as the law of negligence is concerned, those responsible for carrying out works on contaminated land owe a duty of care in terms of the law of negligence, to protect the public from foreseeable risks which may arise from works which are being carried out on the contaminated site. This point is neatly illustrated in *Corby Group Litigation v Corby DC*.[6] In that case a local authority was held to have been in breach of its duty of care to prevent the dispersal of mud and dust, which contained a range of contaminants, from land reclamation sites which the local authority owned and operated. The upshot of this was that pregnant women in the area had become exposed to harmful substances. Children, who were born to some of the women, had physical defects.

Contaminated land: the statutory regime

The current regime which governs contaminated land is contained in the Environmental Protection Act 1990. That regime closely mirrors the statutory nuisance regime, which is now well ingrained in UK environmental law. By way of a general overview, local authorities are primarily responsible for dealing with contaminated land in Scotland. The main responsibility of the local authority is to inspect its area in order to identify contaminated land; to decide what remediation is required; and to act as enforcing authority for all contaminated land which is not designated a special site (in respect of which SEPA bears responsibility).

What is contaminated land?

The expression 'contaminated land' is a term of art (that is, a technical term). It is defined in the Environmental Protection Act 1990[7] (EPA) as any land which appears to the local authority in whose area it is situated to be in such a condition, by reason of substances in, or under the land, that

(a) significant harm[8] is being caused or there is a significant possibility of such harm being caused; or
(b) significant pollution of the water environment is being caused or there is a significant possibility of such pollution being caused.

In determining whether any land appears to be such land, a local authority is required to act in accordance with guidance which is issued by the Scottish Ministers.

Contaminated land and statutory nuisance

Prior to the introduction of the regime, which is specifically aimed at contaminated land, and which we will be discussing, there was no statute which dealt with contaminated land. However, the Public Health (Scotland) Act 1897[9] placed a duty on local authorities to abate certain accummulations and deposits which were a nuisance or injurious or dangerous to health. In the sheriff court case of *Clydebank DC v Monaville Estates Ltd*[10] asbestos had been deposited on the ground of premises prior to the defenders becoming owners of the premises, which were unoccupied. The premises bordered the River Clyde which had exposed the asbestos over a wide area, rendering the asbestos a danger to the public. The court ordered the asbestos to be covered over in order to prevent it continuing to be a danger to public health.

In order to avoid duplication with the statutory nuisance regime,[11] the EPA provides that no matter constitutes a statutory nuisance to the extent that it consists of, or is caused by, any land being in a contaminated state.[12]

Identification of contaminated land
The main responsibility for dealing with contaminated land falls to local authorities in Scotland. A local authority is placed under a duty to inspect its area, from time to time, in order to identify contaminated land and also to enable the authority to decide whether any such land is required to be designated as a special site.[13] In performing this duty, a local authority is required to act in accordance with any guidance which is issued by the

Scottish Ministers.[14] If a local authority identifies any contaminated land in its area, the local authority is required to give notice of that fact to:

(a) SEPA,
(b) the owner of the land,
(c) the person who appears to the authority to be in occupation of the whole or part of the land; and
(d) each person who appears to the authority to be an appropriate person.[15]

If at any time after a local authority has given any person such a notice in relation to any land, it appears to the enforcing authority[16] that another person is an appropriate person, the enforcing authority is required to give notice to that other person:

(a) of the fact that the local authority has identified the land in question as contaminated land; and,
(b) that he appears to the enforcing authority to be an appropriate person.[17]

Special sites
The EPA makes special provision for the identification and designation of special sites. However, the expression 'special site' is not defined in the EPA. If, at any time, it appears to a local authority that any contaminated land in its area might be land which is required to be designated as a special site, the authority is required to decide whether or not the land is land which is required to be designated as a special site, and if the authority decides that the land is required to be so designated, the authority is required to give notice of that decision to the relevant persons.[18] The relevant persons are:

(a) SEPA;
(b) the owner of the land;
(c) any person who appears to the local authority to be concerned in the occupation of the whole or any part of the land; and
(d) each person who appears to that authority to be an appropriate person.[19]

Before making a decision to designate land as a special site, the local authority is required to request the advice of SEPA, and, in making its decision, the local authority is required to have regard to any advice which is given by SEPA in response to that request.[20] If at any time SEPA considers that any contaminated land is land which is required to be designated as a special site, SEPA may give notice of that fact to the local authority in whose area the land is situated.[21] Where such notice is given to a local authority, the authority is required to decide whether the land in question requires to be designated as a special site, or does not require to be so designated.[22] Notice of the decision requires to be given to the relevant persons.

Land is required to be designated as a special site if the Scottish Ministers so prescribe by regulations.[23] The Scottish Ministers are required to determine any disputes between SEPA and a local authority as to whether any land should be designated a special site.[24] The Scottish Ministers have complete powers of review, and can confirm or reverse the decision in relation to the whole or any part of the land to which it relates.[25]

Duty of enforcing authority to require remediation of contaminated land

The EPA places both SEPA, in relation to special sites, and a local authority, in relation to other contaminated land, under a duty to serve a remediation notice on the appropriate person,[26] with such notice specifying what that person is to do by way of remediation, and also the periods within which he is required to do each of the things specified.[27] Different remediation notices which require the carrying-out of different things by way of remediation may be served on different persons in consequence of the presence of different substances in, on, or under any land or the water environment.[28] Where two or more persons are appropriate persons in relation to any particular thing which is to be done by way of remediation, the remediation notice is required to state the proportion (which is determined in accordance with the EPA)[29] of the cost of performing the particular activity which each of them is liable to bear.[30] The relevant enforcing authority may only require to be done that which is reasonable, having regard to the cost which is likely to be involved, and the seriousness of the harm, or the pollution of the water environment in question.[31] In determining how the particular land is to be remediated in any particular case, the standard to which any land, or the water environment, is to be remediated by way of the relevant notice, or what is to be regarded as reasonable, the enforcing authority is required to have regard to Scottish Ministers' guidance.[32]

Who is the appropriate person?

In effect, the EPA, for the purposes of determining which persons should bear responsibility for remediating contaminated land, adopts a procedure which is analogous to that which the EPA uses to deal with statutory nuisances.[33]

The EPA defines the appropriate person for the purposes of remediating contaminated land as:

> Any person or any persons who caused or knowingly permitted the substances, or any of the substances, by reason of which the contaminated land in question is such land to be in, on or under that land.[34]

The EPA emphasises that a person ranks as an appropriate person and is, therefore, liable to remediate the relevant land, only in relation to substances which he caused, or knowingly permitted to be present in, the land in question.[35] However, if no such person has, after reasonable enquiry, been found to bear responsibility for the relevant remediation of the land, the owner or occupier for the time being of the contaminated land in question is the appropriate person.[36] The owner or occupier of the land is, therefore, required to remediate the land in question.[37] The Scottish Ministers can, by way of statutory guidance, exclude certain classes of persons and also certain activities from the scope of the EPA in terms of remediation of contaminated land.[38] The Scottish Ministrs can also apportion remediation costs between the parties.[39]

In *R. (Crest Nicholson Residential Ltd) v Secretary of State for Environment, Food and Rural Affairs*,[40] a site had been contaminated by chemicals which had been deposited on the site by a former owner, R. However, a subsequent owner, C., carried out demolition works on the site. These works exposed the site to rain, thereby accelerating the flushing of the contaminants into the soil. A remediation notice was served on both R. and C. C. sought judicial review of the notice. At first instance it was held that C. had caused the land to be contaminated.

Crest is authority for the proposition that for the purposes of the EPA, a person may be deemed to have caused the relevant land to be contaminated if he creates a state of affairs which facilitates, or materially contributes, to the land in question being contaminated, notwithstanding the fact that the relevant contaminants were present on the land by virtue of the activities of a previous owner.[41] The EPA provides that in circumstances where a person has caused or knowingly permitted any substance to be in, on, or under any land, is deemed to have caused or knowingly permitted there to be in, on, or under that land, any substance which is there as a result of a chemical reaction or biological process affecting that substance.[42]

Furthermore, the remediation of a substance can be required by virtue of the presence of any substance, notwithstanding the fact that such remediation would not have been required to be done simply by virtue of the presence or quantity of that substance which any person caused or knowingly permitted to be present.[43] This would allow an enforcing authority to require remedial action, for example, in circumstances where a water-course could erode adjoining land, thereby exposing contaminants to the danger of the public.[44]

Grant of, and compensation for, rights of entry etc.

A remediation notice may require an appropriate person to do things by way of remediation, notwithstanding that he is not entitled to do those things.[45] An obvious application of this provision would be that the notice could require the appropriate person to enter the land of a neighbouring proprietor to carry out the necessary works. Any person whose consent is required before the necessary works are carried out is required to either grant. or join in granting, such rights in relation to the relevant land or the water environment, as will enable the appropriate person to comply with any requirements which have been imposed by the remediation notice.[46] Before the notice is served, the enforcing authority is required to attempt to consult every person who appears to the authority:

(a)   to be the owner or occupier of any of the relevant land or water environment,[47] and
(b)   to be a person who might be required to grant or join in granting any such rights.[48]

However, there is no need to consult such persons if it appears to the enforcing authority that the contaminated land is in such condition, by reason of substances in, on or under the land, that there is imminent danger of serious harm, or serious pollution of the water environment being caused.[49]

Restrictions on serving remediation notices

The EPA makes certain restrictions on serving remediation notices. For example, the enforcing authority is required to make reasonable endeavour to consult:

(a)   the person on whom the notice is to be served;
(b)   the owner of any land to which the notice relates;
(c)   any person who appears to that authority to be in occupation of the whole or any part of the land; and
(d)   any person of such other description as may be described, concerning what is to be done by way of remediation.[50]

Furthermore, an enforcing authority may not serve a remediation notice as long as any one, or more, of the following conditions apply in the particular case, that is to say:

(a)   the authority is satisfied that, in consequence of the provisions of the EPA relating to cost of remediation and seriousness of the harm or of pollution to the water environment,[51] that there is nothing by way of remediation which could be specified in a remediation notice served on that person;

(b)   the authority is satisfied that appropriate things are being, or will be done, by way of remediation without the service of a remediation notice on that person;

(c)   it appears to the authority that the person on whom the notice would be served is the authority itself; or

(d)   the authority is satisfied that the powers which are conferred on it by the EPA[52] to do what is appropriate by way of remediation, are exercisable.[53]

Restrictions on liability for the pollution of controlled waters

Certain restrictions also apply where land is contaminated by reason of substances in, on, or under the land, that significant pollution of the water environment is being caused, or there is a significant possibility of such harm being caused. However, no remediation notice may be served on the appropriate person in such circumstances, in so far as that notice requires him to remediate either the land or the water environment.[54] A similar exclusion applies where a person permits or has permitted, or might permit, water from an abandoned mine,[55] or part of a mine, to enter the water environment, or to reach a place from which it is or, as the case may be, was likely, in the opinion of the enforcing authority, to enter the water environment.[56] However, such an exclusion does not apply to either the owner or former operator of any mine if the mine in question became abandoned after 31 December 1999.[57]

In the case of land which falls to be regarded as contaminated by virtue of the land causing significant pollution of the water environment, the enforcing authority may itself carry out remedial work under the EPA, but the authority is not entitled to recover costs from any person in carrying out works which the authority is precluded by the EPA[58] from requiring that person to do.[59]

Liability for contaminating substances which escape to other land

Land may be contaminated by substances[60] which escape to other land. The EPA makes provision for such circumstances.

A person who has either caused or has knowingly permitted any substances to be in, on or under any land, is also taken for the purposes of

Part IIA of the EPA, to have caused, or, as the case may be, knowingly permitted, those substances to be in, on or under any land to which they appear to have escaped.[61] The EPA makes provision, in any case, where it appears to the enforcing authority that any substances either are, or have been either in, or on any land (that is, 'land A'), as a result of their escape (whether directly or indirectly) from other land in, on, or under which a person caused or knowingly permitted them to be.[62] In such circumstances no remediation notice may require a person who is the owner or occupier of land A (and who has not caused or knowingly permitted the substances in question to be in, on or under land A) to do anything by way of remediation to any land (or the water environment) of which he is the owner or the occupier, in consequence of land A appearing to be in such condition, by reason of the presence of those substances in, on or under it, that significant harm, or significant pollution of the water environment is being caused, or there is a significant possibility of such harm or pollution being caused.[63] In the case of land ('land B') on which the presence of substances has been caused as a result of their escape from land A to land B, the condition of the latter appearing to be caused by the presence of those substances in, on or under it, that significant harm, or the significant possibility of such harm or pollution is being caused, no remediation notice may require anything of remediation, of either the owner or occupier of land A, provided that he neither caused nor knowingly permitted the substances in question to be in, on or under land A, unless he is also the owner or occupier of land B.[64]

In any case, where one person (person A) has either caused or knowingly permitted any substances to be in, on or under any land, and another person (person B) (who has not caused or knowingly permitted those substances to be in, on or under that land) becomes the owner or occupier of that land, and the substances or any of such substances which person A has knowingly permitted to be in, on or under any land, have appeared to escaped to other land, no remediation notice may require person B to do anything by way of remediation to that other land in consequence of the acts or omissions of person A, except to the extent that person B has either caused or knowingly permitted the escape.[65]

However, in circumstances where substances have escaped from one parcel of land to another, the enforcing authority may itself carry out remedial work on the relevant land.[66] In such circumstances, the enforcing authority may not recover any costs which are incurred by the authority in carrying out the relevant remedial works, the need for which has been occasioned by such escapes, and in relation to which the relevant person may not be required to carry out by virtue of the above provisions.

Appeals against remedial notices

The EPA makes provision for appeals against a remediation notice which has been served. A person on whom a remediation is served may, within a period of twenty-one days, which begins on the day on which the notice is served, appeal to the sheriff, by way of summary application, if the notice was served by a local authority, or to the Scottish Ministers, if the remediation notice was served by SEPA.[67] Both the sheriff and the Scottish Ministers have complete powers of review and either may quash the notice, on being satisfied that there is a material defect in the notice.[68] Subject to such proviso, the sheriff or the Scottish Ministers may confirm the remediation notice either with or without modification, or they may quash it. Furthermore, either the sheriff or the Scottish Ministers may extend the period which is specified in the relevant notice for doing what the notice requires to be done.[69]

The Scottish Ministers may make regulations which, *inter alia*, make provision for the grounds on which an appeal can be made, and also the procedure which governs the appeal.[70]

Offence of not complying with remediation notice

It is an offence for a person on whom an enforcing notice is served to fail, without reasonable excuse, to comply with any requirements of such notice.[71] In the case of a remediation notice which has been served on two or more persons, in respect of the requirement which has not been complied with, in relation to the proportion of the cost which the person who is charged with the offence is liable to bear, it is a defence for that person to prove that the only reason why he has not complied with the requirement, is that one or more of the other persons who are liable to bear a proportion of that cost either refused or was not able to comply with that requirement.[72]

Finally, if the enforcing authority is of the opinion that proceedings for an offence would afford an ineffectual remedy against a person who has failed to comply with any requirements of a remediation notice which that authority has served on him, the authority may take proceedings in any court of competent jurisdiction for the purposes of securing compliance with the remediation notice.[73] Normally, the remedy which would be sought by the enforcing authority would be an interdict.

Powers of enforcing authority to carry out remediation

The EPA confers powers (subject to certain exceptions)[74] on an enforcing authority itself, to carry out remedial works in relation to the relevant land[75] or the water environment.[76] Such powers of remediation can be used in a variety of circumstances, including the following:

(i) where the enforcing authority considers it necessary to do anything by way of remediation for the purpose of preventing the occurrence of any serious harm, or serious pollution of the water environment, of which there is imminent danger;
(ii) where a person on whom the enforcing authority serves a remediation notice, fails to comply with any of the requirements of the notice;
(iii) where no person has (after reasonable enquiry) been found who is an appropriate person on whom a remediation notice can be served.[77]

The enforcing authority has wide powers (subject to certain exceptions)[78] of remediation in terms of the EPA.[79] Finally, the EPA makes provision for the recovery of the cost of remediation from the appropriate person by the enforcing authority.[80]

Registers

Every enforcing authority is under a duty to maintain a register which contains prescribed[81] particulars either of, or relating to, *inter alia*, remediation notices which have been served by that authority; appeals against such notices; remediation notices which have been served by that authority; appeals against such notices; and notices which designate land as a special site.[82] Finally, provision is made for the exclusion from the register of information which affects national security,[83] and, also, the exclusion from the register of certain confidential information.[84]

Reports by SEPA on contaminated land

SEPA is required periodically, and if so requested by the Scottish Ministers, to prepare and publish a report on the state of contaminated land in Scotland.[85] SEPA may request a local authority to furnish SEPA with such information as it requires to enable it perform this function.[86]

Site-specific guidance by SEPA

SEPA is empowered to issue guidance to any local authority in relation to either the exercise or the performance of SEPA's powers and duties under Part IIA of the EPA in relation to any particular contaminated land.[87] The relevant local authority is required to have regard to such guidance when it either exercises or performs those powers or duties in relation to the relevant land. A local authority is required, at the written request of SEPA, to furnish it with such information as SEPA may require for the purpose of giving such guidance.[88]

Power of Scottish Ministers to issue guidance

The Scottish Ministers may issue guidance to SEPA with respect to the exercise or performance of SEPA's powers and duties under Part IIA.[89] In turn, SEPA is required to have regard to such guidance in exercising its powers and duties.

Conclusions

There is a pronounced paucity of case law on the law relating to contaminated land. The legislation, indeed, is also complex. One of the complexities stems from the fact that two separate regulatory bodies (namely, SEPA and local authorities) have responsibility for contaminated land. Perhaps, it might have been simpler to have given SEPA exclusive responsibility for enforcing the provisions of Part IIA? This would conduce to a more consistent approach to contaminated land regulation and remediation in Scotland. Furthermore, and somewhat surprisingly, there has been no comprehensive survey of contaminated land in Scotland. Therefore, both the nature and the extent of the problem are unknown. This state of uncertainty has ramifications in terms of public accountability. The general public is simply not in a position to effectively assess whether the relevant enforcing authority is adequately performing its duties in relation to contaminated land. We see here, of course, similarities with noise pollution, which we have already discussed.[90]

Summary

- Land may become contaminated in a variety of ways.
- The current regime which governs contaminated land is contained in the Environmental Protection Act 1990 (EPA). This regime closely mirrors the statutory nuisance regime of that Act.
- The main responsibility for dealing with contaminated land falls to local authorities in Scotland.
- SEPA is responsible for dealing with special sites.

The EPA places both SEPA, in relation to special sites, and a local authority, in relation to other contaminated land, under a duty to serve a remediation notice on the appropriate person.

Notes

1. S. Tromans and R. Turrall-Clarke, *Contaminated Land*, 2nd edn (Thomson/ Sweet and Maxwell, 2008) at 3.
2. M. Beckett in T. Cairney (ed.), *Contaminated Land*, 2nd edn (Thomson/Sweet and Maxwell, 2008) at 3.
3. R. Lazarus, *The Making of Environmental Law* (University of Chicago Press, 2004) at 107.
4. HC Environment Committee, Session 1989-1990, First Report, Contaminated Land, vol. 1 para 12 (HC 170-1).
5. See, e.g., *Gemmill's Trustees v Alexander Cross and Sons* 1906 14 SLT 576 which appears to have been decided in terms of the rule in *Rylands v Fletcher* in contrast to the law of nuisance. In *RHM Bakeries Ltd v Strathclyde Regional Council* 1985 SC (HL) 17 the House of Lords held that the rule in *Rylands v Fletcher* has no application in the law of Scotland.
6. [2009] EWHC 1944.
7. Environmental Protection Act 1990 (EPA) s 78A(2).
8. 'Harm' is defined as harm to the health of living organisms or other interference with the ecological systems of which they form part and, in the case of man, includes harm to his property; ibid s 78A(4). 'Harm' in relation to the water environment has the same meaning as in s 20(6) of the Water Environment and water Services (Scotland) Act 2003; s 78A(4A). The question as to what harm or pollution of the water environment is to be regarded as significant and whether the possibility of significant harm or of significant pollution of the water environment which is being caused, is significant is to be determined in accordance with Scottish Government statutory guidance; ibid. s 78A(5). The latest statutory guidance was published by the Scottish Government in June 2006 (SE/2006/44).
9. Section 16(5).(repealed).
10. 1982 SLT (Sh Ct) 2.
11. See Chapter 3.
12. EPA s 79 (1A). Land is deemed to be in a contaminated state if it is in such a condition, by reason of substances in, on or under that land that (a) significant harm is being caused or there is a significant possibility of such harm being caused; or (b) significant pollution of the water environment is being caused or there is a significant possibility of such pollution being caused; Ibid. s 79(1B).
13. Ibid. s 78B(1).
14. Ibid. s 78B(2).
15. Ibid s 78B(2). 'Appropriate person' means any person determined in accordance with s 78F of the EPA to bear responsibility for anything which is to be

done by way of remediation in any particular case; Ibid s 78A(9) (see below p. 201-3 incl.)

16. 'Enforcing authority' means (a) in relation to a special site, SEPA; (b) in relation to contaminated land other than a special site, the local authority in whose area the land is situated; ibid. s 78A(9).
17. Ibid. s 78B(4).
18. Ibid. s 78C(1).
19. Ibid. s 78C(2).
20. Ibid. s 78C(3).
21. Ibid. s 78C(4).
22. Ibid. s 78C(5).
23. Ibid. s 78C(8). See the Contaminated Land (Scotland) Regulations 2000 (SSI 2000 No 178) 2.
24. EPA s 78D(1).
25. Ibid. s 78D(4). The Scottish Government is required to give notice of its decision to both the relevant persons and also to the local authority.
26. 'The appropriate person' is defined in s 78F (below).
27. EPA s 78E(1).
28. Ibid. s 78E(2).
29. Ibid. s 78F(7) which provides that where two or more persons are appropriate persons, they are liable to bear the cost of doing that thing in such proportions which are determined by the enforcing authority in accordance with Scottish Government guidance. See note 10 above.
30. EPA s 78F(3).
31. Ibid. s 78F(4).
32. Ibid. s 78(5).
33. See p. 44-51 incl.
34. Ibid. s 78F(2).
35. Ibid. s 78F(3). In *R. (National Grid Gas plc) v Environment Agency* [2007] 1 WLR 1780, coal tar residues from the production of coal gas were deposited underground at a gas works which were operated by a private gas company. The company was nationalised in 1948. All property, rights and liabilities of the company passed to a state-owned gas utility. Gas production was subsequently stopped at the works. In 1965 the site was sold for housing. In 1986 both the assets and the liabilities of the company passed to a public limited company, British Gas, part of whose undertaking later devolved upon the claimant. In 2005 the site was designated as contaminated land by the Environment Agency. The Environment Agency notified the claimant that it was an appropriate person in terms of the EPA. The House of Lords held that the liabilities which were imposed on British Gas in 1986 were those which existed immediately before the transfer which took place on that date.

Such liabilities could not include liabilities which came into existence nine years later under the Environment Act 1995 (which amended the EPA). In short, it could not be plausibly argued that the claimant had either caused or knowingly permitted the substances to be present on the land.

36. EPA s 78F(4).
37. Ibid. s 78F(5).
38. Ibid. s 78F(6). See Statutory Guidance Annex 3 Part D.
39. Ibid. s 78F(7). See Statutory Guidance Annex 3 Part D. See also *R. (on the application of Redland Minerals Ltd) v Secretary of State for the Environment, Food and Rural Affairs* [2011] Env LR 2. In this case, where a site had been contaminated by its first owner, but the subsequent owner had, by its demolition works, exposed the site to rain, which accelerated the flushing of the contaminants to lower levels, there was no simple causative mechanism which allowed apportionment of liability between the owners for costs. Therefore, the length of their respective occupation of the site would, instead, form the basis for apportionment.
40. [2011] Env LR 2. For an analysis of this case see (2010) 140 SPEL 90.
41. For a discussion of *Crest*, see E. Lochery,'Causing contamination' (2010) 140 SPEL 90.
42. EPA s 78F(9). In *Circular Facilities (London) Ltd v Sevenoaks DC* [2005] Env LR 35 it was held that the relevant person need only have knowledge of the substance in question. He need not have been aware of the possibility that a chemical reaction or process could lead to the land in question being contaminated.
43. EPA s 78F(10).
44. See, e.g., *Clydebank District Council v Monaville Estates Ltd* 1982 SLT (Sh Ct) 2.
45. EPA s 78G(1).
46. Ibid. s 78G(2).
47. 'Relevant land or water environment' means:
    (a) the contaminated land in question;
    (b) the water environment affected by that land; or
    (c) any land adjoining or adjacent to that land or water environment; ibid. s 78G(7).
48. Ibid. s 78G(3).
49. Ibid. s 78G(4).
50. Ibid. s 78H(1).
51. Ibid. s 78E(4)(5).
52. Ibid. s 78N (see below).
53. Ibid. s 78H(5).
54. Ibid. s 78J(1)(2).
55. 'Mine' has the same meaning as in the Mines and Quarries Act 1954.

56. EPA s 78J(3).
57. Ibid. s 78J(4).
58. Ibid. s 78J(2)(3).
59. Ibid. s 78J(7).
60. 'Substance' means any natural or artificial substance, whether in solid or liquid form, or in the form of a gas or vapour; s 78A(7).
61. Ibid. s 78K(1).
62. Ibid. s 78K(2).
63 Ibid. s 78K(3).
64. Ibid. s 78K(4).
65. Ibid. s 78K(5).
66. Ibid. s 78K(6).
67. Ibid. s 78L(1).
68. Ibid. s 78L(2).
69. Ibid. s 78L(3).
70. Ibid. s 78L(4)(5).
71. Ibid. s 78M(1). Provision is made for penalties which may be imposed for such an offence; Ibid. s 78(3)(4).
72. Ibid. s 78M(2).
73. Ibid. s 78M(5).
74. The exceptions are contained in s 78YB of the EPA.
75. 'Relevant land or the water environment' means (a) the contaminated land in question; (b) the water environment affected by that land; or (c) any land adjoining or adjacent to that land or that water environment; ibid. s 78N(5).
76. EPA s 78N(1)(2).
77. Ibid. s 78N(3).
78. The exceptions are contained in s 78E(4)(5) of the EPA.
79. Ibid. s 78N(4).
80. Ibid. s 78P.
81. I.e. prescribed by the Scottish Government; ibid. s 78R(2).
82. Ibid. s 78R(1).
83. Ibid. s 78S.
84. Ibid. s 78T.
85. Ibid. s 78U(1).
86. Ibid. s 78U(2).
87. Ibid. s 78V(1).
88. Ibid. s 78V(3).
89. Ibid. s 78W(1).
90. See Chapter 4

CHAPTER 8

Water

The common law has addressed the problem of causing water pollution by imposing liability for the erection of *opera manufacta* (or new works). This branch of the law is of limited practical significance. Causing water pollution can also rank as a nuisance at common law. However, private action at common law really only scratches the surface of the problem of water pollution. The satisfactory quality of water can only be secured by effective regulation. Currently, the law is largely EU-driven. The most important Directive in terms of the regulation of water pollution is the Water Framework Directive. The Water Environment and Water Services (Scotland) Act 2003 makes specific provision for the pollution of water. Whereas formerly the law placed emphasis on regulating polluting matter entering watercourses, currently potential polluting activities ('controlled activities') the form of regulation varying in relation to the capacity of the relevant activity to pollute a watercourse.

Introduction

We have already looked at the problems concerning water pollution which confronted the Victorians.[1] In this chapter we discuss the modern legal controls over water in Scotland. First, we turn our attention to the common law controls, and then look at the relevant statutory controls of the pollution of water.

Liability under the common law

Liability for causing pollution by erecting *opera manufacta* (or new works)

It is now well established that, in contrast to the law of England,[2] as far as liability in nuisance is concerned, in order to succeed, the pursuer requires to aver and prove *culpa* (or fault) on the part of the defender.[3] However, in the Inner House case of *Kennedy v Glenbelle Ltd*,[4] Lord Hope, basing his authority on *Chalmers v Dixon*,[5] expressly recognised that the law would impute *culpa* or fault on the part of the defender if the harm which the former sustained derived from an *opus manufactum* (or new works) which the defender had brought into existence on his land. In short, according to his Lordship, the law would impose strict liability (in effect, by so imposing blame) on the defender in such circumstances. The vast majority of cases which concern liability for *opera manufacta* centre around circumstances where the natural flow of a stream has been affected by the construction of a dam, embankment or the like, the upshot of which is that the property of the riparian proprietors downstream is flooded.[6] However, there are instances of the doctrine of *opus manufactum* being successfully invoked by riparian proprietors against watercourse pollution.

For example, in the Inner House case of *Montgomerie v Buchanan's Trustees*[7] the defender erected premises on his land and conveyed the sewage from the premises into a streamlet which passed through subjacent property. As a consequence, the water in the stream which had formerly been fit for the use of cattle and also for domestic purposes (that is, the primary uses of the water) became polluted and unfit for these purposes. The pursuer, a proprietor of land which adjoined the stream, raised an action in nuisance against the defendant. In deciding in favour of the pursuer, the court held that, given the fact that the primary use of the stream was water, the introduction of sewage into that stream had, in effect, interfered with that use. In coming to this conclusion, the court seemed to set some store by the fact that the adverse state of affairs has come about by the introduction of an *opus manufactum* on the land of the defender.

Another example of the courts enlisting the aid of the doctrine of *opus manufactum* is seen in the Inner House case of *Fleming v Gemmill*.[8] Here, the proprietors of workmen's houses erected earth closets and washhouses for the use of their tenants. Although the drains which served the houses were intended solely to receive waste water from the washhouses and sinks of the premises, they were actually used as a means of disposing of sewage by the tenants. The upshot of this was that the stream, into which the drains discharged, became polluted, to the injury of cattle which watered at the stream. After stating that 'it would be childish not to suppose from the known habits of such persons as the tenants of these cottages, that pollution would ensue', the Lord President (with whom the court concurred) held the defenders liable by reason of the fact that they had erected an *opus manufactum* or new works.[9] Again, in the Inner House case of *Montgomerie v Buchanan's Trustees*[10] the defender, a proprietor of land, erected houses on his land. He introduced running water into the houses. He also constructed drains to serve the houses. The drains discharged effluent from the houses into a stream which became polluted. An action was raised by a subjacent proprietor through whose land the stream flowed. An interdict was granted to the pursuer, prohibiting the defender from polluting the stream. According to the Lord President, the pollution of the stream had come about by an 'artificial operation by which the pollution is created and directed into the stream'.[11] The judgment of Lord Ivory is particularly interesting. According to his Lordship:[12]

> You are not entitled to clear your ground of nuisance and make your neighbour bear the ill consequences of it. Nature has not been left here to do her own work, and man has interfered to make an *opus manufactum*. The French Code provides that the land of inferior proprietors shall receive the water flowing naturally from the lands of the superior proprietors-*sans que la main de l'homme y ait contribute*. Now in this case, the hand of man has contributed to make this nuisance, and that has taken it out of the legal servitude arising out of the natural locality of the subject.

Montgomerie is also authority for the proposition that the works in question do not require to be huge in dimension in order to fall within the scope of the rule.

By way of conclusion, on this subject, the law relating to *opera manufacta* represents a grey area of the law of Scotland and, in the view of the author, is limited to harm caused by works which are situated on streams.

Liability in nuisance

The introduction of polluting matter into a stream can also constitute a nuisance in law. *Duke of Buccleuch v Cowan*[13] concerned the pollution of the River Esk by waste from several paper mills which were situated on its banks. The defendant was the proprietor of one mill. The pursuer owned land through which the river flowed. Before 1835 the water in the river had been pure in nature. However, with the passage of time, the river became polluted. The Inner House held that, whereas a riparian proprietor could use the water in the stream as he chose, he was required to send to proprietors downstream water which was undiminished in quantity and unimpaired in quality. However, this obligation was subject to the condition that the use to which the upper proprietor could use the stream could not interfere with the primary use (which would vary with the particular stream) of the stream which the Inner House described as including washing, bleaching and cooking and watering cattle, by polluting the stream.[14] However, the Inner House held that there was no absolute standard of water quality in law. Furthermore, it was irrelevant for the defender to argue that his contribution to the adverse state of affairs complained of would not, in itself, have constituted a nuisance.

The House of Lords had the opportunity to discuss colliery waste river pollution in *John Young and Co v The Bankier Distillery Co.*[15] In that case, the pursuers operated a distillery which used water from a burn for distilling. Whereas the water in the burn had been fit for its primary purposes and was suited to distilling on account of its softness, the water had ceased to be so after the defenders began to discharge colliery waste into the stream. The House held that the pursuers were entitled to an interdict, on the basis that the defenders had altered the natural character of the water in such a way as to make it unsuitable for the purposes of the pursuer. In the view of the author, this decision underscores the point that, at common law, what ranks as a nuisance in general is often fact-sensitive, especially in relation to water pollution. Indeed, Burn-Murdoch argues in the context of water pollution that water in a river may be fit for primary purposes of drinking and other domestic uses, or, the water in another river may simply be fit for secondary purposes of industrial use.[16] A pollution of the former which would rank as a nuisance may not so rank in relation to the latter. The learned author bases this view on the fact that in determining if a given state of affairs ranks as a nuisance, one is required to take into account the degree and locality of the relevant adverse state.

There are certain defences which the defender may invoke in an action for nuisance. These are the defences of statutory authority, prescription, and acquiescence. Lack of space precludes discussion of these defences (which the author has discussed elsewhere)[17] in this work.

The author must observe that no empirical research has been undertaken in Scotland, as to whether interdicts were effective at all in securing the prevention of pollution of the relevant watercourse. Attention should also be drawn to the fact that local authorities were, arguably, the greatest water polluters of the nineteenth century. For example, rivers such as the Water of Leith in Edinburgh were simply used as open sewers to discharge effluent from municipal sewers.[18] By way of conclusion, as was the case with air pollution,[19] the law of nuisance was a rather ineffectual instrument in the battle against water pollution. The remedies, normally in the form of interdicts, simply scratched at the surface of the problem. What was really required was effective state regulation of water pollution, to which we now turn our attention.

Statutory controls over water pollution

Introduction

The first major UK statute to strike at the problem of river pollution was the Salmon Fisheries Act 1861. The Act made it an offence to discharge sewage into salmon fishing waters. Whereas the obvious intention of that Act was to prevent harm to fishing interests, the Rivers Pollution Prevention Act 1876,[20] which made provision for offences relating to solid matter in streams, sewage pollution and manufacturing pollution, was passed in the interests of public health and amenity.[21] Somewhat surprisingly, the next major reform of water pollution did not take place until after the Second World War, with the passing of the Rivers (Prevention of Pollution) Act 1951. This Act placed a duty on the Secretary of State to promote the cleanliness of Scotland's rivers. The Act also instituted rivers purification boards to regulate the pollution control regime which the Act had instituted. The next major enactment which concerned pollution of watercourses was the Control of Pollution Act 1974. That Act made it an offence either to cause or knowingly permit poisonous, noxious or polluting matter to enter a watercourse.

The European Union

The Water Framework Directive

EU water policy is about forty years old.[22] EU law and policy relating to water has been the primary driver behind reform across the UK for thirty years.[23] Speaking generally, EU Directives which concerned water pollution could be categorised as those which controlled the discharge of specific substances to either surface waters or groundwater, Directives which specified quality standards for waters which were to be used for specific purposes, and Directives which controlled specific polluting activities. Currently, the most important directive in terms of the regulation of water pollution is the Water Framework Directive (WFD).[24] The WFD adopts a more holistic and revolutionary approach to the regulation of water pollution and water management than previous EU directives, and indeed, than UK national law, in which the approach to water pollution regulation has largely been sectorial. The preamble to the Directive commences in a poignant (but at the same time, rather aspirational) tone by stating that, 'water is a not a commercial product like any other, but rather a heritage which must be protected, defended and treated as such'.[25] The purpose of the WFD is to establish a framework for the protection and securement of good ecological status of inland surface waters, transitional waters and groundwater.[26] In making operational the programmes and measures which are specified in the river basin management plans for surface waters, a Member State is required to prevent the deterioration of the status of all bodies of surface water bodies.[27] For surface waters a Member State is required (subject to certain exceptions) to prevent the deterioration of the status of such waters. As far as groundwater is concerned, a Member State must take such measures to prevent or limit the input of pollutants into the groundwater to ensure that it does not deteriorate. A Member State is required to ensure that a river basin management plan is produced for each river basin lying entirely within its territory.[28]

The WFD is implemented in Scotland by the Water Environment and Water Services (Scotland) Act 2003 which is now discussed.

Water Environment and Services (Scotland) Act 2003

Introduction
By way of a brief overview, Part 1 of the Water Environment and Services (Scotland) Act 2003 (WEWS) implements the WFD in Scotland. However, WEWS is of broader scope than the WFD in that the former also establishes a framework for a comprehensive review of water pollution in Scotland. Scotland began the WFD process from a much lower starting-point than England in that there has been neither a history of statutory catchment management nor any comprehensive abstraction controls.[29] WEWS also introduces a new system of combined water use licences to manage discharges, abstractions, impoundments and river engineering (collectively known as 'controlled activities').

River basin management planning
WEWS makes provision for the establishment of river basin districts in Scotland. The Scottish Ministers are placed under a duty to designate, by order, one or more river basin districts (RBD) in Scotland.[30] The Water Environment and Water Services (Scotland) Act 2003 (Designation of Scotland River Basin District) Order 2003[31] designates a single RBD which covers most of Scotland. There are also two cross-border RBDs with England. The Scottish Environment Protection Agency (SEPA) was required to carry out a 'characterisation' of each RBD by 22 December 2004.[32] WEWS defines a characterisation as an analysis of the characteristics of the water environment, a review of the impact of human activity on the status of the water environment, and an economic analysis of water use.[33] SEPA was required to review and, where necessary, update each characterisation by December 2013 and by the end of every six years

thereafter.[34] The Scottish Ministers have powers to make regulations to provide for further provisions as to the characterisations and reviews which SEPA is required to carry out.[35] The Water Environment (River Basin Management Planning: Further Provision) (Scotland) Regulations 2013[36] make further provision towards implementing the WFD, the environmental quality standards in the field of water policy Directive[37] (the 'Priority Substances Directive') and also the requirements of the Groundwater Directive.[38]

The Scottish Ministers may, by order, designate an area of coastal water or transitional water as a shellfish protected area in terms of the WEWS.[39]

SEPA is placed under a duty to monitor the status of the water environment in the relevant district and also the relevant territorial water which is adjacent to the RBD.[40] SEPA must also prepare a programme (a 'monitoring programme') for monitoring the status of the water environment and relevant territorial water.[41] SEPA is required to set environmental objectives for each body of water in a RBD, and also for each shellfish protected water within the RBD.[42] SEPA is also required to prepare a programme of measures which are to be applied in order to meet these objectives. SEPA is also required to prepare a RB management plan for each RBD.[43] The relevant river basin management plan requires to undergo a consultation process, and also requires to be submitted to and approved by the Scottish Ministers.[44] In 2005 SEPA prepared a strategy for the Scottish RBD. In 2009 the first Scotland River Basin Management Plan was published. At the time of writing[45] a second Scotland River Basin Management Plan is out for public consultation.

Control of water pollution

WEWS makes specific provision for the protection of water pollution. The Scottish Ministers are empowered to make regulations which regulate controlled as is considered necessary or expedient in order to protect the water environment.[46] The Water Environment (Controlled Activities) (Scotland) Regulations 2011[47] have been made under the WEWS. The main provisions of the former will now be discussed.

The Water Environment (Controlled Activities) (Scotland) Regulations 2011

The Water Environment (Controlled Activities) (Scotland) Regulations 2011 (CAR) apply, *inter alia,* to activities (that is, 'controlled activities') which are likely to cause pollution of the water environment, the direct or indirect discharge, and any activity likely to cause a direct or indirect

discharge, into groundwater of any hazardous substance or other pollutant, and also any other activity which, directly or indirectly, has or is likely
to have a significant adverse impact on the water environment.[48] CAR
prohibits any person to either to carry on, or permit others to carry on, a
controlled activity except in so far as that activity is authorised under the
regulations and the relevant activity is carried on in accordance with that
authorisation.[49] Whilst the main thrust of CAR is to prevent water pollution, the ambit of CAR is wider. A duty is imposed on any person who is
carrying on a controlled activity which is authorised under the regulations
to take all reasonable steps to secure both efficient and sustainable water
use.[50]

The authorisation system

BINDING RULES

The least onerous form of authorisation, in terms of CAR, takes the form
of the application of binding rules. A controlled activity is automatically
authorised if the activity is carried out in conformity with such rules.[51]
Controlled activities which fall to be regulated by binding rules are activities which have a potentially less serious negative impact on the water environment. Such activities include the construction or extension of any well;
the dredging of a river, burn or ditch; the construction of minor bridges;
and the discharge of surface water run-off from a surface water drainage
system.

REGISTRATION

A more onerous form of authorisation takes the form of registration. SEPA
may authorise a controlled activity, which falls within the scope of CAR,
by registering the controlled activity.[52] SEPA can effectively regulate the
relevant controlled activity by imposing conditions as it considers expedient for protecting the water environment.[53] The authorisation requires to
be given by registering the following particulars in a register which is maintained by SEPA in terms of CAR.[54] The relevant particulars are:

(a)   the activity authorised;
(b)   the conditions which SEPA has imposed; and
(c)   the date of authorisation.[55]

WATER USE LICENCE

The most onerous form of authorisation takes the form of a water use
licence. SEPA may authorise a controlled activity by imposing appropriate
conditions in the licence.[56] SEPA is under a duty to impose such conditions

it considers necessary for the protection of the water environment.[57] A condition which is imposed may require the applicant to carry out works or do other things in relation to land which is not within his ownership or control.[58] In such a case, it is the responsibility of the applicant to obtain all consents which are necessary in order to allow the condition to be complied with.[59] When SEPA is considering whether to grant a licence or considering the conditions which are to be attached to a licence, it is required to have regard to all the controlled activities which are being carried on in the area of the water environment which is likely to be affected by the controlled activity to which the application relates.[60] In this way, the cumulative effects from the relevant controlled activities can be taken into account. However, as has been pointed out, the beneficial effect of this provision is, to some extent, limited in that there might be a range of other impacts which are indirectly affecting the water environment such as emissions to air from industrial installations.[61]

SEPA may also take into account any agreement which is reached between different persons concerning controlled activities which are carried on in the relevant area of the water environment.

Power of SEPA to impose authorisation

SEPA may impose an authorisation in certain circumstances. First, an authorisation can be imposed in circumstances where it appears to SEPA that a person is carrying on a controlled activity which is not registered or licensed in terms of the CAR.[62] Secondly, SEPA may impose an authorisation if the relevant activity is authorised by way of binding rules, but that additional measures are required to protect the water environment. Thirdly, an authorisation may be imposed if SEPA is of the opinion that the relevant activity which is authorised by way of registration should be authorised by means of a water use licence (or vice versa). In any of these circumstances SEPA may treat the activity as one in respect of which an application has been made and can grant an authorisation by means of registration or by a water use license.

Applications for authorisation

An application for authorisation requires to be made in writing to SEPA.[63] If SEPA considers that the controlled activity is likely to have a significant adverse impact on the water environment, SEPA must require the relevant application to be accompanied by certain information which includes: a description of the controlled activity; a description of the measures which are envisaged to mitigate and, if possible, remedy significant adverse impacts on the water environment, and an outline of the main

activities which have been studied by the applicant; and also an indica-
tion of the main reasons for the choice which has been made, taking into
account the environmental effects.[64] However, SEPA must only request
such information if it is reasonably necessary to determine the application, and the request is also reasonably capable of being compiled by
the applicant, having regard amongst others, to current knowledge and
methods of assessment.[65] Before making an application, the applicant may
request SEPA to provide an opinion as to what information must accompany the application.[66] SEPA must, after being so requested, provide that
information. However, SEPA is under no such duty if it considers that
it has not been provided with sufficient information to allow it to provide an opinion.[67] In such circumstances, SEPA is required to notify the
applicant of the points in respect of which further information is required.
In the face of the applicant failing to provide such information, SEPA is
under no duty to provide an opinion.[68] If SEPA considers that the controlled activity is likely to have a significant adverse impact on the water
environment, SEPA must, in preparing its opinion, consult both with the
applicant and also with any public authorities which, in SEPA's opinion
are, by virtue of their specific environmental responsibilities, to have an
interest in the application.[69] SEPA must then consider any information or
representations which are made by such authorities.[70] Furthermore, SEPA
is required to publicise the application.[71] SEPA may also request further
information from the applicant.[72] Importantly, SEPA may carry out any
examination or investigation which it considers necessary in order to allow
it to make a determination in respect of an application.[73]

Determination of application
Before SEPA determines an application, SEPA is required to assess the
risk to the water environment which is posed by the carrying-on of the
relevant activity.[74] If SEPA considers that the application is in respect of
an activity which either has, or is likely to have, a significant adverse effect
on the water environment, SEPA is required to assess the indirect effects of
that impact on any other aspects of the environment which is likely to be
significantly affected. SEPA is also required to consider any likely adverse
social and economic effects of that impact and of any indirect environmental effects which are associated with the carrying-on of that activity. SEPA
must also consider the likely environmental, social and economic benefits
of the activity; the impact of the controlled activity on the interests of other
users of the water environment. Furthermore, SEPA is required to assess
what steps may be taken in order to ensure efficient and sustainable water
use. Finally, SEPA is required to apply the requirements and also have

regard to the provisions of certain legislation, including the Groundwater Directive.

If the application relates to the carrying-on of more than one controlled activity, SEPA may grant or refuse the application in relation to any one or more of these activities.[75] SEPA must either grant or refuse an application to carry on an activity or, as the case may be, each of the activities which are referred to in the application.[76] The applicant must be notified of SEPA's decision. If SEPA refuses to grant an application either in whole or in part, SEPA must, when notifying the applicant of its refusal, give reasons for doing so.[77] If SEPA determines an application for a controlled activity which SEPA considers is likely to have a significant impact on the water environment, SEPA is required to make available to the public its decision, the main reasons for it, the matters which were considered in making the decision and, finally, if the application is granted, details of any measures which will be taken in order to mitigate the significant environmental impact.[78]

Call-in powers of Scottish Ministers
The Scottish Ministers may call in particular applications of a class or description which is specified in the relevant direction or the Scottish Ministers can call in a particular application.[79] However, SEPA requires to be consulted before such powers are exercised.[80] The Scottish Ministers have the power to hold a public inquiry into a called-in application.[81] When the application is determined, the Scottish Ministers are required to direct SEPA to either grant or refuse to grant the relevant application for either authorisation, or variation or surrender of authorisation.[82]

Review of authorisations, etc.
SEPA is placed under a duty to periodically review authorisations which have been granted, either by way of a registration of the relevant activity, or by way of a water use licence.[83] SEPA is also required to the general binding rules which are applicable to controlled activities.[84]

Variation of authorisations
The CAR makes provision for the variation of authorisations, at the instance of SEPA itself or at the request of the relevant responsible person or operator.

As far as the first form of variation is concerned, SEPA may vary an authorisation which has been granted in the form of a registration or in the form of a water use licence whether or not under a review of the authorisation.[85] Such a variation may include removing adding or amending any condition of an authorisation.[86] When SEPA is considering varying an authorisation, the variation falls to be treated as an application for authorisation under the CAR, and in turn, the responsible person[87] or operator is the relevant applicant.[88] SEPA is then required to determine whether or not to grant the variation.[89] If SEPA determines to grant the variation, SEPA is required to serve notice on the applicant such notice specifying the variations which have been made to the authorisation and also the date on which the variations are to take effect, such a date being not less than three months from the date on which the notice was served.[90] If SEPA determines not to grant an authorisation, reasons for so doing require to be given to the applicant.[91]

As far as the second form of variation is concerned, the relevant responsible person or operator may apply to SEPA for a variation of an authorisation which has been granted in the form of a registration or a water use licence.[92] As is the case with a variation which has been initiated by SEPA itself, the application falls to be treated as an application for an authorisation.[93] SEPA must either grant or refuse to grant the application.[94] If SEPA refuses to grant an authorisation, it is required to give reasons for such refusal. As is the case where SEPA itself initiates the variation, SEPA, on granting the application, is required to serve notice on the applicant specifying the variations which are being made to the authorisation and also the date on which the variations are to take effect, such date being not less than three months from the date on which the notice was served.[95]

Transfer of authorisation

A responsible person may jointly with another person apply to transfer an authorisation which has been granted in the form of a water use licence, either in whole or in part, to that other person.[96] SEPA may not grant an application for the transfer of such a licence unless SEPA is satisfied that the person to whom the authorisation will be transferred will secure compliance with the terms, limitations and conditions which are specified in the authorisation or relevant part thereof.[97] SEPA is required to determine the application within two months, or such longer period as may be agreed with the applicant in writing.[98] SEPA is required to notify the applicant of its decision, and if SEPA refuses the application, SEPA is required to give reasons for its decision.[99] If SEPA fails to determine the application within the requisite period, the application is deemed to have been granted.[100]

Surrender of authorisation

The CAR makes provision for the surrender of an authorisation which takes the form either of registration or water use licence. In circumstances where it is intended to cease the relevant activity or the activity has ceased, if the authorisation is by way of registration, the operator is required to notify SEPA of the intention to cease the authorised activity and also the date on which it will cease as soon as that information is known to the operator, and in any event, notify SEPA within seven days of the cessation of the activity.[101]

If, however, the authorisation is by way of a water use licence, the person responsible is required to apply to SEPA to surrender the licence.[102] In such a case the application falls, in effect, to be treated as if it were an application for an authorisation.[103] Before SEPA determines whether to grant or to refuse such an application, SEPA is required to assess the risk which is posed to the water environment by the cessation of the relevant activity.[104] SEPA is also required to take account of any steps which are (a) necessary in order to avoid any risk of adverse impact on the water environment which results from the cessation of the activity, and (b) leave the relevant part of the water environment which is affected by the authorised activity in a state which will permit compliance with any relevant requirements of certain specified legislation.[105] SEPA is required to give notice of its determination of an application to surrender an authorisation within a period of three months, or such longer period as may be agreed with the applicant in writing.[106] If SEPA fails to determine the application within the specified period, the application is deemed to have been granted at the end of such period.[107]

Suspension and revocation of authorisation
SEPA may suspend or revoke an authorisation, either in whole or in part, by serving a notice on the responsible person or operator.[108] In the case of a partial suspension or partial revocation, the notice requires to specify: (a) the extent to which the authorisation is being suspended or revoked, (b) the date (which must be at least twenty-eight days from the date on which the notice is served) on which the suspension or revocation is to take effect, and (c) the reasons for the suspension or revocation.[109] The authorisation ceases to have effect, either in whole or in part, from the date which is specified in the notice.[110] However, SEPA may lift the suspension of an operation by serving a notice either on the person responsible or operator.[111] The notice is required to specify, in relation to a partial suspension, the extent to which the authorisation remains suspended; the date on which any form of suspension takes effect; and the reasons for lifting any suspension.[112]

Monitoring and enforcement etc.

The overall duty to monitor and also enforce the CAR regime falls on SEPA.[113] However, in relation to the Northumbria River Basin District[114] and the Solway Tweed River Basin District,[115] SEPA is required to consult and collaborate, as is necessary, with the Environment Agency.[116] SEPA is empowered to carry out examinations and investigations which it deems necessary through such persons as it deems appropriate for enforcing the relevant regulations.[117]

The CAR regime makes provision for enforcement by way of enforcement notices. SEPA may serve an enforcement notice on the relevant person where such a person has carried out a controlled activity, is carrying out or is likely to carry out a controlled activity, and SEPA is of the opinion that the activity:

(i)   has contravened, is contravening or is likely to contravene an authorisation under the CAR,

(ii) has caused, is causing or is likely to cause significant adverse impacts on the water environment, or any part of it,

(iii) has caused, is causing or is likely to cause an indirect discharge into groundwater of any hazardous substance or any other pollutant.[118]

SEPA is empowered to serve a notice on the responsible person or the operator specifying:

(a) the activity,

(b) if SEPA is of the opinion that the activity has contravened, is contravening or is likely to contravene an authorisation under CAR, the matters which constitute the contravention or likely contravention,

(c) if SEPA is of the opinion that the activity has caused, is causing or is likely to cause a significant adverse impact on the water environment, the nature of that impact,

(d) if SEPA is of the opinion that the activity has caused, is causing or is likely to cause a direct or indirect discharge into groundwater of any hazardous substance, or any other pollutant, details of that discharge or indirect discharge,

(e) the steps which are to be taken by the person responsible or the operator which SEPA considers to be necessary or appropriate to prevent, mitigate or reduce or remedy the contravention of the authorisation, the adverse impact on the water environment, or the direct or indirect discharge into the water environment.

SEPA must revoke an enforcement notice if:

(a) the contravention or likely contravention of an authorisation has ceased and is unlikely to recur,

(b) the adverse impacts or likely adverse impacts of the water environment have ceased and are unlikely to recur and any remedial mitigating or preventative steps which are required by SEPA have been carried out,

(c) the direct or indirect or likely direct or indirect discharge to groundwater has ceased and is unlikely to recur and any remedial mitigating or preventative steps which have been required by SEPA have been carried out.[119]

Remedial action by SEPA

If SEPA considers that an enforcement notice should be served, SEPA is entitled to take any steps that would be identified in that notice, or secure that those steps are taken, either if it considers it is necessary to do so forthwith, or it appears to SEPA, after reasonable enquiry, that no person can be found on whom to serve such notice.[120] If SEPA has either carried out or has secured the carrying-out of an investigation in order to establish whether or not an enforcement notice is necessary and, if necessary, on whom such notice requires to be served, or SEPA has taken steps or secured that steps (which would have been identified in the enforcement notice) have been carried out, SEPA may recover the costs from the responsible person or operator who has carried out or is likely to carry out the activity in respect of which the notice would have been served.[121]

Enforcement by the courts

If SEPA is of the opinion that proceedings for an offence for failing to comply with the requirements of an enforcement notice would afford an ineffectual remedy against any person, SEPA may take proceedings before any court of competent jurisdiction in order to secure compliance with the notice.[122]

Information and registers

The Scottish Ministers may, by notice, require SEPA to furnish it with such information about the discharge of its functions in terms of the CAR as the former may require.[123] SEPA may itself serve a notice on any person requiring that person to furnish the former within the period which is specified in the notice, any information which SEPA reasonably considers is necessary for the purpose of any function which is conferred on SEPA by the Water Environment and Water Services (Scotland) Act 2003, the Water Environment (Water Framework Directive) (Northumbria River District Basin) Regulations 2003,[124] the Water Environment (Water Framework Directive) (Solway Tweed River Basin District) Regulations 2004,[125] and the CAR.[126]

The information which a person may be required to furnish SEPA must include information which, although it is not in possession of that person, or would not otherwise come into possession of that person, is information which it is reasonable to require that person to obtain for the purpose of complying with the information notice.[127] However, nothing in the afore-mentioned provisions authorises either the Scottish Ministers or SEPA to require the disclosure of anything which a person would be entitled to refuse to disclose on grounds of confidentiality in proceedings in the Court of Session.[128]

SEPA is required to maintain a register which contains specified information.[129] The CAR makes provision for the exclusion of commercially confidential information from the register.[130]

Appeals, offences etc.
The following persons can appeal to the Scottish Ministers against the decision of SEPA:

(a)   a person who has been refused the grant of authorisation of a controlled activity, or is deemed to have been refused the grant of such authorisation,

(b)   a person who has been granted a form of registration which is different from the form of authorisation which that person believes ought to have been granted,

(c)   a person who is aggrieved by the terms and conditions which are attached to an authorisation,

(d)   a person who has been served with a variation notice, or a person who is aggrieved with the conditions which are attached to such a notice,

(e)   a person who has been refused the variation of an authorisation,

(f)   a person who has been granted the variation of an authorisation but that person is aggrieved by the removal, addition or amendment of any condition which is pursuant to that variation,

(g)   a person whose application to effect a transfer of authorisation has been refused, or a person who is aggrieved by the conditions which are attached to that person's authorisation to take account of such a transfer,

(h)   a person whose application to surrender an authorisation has been refused or a person who is aggrieved by the conditions which are attached to the authorisation in order to take account of the surrender,

(i)   a person whose authorisation has been suspended or revoked,

(j)   a person on whom an enforcement notice has been served,

(k)   if SEPA has determined that information is not commercially confidential, the person to whom or whose business that information relates.[131]

The CAR make provision for a number of offences, amongst which is the offence for a person to:

(i)   contravene reg 4,

(ii)   fail to comply with a general binding rule,

(iii) fail to comply with or contravene a registration, including any condition which has been imposed,

(iv)   fail to comply with or contravene a water use license, including any condition which has been imposed,

(v)   fail to comply with an enforcement with an enforcement notice.[132]

Provision is made for offences which have been committed by a body corporate, a limited liability partnership, and a Scottish partnership (other than a limited liability partnership).[133]

Where an offence by any person is due to the act or default of some other person, that other person may be charged with and convicted of the offence, whether or not proceedings are taken against the first mentioned person.[134]

Provision is also made for defences to the principal offences under the CAR. A person is not guilty of any such offence if:

(a)   the contravention is the result of:

(i)   an accident which could not have reasonably been foreseen,

(ii)   natural causes or *force majeure* which are exceptional or could not reasonably have been foreseen,

(iii) an act or omission by a category 1 or 2 responder[135] that is reasonably necessary to protect people, property or the environment from imminent risk of serious harm,

(b)   all practical steps are taken to prevent deterioration of the water environment,

(c)   all practical steps are taken as soon as reasonably practicable to restore the water environment to its condition prior to the contravention, and,

(d)   particulars of the contravention are furnished to SEPA as soon as practicable after it occurs.[136]

Where a person is convicted of a principal offence under the CAR which has an adverse impact on the water environment, and it appears to the court that it is in the power of that person to either mitigate or remedy such an impact, the court may, either in addition to or instead of imposing any punishment, order that person within a specified period to take steps which are specified in the order, to remedy those matters.[137] Before making the order the court is required to have regard to any representations of SEPA as to the steps which are required to mitigate or remedy the adverse impact.[138]

Sewerage

We have already observed the public health problems which can arise from ineffective sewerage and drainage.[139] We have also seen how legislation gave local authorities increasing powers to make adequate provision for the sewerage of their areas. Increasingly, over the twentieth century, larger local authority units were charged with the responsibility of providing adequate sewerage to their respective areas. The Sewerage (Scotland) Act 1968[140] ('the Act') which, in effect, radically reformed the law relating to sewerage and drainage (which had experienced little substantive change since 1897 with advent of the Public Health (Scotland) Act 1897)[141] in Scotland. At present, Scottish Water (SW) is the authority responsible for the provision of sewerage in Scotland. The main provisions of the Act are now discussed.

Duties and powers of SW to provide sewerage etc.
Scottish Water is placed under a duty to provide such public sewers[142] and public sustainable urban drainage (SUD) systems[143] as may be necessary for effectually draining its area of domestic sewage,[144] surface water,[145] and trade effluent,[146] and to make such provision, by way of sewage treatment works,[147] or otherwise, as may be necessary for effectually dealing with the contents of its sewers and SUD systems.[148] Scottish Water is under a duty to take its public sewers to such point or points as will enable owners of the premises which are to be served by the sewers to connect their drains or private sewers with the public sewers at a reasonable cost.[149] However, SW is under no such duty if it has contracted with a private provider to carry out this duty.

Duty to maintain etc. sewers

Scottish Water has a duty to inspect, maintain and repair, cleanse and empty, ventilate and, where appropriate, renew all sewers, SUD systems, sewage treatment works, and other works which are vested in it by virtue of the Sewerage (Scotland) Act 1968 or the Water Industry (Scotland) Act 2002.[150] In the House of Lords case of *RHM Bakeries v Strathclyde Regional Council*[151] it was held that the duty to maintain a public sewer was not absolute.[152]

The Sewerage (Scotland) Act 1968 ('the Act') allows SW to construct a public sewer or SUD system, in on or under any road or under any cellar or vault below any road or in, on or over any land not forming part of a road.[153] Furthermore, SW may construct public sewage treatment works in or on any land either held by it or appropriated for that purpose. Before commencing the construction of a sewer or SUD system in, on or over any land not forming part of a road, SW is required to serve notice of its intention on the owner and occupier of the relevant land with a description of the proposed works and the right to object thereto.[154] However, within a period of three months after the service of the notice, if the owner[155] or the occupier objects to the proposed works, and that objection is not withdrawn, SW may not execute the works without their consent. In such circumstances SW may refer the matter to the sheriff by summary application. In turn, the sheriff may refuse consent, or he may grant consent either unconditionally or subject to such terms and conditions as he considers just. The decision of the sheriff is final. The sheriff has complete powers of review. In other words, he is not simply confined to considering whether SW has complied with the requisite statutory procedure.[156]

SW may authorise a person to construct on its own behalf a public sewer, whether or not it connects with its own sewers or sewage treatment works:

(1) in, under or over any road or under any cellar or vault below any road,

(2) in, on or over any land which does not form any part of a road and is not land in respect of which he is owner, lessee or occupier.[157]

In such a case, the same notification procedure, as described above, applies to the relevant authorised person as applies to SW.[158] In giving its authorisation to another person to execute such works, or, in relation to any sewer or SUD system, not being a sewer or SUD system which is being constructed on behalf of SW (the construction of which does not require such authorisation), SW may, in the case where a proposed sewer or SUD will connect with either its sewer, SUDs or sewage treatment works, determine (by written notice) that all or part of the sewer or SUD will not vest in SW under the Act,[159] but rather in him.[160] However, SW may, either then or at some later date, enter into an agreement under which the relevant sewer or SUD is to vest in SW.

Scottish Water powers to close, alter etc. public sewers

Scottish Water is given the power to close, alter or replace any sewer, SUD system, sewage treatment works or other works vested in it either under the Sewerage (Scotland) Act 1968 or under the Water Industry (Scotland) Act 2002.[161] However, before any person who is lawfully using the relevant sewer etc. is deprived of such use, SW is required to provide a sewer etc. which functions equally effectively as the sewer etc. which has been taken out of use. Furthermore, SW is required to carry out, at its own expense, any work which is necessary to connect his drain or private sewer with the sewer or works so provided.

Agreements between SW and roads authorities

In order to provide coherence and overall efficiency of the sewerage system, a roads authority may enter into an agreement with SW as to the provision, management, maintenance or use of their sewers, SUD systems or drains for the conveyance of water from the surface of a road or the surface from any premises.[162] However, neither the roads authority nor SW may unreasonably refuse to enter into such an agreement for such purposes or unreasonably insist upon terms and conditions which are unacceptable to the other party.[163] Any dispute as to whether either the relevant roads authority or SW is acting unreasonably requires to be determined by the Scottish Government, whose decision is final.

Agreement to provide sewers etc.

If SW is satisfied that premises are to be constructed in its area, it may enter into an agreement with that person as to the construction as to the provision by that person or by SW of sewers, SUD systems and sewage treatment works to serve those premises.[164] The relevant agreement may specify both the terms and conditions on which the work is to be carried out, including provision as to the taking-over by SW of SUD systems and sewage treatment works so provided. Importantly, the agreement is enforceable against SW by the owner or occupier of the relevant premises for the time being.

SW may enter into such an agreement only if it has no duty to provide public sewers to the premises under s 1 of the Act.[165]

Right of owners and occupiers of premises to connect etc. with public sewer

The owner of any premises has the right to connect his drains, private sewers and private SUD systems with the sewers, SUD systems or sewage treatment works of SW.[166] In turn, the occupier of the relevant premises is entitled to use such private drains, private sewers and private SUD systems to discharge both domestic sewage and surface water from the premises into the public sewer, SUD systems or sewage treatment works. However, the relevant owner does not have the right to connect his drains, private sewers and private SUD systems or sewage treatment works with the drains, sewers or SUD systems of SW unless the intervening land is land through which the owner is entitled to construct a drain, sewer or SUD system.[167]

The owner who proposes to connect his drains, SUD systems, or sewage treatment works of SW or to alter a drain, sewer or SUD system which is connected with such sewer, SUD system or works in such a manner as to interfere with them, is required to give SW notice of his proposals.[168] SW must, within twenty-eight days, refuse permission for the relevant connection or alteration, or grant such permission subject to such conditions as it thinks fit. Any such permission may, in particular, specify the mode and point of connection and, where there are separate public sewers for foul water and surface water, prohibit the discharge of foul water into the sewer which is reserved for surface water and vice versa. If SW either refuses such permission or grants it subject to conditions, the owner must be informed of the reasons for such a decision and also of his right of appeal.[169] The owner who is aggrieved by the decision of SW has the right of appeal to the Scottish Ministers.[170] The Scottish Ministers may confirm the decision, and any such conditions, either with or without modification, or it may refuse to confirm the decision. In *Tayside Regional Council v Secretary of State for Scotland*[171] it was held that in determining an appeal, provided that the rules of natural justice were complied with, the Secretary of State was not confined to considering matters which had been given as grounds for refusal of permission. The Secretary of State could consider other factors.

It is an offence for a person to connect (or alter) a drain, sewer, or SUD system to the sewers, SUD systems or works of SW without the necessary permission.[172]

Power of Scottish Water to direct manner of construction of works

Where the owner of any premises proposes either to construct a drain, sewer, or SUD system in relation to which notice has been given to SW,[173] or he proposes to construct a sewage treatment works in respect of which notice has been given to SW,[174] SW may, if it considers that the proposed drain, sewer, SUD system or works either is, or is likely to be, needed to form part of a general sewerage system which it either has provided or proposes to provide, direct him to construct the drain, sewer, SUD system or works in a manner differing from that in which he proposes to construct the drain, sewer, SUD system or other works.[175] The person to whom such a direction is given can appeal to the Scottish Ministers who may either disallow the direction or allow it, with or without modification.[176] Where SW has issued a direction, SW is required to pay to the person who is constructing the drain, sewer, SUD system or sewage treatment works, the extra expenses which are reasonably incurred by him in complying with the direction.[177] Until the drain, sewer, SUD system or works become vested in SW, it is required to pay him any expenses which are reasonably incurred by him in repairing operating or maintaining the drain, sewer, SUD system or works as may be attributable to its direction having been made and complied with. Any dispute as to the amount of payment which SW requires to make to the person who has carried out the relevant work may be referred to the sheriff, whose decision on the matter is final. It is made an offence for any person who has been directed by SW to construct a drain, sewer, SUD system or sewage treatment works in a particular manner to construct them otherwise than in accordance with the direction or any modified direction.[178]

Power to remedy defects in drains etc.

Power is given to both SW and a local authority to require, by notice, the owner or occupier of any premises to remedy any defect[179] in any drain, SUD system, sewage treatment works (other than drains, SUD systems or works which are vested in SW) within a reasonable time.[180] A person served with a notice can refer the matter to the sheriff who can issue such directions as he thinks fit and whose decision on the matter is final.[181]

In the face of the owner or occupier failing to comply with the terms of the notice, SW or the local authority can carry out the relevant works and recover the costs from the person on whom the notice was served.[182]

Vesting of sewers etc. in Scottish Water

One of the most important provisions of the Act relates to the vesting of sewers etc. in SW. The following vest in SW:

(a)   All sewers, SUD systems, and sewage treatment works constructed by it at its expense in terms of its general duties to provide sewerage in its area,

(b)   All junctions with its sewers, whether constructed at the expense of SW or otherwise,

(c)   All private sewers and private SUD systems connecting with its sewers or sewage treatment works,

(d)   All sewage treatment works and SUD systems which SW takes over by agreement or otherwise.[183]

Vesting of certain private sewers etc.

The vesting of private sewers, the construction of which has been authorised by SW, has already been discussed.[184]

Furthermore, there vests in the person whom SW authorises under the Act[185] to construct a sewer which does not connect with SW's sewers or sewage treatment works, that sewer.[186] That sewer remains his property and he is solely responsible for its management, maintenance and renewal. However, SW may enter into an agreement that the sewer, SUD system or any part of it is to vest in SW.[187]

Power of Scottish Water to take over private sewage treatment works

Scottish Water may take over either the whole or part of any private sewage treatment works or private SUD system by agreement with the owner or, failing such agreement, by compulsion.[188] If SW wishes to adopt the latter means of acquiring the works or SUD, SW is required to intimate its intention to do so by notice. Such notice may include conditions which relate to compensation by it.[189] The notice must inform the owner of his right of appeal to the Scottish Ministers. If such an appeal is made, the Scottish Ministers may confirm the proposals of SW and any conditions so specified, either with or without modification, or the former may refuse to confirm them.[190] All works which are taken over by SW then vest in it.[191]

Trade effluents

It is important that effluent from industrial sources is controlled in order to prevent the sewage treatment works into which the effluent flows being adversely affected. Another reason for the need for such a form of regulation is to protect sewer workers from harm. Part II of the Act allows SW to regulate the discharge of trade effluent into public sewers.

Right to discharge into public sewers

The occupier of any trade premises within the area of SW has the right to discharge any trade effluent[192] from the premises into a sewer or sewage treatment works of SW.[193] However, the right of the occupier to discharge trade effluent into such a sewer or works is circumscribed by the provision that any occupier who discharges such effluent into the sewers or sewage treatment works of SW without the consent of SW (where such consent is required) or contrary to any direction or condition which is imposed under the Act, commits an offence.[194]

Control of new discharges

The Act makes specific provision in relation to new discharges[195] of trade effluent into public sewers or the sewage treatment works of SW. The occupier of trade premises who proposes to make a new discharge of trade effluent from those premises into the sewers or sewage treatment works of SW requires to obtain its consent.[196] SW may refuse its consent, or may grant its consent either unconditionally or subject to such conditions as SW thinks fit.[197] Whereas SW has wide discretion as to the conditions it can impose in granting consent, the Act specifies a wide variety of conditions which SW can impose on granting such consent. There include conditions relating to the sewers into which any trade effluent can be discharged, the nature or composition of any trade effluent which may be discharged, and the daily quantity and maximum hourly rate at which such effluent may be discharged.[198]

The applicant can appeal to the Scottish Ministers against a decision of SW to refuse its consent or against any conditions which SW attaches to such consent.[199] The decision of the Scottish Ministers is deemed to be that of SW from whose decision the appeal is made.[200] The decision by the Scottish Ministers is final.[201] However, at any stage of the proceedings of the appeal, the Scottish Ministers may, and if so directed by the Court of Session, must, state a case for the opinion of the Court on any question of law which arises in the proceedings. Pending a decision on any appeal to the Scottish Ministers, a discharge of trade effluent may continue to be made in accordance with the conditions then applying.[202]

Review of consents etc.

Scottish Water may, and when requested to do so by the occupier of the relevant premises, review by direction a decision which SW has made regarding consents, conditions and refusals.[203] Before making any direction, SW is required to take into account any representations which have been made by the occupier.[204] However, no review may take place until two years after SW has made a decision as to whether consent should be granted or two years after the previous review, unless the applicant has otherwise agreed in writing.[205]

Existing discharges
The Act also makes provision for the control of existing discharges[206] of effluent from trade premises. Any dispute between SW and the person making the discharge as to whether the discharge is an existing discharge requires to be determined by the sheriff, against whose determination an appeal lies to the Court of Session.[207] Except where SW and the person who is making the discharge agree otherwise, an existing discharge is allowed to continue.[208]

Review of existing discharges
Scottish Water may, and when requested by the person who is making the discharge, review the making of an existing discharge, and SW may direct that any condition of the discharge is either unconditional or subject to such conditions as it thinks fit to impose.[209] Furthermore, SW may by direction, from time to time, and when requested by the person making the discharge, review such a direction.[210] However, unless SW and the person who is making the direction otherwise agree in writing, reviews may not take place at intervals which are less than two years. An appeal lies to the Scottish Ministers against such a direction.[211] A similar procedure to that which relates to a direction concerning a new discharge, applies to such an appeal.[212] However, where SW has directed that the continuation of a discharge is subject to conditions which did not previously apply to the making of the discharge, and an appeal is made against the imposition of those conditions, SW requires to establish that the circumstances of the making of the discharge or its reception, treatment or disposal are so altered as compared with those which pertained before 16 May 1973, that it is reasonable that those conditions should be imposed.

Under the Urban Waste Water Treatment (Scotland) Regulations 1994[213] SW is under a general duty to ensure that as far as its functions under the Act which relate to trade effluents with respect to the discharge of industrial waste water,[214] to secure that the provisions of the Regulations are met in relation to that discharge. Furthermore, SW is required to review, and if necessary, for the purposes of complying with the Regulations, modify, any consent which has been granted under the Act.[215] Furthermore, any directions which have been made in relation to such consents also require to be reviewed for the same purposes.

Public register
Scottish Water is required to maintain a register for the purposes of the Act.[216] The register is required to contain certain prescribed information.[217]

The Act makes provision for the exclusion from the register of information which affects national security.[218]

Summary

- At common law an action can be founded on harm which the pursuer sustains by virtue of pollution of a watercourse which has been caused by the erection of an *opus manufactum* (new works) or an activity which the defender is conducting on his land.
- Law and policy relating to water pollution is currently EU-driven.
- The most important Directive relating to the pollution of water is the Water Framework Directive (WFD).
- The Water Environment and Water Services (Scotland) Act 2003 (WEWS Act) implements the WFD.
- The WEWS Act makes special provision for the prevention of water pollution.
- Activities which could potentially threaten the purity of watercourses, 'controlled activities' are regulated under the CAR regulations by SEPA through a system of binding rules, registration and licensing.
- The CAR regime is enforced by enforcement notices.
- Scottish Water (SW) is responsible for the provision of sewerage in Scotland.
- SW is placed under a statutory duty to effectively drain its area.
- SW has special control over trade effluents.

Notes

1. See p. 3-4 incl.
2. See *Cambridge Water Co v Eastern Counties Leather* [1994] 2 AC 264.
3. See, e.g., *RHM Bakeries (Scotland) Ltd. v Strathclyde Regional Council* 1985 SC(HL) 17.
4. 1996 SC 95 at 99.
5. (1876) 3 R 461.
6. See, e.g., *Potter v Hamilton and Strathaven Railway Co* (1864) 3 M 83. See also *Kerr v Earl of Orkney* (1857) 20 D 298.
7. (1853) 15 D 853.
8. 1908 SC 340.
9. Ibid. at 349. For a discussion of liability for *opera manufacta* see F. McManus, 'Liability for opera manufacta (new works) in Scots law' 1998 Jur Rev 281.
10. 1853 15 D 853.
11. Ibid. at 859.

12. Ibid. at 860.
13. (1866) 5 M 214.
14. Ibid. at 217.
15. 1893 AC 691.
16. H. Burn-Murdoch, *The Scots Law of Interdict* (W. Hodge, 1933) at 204.
17. See F. McManus, 'Common law nuisance', in F. McManus (gen. ed.), *Environmental Law in Scotland* (W. Green/SULI) paras 3.64-3.72. See also, F. McManus and E. Russell *Delict*, 2nd edn (Edinburgh University Press, 2011) p. 161-4.
18. For a discussion of the effectiveness of injunctions against municipal authorities in England during the nineteenth century, see L. Rosenthal, *The River Pollution Dilemma in Victorian England* (Ashgate, 2014).
19. See p. 101.
20. Repealed.
21. For a more detailed discussion of the development of the statutory controls over river pollution in Scotland, see S. Hendry, 'Water resources and water pollution', in F. McManus (gen. ed.), *Environmental Law in Scotland* paras 6.20-6.23.
22. L. Kramer, *EU Environmental Law*, 7th edn (Sweet and Maxwell) para 7-01.
23. Ibid. at para 6.24.
24. Directive 2000/60/EU.
25. Ibid. Preamble, para 1.
26. Ibid. Art 1. These different types of water are defined in Art 2.
27. Ibid Art 4.
28. Ibid. Art 13.
29. S. Hendry (note 21) at para 6.42.
30. Water Environment and Water Services (Scotland) Act 2003, s 4(1).
31. SSI 2003 No 610, Art 2.
32. Water Environment and Water Services (Scotland) Act 2003, s 5(1).
33. Ibid. s 5(2).
34. Ibid. s 5(3).
35. Ibid. s 5(5).
36. SSI 2013 No 323.
37. Directive 2008/105/EC.
38. Directive 2006/118/EC.
39. Water Environment and Water Services (Scotland) Act 2003, s 5A(1). See the Water Environment (Shellfish Water Protected Areas: Environmental Objectives etc.) (Scotland) Regulations 2013 (SSI 2013 No 325).
40. Ibid. s 8(1).
41. Ibid. s 8(2).
42. Ibid. s 9(1).

43. Ibid. s 10(1).
44. Ibid. regs 11-14.
45. January 2015.
46. Water Environment and Water Services (Scotland) Act 2003, s 20(1).
47. SSI 2011 No 209 (as amended).
48. Ibid. reg 3(1).
49. Ibid. reg 4.
50. Ibid. reg 5.
51. Ibid. reg 6(1) and Sched 3.
52. Ibid. reg 7(1).
53. Ibid. reg 7(2).
54. Ibid. reg 7(3).
55. Ibid. reg 7(4).
56. Ibid. reg 8(1).
57. Ibid. reg 8(2).
58. Ibid. reg 8(3).
59. Ibid. reg 8(4).
60. Ibid. reg 8(5).
61. SME 'Environment' (re-issue) para 450.
62. Water Environment (Controlled Activities) (Scotland) Regulations 2011, reg 10(1).
63. Ibid. reg 11(1).
64. Ibid. reg 11(2).
65. Ibid. reg 11(3).
66. Ibid. reg 11(4).
67. Ibid. reg 11(6).
68. Ibid. reg 11(7).
69. Ibid. reg 11(8).
70. Ibid. reg 12(3).
71. Ibid. reg 13.
72. Ibid. reg 14(1).
73. Ibid. reg 14(3).
74. Ibid. reg 15(1).
75. Ibid. reg 15(2).
76. Ibid. reg 15(3).
77. Ibid. reg 15(4).
78. Ibid. reg 15(6).
79. Ibid. reg 20(1).
80. Ibid. reg 20(2).
81. Ibid. reg 20(3).
82. Ibid. reg 20(5).

83. Ibid. reg 21(1). SEPA are required, in carrying out the relevant review, to take into account any directions of the Scottish Ministers. See the Scotland River Basin District (Surface Water Typology, Environmental Standards, Condition Limits and Groundwater Threshold Values) Directions 2009, and the Solway Tweed River Basin District (Surface Water Typology, Environmental Standards, Condition Limits and Groundwater Threshold Values) Directions 2009.

84. Ibid. reg 21(2).

85. Ibid. reg 22(1).

86. Ibid. reg 22(2).

87. The 'responsible person' is the person who is responsible for complying with a water use licence; reg 2(1).

88. Ibid. reg 23(1).

89. Ibid. reg 23(2).

90. Ibid. reg 23(3).

91. Ibid. reg 23(4).

92. Ibid. reg 24(1).

93. Ibid. reg 24(2).

94. Ibid. reg 24(3).

95. Ibid. reg 24(4).

96. Ibid. reg 25(1).

97. Ibid. reg 25(3).

98. Ibid. reg 25(4).

99. Ibid. reg 25(5).

100. Ibid. reg 25(6).

101. Ibid. reg 27(1)(2).

102. Ibid. reg 27(3).

103. Ibid. reg 27(4).

104. Ibid. reg 27(5).

105. The relevant legislation is specified in Part 1 of Sched 4 to the CAR.

106. Ibid. reg 28(1).

107. Ibid. reg 28(5).

108. Ibid. reg 29(1).

109. Ibid. reg 29(2).

110. Ibid. reg 29(3).

111. Ibid. reg 29(4). In such a case the authorisation has effect from the date which is specified in the notice; ibid reg 29(6).

112. Ibid. reg 29(5).

113. Ibid. reg 31(1).

114. See the Water Environment (Water Framework Directive) (Northumbria River Basin District) Regulations 2003 (SI 2003 No 3245).

115. See the Water Environment (Water Framework Directive) (Solway Tweed River Basin District) Regulations 2004 (SI 2004 No 99).
116. Ibid. reg 31(2).
117. Ibid. reg 31(3). The relevant regulations are CAR and also the regulations cited in notes 114 and 115 above.
118. Ibid. reg 32(1)(2).
119. Ibid. reg 32(4).
120. Ibid. reg 33(1).
121. Ibid. reg 33(2). The CAR states '. . . in respect of which the notice is served' which must be an error!
122. Ibid. reg 35.
123. Ibid. reg 36(1).
124. SI 2003 No 3245
125. SI 2004 No 99.
126. Ibid. reg 36(2).
127. Ibid. reg 36(3).
128. Ibid. reg 36(4).
129. Ibid. reg 37(1). The information which is required to be included in the register is specified in Sched 8 to the CAR.
130. Ibid. regs 38-42.
131. Ibid. reg 50.
132. Ibid. reg 44(1).
133. Ibid. reg 45(1).
134. Ibid. reg 46.
135. In terms of the Civil Contingencies Act 2004.
136. CAR reg 48.
137. Ibid. reg 49(1).
138. Ibid. reg 49(2).
139. See p. 4-5 incl.
140. As amended.
141. Repealed.
142. 'Public sewer' means any sewer which is vested in Scottish Water; Sewerage (Scotland) Act 1968, s 59(1). A 'sewer' is defined as not including a drain but includes all sewers, pipes and drains used for the drainage of buildings and yards appurtenant to buildings. 'Drain' in relation to premises means any pipe or drain within the curtilage of those premises for the drainage of those premises used solely for or in connection with the drainage of one building or of any building or yards appurtenant to buildings within the same curtilage; ibid. reg 59(1). For a meaning of 'curtilage' see note 145 below.
143. A 'public SUD system' is a SUD system which is vested in Scottish Water; ibid. s 59(1).

144. 'Domestic sewage' in relation to any area or premises means sewage which is not surface water or trade effluent; ibid. s 59(1).

145. 'Surface water' means the run-off from roofs and any paved ground surface within the curtilage of premises; ibid. s 59(1). The word, 'curtilage' is not defined in the Act. However, in *Dyer v Dorset County Council* [1998] 3 WLR 213 it was held that the word 'curtilage' connoted a small area forming part or parcel with a house or building which it contained or to which it was attached. See also *McAlpine v Secretary of State for the Environment The Times*, 6 December 1994. In the Inner House case of *Sinclair-Lockhart's Trustees v Central Land Board* 1951 SC 258 at 264 Lord Mackintosh was of the opinion that the word 'curtilage' connoted land which is used for the comfortable enjoyment of a house.

146. 'Trade effluent' means any liquid, with or without particles of matter of suspension therein which is wholly or in part, produced in the course of trade or industry which is carried on in trade premises, and in relation to trade premises means any such liquid as aforesaid which is so produced in the course of any trade or industry at those premises. 'Trade and industry' for the purpose of the definition of 'trade effluent' includes premises which are used or are intended to be used in whole or in part, for carrying on agriculture, horticulture or scientific research or experiment or as a hospital or as accommodation which is provided by a home care service; ibid. s 59(1).

147. 'Sewage treatment works' means any works, apparatus or plant used for the treatment or disposal of sewage, and includes a septic tank but does not include a SUD system; ibid. s 59(1).

148. Ibid. s 1(1).

149. Ibid. s 1(2).

150. Ibid. s 2.

151. 1985 SC (HL) 17.

152. For a discussion on the potential liability in nuisance of Scottish Water for harm which is caused by overloaded sewers, see F. McManus, '*Marcic* rules OK? Liability in the law of nuisance in Scotland for overloaded sewers.' (2008) 19 *Water Law* 61.

153. Ibid. s 3(1).

154. Ibid. 3(2).

155. 'Owner' means the person who, for the time being is entitled to receive or would be entitled to receive, the rents of the premises, and includes a trustee, factor, tutor or curator, and in the case of public or municipal property applies to the persons to whom the management thereof is entrusted. 'Occupier' means the person in occupation or having the charge, management or control of premises, either on his own account or as the agent of another person; ibid. s 59(1).

156. See *Central Regional Council v Barbour European Ltd* 1982 SLT (Sh Ct) 49.
157. Sewerage (Scotland) Act 1968, s 3A(1).
158. Ibid. s 3A(1).
159. Ibid. s 16(1).
160. Ibid. s 3A(2).
161. Ibid. s 4.
162. Ibid. s 7(1).
163. Ibid. s 7(3).
164. Ibid. s 8(1).
165. Ibid. s 8(2).
166. Ibid. s 12(1).
167. Ibid. s 12(2).
168. Ibid. s 12(3).
169. Ibid. s 12(4).
170. Ibid. s 12(5).
171. 1996 SLT 473.
172. Ibid. s 12(8).
173. Under s 12(3) above.
174. Under s 14(2) below.
175. Ibid. s 14(1).
176. Ibid. s 14(3).
177. Ibid. s 14(5)
178. Ibid. s 14(6).
179. 'Defect' includes any obstruction in a drain, SUD or sewage treatment works; ibid. s 15(5).
180. Ibid. s 15(1).
181. Ibid. s 15(2).
182. Ibid. s 15(3).
183. Ibid. s 16(1).
184. See p. 231-2 incl.
185. Ibid. 3A(1).
186. Ibid. s 16A(1).
187. Ibid s 16A(1).
188. Ibid. s 17(1).
189. Ibid. s 17(2).
190. Ibid. s 17(3).
191. Ibid. s 17(4).
192. 'Trade effluent' means any liquid, either with or without particles of matter in suspension therein, which is wholly or in part produced in the course of any trade or industry carried on at trade premises, including trade waste water or waters heated in the course of any trade or industry and, in rela-

tion to any trade premises, means any such liquid as aforesaid which is so produced in the course of any trade or industry carried on at those premises. 'Trade or industry' for the purpose of the definition of 'trade effluent' includes agriculture, horticulture and scientific research or research or experiment, the carrying-on of a hospital and the provision of a care home service. The definition of 'trade premises' includes premises used or intended to be used in whole or in part for carrying on agriculture, horticulture or scientific research or experiment, or as a hospital or as accommodation provided by a care home service. Ibid. s 59(1).

193. Ibid. s 24(1).
194. Ibid. s 24(2).
195. 'New discharge' means a discharge from trade premises into the sewers or sewage treatment works of SW of trade effluent where the discharge:
    (i)   has not previously been lawfully made into such sewers or works, or
    (ii) not being an existing discharge as defined by s 33(1) of the Act, and has become substantially altered in nature or composition or whose nature or composition has been substantially increased since 16 May 1973, or
    (iii) has been discontinued for a period of two years or more, the whole or part of which period occurs after 16 May 1973 and is thereafter resumed; ibid. s 25.
196. Ibid. s 26.
197. Ibid. s 29(1).
198. Ibid. s 29(3).
199. Ibid. s 31.
200. Ibid. s 51(4).
201. Ibid. s 51(5).
202. Ibid. s 51(6).
203. Ibid. s 32(1).
204. Ibid. s 32(3).
205. Ibid. s 32(5).
206. An 'existing discharge' means a discharge of trade effluent from trade premises into the sewers or sewage treatment works of a local authority which was lawfully within two years prior to 16 May 1973, provided that where before the said date the local authority and the person making the discharge have agreed that after that date the nature or composition may be altered or the temperature, volume or rate of discharge may be increased, any discharge made in accordance with such agreement falls to be treated as an existing discharge; Ibid. s 33(1).
207. Ibid. s 33(2).
208. Ibid. s 34.
209. Ibid. s 36(1).

210. Ibid. s 36(2).
211. Ibid. s 36(3).
212. Ibid. s 36(4).
213. SI 1994 No 2842 reg 7(1).
214. 'Industrial waste water' means any waste water which is discharged from premises used for carrying on any trade or industry, other than domestic waste water and run-off waste water; ibid. reg 2(1).
215. Ibid. reg 7(5).
216. Ibid. s 37A(1).
217. Ibid. s 37A(2). The Trade Effluent (Registers)(Scotland) Regulations 1998 No 2533 prescribe the particulars which require to be entered in the register.
218. Ibid. s 37B.

CHAPTER 9

Integrated Pollution, Prevention and Control and Permitting

The regulation of pollution has traditionally been piecemeal, with different bodies having the responsibility of enforcing the law. However, such an uncoordinated approach to regulation is conducive to practical problems.

Currently the Pollution Prevention and Control Act 1999 makes provision for the Scottish Environment Protection Agency (SEPA) to regulate installations which have the potential to pollute the environment.

Introduction

In this chapter we discuss integrated pollution prevention and control and permitting. The regulation of pollution was traditionally piecemeal in the United Kingdom as a whole. This is a legacy of its Victorian origins.[1] Not only were a variety of different agencies involved in regulating various forms of pollution from both industrial and other sources, but often different agencies would be involved in regulating different forms of pollution from the same premises. For example, local authorities were, and still are, responsible for enforcing the provisions of the Clean Air Act 1956 in relation to grit and dust from certain industrial premises into the atmosphere, whereas the regulation of river pollution from the same premises fell to be regulated by the relevant rivers purification authority. In other words, the relevant agency simply possessed the statutory authority to regulate pollution into one medium. The disadvantage of such a fragmented approach to the control of pollution is that effective enforcement action by one agency may simply cause another environmental problem which falls to be dealt with by another agency. For example, consider a situation where a local authority requires the occupier of a factory to install grit arrestment plant in order to reduce the pollution from a chimney which serves a boiler in the factory. The arrestment plant which is subsequently installed uses water to extract the grit etc. from the relevant boiler. The resultant effluent is retained in settling tanks prior to being discharged into a watercourse. However, the filters at the outlet from the tank becomes blocked, the upshot of which is that the watercourse becomes polluted. The water pollution would require to be regulated by another agency. This problem in environmental regulation was recognised by the Royal Commission on Environmental Pollution in 1976.[2]

The first attempt which was made by Parliament to deal holistically with environmental pollution – that is to say, which took into account the environment as a whole – was the Control of Pollution Act 1974 (COPA) which dealt with waste, water, noise and atmospheric pollution. A good example of such a holistic approach to regulating pollution can be illustrated in the Act's approach to waste disposal. Under Part 1 of COPA,[3] a waste disposal authority, when it was considering whether to grant a waste licence, was required to refer the proposal to the relevant river purification authority and also to take into account representations which were made by the latter.

The move to a more integrated approach to pollution control continued in the form of the Environmental Protection Act 1990 (EPA).[4] The EPA has been described as the most significant British legislative effort so far, to achieve a comprehensive and all-embracing system of control over all (or at least most) aspects of certain potentially polluting processes.[5] In essence, the EPA dealt with processes and discharges which affect all environmental media. The EPA allowed certain industrial processes (described as 'prescribed processes') which could have a detrimental effect on the environment to be regulated. It was the intention of the EPA to make industries which posed a significant threat to the environment in general, such as petrochemical works, cement works and oil refineries, to be regulated by central government by way of integrated pollution control (IPC), and industries which posed a threat in terms of polluting the atmosphere to be regulated by local authorities by way of local authority air pollution control (LAPC). However, as far as Scotland is concerned, SEPA was solely responsible for enforcing both IPC and LAPC. In summary, the EPA allowed SEPA to regulate prescribed processes by authorising such processes and to attach conditions to such authorisations. In addition to this, the EPA had its own enforcement machinery which made provision for SEPA to serve both enforcement and prohibition notices. A new regime was instituted by the Pollution Prevention and Control Act 1999. The intention of the Act was to create a single unified pollution control regime, where, otherwise, the UK would have had two or three.[6] The Act is, in effect, simply a framework Act. The provisions of the Act are currently 'fleshed-out', as it were, by the Pollution Prevention and

Control (Scotland) Regulations 2012.[7] The Regulations make provision for an integrated pollution control regime for Scotland. The Regulations implement the Industrial Emissions Directive.[8] Other environmentally-polluting activities are also covered by the Regulations.

By way of a brief overview, the regime which is established by the Regulations requires that a person who operates an installation or mobile plant which falls within the scope of the Regulations is authorised to do so by a permit which is granted by SEPA. SEPA can also attach conditions to a permit in order to ensure that the installation does not present a significant threat to the environment. Provision is also made for both the transfer and variation of permits. Finally, the Regulations give SEPA the power to serve enforcement and suspension notices on the holder of a permit in order to secure compliance with the Regulations.

The Pollution Prevention and Control (Scotland) Regulations 2012

The Pollution Prevention and Control (Scotland) Regulations 2012 ('the Regulations') apply to all installations[9] which include mobile plant and which carry out an activity listed in Annex 1 to the Industrial Pollution Directive which is transposed by Schedule 1 and 2 of the Regulations. These schedules divides installations into 'Part A' processes and 'Part B' processes. Part A processes have the capacity to pollute the atmosphere, water and also land. Part B processes simply have the capacity to pollute the atmosphere. Part A installations are, therefore, subject to integrated pollution prevention and control (IPPC), whereas Part B installations are subject to local air pollution control. However, SEPA is the relevant enforcing authority for both Part A and Part B installations.[10] No person may operate a Part A or a Part B installation, or any mobile plant or a solvents installation, unless authorised to do so by a permit.[11]

Applying for a permit

SEPA must, on receiving an application which is submitted in conformity with the requirements of the Regulations, either grant a permit subject to the conditions which are required, or authorised to be imposed by or under the Regulations, or the Landfill (Scotland) Regulations 2003,[12] or, SEPA may refuse the application.[13] However, SEPA is required to refuse an application if it considers that the applicant will not be the person who will have control over the operation of the relevant installation or mobile plant, after the grant of the permit, or, that the applicant will not ensure that the installation or mobile plant is operated so as to comply with the conditions which would be included in the permit.[14] A permit may authorise the operation of more than one Part A or Part B installation, mobile plant, or solvents installation on the same site if operated by the same operator.[15]

SEPA may include a condition in a permit which imposes a limit on the amount or composition of any substance which is produced or utilised during the operation of the installation or mobile plant in any period, or which is supplemental or incidental to other conditions which are contained in the permit.[16] SEPA may exercise such a power separately from any requirement or power to include a condition in a permit which is provided for elsewhere in the Regulations.[17] However, in order to avoid duplication, SEPA may not include any condition in a permit for the purpose only of securing the health of persons at work.[18] Furthermore, where emissions of a pollutant are subject to conditions which are imposed for the purposes of the Greenhouse Gas Emissions Trading Scheme Regulations,[19] SEPA may not include an emission limit value in a permit unless the installation is excluded from the ETS regime or SEPA considers the emission limit value is necessary in order to ensure that no significant local pollution is caused.[20]

SEPA may grant a permit in respect of a specified waste management activity only if it is satisfied that the applicant is a fit and proper person to carry out the activity, and that planning permission is in force under the Town and Country Planning (Scotland) Act 1997 where such permission is required.[21] In determining whether a person is a fit and proper person, SEPA is required to do so by reference to the ability of the person concerned to fulfil the conditions of the permit which apply, or will apply, to the carrying-out of that activity.[22]

A person is not a fit and proper person if, in particular, it appears to SEPA that:

(a)   the person or a relevant person[23] has been convicted of a relevant offence,

(b)   the person has not made adequate financial provision to ensure that obligations arising from the permit in relation to the activity are met, and any closures procedures required under the permit are followed,

(c)   the person and all staff who are engaged in carrying out such an activity will not be provided with adequate professional technical development and training, or

(d)   the management of such an activity will not be in the hands of a technically competent person.[24]

However, para (4)(a) does not apply where SEPA considers it appropriate to treat the person as being a fit and proper person.[25] Furthermore, para

(4)(b) does not apply in respect of landfill sites which are specified in regulation 6 of the Landfill (Scotland) Regulations 2003.[26]

Permits may only be transferred and also cease to have effect in accordance with the provisions of the Regulations.[27]

Conditions: general principles

The Regulations require general principles to apply to all permits.[28] In determining the conditions which apply to a permit which relate to both Part A and Part B installations and mobile plant, SEPA is required to ensure that all the appropriate preventative measures are taken against pollution, in particular through application of the best available techniques,[29] and that no significant pollution is caused.[30] As far as Part A installations are concerned, additional general principles apply.[31] These principles are that:

(a)   installations should be operated in such a way that-
   (i)   waste generation is prevented, and where waste is produced it is, in order of priority and in accordance with the Waste Framework Directive prepared for re-use, recycled, recovered or, where that is technically and economically impossible, disposed of while avoiding or reducing any impact on the environment,
   (ii)   energy is used efficiently, and
   (iii) the necessary measures are taken to prevent accidents and limit their consequences, and
(b)   the necessary measures are taken on final cessation of activities to avoid any pollution risk, and to return the site of the installation to a satisfactory state.

Conditions: general provisions

The Regulations go on to require general conditions to be included in permits. SEPA is required to include a condition in a permit for a Part A or Part B installation or any mobile plant that the operator must use the best available techniques (BAT)[32] for preventing or, where that is not practicable, reducing emissions from an installation or mobile plant.[33] However, in order to avoid duplication, this requirement does not apply to the extent that any other condition of a permit, or a standard rule,[34] which has the effect as a standard rules condition, has the same effect.[35]

As far as conditions which apply to a Part A installation are concerned, SEPA is required to include in a permit the conditions which it considers appropriate to comply with the provisions of reg 23(2), and also to ensure that by means of the principles which are enshrined in reg 22, a high level of protection for the environment as a whole, taking particular account for that purpose of the general principles in reg 21.[36] Regulation 23(2) requires a permit for a Part A installation to include, *inter alia*, conditions:

(i) aimed at minimising long-distance or transboundary pollution,
(ii) ensuring, where necessary, appropriate protection of the soil and groundwater, including requirements for the regular maintenance and surveillance of measures taken to prevent emissions to soil and groundwater, and
(iii) ensuring, where necessary, appropriate monitoring and management of waste produced by the installation,
(iv) setting out suitable emission monitoring requirements specifying measurement methodology, frequency, and evaluation procedure.
(v) requiring the operator to supply SEPA regularly, and at least annually, with results of the monitoring of emissions,
(vi) requiring the operator to inform SEPA, without delay, of any incident or accident which significantly affects the environment.

As far as conditions which apply to Part B installations and mobile plant are concerned, SEPA is required to include in the relevant permit the conditions which SEPA considers appropriate, when taken with the principles which are enshrined in reg 22, for the purpose of preventing or, where that is not practicable, reducing emissions into the air, taking particular account for that purpose of the general principles which are set out in reg 21(2).[37]

As far as both Part A and Part B installations are concerned, SEPA may include in a permit a condition which requires an operator to carry out works, or do other things in relation to land which does not form part of the site of the installation, an 'off-site' condition, whether or not the operator is not entitled to carry out such works or to do that thing in relation to the land.[38] This power would, for example, allow SEPA to include a condition in a permit to require the relevant operator to construct a drain in land which is owned by another, which adjoins the installation.

The person whose consent would be required to carry out such works etc. must either grant, or join in granting, the operator such rights in relation to the land as will enable the operator to comply with an off-site condition.[39]

Conditions: emission limit values and environmental quality standards
SEPA is required to ensure that a permit either for a Part A or a Part B installation or a mobile plant includes certain conditions which relate to emissions[40] from the installation.[41] In summary, a permit is required to

include emission limit values[42] for polluting substances which are listed in Sched 5, and also other polluting substances which are likely to be emitted in significant quantities from an installation or any mobile plant, having regard for that purpose to the nature of the pollutant, and, in the case of a Part A installation, the potential for emissions to transfer pollution from one environmental medium to another.[43] SEPA may supplement or replace an emission limit value by an equivalent parameter or technical measure which ensures an equivalent level of protection for the environment.[44] An emission limit value must apply at the point at which the emissions leave the installation or mobile plant, any dilution before that point being disregarded for the purpose of determining the value.[45] An emission limit value may apply to groups of pollutants rather than to individual pollutants.[46]

The Regulations also make specific provision for the implementation of EU Directives including that part of the Industrial Emissions Directive relating to large combustion plants, installations which produce titanium oxide, volatile organic compounds (VOCs) and solvents.[47]

Standard rules

The Regulations make provision for the rule-making authority (namely, SEPA or the Scottish Ministers)[48] to make standard rules to apply generally to installations or mobile plants.[49] The rule-making authority is required to ensure that when either making or revising standard rules, the rules give effect to the best available techniques for preventing, or where that is not practicable, reducing, emissions from an installation or any mobile plant.[50] A rule-making authority may only make or revise standard rules if it is satisfied that the operation of an installation or any mobile plant will, to the extent that it is covered by a standard rules condition, result in the same level of environmental protection, and in the case of a Part A installation, the same level of integrated pollution prevention and control, as would result were 'tailor-made' conditions made applicable under Regulations.[51] A rule-making authority is required to keep standard rules which are made by the authority under review and revise any such rules whenever it considers necessary to do so in order to follow developments in best available techniques or ensure compliance with the Industrial Emissions Directive.[52] The rule-making authority is required, before making, revising or revoking standard rules, to consult those whom it considers representative of the interests of those communities which are likely to be affected by the proposed rules, relevant operators and also other interested parties.[53]

Review of permits

SEPA is required to review the conditions of a permit, *inter alia*, if:

(i)   the pollution which is caused by an installation or mobile plant is of such significance that the emission limit values in the permit need to be revised, or new emission limit values need to be included,

(ii) if the operational safety of the activities which are carried out in the installation or mobile plant requires other techniques to be used,

(iii) where it is necessary to comply with a new or revised environmental standard in accordance with Art 18 of the Industrial Emissions Directive.[54]

Notwithstanding the above, SEPA is under a general duty to periodically review the conditions of a permit and may also review the conditions of a permit at any other time.[55] SEPA is required, in carrying out a review of the conditions of a permit, to have regard to the results of emissions monitoring and other data that enables a comparison with the best available techniques (including, if applicable, techniques which are described in BAT conclusions)[56] and, in addition, SEPA is required to ensure that the permit complies with the Industrial Emissions Directive, if necessary by variation or revocation of the permit.[57]

Variation of permits

SEPA may vary a permit if it considers it necessary to do so in order to ensure that the permit complies with the Regulations or the Landfill Regulations.[58] SEPA may vary the conditions at any other time.[59] The operator of an installation or mobile plant may apply to SEPA for a variation of the permit.[60] If SEPA varies a permit, notice of the variation requires to be given to the operator in the form of a variation notice which requires to specify the variations of the conditions of the permit and also the date on which the variation is to take effect.[61] SEPA is required to give notice to the operator if the application for variation is refused.[62]

Transfer of permit

The Regulations make provision for the transfer of a permit from the current holder to another. Before a transfer can take place, both the existing and the proposed permit holders are required to make a joint application to SEPA to approve the transfer of either all or part of a permit.[63] SEPA is required to approve the application for transfer unless it considers that the proposed holder will not be the person with control of the operation of the installation or mobile plant after any transfer, or, in the case of a permit which authorises the carrying-out of a specified waste management activity, that the proposed holder is not a fit and proper person for the purposes of reg 18 or that the proposed holder will not ensure compliance with the permit conditions.[64] SEPA may only vary the conditions of a permit if it considers it necessary to do so to take account of the transfer.[65]

Surrender of permit

The operator of a Part A installation may apply to surrender either all or part of a Part A installation.[66] SEPA is required to determine the application within three months, that period beginning on the date of receipt of the application, or such longer period as either SEPA and the operator may agree in writing.[67] SEPA is required to approve an application for the surrender of a permit if it is satisfied that all appropriate measures have been taken to:

(a) avoid pollution risk[68] which results from the operation of the installation,

(b) return the site to a satisfactory state, taking into account the technical feasibility of the measures,

(c) remove, control, contain or reduce any relevant hazardous substance in soil or groundwater so that the site, taking into account its current or approved future use, ceases to pose a significant risk to human health or the environment.[69]

SEPA is required to give notice (that is, the 'determination notice') of either approval or rejection of the application to the operator.[70] The permit, or part of the permit, ceases to have effect on the date which is specified in the determination of the notice.[71] Finally, SEPA may vary a condition of the relevant permit if SEPA considers it necessary to do so as a result of the approval of a partial surrender of the permit.[72] In such a case, the condition, as varied, has effect on the date which is specified in the determination notice.

As far as the surrender of permits, other than Part A permits, is concerned, the relevant operator of the installation or mobile plant may give notice (that is, the surrender notice) to SEPA of the surrender of all or of any part of a permit.[73] The date on which the surrender is to take place must be at least twenty-eight days after the date on which the surrender notice is served on SEPA.[74] Finally, the permit ceases to have effect on the date which is specified in the surrender notice, or, in the case of a partial surrender, on that date.[75] Where SEPA considers it necessary to vary the conditions of the permit in order to take account of the partial surrender of the permit, the permit ceases to have effect on the later of the date of the surrender notice or the date of the variation of remaining part of the permit.

Revocation of permit

SEPA may, at any time, revoke either all or part of a permit by serving a notice (a revocation notice) on the relevant operator.[76] In particular, SEPA may serve a revocation notice where a permit authorises the carrying out of a specified waste management activity, and it appears to SEPA that the operator has ceased to be a fit and proper person by reason of:

(i)   the operator or a relevant person having been convicted of a relevant offence within the meaning of regulation 18 of the Regulations, or,

(ii) the management of the activity ceasing to be in the hands of a technically competent person.[77]

SEPA may also serve a revocation notice where the holder of the permit has ceased to be the operator of the installation or plant which is covered by the permit. The power SEPA possesses to revoke permits is wide. SEPA may revoke a permit either entirely, or only to the extent that it authorises the operation of some of the installations or mobile plant to which it applies, or SEPA may revoke a permit only to the extent that it authorises the carrying-out of some of the activities which may be carried out in an installation or by means of mobile plant to which it applies.[78] A revocation notice must specify the date on which the revocation takes effect (which must be at least twenty-eight days after the date on which the notice is served) and, in the case of a partial revocation, the extent to which the permit is being revoked.[79]

Where a permit for a Part A installation is revoked, either entirely or partially, and, furthermore, SEPA considers that the operator must take steps in respect of the installation, when once no longer operating, to:

(a)   avoid any pollution risk resulting from the operation of the installation on the site,

(b)   return the site to a satisfactory state, taking into account the technical feasibility of the steps, or

(c)   remove, control, contain or reduce any relevant hazardous substance in soil or groundwater, so that the site, taking into its current or future use, ceases to pose a significant risk to human health or the environment,

the revocation notice is required to specify any steps which must be taken in relation to the site, or part of the site, where applicable, that are further to those which are required by the permit.[80]

The permit ceases to have effect, in so far as it requires the above steps to be taken, until SEPA issues a certificate of completion, which states that SEPA is satisfied that such steps have been taken, those steps falling to be treated as conditions (as well as those which are actually contained in the permit) of the relevant permit[81] SEPA may withdraw a revocation notice before the date on which the revocation has effect.[82]

Enforcement notices

SEPA may serve an enforcement notice on the operator of an installation or mobile plant in respect of which a permit is granted if it considers that:

(a) the operator has contravened, is contravening, or is likely to contravene any condition of a permit, or
(b) an incident, or accident, which significantly affects the environment has occurred as a result of the operation of the operation of the installation or mobile plant.[83]

The enforcement notice is required to:

(a) state why SEPA considers that there is, or is likely to be, such a contravention,
(b) specify the matter which constitutes the contravention, or the matter which make it likely that the contravention will arise (as the case may be) and
(c) specify the steps which the operator must take in order to remedy the contravention, or to remedy the matter which makes it likely that the contravention will arise (as the case may be).[84]

The enforcement notice is required to specify the steps which the operator must take:

(a) to limit the environmental consequences of the incident or accident, and
(b) to prevent further possible incidents or accidents.[85]

The steps which may be specified in an enforcement notice may, without prejudice to the generality reg 55(3), include steps which must be taken to remedy the effects of any pollution which is caused by the contravention.[86] The operator of the relevant installation or mobile plant is required to comply with an enforcement notice.[87] SEPA may withdraw an enforcement notice at any time.[88]

Suspension notices

The Regulations also make provision for the issuing suspension notices by SEPA. SEPA must issue such a notice if it considers that any aspect of the operation of the installation or mobile plant:

(a)   poses an immediate danger to human health,
(b)   threatens to create an immediate significant adverse effect upon the environment, or
(c)   involves some other risk of pollution.[89]

However, SEPA may not serve a suspension notice where SEPA intends to arrange for steps[90] to be taken under the Regulations.[91] The obligation which is placed on SEPA to issue a suspension notice applies whether or not the particular manner of operation is either regulated by, or contravenes, a condition of the relevant permit.[92] SEPA may also issue a suspension notice to an operator of a waste management activity if SEPA considers that the operator has ceased to be a fit and proper person in relation to those activities by reason of management of those activities having ceased to be in the hands of a technically competent person.[93] The relevant suspension notice is required to state why SEPA considers that the suspension notice is required, and, in the case of a suspension notice which is served under reg 56(1), the notice is required to specify:

(i)   the nature of the harm which is being (or may be) caused by the operation of the installation or mobile plant,
(ii)   the steps that must be taken to remedy the harm or remove a risk, and
(iii) the period within which those steps must be taken.[94]

The suspension notice is also required to state the extent to which the permit ceases to have effect to authorise the operation of the installation or mobile plant, or the carrying-out of an activity in the installation, or by means of the mobile plant, and, where the permit is to continue to have effect to authorise an activity, any steps, which are in addition to those which are already required under the permit, which are required to be taken in carrying out that activity. The operator of the installation or mobile plant must comply with a suspension notice.[95] The relevant permit ceases to have effect, to the extent which is stated in the suspension notice on the service of the notice.[96] SEPA may withdraw a suspension notice at any time, and must withdraw the notice if SEPA is satisfied, in the case of a suspension notice which has been issued in terms of reg 56(1), that the steps which are required by the notice have been taken, and, in the case of a notice which has been issued in terms of reg 56(4), that the management of the activities is in the hands of a technically competent person.[97]

SEPA has published a policy statement relating to its enforcement policy.[98]

Power to prevent or remedy pollution

SEPA is empowered to arrange for steps to be taken in order to remove an imminent risk of serious pollution if SEPA considers that the operation of any installation or mobile plant which is regulated by a permit, or the operation in a particular manner, involves such a risk.[99] SEPA may also arrange for steps to be taken towards remedying the effects of pollution which is caused by the commission of an offence which comprises of the failure to comply with either the requirement of a permit, or a failure to comply with the condition of a permit, or the failure to comply with the requirements of an enforcement notice or a suspension notice, or a closure notice in terms of the Landfill Regulations.[100] In such circumstances, SEPA is required to give at least seven days' notice to the relevant operator before such steps are taken.[101] SEPA may recover the cost of taking such remedial action from the relevant operator of the installation or mobile plant.[102] However, no costs fall to be recovered if, in relation to steps which are taken in order to remove imminent risk of serious pollution, the operator shows that there was no such imminent risk. Furthermore, no costs can be recovered if the operator can show that such costs have been unnecessarily incurred by SEPA.[103]

Appeals

The Regulations make provision for appeals to the Scottish Ministers against various decisions of SEPA.[104] A person may appeal against the relevant decision of SEPA in the following circumstances, namely, where:

(a)   an application for a permit has been refused,
(b)   an application for the variation of a permit has been refused,
(c)   conditions which have been attached to a permit, or by a variation notice following an application by the operator,
(d)   an application for a transfer of a permit has been refused or conditions have been attached to a permit in order to take account of such transfer,
(e)   an application to surrender a permit has been refused or conditions have been attached to a permit in order to take account of the surrender,
(f)   a request to begin closure procedure is not approved under the Landfill (Scotland) Regulations 2003.[105]

Furthermore, a person who is served with:

(a)   a variation notice, other than in respect of an application for variation,
(b)   a revocation notice,
(c)   an enforcement notice,

(d)   a suspension notice, or,
(e)   a closure notice under the Landfill (Scotland) Regulations,

may appeal to the Scottish Ministers.[106] There is no right of appeal where SEPA's decision gives effect to directions which are given to SEPA by either the Scottish Ministers or the sheriff.[107]

On determining an appeal against a decision of SEPA under reg 58(1), the Scottish Ministers may:

(a)   affirm the decision,
(b)   where the decision was a refusal to grant a permit or to vary the conditions of a permit, direct SEPA to grant the permit or to vary the conditions of the permit,
(c)   where the decision was as to the conditions which were attached to a permit, quash all or any of the conditions of the permit,
(d)   where the decision was a refusal to effect the transfer or to accept the surrender of a permit, direct SEPA to effect the transfer or to accept the surrender.[108]

Where the Scottish Ministers give directions as to the conditions which are to be attached to the permit under (b) or (c) above, the Scottish Ministers may give SEPA directions as to the conditions which are to be attached to the permit. In giving such directions, the Scottish Ministers possess identical powers to those of SEPA.[109]

On determining an appeal against a notice in terms of reg 58(2), the Scottish Ministers may quash or affirm the notice, and, if affirming it, may do so either in its original form or with such modifications as they think fit.[110] Both SEPA and any person who is affected by the relevant determination of the Scottish Ministers may appeal to the sheriff.[111] The appeal requires to be made by summary application within twenty-one days from the date of the decision of the Scottish Ministers.[112] The sheriff may, in disposing of the appeal, take any step which was available to the Scottish Ministers above.[113] The determination of an appeal by the Scottish Ministers or the disposal of an appeal by the sheriff, in relation to a decision to include a standard rules condition in a permit, does not affect the continued validity of the relevant standard rules.[114] Furthermore, the bringing of an appeal in relation to the conditions which are attached to a permit does not suspend the operation of the condition.[115] Again, the bringing of an appeal does not suspend the operation of an enforcement notice, a suspension notice or a variation notice. In an appeal against a variation notice, the notice, if affirmed, does not take effect for a period of twenty-one days or from the withdrawal of the appeal.[116]

Directions by Scottish Ministers
The Scottish Ministers can give SEPA a direction, which may be either of a general or of a specific character, in relation to the carrying-out of its functions under the Regulations or under the Landfill Regulations.[117] SEPA may be directed to exercise, or refrain from exercising generally, any functions under the Regulations or the Landfill Regulations, or to exercise, or refrain from exercising, any function in such circumstances, or in such manner, as may be specified, or as to the objectives which are to be achieved by any condition of a permit.[118] Where the Scottish Ministers receive information from another Member State in relation to the operation of an installation outside the UK, the Scottish Ministers must direct SEPA to take such steps as SEPA considers appropriate for the purposes of bringing the information to the attention of those in Scotland who are likely to be affected by the operation of the installation, and providing such persons with an opportunity to comment on that information.[119] SEPA is placed under a duty to comply with any such direction.[120] The Scottish Ministers may also issue guidance to SEPA in relation to the carrying-out of any of its functions under the Regulations or the Landfill Regulations.[121] SEPA is required to have regard to such guidance in carrying out its functions under the Regulations or the Landfill Regulations.[122]

Emission plans
The Scottish Ministers may make plans for the setting of limits on the total amount in any period of emissions from all or any description of source within Scotland, and the allocation of quotas which relate to such emissions.[123] However, such plans do not apply to an emission plan which is made under the Large Combustion Plants (National Emission Reduction Plan) Regulations.[124]

Provision of information to Scottish Ministers and SEPA
The Scottish Ministers may, by written notice, require SEPA to provide such information about the discharge of any function of SEPA under the Regulations or the Landfill Regulations, as is specified in the notice.[125] Furthermore, either the Scottish Ministers or SEPA may require any person to provide such information as is specified in the notice.[126]

Public registers
SEPA is required to maintain a public register of a variety of particulars including particulars relating to applications for a permit, particulars of permits, particulars which relate to the variation, transfer and surrender of permits, appeals, enforcement notices, and closure notices under the

Landfill Regulations.[127] SEPA is required to secure that the register is available at all times for inspection by the public free of charge.[128] The Regulations make provision for the exclusion from the register of information which affects national security,[129] and also confidential information.[130]

Offences
The regulations make provision for a variety of offences including:

(i)   operating an installation without a permit,
(ii) failing to comply with or contravene a permit,
(iii) failing to comply with a closure notice under the Landfill Regulations.[131]

Summary

*   The Pollution Prevention and Control Act 1999 creates a single unified pollution control regime. The Act is a framework Act. It is 'fleshed-out' by the Pollution Prevention and Control (Scotland) Regulations 2012.
*   The Regulations institute a system of permitting of installations.
*   SEPA has sole responsibility for regulating Part A and Part B processes.

Notes

1. See, generally, Chapter 1.
2. See Fifth Report of the Royal Commission on Environmental Pollution, 'Air Pollution Control: an Integrated Approach', Cmnd 6731 (1976).
3. COPA 1974 s 5(5) (repealed).
4. For a useful general overview of the EPA see J. Blair, 'Integrated Pollution Control', in C. Reid, *Environmental Law in Scotland*, 2nd edn (W. Green, 1997) at 92. See also F. McManus, 'Pollution prevention and control' paras 11.01-11.57, in F. McManus, *Environmental Law in Scotland* (W. Green/SULI, looseleaf).
5. Ibid. at 92.
6. Lord Whitty, House of Lords, Hansard, vol 595, col 778.
7. SSI 2012 No 360.
8. Directive 2010/75/EU (recast).
9. 'Installation' means (a) a stationary technical unit where one or more activities listed in Schedules 1 or 2 are carried out, and (b) any other location on the same site where any other directly associated activities are carried out; Pollution Prevention and Control (Scotland) Regulations 2012 (SSI 2012 No 360), reg 2(1).

10. Pollution Prevention and Control (Scotland) Regulations 2012, reg 10.
11. Ibid. reg 11(2).
12. SSI 2003 No 235 (as amended).
13. Ibid. reg 13(1).
14. Ibid. reg 13(2).
15. Ibid. reg 14(1).
16. Ibid. reg 15(1).
17. Ibid. reg 15(2).
18. Ibid. reg 15(3).
19. Greenhouse Gas Emissions Trading Scheme Regulations 2005 (SI 2005 No 925) revoked by SI 2012 No 3038 but subject to transitional provisions in the latter.
20. Pollution Prevention and Control (Scotland) Regulations 2012, reg 17(1).
21. Ibid. reg 18(1).
22. Ibid. reg 18(3).
23. 'Relevant person' means in relation to the holder or proposed holder of a permit
    (a) any person who has been convicted of a relevant offence carried out
         (i)   in the course of that person's employment by the holder or proposed holder, or
         (ii) In the course of the carrying-on of any business by a partnership, one of the members of which was the holder or proposed holder,
    (b) a body corporate which has been convicted of a relevant offence committed when the holder or proposed holder was a director, manager, secretary or other similar officer of that body corporate (including, where the affairs of the body corporate are managed by its members, one of those members) or,
    (c) where the holder is a body corporate, a person who is a director, manager, secretary or other similar officer of that body corporate (including, where the affairs of the body corporate are managed by its members, one of those members) and who
         (i)   has been convicted of a relevant offence, or
         (ii) was a person holding such an office in another body corporate at a time when a relevant offence for which that body corporate has been convicted, was committed, and 'relevant offence' means an offence which is prescribed under s 74(6) of the Environmental Protection Act 1990 for the purposes of s 74(3)(a) of that Act; ibid reg 18(7).
24. Ibid. reg 18(4).
25. Ibid. reg 18(5).
26. SSI 2003 No 235.

27. Pollution Prevention and Control (Scotland) Regulations 2012 (SSI 2012 No 360) reg 19.

28. Ibid. reg 21(1).

29. The expression 'best available techniques' mean the most effective and advanced stage in the development of activities and their methods of operation which indicates the practical suitability of particular techniques for providing the basis for emission limit values and other permit conditions designed to prevent and, where that is not practicable, to reduce emissions and the impact on the environment as a whole; ibid. reg 4. 'Available techniques' means those techniques which have been developed on a scale which allows implementation in the relevant industrial sector, under economically and technically viable conditions, taking into consideration the cost and advantages, whether or not the techniques are used or produced inside the United Kingdom, as long as they are reasonably accessible to the operator; ibid. reg 4.

30. Ibid. reg 21(2).

31. Ibid. reg 21(3).

32. 'Best available techniques' mean the most effective and advanced stage in the development of activities and their methods of operation which indicates the practical suitability of particular techniques for providing the basis for emission limit values and other permit conditions designed to prevent and, where that is not practicable, to reduce emissions and the impact on the environment as a whole; ibid. reg 4.

33. Ibid. reg 22(1).

34. See p. 253 for a discussion of standard rules.

35. Ibid. reg 22(2).

36. Ibid. reg 23(1)(a).

37. Ibid. reg 23(1)(b).

38. Ibid. reg 24(1).

39. Ibid. reg 24(2.)

40. 'Emission' means in relation to (a) Part A installations, the direct or indirect release of a substance, a vibtration, heat or noise from individual or diffuse sources in an installation into the air, water or land; (b) Part B installations, the direct release of a substance or heat from individual or diffuse sources in an installation into the air; (c) mobile plant, the direct release of a substance or heat from the plant into the air; and (d) a solvent activity – (i) the direct release of a substance in waste gases into the air from individual or diffuse sources forming part of that activity, and (ii) the direct or indirect release of fugitive emissions; ibid. reg 2(1).

41. Ibid. reg 25(1).

42. 'Emission limit value' means the mass, expressed in terms of specific param-

eters, concentration or level of an emission, which may not be exceeded during one or more periods of time; ibid. reg 2(1).

43. Ibid. reg 25(2).
44. Ibid. reg 25(3).
45. Ibid. reg 25(4).
46. Ibid. reg 25(5).
47. Ibid. regs 26-35.
48. Ibid. reg 2(1).
49. Ibid. reg 36(1).
50. Ibid. reg 36(1).
51. Ibid. reg 36(3).
52. Ibid. reg 36(4).
53. Ibid. reg 38(1).
54. Ibid. reg 44(1).
55. Ibid. reg 44(3)(4).
56. 'BAT' conclusions' means a document containing the parts of a BAT reference document laying down the conclusions on best available techniques, their description, information to assess their applicability, the emission levels associated with the best available techniques, associated monitoring, associated consumption levels and, where appropriate, relevant site remediation measures; ibid. reg 4.
57. Ibid. reg 44(5).
58. Ibid. reg 46(1).
59. Ibid. reg 46(2).
60. Ibid. reg 46(3).
61. Ibid. reg 46(8).
62. Ibid. reg 46(10).
63. Ibid. reg 47(2).
64. Ibid. reg 47(8).
65. Ibid. reg 47(11).
66. Ibid. reg 48(1). For the purposes of the regulation, a Part A installation does not include that part of an installation where a relevant waste activity is carried out; ibid. reg 48(13).
67. Ibid. reg 48(5).
68. 'Pollution risk' includes only those risks which arise from the carrying-out of an activity under the permit after the date of the permit, and, in respect of a specified waste management activity, only those risks which arise after the relevant date; ibid. reg 48(13).
69. Ibid. reg 48(8).
70. Ibid. reg 48(9).
71. Ibid. reg 48(10).

72. Ibid. reg 48(11).
73. Ibid. reg 49(2).
74. Ibid. reg 48(4).
75. Ibid. reg 49(5).
76. Ibid. reg 50(1).
77. Ibid. reg 50(2).
78. Ibid. reg 50(3).
79. Ibid. reg 50(4).
80. Ibid. reg 50(5).
81. Ibid. reg 50(7).
82. Ibid. reg 50(8).
83. Ibid. reg 55(1).
84. Ibid. reg 55(2).
85. Ibid. reg 55(3).
86. Ibid. reg 55(5).
87. Ibid. reg 55(6).
88. Ibid. reg 55(7).
89. Ibid. reg 56(1).
90. Ie steps which are taken under reg 57(1) (see below).
91. Ibid. reg 56(2).
92. Ibid. reg 56(3).
93. Ibid. reg 56(4).
94. Ibid. reg 56(5).
95. Ibid. reg 56(6).
96. Ibid. reg 56(7).
97. Ibid. reg 56(8).
98. See Policy No 5 Enforcement Policy (SEPA, undated).
99. Pollution Prevention and Control (Scotland) Regulations 2012 (SSI 2012 No 360) reg 57(1).
100. Ibid. reg 57(2).
101. Ibid. reg 57(3).
102. Ibid. reg 57(4).
103. Ibid. reg 57(5).
104. Ibid. reg 58(1).
105. Ibid. reg 58(1).
106. Ibid. reg 58(2).
107. Ibid. reg 58(3).
108. Ibid. reg 58(4).
109. Ibid. reg 58(13).
110. Ibid. reg 58(5).
111. Ibid. reg 58(6).

112. Ibid. reg 58(7).
113. Ibid. reg 58(8)
114. Ibid. reg 58(9).
115. Ibid. reg 58(10).
116. Ibid. reg 58(11).
117. Ibid. reg 60(1).
118. Ibid. reg 60(2).
119. Ibid. reg 60(3)
120. Ibid. reg 60(5).
121. Ibid. reg 61(1).
122. Ibid. reg 61(2).
123. Ibid. reg 62(1).
124. SI 2007 No 3476 (as amended).
125. Pollution Prevention and Control (Scotland) Regulations 2012.
126. Ibid. reg 63(1).
127. Ibid. reg 64(1).
128. Ibid. reg 64(3).
129. Ibid. reg 65.
130. Ibid. reg 66.
131. Ibid. reg 67(1).

CHAPTER 10

Planning and Pollution Control

The Scottish Government sets out its planning policy in the National Planning Framework.

Planning authorities are responsible for granting planning permission. The capacity of a development to pollute the environment is a material consideration in determining a planning application. A planning authority can attach conditions to the grant of planning permission to regulate pollution from the development. Special controls exist for the control of hazardous substances.

Certain forms of development may require an environmental impact assessment.

Introduction

In this chapter, attention turns to the role which is played by town and country planning in regulating pollution. However, prior to specifically addressing this subject, it is desirable to briefly discuss the subject of planning generally. Whilst, as we have already observed,[1] town and country planning has its origins in the mid-nineteenth century, the modern system of planning was founded in 1947. The Town and Country Planning Act 1947[2] and the Town and Country Planning (Scotland) Act 1947,[3] in effect, introduced a new system for the regulation of the development of land in the United Kingdom. Indeed, the town and country planning legislation of 1947 has been described as a 'daring experiment in social control of the environment'.[4] In essence, the legislation vested the regulation of the development of land in the state. Put simply, if one wanted to develop land, one required planning permission. Whereas the Scottish Government has responsibility for national planning policy, planning authorities, namely local authorities, are responsible for granting planning permission for particular projects.[5] The role of both the Scottish Government and planning authorities is now discussed, with special reference to pollution control.

Scottish Government planning policy

The subject of town planning is a devolved function under the Scotland Act 1998. The most important function which the Scottish Government performs in relation to planning is the formulation of national planning policy. The Scottish Government sets out its planning policies in the National Planning Framework, Scottish Planning Policy and Circulars.[6]

The National Planning Framework 3 (NPF3) (which was approved by the Scottish Parliament in 2014) emphasises that planning has a key role to play in reducing greenhouse gas (GHG) emissions so that Scotland will meet the target of 80 per cent reduction of GHGs by 2050.[7] The Scottish Government sees both terrestrial and marine planning as playing a key role in meeting these targets by facilitating development, linking generation with consumers and guiding new infrastructure to appropriate locations.[8]

The current Scottish Government's Planning Policy (SPP), which sits side by side with the National Planning Framework, was published in 2014.[9] The legal significance of the SPP is that Scottish Government planning policy ranks as a material consideration which a planning authority requires to take into account when it determines a planning application for the development of land. However, the weight which should be accorded to the SPP rests at the discretion of the individual planning authority.

The SPP supplements the aims of the Scottish Government, which are contained in NPF3, to transform Scotland to a low-carbon economy.[10] The Scottish Government aims, *inter alia*, to derive 30 per cent of overall energy demand from renewable energy by 2020, 11 per cent of heat demand from renewable sources by 2020 and also the equivalent of 100 per cent of electricity demand by 2020. In order to meet these objectives, development plans should seek to ensure that an area's full potential for electricity and heat from renewable sources is achieved in line with national climate change targets.[11] As far as the problem which is posed to the environment by waste is concerned, the planning system should, *inter alia*, promote developments which minimise the unnecessary use of primary materials and also promote the efficient use of secondary materials and support the achievement of Scotland's zero waste targets.[12] Furthermore, development plans should give effect to the aims of Scotland's Zero Waste Plan and promote the waste hierarchy.[13]

In addition to the subject of waste and renewable energy, the Scottish Government has also issued specific guidance in relation to air quality and land use planning.[14] The land use planning system is regarded by the Scottish Government as integral to improving air quality. In circumstances where an emission source is not regulated by SEPA under the integrated pollution prevention and control regime,[15] or by a local authority, in terms of the Clean Air Act 1993, planning authorities should consider attaching appropriate conditions to the grant of planning permission. Mention should also be made of the guidance which has been issued by the Scottish Government to planning authorities as to how the planning system may be used in order to reduce noise from new developments.[16]

The control of development: planning and pollution control

A proposed development may pose a potential source of pollution to the general environment by reason of the activities which are to take place on the relevant land. For example, a proposed factory could potentially pollute the atmosphere by fumes or noise. The advantage of the development management system as a mechanism for pollution prevention is that polluting activities can be prevented at source.[17] It is an anticipatory control which exemplifies the preventative principle. Indeed, it has been argued that the UK can claim to have adopted the principle long before such a principle became fashionable and also before it featured in EU policy.[18]

The obvious question which has to be asked at the outset is whether a planning authority can take pollution from the proposed development into account when it is considering a planning application. Before we examine the relevant case law it should be borne in mind that in the vast majority of cases, premises which have the capacity to pollute the atmosphere, water or land will fall to be regulated by SEPA.[19]

Material considerations

The Town and Country Planning (Scotland) Act 1997[20] requires a planning authority, when it is determining a planning application, to take into account the relevant development plan, in so far as it is material to the application, and also any other material considerations. Unfortunately, however, the Act does not define the term 'material consideration'. One, therefore, requires to determine, first, if the planning authority regard as a material consideration the pollution which the relevant proposed development will cause, and, secondly, to what extent, if any, the planning authority, if it did regard pollution as a material consideration, could take into account the powers which SEPA possesses to deal with pollution from the premises? As far as the second limb of the question is concerned, what we are, in essence, considering is the relationship between planning controls and other environmental regulatory regimes. However, that relationship is not particularly clear.[21]

These issues were discussed in the English Court of Appeal case of *Gateshead Metropolitan BC v SoS for the Environment*.[22] The court was required to address, first, whether potential pollution from the relevant development ranked as a material consideration, and, secondly, what significance, in terms of planning law, should be accorded to the regulatory regime which would come into effect after the plant became operational.

The *Gateshead* case concerned a planning application by the Northumbrian Water Group (NWG) for the construction and operation of a waste incineration plant. It was necessary for the prospective operators of the plant to obtain both planning permission and also, by virtue of the operation being a prescribed process in terms of Part 1 of the Environmental Protection Act 1990 (EPA), authorisation by HM Inspectorate of Pollution (HMIP, now the Environment Agency). Planning permission was refused by the planning authority on the grounds that potential pollution from the incinerator would have a negative impact on the environment. NWG appealed to the Secretary of State (SoS). An inquiry into the appeal was heard. The inspector recommended that permission be refused. However, the SoS disagreed with the inspector's recommendation. The SoS took the view that the concerns about atmospheric pollution could be addressed by the HMIP by using its powers under the EPA. The SoS therefore granted outline planning permission, subject to conditions. The local authority appealed against his decision, *inter alia*, on the grounds that the SoS had misunderstood both the powers and functions of HMIP.

The key issue which fell to be determined by the court was to what extent, if any, the SoS was entitled to set store by the provisions of the EPA in determining whether to grant NWG planning permission for the incinerator. In short, should the powers which the HMIP could use in terms of the EPA in order to regulate atmospheric pollution from the plant, rank as a material consideration in planning terms? In a judgment which, in the author's opinion, is (with respect) notable for its lack of clarity, Glidewell LJ tacitly accepted that indeed, the planning authority could set store by the powers which the HMIP possessed in terms of the EPA, when the former was determining whether planning permission could be granted for the incinerator.[23] For His Lordship, the SoS was justified in concluding that issues which had been raised at the planning inquiry which related to the atmospheric pollution from the plant, could be addressed by the HMIP and could also be adequately dealt with by that body. In the last analysis, the decision of the SoS could not be impugned.[24]

The inter-relationship between pollution, planning controls and the relevant regulatory pollution control regime came to be discussed again in *R. v Bolton MBC ex p Kirkman*.[25] In that case the claimant contended that when the defendant planning authority was determining a planning application, it had failed to address, *inter alia*, potential pollution from a proposed waste incinerator. Carnwath J (as he then was) held that the impact of discharges from the incinerator ranked as a material consideration in terms of planning law.[26] However, in considering that issue, the planning authority was entitled to take into account the system of controls under the integrated pollution control regime (IPC) of the EPA, unless it appeared to the planning authority that the discharges in question would, or would probably, be unacceptable to the Environment Agency, it would be a proper course of action for the planning authority to leave that matter to be dealt with under the IPC regime.[27]

Again, in *Hopkins Developments Ltd v First Secretary of State and North Wiltshire DC*[28] it was held that the impact of air emissions from a proposed cement works was capable of being a material consideration. However, in considering that issue, the planning authority was entitled to take into account the pollution control regime which would be applicable. Thus, in appropriate cases, planning authorities could use their discretion to leave pollution control to the relevant pollution control authorities but planning authorities were not obliged, as a matter of law, to do so. Furthermore, it was the view of the court that planning authorities should focus on the impact of emissions from premises rather than the control of the relevant processes or the emissions themselves.

Planning conditions

On granting planning permission for the development of land, a planning authority can, *inter alia*, attach such conditions, as it thinks fit.[29] A planning authority can use such powers to reduce the potential negative impact of a proposed development, including reducing pollution from the relevant premises. Whereas a planning authority has fairly wide discretion as to both the nature and the content of a condition it may impose on the grant of planning permission, such discretion is not unfettered. The limits of the powers of planning authorities in imposing planning conditions were set out in the leading House of Lords case of *Newbury DC v SoS for the Environment*.[30] The House held that for a planning condition to be *intra vires* and valid, the relevant condition was, first, required to be for a planning purpose, and not for an ulterior one;, second, required to fairly and reasonably relate to the relevant development; and finally, the condition was required not to be so unreasonable that no reasonable planning authority could have imposed it.

An important Scottish case which illustrates the application of the requirements which were set out in *Newbury* is the Inner House case of *British Airports Authority v SoS for Scotland.*[31] In that case, the British Airports Authority (BAA) had applied to Aberdeen County Council to carry out certain developments at Aberdeen Airport, including the erection of a new terminal building and a new aircraft apron. The SoS confirmed the grant of planning permission by the planning authority, subject to two conditions which were designed to restrict the operational hours at the airport and also regulate the direction of both take-offs and landings of aircraft there. Both conditions were imposed in order to reduce the noise impact from the premises.

An application for planning permission had also been made by British Airways Helicopters Ltd (BAHL) for the erection of a one-storey building in order to provide an office for its flight-operations headquarters at its terminal. In this case, planning permission had been granted to BAHL, subject to a condition which was designed to restrict its operational hours at the terminal.

Bristow Helicopters (BH) had also applied for planning permission to build an extension to its terminal building at the airport in order to provide freight-handling facilities and additional office accommodation. Again, the planning authority had attached a condition to the grant of planning permission, which restricted operational hours at the terminal.

As far as the appeal by BAA was concerned, the court held that both of the conditions which had been imposed fairly and reasonably related to the proposed development, but as far as the condition which sought to regulate the direction of take-offs and landings from the airport was concerned, such a function fell to be exercised not by the SoS, but, rather, by the Civil Aviation Authority. Thus, the second condition was unreasonable and, therefore, *ultra vires*, in as much as no reasonable planning authority could have imposed such a condition.

As far as the appeal by BAHL was concerned, the court held that the condition which related to its operational hours was *ultra vires* on two grounds: first, the condition did not fairly and reasonably relate to the development in question, in that no helicopter took off or landed from any land which was occupied by BAHL; secondly, and in any case, such a condition was pointless and unnecessary in that, since all aircraft took off and landed from runways at the airport, operational hours in relation to such aircraft fell to be regulated by the valid relevant planning condition which had been imposed on BAA.

In the case of the BH appeal, it was held that the condition which sought to restrict operational hours was *ultra vires* in that the impugned condition did not fairly and reasonably relate to the development in question, and in that the proposed increase in office/freight accommodation would not directly lead to an increase in air traffic and, therefore, more noise. In short, the permitted development had no connection with the helicopter operations at the airport. It automatically followed that any conditions, the aim of which were to reduce noise by restricting operational hours from BH's proposed development, were *ultra vires*.[32]

Planning control and hazardous substances

Special planning controls exist in relation to hazardous substances. These controls are now briefly discussed.

Planning (Hazardous Substances) (Scotland) Act 1997

The Planning (Hazardous Substances)(Scotland) Act 1997 places a duty on planning authorities to control hazardous substances.[33] Subject to certain exceptions, the presence of a hazardous substance which is either on, over, or under any land, requires the consent of the planning authority.[34] The Scottish Ministers have power to specify by regulations, *inter alia*, what substances are hazardous substances and the quantity which is to be controlled of any substance.[35] The Town and Country Planning (Hazardous Substances) (Scotland) Regulations 2015[36] specify which substances rank as hazardous for the Act and also the quantity which falls to be controlled.[37] The regulations also make provision for hazardous substances to be exempt from the requirement to have consent of the planning authority.[38] For example, hazardous substances consent is not required for the temporary presence of hazardous substances on land.[39] The applicant for consent is required to notify neighbouring proprietors that he is applying for planning permission.[40] The application is required to be publicised.[41] The applicant is also required to make the statement available for public inspection.[42]

Applications for hazardous substances consent
Before determining an application for consent the planning authority is required to consult a number of public bodies including the Health and Safety Executive, Scottish Natural Heritage, the relevant community council and SEPA.[43] The planning authority may grant hazardous substance consent either unconditionally or subject to such conditions as it thinks fit, or the planning authority may refuse planning permission.[44] In determining the application the planning authority is required to have regard to any material considerations and, in particular, but without prejudice to the generality of the foregoing:

(a)   to any current or contemplated use of the land to which the application relates,
(b)   to the way in which land in the vicinity is being used or is likely to be used,
(c)   to any planning permission that has been granted for development of land in the vicinity,
(d)   to the provisions of the development plan, and
(e)   to any advice which the Health and Safety Executive have given.[45]

In *Eriden Properties LLP v Falkirk Council*[46] the pursuer sought to challenge, by way of judicial review, the grant of a hazardous substances consent which the defender planning authority had granted to Kemfine UK Ltd (K) as the occupier of a chemical works. The pursuer owned and wished to develop land which was situated close to the works in question. The site in question had been granted hazardous substance consent in the past but such consent, by virtue of the provisions of the Act, had been deemed to have lapsed. A new application had, therefore, to be made to the planning authority which duly granted hazardous substances consent to K. The pursuer claimed that the planning authority had, in effect, consulted inadequately with the HSE as to whether the so-called 'consultation zone' (that is to say, the relevant area which was covered by the consent) could be reduced. Lord Clarke, in the Outer House, held that the fact that the site in question had operated for many years under previous consents was a highly relevant material consideration which fell to be taken into account by the planning authority. The planning authority had also balanced the economic benefit to the community against the relevant risks which were posed by the works. In the last analysis, the planning authority had acted reasonably. The petition by way of judicial review, therefore, failed.

Revocation etc. of hazardous substances consent
A planning authority may, by order, revoke a hazardous substances consent, or modify it to such an extent as the planning authority considers expedient, if it appears to it, having regard to any material consideration, that it is expedient to revoke or modify it.[47] The planning authority may also, by order, revoke a hazardous substances consent if it appears to the planning authority:

(a)   that there has been a material change of use of land to which a hazardous substances consent relates,
(b)   that planning permission, or development consent, has been granted for development, the carrying-out of which would involve a material

change of use of such land and the development to which permission relates has been commenced,

(c)   in the case of a hazardous substances consent which relates to only one substance that the substance has not for at least five years been present on, over or under the land to which the consent relates in a quantity which is equal to or exceeding the controlled quantity, or

(d)   in the case of a hazardous substance consent which relates to a number of substances, that none of those substances has, for at least five years, been so present.[48]

The relevant order requires to specify the grounds on which it is made.[49] However, the order does not take effect unless it is confirmed by the Scottish Ministers.[50]

A hazardous substances consent is revoked if there is a change in the person in control of part of the land to which the consent relates, unless an application for the continuation of the consent has previously been made to the planning authority.[51] When an application is made for the continuation of a hazardous consent, the planning authority may modify the consent in any way which it considers appropriate, or it may revoke the consent.[52] In such a case the relevant planning authority is required to compensate the person in control of the whole of the land before the change in control by virtue of which the application was made, in respect of any loss or damage which has been sustained by him and is directly attributable to the modification or revocation.[53]

Directions by Scottish Ministers

The Scottish Ministers may give directions to the effect that applications for hazardous substances consent under the Act be referred to it, instead of the application being dealt with by the relevant planning authority.[54] A direction may be given either to a particular planning authority or to planning authorities generally.[55] Furthermore, the direction may either relate to a particular application or to applications in general. Thereafter, any application in respect of which a direction has effect requires to be referred to the Scottish Ministers.[56] Before the Scottish Ministers determine such an application either the applicant or the planning authority require to be given the opportunity of appearing before a person who is appointed by the Scottish Ministers for the purpose.[57] The decision of the Scottish Ministers on any application which is referred to it is final.[58]

Appeals
An applicant for hazardous substances consent can appeal to the Scottish Ministers against the refusal of an application for such consent, or in respect of an application for any consent, agreement or approval of the authority which is required by a condition which is imposed on the grant of such consent, or against any conditions which are attached to such consent.[59] The Scottish Ministers have complete powers of review and they may either allow or dismiss the appeal, or they may reverse or vary any part of the decision of the planning authority (whether the appeal relates to that part or not), and they may deal with the application as if it had been made to them in the first instance.[60]

Before determining such an appeal the Scottish Ministers are required, if requested by either the applicant or the relevant planning authority, to allow each of them an opportunity of appearing before and being heard by a person who is appointed by the Scottish Ministers for that purpose.[61] The decision of the Scottish Ministers as regards the appeal is final.[62]

Any person who is aggrieved by any decision of the Scottish Ministers either in respect of a direction which has been given under s 18 or an appeal which has been made under s 19, and wishes to question the validity of that decision on the grounds that either such a decision is not within the powers of the Act, or that any of the relevant requirements have not been complied with in relation to that decision, may, within six weeks from the date on which the decision is taken, make an application to the Court of Session.[63] The Court may, if satisfied that the relevant decision is not within the powers of the Act, or that the interests of the applicant have been substantially prejudiced by a failure to comply with any of the relevant requirements[64] in relation to it, quash that decision.[65]

Contravention of hazardous substances control
The Act provides that if there is contravention of hazardous substances control, the appropriate person[66] is guilty of an offence.[67] Such a contravention takes place if:

(a)   a quantity of hazardous substance equal to or exceeding the controlled quantity is or has been present on, over or under land and either -
   (i)   there is no hazardous substances consent for the presence of the substance, or
   (ii)   there is hazardous substances consent for its presence but the quantity present exceeds the maximum quantity which is permitted by the consent, or

(b)   there is or has been a failure to comply with a condition subject to which a hazardous substances consent was granted.[68]

A person guilty of an offence under s 21 is made liable, on summary conviction, to a fine not exceeding £20,000, and on conviction on indictment, to a fine.[69]

The Act makes provision for defences in proceedings for an offence under the section.[70]

The Act makes provision for the issue by the planning authority of contravention notices in respect of apparent contraventions of hazardous substances control.[71]

REGISTERS

A planning authority is required to keep a register which contains certain information which relates to hazardous substances consent including applications for such consent and revocations or modifications of such consent.[72] The register requires to be made available for public inspection.[73]

Environmental impact assessment

Environmental impact assessment (EIA) is a key legal mechanism which has emerged in the last thirty years. It has its origins in the USA in the 1960s.[74] There, it was a response to both the growing environmental movement of that era,[75] and, also, in no small measure, to concerns about the US interstate highway system.[76] EIA enables decision-makers, mainly in the form of planning authorities, as far as Scotland is concerned, to take account of the environmental impact of their decisions. In essence, the importance of EIA is that information about likely environmental impacts of certain development projects, is properly considered before a decision is taken as to whether they should proceed. In essence, EIA is a process or procedure which comprises a drawing-together, in both a formal and systematic way, of an assessment of projects which are likely to have significant environmental effects. This process helps to ensure that the importance of the predicted effects, and the scope for reducing them, are properly understood by the public and the relevant competent authority before it makes its decision.[77] The Scottish Government has described EIA as 'a process by which information about the likely significant environmental effects of a project and the potential for reducing avoiding and off-setting any adverse impacts, is collected and assessed by the developer'.[78] However, the importance of EIA is not simply confined to the benefit of the developer and the relevant planning authority. The use of EIA conduces to transparency on the part of actions which are taken by decision-makers, and also increa.. the opportunities for the public to participate in the planning process.

International law and environmental impact

Brief mention only can be made in this work of EIA in international law.[79] EIA, as a principle, in international law emerged after the 1972 Stockholm Conference, and is now an established international and domestic legal technique for integrating environmental considerations into socio-economic development and decision-making processes.[80] Whereas the process which is to be employed in carrying out an EIA is not set out in any international agreement,[81] at present, many international agreements make provision for what has been described as EIA-type agreements.[82] One of the most important is articulated in Principle 17 of the Rio Declaration of 1992. It states that, 'environmental impact assessment, as a national instrument, shall be undertaken for proposed activities that are likely to have a significant adverse impact on the environment and are subject to a decision of a competent authority'.

Again, Article 4 of the Aarhus Convention (which was ratified by the UK in 2005)[83] requires parties to ensure that public authorities make environmental information available to the public, and that systems are established to ensure that there is an adequate flow of information to both public authorities and the general public about existing and proposed activities which may significantly affect the environment. However, the Convention does not create any substantive environmental rights; rather, the emphasis is on the creation of procedural rights.[84]

There is growing jurisprudence in international law on the subject of EIA. In *Gabcikovo-Nagymaros*[85] (which concerned the interpretation of a treaty which had been concluded between the respective parties, Slovakia and Hungary) the International Court of Justice interpreted the treaty as requiring both the carrying-out of an EIA and a continuing environmental assessment of the relevant project's impact on the environment. Furthermore, in the case of *Argentina* v *Uruguay*[86] (*Pulp Mills* case) which concerned a dispute between Argentina and Uruguay concerning pollution of the River Uruguay, the International Court of Justice recognised EIA as a general principle in international law. The court concluded that it was now a requirement under international environmental law to undertake an EIA where there was a risk that the proposed industrial activity may have significant adverse impact in a transboundary context, in particular, on a shared resource.

EIA Directive and its implementation in Scotland

European Commission's Second Action Programme on the environment in 1977 reiterated the approach which had been expressed in the First Action Programme, namely, that effects on the environment should be taken into account at the earliest possible stage in all the technical planning and decision-making processes.[87] The UK was initially opposed to the European Commission's proposals for a Directive on EIA.[88] Such opposition was largely based on the definition of the projects which would fall within the scope of an EIA Directive and also the delays which the implementation of the Directive would have on the UK planning system.[89] Furthermore, the incoming Conservative government's policy of deregulation, generally, was not conducive to a ready acceptance of the EIA concept. In the last analysis, Directive 85/337/EEC represented a political compromise. The 1985 Directive has been amended subsequently several times and was codified in 2011 by Directive 2011/92/EU which, in turn, has been amended by Directive 2014/52/EU.

The preamble to the 2011 Directive provides that EIA is based on the precautionary principle of preventative action, and also on the principle that environmental damage should, as a priority, be rectified at source, and that the polluter should pay.[90] The preamble also provides that effects on the environment should be taken into account at the earliest possible stage in all technical planning and decision-making processes.

Article 2 requires that Member States adopt all measures which are necessary to ensure that before consent (that is, development consent) is given, projects which are likely to have significant effects on the environment by virtue, *inter alia*, of their nature, size or location, are made subject to a requirement for development consent, and also an assessment with regard to their effects on the environment. Importantly, the article provides that EIA may be integrated into the existing procedures for development consent to projects in Member States.

What is a project?
The directive defines a project as either the execution of construction works or other installations or schemes, or other interventions in the natural surroundings and landscape, including those involving the extraction of mineral resources.[91] Normally, to be classed as a project, there requires to be some form of construction or physical intervention. In *Brussels Hoofdstedilijk Gewest v Vlaams Gewest*[92] the European Court of Justice held that a consent which simply allowed an airport to continue to operate was not a project which fell within the scope of the Directive, on the basis that no works or physical interventions to the airport were involved,

nor did the relevant consent constitute a stage in a procedure which could lead to such works or physical interventions. However, where a proposal is simply part of a larger scheme which, when looked at *in toto,* would constitute a project which falls within the scope of the Directive, an EIA would be required. What is at issue here is what has been referred to as 'salami-slicing', namely, splitting a large development project into smaller units which, looked at in isolation, would fall below the thresholds which would require an EIA.[93] The issue as to whether a given project is part of a larger project is also inextricably linked but, at the same time, conceptually quite separate from the issue as to whether that smaller project has a significant effect on the environment by virtue of the cumulative effects of the projects *in toto.*[94] The Directive is not simply confined to new projects but also includes modification of existing projects.[95]

While the UK courts have never fully discussed the point, *Bowen-West v SoS*[96] is some authority for the proposition that it is a question of fact and planning judgment as to whether or not the proposal is part of a larger scheme.[97]

'Development consent' is defined in the Directive as 'the decision of the competent authority or authorities which entitles the developer to proceed with the project'.[98] However, the Directive does not cover decisions which involve merely the detailed regulation of activities, consent for which has already been given.[99] Generally, a project which falls within the scope of the Directive will fall within the definition of 'development' in terms of the Town and Country Planning (Scotland) Act 1997 and, therefore, be subject to planning control. In such cases, the EIA process is governed by the regulations which we now discuss. As for projects which do not fall within the compass of the 1997 Act, such projects fall to be regulated by separate legislation which incorporates EIA procedure.[100] However, space precludes any discussion here of such legislation.

Town and Country Planning (Environmental Impact Assessment) (Scotland) Regulations 2011[101]

The Town and Country Planning (Environmental Impact Assessment) (Scotland) Regulations 2011 essentially implement Article 2 of the Directive. At the outset it should be observed that the regulations do not employ the term 'project'. Rather, the term 'development' is used to describe the projects which fall to be regulated by the planning regime. The regulations prohibit the Scottish Ministers, or any planning authority, from granting planning permission for an EIA development unless they have taken into consideration environmental information.[102] An EIA development is defined as a Schedule 1 development or a Schedule 2 development which is likely to have significant effects on the environment by virtue of factors such as its nature, size or location.[103]

Schedule 1 development
Schedule 1 of the regulations implements Annex 1 of the Directive. Schedule 1 includes twenty-three different categories of development, including, airports, nuclear power stations and chemical installations. For such developments, an EIA is mandatory unless the development ranks as an exempt development[104] in terms of the regulations.[105] However, each category has its own threshold by means of which one determines whether the development ranks as a Schedule 1 development. Some thresholds take the form of the site size of the development (for example, the construction of new roads) or the output of the installation (for example, waste disposal installations). Any change to a Schedule 1 development also ranks as such a development provided that such a change, in itself, meets the relevant threshold, if any, of the development.[106]

Whether a given development falls within either Schedule 1 or Schedule 2 is a question of law to be determined by the court.[107]

Schedule 2 development
The regulations define a Schedule 2 development as a development, other than an exempt development, of a description which is mentioned in column 1 of Schedule 2 where any part of the development is in a sensitive area,[108] or any applicable threshold or criterion in the corresponding part of column 2 of the table is respectively exceeded or met, in relation to that development.[109] Generally speaking, a Schedule 2 development is one which is likely to have a lesser environmental impact than a Schedule 1 development. Examples of Schedule 2 developments include intensive fish farming, drilling for water supplies, surface storage of fossil fuels and installations for the manufacture of cement.

In determining whether any development is to be classified as a Schedule 2 development, the planning authority is required to take into account, *inter alia*, the characteristics of the particular development, its location, and also the characteristics of its potential impact as well as the cumulation with other development.[110] However, a planning authority has wide discretion as to whether or not any Schedule 2 development requires an EIA. The courts will only intervene if the decision which is taken by the planning authority as to whether an EIA is required is so unreasonable that no planning authority could have reached that decision. In other words, the relevant decision by the planning authority can only be overturned on *Wednesbury* grounds.[111] The rationale for this approach is that the local planning officials and elected members are better placed than judges to evaluate the impact of a project. In this context, the judgment of Carnwath LJ (as he then was) in *R. (Jones) v Mansfield District Council*[112] is worthy of note. After stating[113] that the EIA process is intended to be an 'aid to efficient and inclusive decision-making in special cases, not an obstacle race', his Lordship stated[114] that whether a proposed development will have a significant effect on the environment required the exercise of judgment on planning issues and consistency in the exercise of that judgment in different cases. That was a function for which the courts were ill-equipped.[115]

It may be observed, at this stage, that neither the EIA Directive nor the 2011 regulations define the term 'environment'. In of *R. (Malster) v Ipswich BC*[116] it was held that in determining whether a particular proposed development had a significant effect on the environment (in terms of the English EIA regulations) the planning authority was not obliged to take into account the impact of the development (in this case the proposed development would have cast a 'shadow' on nearby houses) on the amenity of individual occupiers of houses. The court went on to hold that there might be a significant impact upon a particular dwelling or dwellings without there being any likely significant effect on the environment for the purposes of the EIA regulations. This decision, however, has not escaped academic criticism.[117]

In some circumstances, the relevant planning application may contain proposals to mitigate any potential harm accruing from the development in question. Therefore, the question which falls to be answered is to what extent, if any, it is lawful for the planning authority, in deciding whether the proposed development is likely to have a significant effect on the environment, to take into account such mitigating measures. The leading case is the Court of Appeal case of *Gillespie v First Secretary of State*[118] which concerned a proposed redevelopment of a former gasworks. The court held that in considering whether the development posed such a risk, the planning authority was not obliged to ignore the remedial measures which had been submitted along with the development proposal. *R. (Treagus) v Suffolk County Council*[119] is authority for the proposition that the remedial or mitigating measures which can be taken into account by a planning authority can comprise appropriate forms of future regulation of the proposed development. In *Treagus* it was held lawful for a planning authority to take into account the application of the permitting regime which would operate in future.[120]

Screening opinion

A developer may seek what is called a screening opinion, from the planning authority, in order to determine whether an EIA is required for a particular development.[121] If the planning authority fails to make such a determination or adopts an opinion that a development is an EIA development, the person making the request can request the Scottish Ministers to make a screening direction.[122] The regulations make provision for the information which is required to accompany the screening request.[123] The Scottish Ministers are required to make a screening direction within three weeks from the date of the relevant request.[124] Where the planning authority adopts a screening opinion or the Scottish Ministers make a screening direction, full reasons require to be given by either for its decision.[125] Such reasons require to contain sufficient information to allow anyone who is interested to see that proper consideration has been given to the environmental effects of the proposal.[126]

If it appears to the planning authority that a planning application relates either to a Schedule 1 or 2 development and that the development in question has not been subject to either a screening opinion or a screening direction, and that the application is not covered by a environmental statement (see immediately below), the application falls to be treated as a request for a screening opinion.[127]

Environmental statements

An environmental statement is simply a statement by means of which one can assess the environmental effects of a project.[128] The environmental statement has been described as the 'cornerstone' of the EIA regime.[129] For Tromans the importance of the environmental statement lies not just in the information which it contains, but in its presentation to members of the public.[130]

Whilst the Regulations do not prescribe the precise form of the environmental statement, it is required to contain certain information. The environmental statement must contain the particulars in Part 1 of Schedule 4 of the Regulations as are reasonably required to assess the environmental effects of a development, and which the applicant can be reasonably be required to compile, and the environmental statement must also include at least the information referred to in Part 2 of Sched 4.[131] The aspects of the environment which might significantly be affected by a project which are to be contained in the environmental statement are set out in para 3 of Part 1 of Sched 4 and include: human beings, flora, fauna, soil, water, air, climate, landscape, material assets including any architectural or archaeological heritage, and the interaction of any of these factors. Furthermore, under para 4 of Part 1 of Sched 4 the environmental statement should also contain a description of the likely significant effects resulting from use of natural resources, emission of pollutants, creation of nuisances and elimination of waste. Finally, the information which is contained in the environmental statement must be summarised in non-technical language.[132] Advice on preparation of an environmental statement is contained in Planning Circ 3 2011 and also PAN 1/2013.[133]

In the House of Lords case of *Berkeley v Secretary of State for the Environment, Transport and Regions*[134] which concerned a planning application which had been called in by the Secretary of State, the House was required to consider whether, in determining the application, the EIA Directive had been complied with. Whilst the Secretary of State did not have an environmental statement he did have access to, *inter alia*, the developer's statement of a case before the relevant planning inquiry, the planning officer's report to the planning authority and also reports of consultation bodies such as the National Rivers Authority. It was argued that, by reason of the fact that members of the public could cross-reference the relevant documentation (and, by doing so, could be adequately informed of the environmental impact of the proposed development), such documentation was equivalent to an environmental statement. However, this argument was rejected by the House. Lord Hoffman described the process, by means of which one would require to elicit the relevant information, as a 'paper chase'.[135] For his Lordship, in order to comply with the Directive, an environmental statement was required to comprise 'a single and accessible compilation produced by the applicant at the very start of the application process of the relevant environmental information and the summary in non-technical language'.

Another case which neatly emphasises that a developer cannot simply rely on the screening process to circumvent the statutory requirement to provide an adequate environmental statement is *R. (Cooperative Group Ltd) v Northumberland County Council*.[136] There, the relevant developer had submitted an environmental statement which had identified potential environmental issues without addressing the impact which the proposed development would have on them. Instead, the statement simply contained assurances that such issues would be addressed in a future occasion. It was held that the planning authority did not have sufficient material before it to ascertain whether the proposed development would have a significant effect on the environment. The planning decision was, therefore, quashed.

In *R. (Blewett) v Derbyshire CC*[137] the court held that the fact that an environmental statement has failed to provide full information on the environmental impact of a project does not mean that the environmental statement falls outwith the legal definition of an environmental statement. In that case Sullivan J stated:

> In an imperfect world it is an unrealistic counsel of perfection to expect that an applicant's environmental statement will always contain the 'full information' about the environmental impact of a project. The Regulations are not based upon such an unrealistic expectation. They recognise that an environmental statement may well be deficient, and make provision through the publicity and consultation process for any deficiencies to be identified so that the resulting 'environmental information' provides the local planning authority with as full a picture as possible.

Furthermore, the courts accord planning authorities wide discretion as to the content of an environmental statement. This approach is neatly illustrated in *R. (Kent) v First Secretary of State.*[138] Here, the claimant was an objector to a proposed waste development. The First Secretary had called in the relevant planning application and had granted planning permission for the development. However, K. claimed that the hazardous waste which was to be dumped on the site was not described with sufficient particularity in the environmental statement. It was further claimed that the environmental statement was defective in that it had not included a quantitative risk assessment. It was held, however, that whereas an environmental statement was required to contain sufficient information to allow a planning authority to make an informed judgment as to whether development would have significant effects on the environment, it fell to the relevant planning authority to decide if information in the environmental statement was sufficient for this purpose, subject to review on *Wednesbury* grounds.[139]

Environmental statements and planning applications
Where an EIA application has been submitted to a planning authority but the application is not accompanied by an environmental statement, the planning authority is required to notify the applicant that an environmental statement is required.[140]

An applicant who receives such a notice can write to the planning authority, either stating that he accepts its views and that he is providing an environmental statement, or that he is writing to the Scottish Ministers to request a screening direction.[141] If the applicant fails to write to the planning authority within a period of three weeks, such period commencing on the date of the notice, the application falls to be treated as having been refused (unless the Scottish Ministers have made a screening direction to the effect that the development is not an EIA development) at the end of that period.[142] In that event, such a deemed refusal deprives the applicant both of the right of appeal against the refusal of planning permission and the right of having the decision reviewed in terms of ss 43A(8) and 47 of the Town and Country Planning (Scotland) Act 1997 ('the Act'), respectively. If the planning authority has given notice to the applicant in terms of reg 9(1), the authority is required to refuse the application if the applicant fails to submit an environmental statement.[143]

In the case where the Scottish Ministers have either called in a planning application or where an appeal has been made to the Scottish Ministers against a decision (or failure to make a decision) by a planning authority, and it appears to the Scottish Ministers that the application is either a Sched 1 or 2 application and the development in question has not been the subject of a screening opinion or screening direction, and that the application is not accompanied by an environmental statement, the Scottish Ministers can request that the applicant provides relevant information.[144]

Environmental statements and planning referrals

Similar provisions to those which have just been outlined above, apply where a planning application has been referred to the Scottish Ministers which, in turn, consider that the application is an EIA application, but, at the same time, the application is not covered by an environmental statement.[145] The applicant must be notified in writing (within three weeks of the date of the application, or such longer period as is required) that an environmental statement is required and a copy of the notification must be sent to the planning authority.[146] An applicant who receives such notification may, within a period of three weeks which begins on the date of notification, write to the Scottish Ministers, stating that an environmental statement will be provided and the applicant may also request the Scottish Ministers to make a scoping direction.[147] If the applicant fails to write to the Scottish Ministers, the Scottish Ministers are under no duty to deal with the application, and, at the end of the three-week period, the applicant requires to be notified in writing that no further action is to be taken on the application.[148] If the Scottish Ministers have given such notification and the applicant fails to provide an environmental statement, the Scottish Ministers are required to refuse the planning application.[149]

Planning reviews and environmental statements

If, in considering a review (that is, a review of planning decisions and failure to take such decisions) in terms of the Act,[150] a planning authority is of the view that the application is an EIA application and is not covered by an environmental statement, the planning authority is required to inform the applicant that an environmental statement is required.[151] The applicant then has three weeks, from the date of notification, to write to the planning authority stating that he accepts its decision and, as a consequence, will provide an environmental statement, or will request a screening direction from the Scottish Ministers.[152] If the applicant fails to write to the planning authority, unless the Scottish Ministers have made a screening direction that the development is not an EIA development, the permission sought is to be deemed to be refused.[153] The consequence of this is that the applicant forfeits the right to appeal, against the decision of the planning authority, in terms of s 47 of the Act, to the Scottish Ministers. After such notification has been given to the applicant, unless the Scottish Ministers has made a screening direction to the effect that the development is not an EIA development, the planning authority may only refuse planning permission if the applicant does not submit an environmental statement.[154]

Scoping opinion

A developer who intends to make an EIA application can request that the planning authority adopts a scoping opinion.[155] A scoping opinion is simply a request that the planning authority informs the developer of the information which is to be included in an environmental statement.[156] The planning authority has five weeks to adopt a scoping opinion, or such longer period as may be agreed with the person who made the request.[157] In the face of the planning authority failing to adopt a scoping opinion, the developer may request the Scottish Ministers to make a scoping direction.[158]

Environmental statements and publicity, consultation etc.

Whereas there is no need for the applicant to consult anyone prior to submitting an environmental statement, it is good practice to do so. However, the planning authority, on receipt of an environmental statement, is required, *inter alia*, to send a copy of the environmental statement to the Scottish Ministers and also to each consultation body and the appropriate authority.[159] Copies of the environmental statement have also to be made available to the general public.[160] Finally, both the Scottish Ministers and a planning authority may request a person who has made an EIA application to provide further information, in which case the applicant is under a duty to do so.[161]

Conclusions on the EIA

The EIA (despite the plethora of case law which the topic has generated) is simply a procedure with which the relevant planning authority requires to comply, prior to making a decision as to whether a proposed development should be given planning permission. The EIA process ensures that the environmental impacts of a proposal are taken into account by the planning authority. Furthermore, the facts which are elicited by an EIA simply rank as a material consideration in planning law and, as such, the weighting (or importance) which the relevant planning authority accords to the EIA is at the discretion of the relevant planning authority and, as such, only challengeable on *Wednesbury* grounds.[162] It automatically follows, of course, that an EIA can conclude that a proposed development would have a significant effect on the environment (that is, a so-called 'negative EIA'), but, notwithstanding this fact, the planning authority can quite legitimately decide to give planning permission to the relevant development. However, frequently this basic principle escapes many of the pressure groups challenging proposed developments. Indeed, such groups often regard the EIA as a formidable hurdle which developers require to overcome in order to obtain planning permission. This, of course, is not so. Rather, the EIA is a facilitative process which, in theory but not often in in practice, should result in sounder planning decisions. In this context, Tromans observes[163] of the EIA and the strategic environmental impact assessment (SEA) (discussed below) that:

> They present procedural requirements which decision-makers can all too easily get wrong. They provide a handle for objectors to grasp, which may, if successful, result in the consent being quashed and the whole project derailed, or, if unsuccessful, will at least have provided the objectors with the satisfaction, or otherwise, of their day in court. Developers may, understandably, view the system as somewhat akin to a game of snakes and ladders, with themselves as the potential loser.

Strategic environmental impact assessment

Introduction

Essentially, a strategic environmental impact assessment (SEA) is an assessment of the potential environmental impacts of plans and programmes on the environment by competent authorities. The SEA has its origins in the US with the passing of the National Environmental Policy Act 1969 (NEPA) in which, as we have seen above, the EIA also has its origins. However, whereas the EIA operates at the micro level, the SEA operates at a macro, or strategic, level. Like the EIA, the SEA is purely procedural in nature. Again, as is the case with the EIA, simply because significant environmental effects are identified and assessed prior to the adoption of the relevant plan or programme, does not mean those effects will be avoided as a result of the SEA procedure.

The SEA Directive 2001/42/EC

Introduction

As is the case with the EIA, domestic UK law is EU-driven. Tromans observes that the SEA Directive (it should be noted that the word 'strategic' does not feature at all in the text of the Directive) was born of a need to make mandatory, and at the same time, harmonise, the SEA across the EU.[164] An important basis of the Directive is the precautionary principle, which is now a well engrained principle in EU law and policy.[165] The basic objective of the Directive is to provide for a high level of protection of the environment in the preparation and/or adoption of plans and programmes with a view to promoting sustainable development by ensuring that an environmental assessment is carried out in respect of plans and programmes, which have a significant effect on the environment.[166] It is up to Member States to decide whether the relevant plan or programme has such an effect.[167] Essentially, the objective of the Directive is to contribute to more transparent decision-making and to allow contributions to the development of a strategic plan by the public.[168] Whereas the EIA process is downstream, the SEA process is upstream and identifies options at an early planning stage.[169] The purpose of the SEA is to ensure that major effects on the environment are not predetermined by earlier planning measures before the EIA stage is reached.[170]

Scope of the SEA

It is mandatory for an environmental assessment to be carried out for all plans and programmes which are prepared for agriculture, forestry, fisheries, energy, waste management, industry, water management, telecommunications, tourism, town and country planning or land use, and which set the framework for projects for which an EIA is required, or which in view of the likely effect on sites is likely to require an assessment in terms of the Habitats Directive.[171] It can be seen, of course, that the 2001 Directive makes an important link between SEA and EIA. The criteria which require to be taken into account, in determining whether the plan or programme will have a significant effect on the environment, are set out in Annex II to the Directive, and include having regard to the duration, cumulative nature of effects, risks to human health and environment, natural considerations, and cultural heritage. The SEA requires to be carried out during preparation of the plan or programme before its adoption or submission to the relevant legislative procedure.[172]

Meaning of 'plans and programmes'

Plans and programmes are defined as those which are prepared and adopted at both national and local levels, and importantly, include modifications to such plans which are required by legislative, regulatory or administrative provisions.[173] In *Inter-Environment Bruxelles ASBL v Région de Bruxelles-Capitale*[174] it was held that for a plan or programme to fall within the scope of the Directive the relevant plans or programme need not be mandatory or compulsory. Furthermore, it was held that the adoption or revocation of a plan or programme included their partially or totally repeal. In *Cala Homes (South) Ltd v Secretary of State for Communities and Local Government.*[175] Sales J stated (*obiter*) that the revocation of a plan came within the scope of the Directive. However, in the Northern Ireland Court of Appeal case of *Central Craigavon Ltd v Dept of Environment for Northern* Ireland[176] it was held that a draft planning policy statement did not require a SEA since the formulation of the statement was not mandatory. Again, in *R. (Cala Homes (South)) Ltd v Secretary of State for Communities and Local Government*[177] it was held that a ministerial circular letter to planning authorities was not a plan or programme which fell within the scope of the Directive.

The issue as to what constitutes a plan or programme which falls within the scope of the Directive was considered by the Supreme Court in *Walton v The Scottish Ministers.*[178] This case concerned a challenge to the Aberdeen Western Peripheral Route (AWPR) road scheme. In 1996 the local roads authorities decided on a corridor for part of the AWPR. In 2001 a non-statutory regional partnership, the Modern Transport System (MTS) which included roads authorities, was formed in order to develop a road strategy for the north-east of Scotland. That strategy was described in a report which was published by MTS. However, the Scottish Ministers announced the adoption of a new scheme for a 'Fastlink' road which connected Stonehaven to the AWPR. The scheme was treated as a project for which an EIA was required. A public inquiry was held but its remit was restricted to technical and environmental issues. The pursuer argued that the decision by the Scottish Government to construct Fastlink was a modification of a plan or programme within the meaning of the SEA Directive. However, the Supreme Court held that the decision to construct Fastlink was not the modification of a plan or project which fell within the scope of the SEA Directive and, furthermore, did not set either the legal or the administrative framework for future projects since the decision had been implemented in accordance with roads legislation.[179] The court, therefore, was not required to decide whether the MTS was a plan or programme which fell within the scope of the Directive. Lords Reed and Hope reserved their opinions on the matter. However, while Lord Carnwath also reserved his opinion, his Lordship had 'serious doubts' as whether to the MTS amounted to a 'plan or programme' which fell within the scope of the SEA Directive since the MTS lacked the requisite formality.[180]

The Supreme Court had another opportunity to determine the meaning of the expression 'plan or programme' in *R. (Buckinghamshire CC) v Secretary of State for Transport*.[181] Here, the basic facts were that the Secretary of State for Transport published a command paper which was entitled 'High Speed Rail: Investing in Britain's Future – Decisions and Next Steps' (DNS)[182] which set out the government's strategy for the promotion, construction and operation of High Speed Two (HS2), a new national high speed rail network from London to Birmingham, Manchester and Leeds. One of the issues which fell to be decided was whether the DNS constituted a plan or programme which set the framework for development consent and was also required by administrative provisions. If so, an SEA should have been carried out before the DNS was adopted.

Lord Carnwath, who gave the main judgment, 'was prepared to proceed . . . or at least there was a referable issue (ie referable to the ECJ)' as to whether the DNS was a plan or programme for the purposes of the Directive.[183] He then went on to consider whether the DNS 'set the framework' for the purposes of Art 3. His Lordship concluded[184] that since the DNS did not constrain the decision-making process of the authority responsible (that is, Parliament) the DNS fell outwith the scope of the Directive.

For Lord Sumption (who tacitly accepted that the DNS was a 'plan or programme')[185] in order to fall within the scope of the SEA Directive, the plan or programme must comprise a 'policy framework' which operates as a constraint on the discretion of the authority responsible for making the decision about development consent. His Lordship went on to state that the plan or programme must, at least, limit the range of discretionary factors which can be taken into account in making that decision or affect the weight to be attached to them. In the last analysis, the DNS was nothing more than a proposal.[186]

Environmental report

Where a SEA is required, an environmental report must be prepared.[187] The environmental report identifies, describes and evaluates the likely significant effects on the environment of implementing the plan or programme, together with reasonable alternatives. The information which requires to be provided in the report is contained in Annex 1 to the Directive. The environmental report must include a non-technical summary.

SEA and Scotland

The 2001 Directive is implemented in Scotland by the Environmental Assessment (Scotland) Act 2005 (The 'Act').[188] The SEA regime is similar to the EIA regime which has just been discussed. The Act requires 'responsible authorities' (namely, public bodies) to conduct an environmental assessment in respect of new 'qualifying plans and programmes'.[189] The Act covers the plans and programmes which are subject to preparation or adoption by a public body (whether at national, regional or local level), and also includes modifications to such plans and programmes.[190] However, a qualifying plan or programme is only such if it relates to matters of a public character.[191] A qualifying plan or programme is one which is prepared for agriculture, forestry, fisheries, energy, industry, transport, waste management, water management, telecommunications, tourism, town and country planning and land use and, importantly, sets the framework for the projects which are contained in Schedule 1 to the Act. Schedule 1 contains a list of activities, including thermal power stations, nuclear power stations, waste incineration plants, and quarries and open-cast mining.[192] An SEA is also required if, in view of the likely effects on sites, it requires an assessment under the Habitats Directive, or if the qualifying plan or programme does not fall within the aforementioned categories but, nonetheless, sets the framework for future development consents of programmes.

The Act makes provision for the exclusion of certain plans and programmes.[193] Plans and programmes which relate to individual schools are exempt from the requirement to have an EA.[194] The Scottish Ministers may, by order, also exempt plans and programmes from the requirement to have an EA if it believes that the plan or programme will have no or minimal effect on the environment.[195]

Pre-screening

Plans and programmes which fall out-with the scope of the SEA Directive require to be pre-screened by the responsible authority in order to find out if plans or programmes have no or minimal impact on environment.[196] In determining whether the plan or programme has such an impact, the responsible authority requires to apply the criteria set out in Schedule 2.[197] If plan or programme has no such impact the responsible authority is required to inform the consultation authorities of that fact.[198] s 7(3).

Exemption: screening
Certain other plans and programmes which determine the use of small areas of land at local level, or minor modifications of plans and programmes, require to be formally screened to ascertain if they are to have significant environmental effects, and therefore require a full EA.[199] In determining whether the plan or programme has such effects the responsible authority is required to apply the criteria in Schedule 2.[200] If the responsible authority decides that an EA is not required for a plan or programme, reasons require to be stated.[201]

Screening procedure
Before making a decision under s 8(1) the responsible authority is required to prepare a summary of its views as to whether the plan or programme is likely to have significant environmental effects.[202] The summary requires to be sent to each consultation body.[203] The consultation body has twenty-eight days to respond to the responsible authority.[204] If the consultation authorities agree with the responsible authority that the plan or programme is unlikely to have a significant effect on the environment, or is likely to have a significant effect on the environment, the responsible authority is required to make a determination to that effect.[205] If the parties fail to agree, the matter is referred to the Scottish Ministers.[206] In such a case, the Scottish Ministers make the relevant determination.[207]

Screening publicity
Within twenty-eight days of a determination having been made under s 8(1), either by the responsible authority or the Scottish Ministers, the former must send a copy of the determination to the consultation authorities together with relevant reasons.[208] A copy of the determination requires to be made available for inspection by public, and also must be displayed on the responsible authority's website and published in a local newspaper.[209]

Preparation of environmental report
The responsible authority is required to prepare an environmental report for any qualifying plan or programme.[210] The report must identify, describe and evaluate the likely significant effects on the environment of implementing the plan or programme, and also identify reasonable alternatives to the plan or programme.[211] Schedule 3 specifies the information which is required to be contained in the report.

Scoping
Before deciding on the level of detail of the information which is to be included in an environmental report and the consultation period it intends to specify under s 16 (below), the responsible authority is required to send each consultation authority sufficient information of the qualifying plan or programme to allow the latter to form a view of those matters.[212] The latter has five weeks to respond.[213] The environmental report requires to be given local publicity.[214]

Environmental report
In preparing plans or programmes, the responsible authority is required to take account of the environmental report and of any views expressed on it.[215] Once adopted, copies of the environmental report must be made publicly available.[216] The responsible authority is also required to monitor the significant environmental effects of the implementation of the qualifying plan or programme, and if unforeseen adverse effects are identified, undertake appropriate remedial action.[217]

Summary

- The potential for a proposed development to cause pollution is a material consideration in terms of planning law.
- In granting planning permission a planning authority can attach conditions to regulate pollution from the proposed development.
- There are additional planning controls for hazardous waste.
- The environmental impact assessment (EIA) has its origins in the USA. The Town and Country Planning (Environmental Impact Assessment) (Scotland) Regulations 2011 make provision for the EIA of certain developments which may pose a threat to the environment.
- The EIA is simply a procedure which must be followed by the planning authority. There can be a negative EIA in the face of which the planning authority can lawfully grant planning permission.
- The Environmental Assessment (Scotland) Act 2005 makes provision for strategic environmental impact assessment (SEA).
- The SEA is required for plans and programmes of a public character.

Notes

1. See p. 1.
2. Repealed.
3. Repealed.

4. J. Rowan-Robinson, *Scottish Planning Law and Procedure* (W. Green/SULI) at 13, citing C. Haar, *Land-Use Planning in Free Society* (Harvard University Press, 1951).

5. Scotland's two National Parks Authorities are the planning authorities for national parks.

6. For a general overview of the role of the Scottish Government in relation to planning, see R. McMaster et al., *Scottish Planning Law*, 3rd edn (Bloomsbury, 2014) paras 2.34-2.37.

7. National Planning Framework 3, paras 3.1-3.40.

8. Ibid. para 3.12.

9. Scottish Government June 2014.

10. Ibid. para 154.

11. Ibid. para 155.

12. Ibid. para 176.

13. Ibid. para 178. See also NPPG 10 Planning and Waste Management (Scottish Government, 1996) and PAN 63 Waste Management Planning (2002).

14. Scottish Government, Air Quality and Land Use Planning (2004).

15. See Chapter 9.

16. See PAN 1/2011 Planning and Noise.

17. M. Purdue, 'The relationship between development control and specialist pollution controls: which is the tail and which the dog? [1999] JPL 585.

18. See M. Purdue, 'The impact on planning law', in J. Holder, *Impact of EC Environmental Law in the UK* (Wildy, 1997) 231 at 232.

19. The Scottish Government has issued guidance on the relationship between planning controls and environmental regulation (see PAN 51 Revised, 2006). For a useful, if slightly dated, discussion of the inter-relationship of planning and pollution control, see J. Pugh-Smith, 'The local authority as a regulator of pollution in the 1990s' [1992] JPL 103 and S. Tromans, 'Town and country planning and environmental protection' [1992] JPL *Occasional Paper* at [6].

20. Town and Country Planning (Scotland) Act 1997, s 37(2).

21. V. Moore, *A Practical Approach to Planning Law*, 9th edn (Oxford University Press) at 248.

22. [1994] Env LR 37.

23. Ibid. at 49.

24. For an analysis of this case, see K. Mylrea, 'Drawing the dividing line between planning control and pollution control' (1994) 6 JEL 93.

25. [1998] JPL 787.

26. Ibid. at 795.

27. An appeal to the Court of Appeal was dismissed.

28. [2007] Env LR 14.
29. Town and Country Planning (Scotland) Act 1997, s 37(1). See Scottish Government (1998) Circ 4/1998 – The Use of Conditions in Planning Permissions'.
30. [1981] AC 578.
31. 1979 SC 200.
32. See also *North East Fife DC v SoS for Scotland* 1992 SLT 373.
33. Planning (Hazardous Substances) (Scotland) Act 1997 s 1.
34. Ibid. s 2(1).
35. Ibid. s 3(1).
36. SI 2015 No 181.
37. Ibid reg 3(1).
38. Ibid. reg 4.
39. Ibid. reg 4(1).
40. Ibid. reg 6.
41. Ibid. reg 7.
42. Ibid. reg 9.
43. Ibid. reg 11.
44. Planning (Hazardous Substances) (Scotland) Act 1997 s 7(1).
45. Ibid. s 7(2).
46. 2007 SLT 966. See (2007) 124 SPEL 139.
47. Planning (Hazardous Substances) (Scotland) Act 1997 s 12(1).
48. Ibid. s 12(2).
49. Ibid. s 12(4).
50. Ibid. s 13(1).
51. Ibid. s 15(1).
52. Ibid. s 16(1).
53. Ibid. s 17.
54. Ibid. s 18(1).
55. Ibid. s 18(2).
56. Ibid. s 18(3).
57. Ibid. s 18(4).
58. Ibid. s 18(5).
59. Ibid. s 19(1).
60. Ibid. s 19(5).
61. Ibid. s 19(6).
62. Ibid. s 19(8).
63. Ibid. s 20(1).
64. For the purposes of the section, 'relevant requirements', in relation to any decision, means any requirements of the Act or the principle Act (namely, the Town and Country Planning (Scotland) Act 1997 or of the Tribunals

and Inquiries Act 1992 or of any order, regulations or rules which are made under the Town and Country Planning (Hazardous Substances) (Scotland) Act 1997 or under either of those Acts which are applicable to the decision; s 20(4).

65. Ibid. s 20(3).
66. The appropriate person means
    (a) in relation to a contravention falling within paragraph (a) of subsection (2),
        (i) any person knowingly causing the substances to be present on, over or under the land;
        (ii) any person allowing it to be so present, and
    (b) in relation to a contravention falling within para (a) or (b) of that subsection, the occupier of the land; ibid. s 21(3).
67. Ibid. s 21(1).
68. Ibid. s 21(2).
69. Ibid. s 21(4).
70. Ibid. s 21(6)-(8).
71. Ibid. ss 22 and 23.
72. Ibid. s 27(1).
73. Ibid. s 27(2).
74. See the US National Environmental Policy Act 1969. The USA, along with Canada and the European Union, is said to have the most sophisticated legislation on EIA; see P. Birnie et al., *International Law and the Environment*, 3rd edn (Oxford University Press, 2009) at 166.
75. See R. Carson, *Silent Spring* (1962).
76. S. Tromans, *Environmental Impact Assessment*, 2nd edn (Bloomsbury, 2012) at 2.
77. Department of Environment (now DEFRA) Circ. 02/1999 *Environmental Impact Assessment* para 9.
78. Scottish Government, Users Guide to the Environmental Impact Assessment (Scotland) Regulations 2011 (Scottish Government website, n. d.).
79. For a general discussion of the EIA in international law, see P. Sands et al., *Principles of International Environmental Law*, 3rd edn (Cambridge University Press) ch. 13, and P. Birnie et al. (note 74) at 164-89.
80. P. Sands (note 78) at 601.
81. P. Birnie et al. (note 74) at 174.
82. S. Bell and D. McGilivray, *Environmental Law*, 8th edn (Oxford University Press, 2013) at 455.
83. For a comprehensive discussion of the Aarhus Convention, see F. McCartney, 'The Aarhus Convention and Scots law', in F. McManus (ed.), *Environmental Law in Scotland* (W. Green/SULI) ch. 16.

84. F. McCartney (note 82) at 16.02.
85. (1997) ICJ Reports 7.
86. *Pulp Mills on the River Uruguay* (Argentina v Uruguay) (Judgment) General List no 135, 20 April 2010 38.
87. European Community Policy and Action Programme on the Environment, OJ C139, 13.6.1977 p. 1, para [203].
88. For a discussion of the opposition of the UK government, see S. Tromans (note 75) at 2.19.
89. S. Tromans (note 75) at 2.19.
90. Directive 2011/92/EU, Preamble, para 2.
91. Ibid. Art 1.
92. [2011] ENV LR 26.
93. See, e.g., *Commission v Spain* [1993] ECR 1-5997.
94. See p. 282.
95. See, e.g., *R. (Baker) v Bath and North East Somerset Council* [2009] EWHC 595.
96. [2012] Env LR 22.
97. See also *R. v Swale BC ex p RSPB* [1991] JPL 39 and *R. (Save Britain's Heritage) v SoS for Communities and Local Government* [2014] Env LR 9.
98. Ibid. Art 1
99. *R v North Yorkshire Council* [1999] Env. LR 623 at 630 (*per* Lord Hoffman). See also *R v SoS ex p Greenpeace Ltd.* [1999] 4 All ER 352.
100. See, e.g., the Environmental Impact Assessment and Natural Habitats (Extraction of Minerals by Marine Dredging) (Scotland) Regulations (SSI 2007 No 485) (as amended).
101. SSI 2011 No 139.
102. Ibid. reg 3. Environmental information is defined as 'any environmental statement and any additional information, any representations made by any body required by these Regulations to make representations and any representations duly made by any other person about the environmental effects of a development'; ibid. reg 2(1).
103. Ibid. reg 2(1).
104. An exempt development is a development in respect of which the Scottish Government has made a direction in terms of reg 5(4).
105. Ibid. reg 2(1).
106. Ibid. Sched 2 para 23.
107. *R. (on the application of Goodman) v Lewisham LBC* [2003] Env LR 28.
108. The expression sensitive area is defined in reg 2(1) and includes sites of special scientific interest.
109. Ibid. reg 2(1).
110. Ibid. reg 5(6) and Sched 3.
111. *R. (Malster) v Ipswich BC* [2002] Env LR D7. See also *R. (Kathro) v Rhonda*

Cynon Taff BC [2002] Env LR 15, *Hockley v Essex CC* [2014] EWHC 4051 and *R. (Lyon) v Cambridge CC* [2012] Env LR 11.

112. [2003] EWCA Civ 1408.
113. Ibid. at [58].
114. Ibid. at [61].
115. See also *River Faughan Anglers Ltd Application for Judicial Review*, Re [2014] NIQB 34 and *R. (Loader) v SoS* [2012] EWCA Civ 869.
116. [2002] Env LR D7.
117. See Bell et al., *Environmental Law*, 8th edn (Oxford University Press, 2013) at 471.
118. [2003] Env LR 30.
119. [2013] Env LR 36.
120. See also *R. (Catt) v Brighton and Hove City Council* [2006] EWHC 1337. For a discussion of *Catt*, see (2008) 125 SPEL 20. See also *R. (Champion) v North Norfolk DC* [2014] Env LR 23.
121. Town and Country Planning (Environmental Impact Assessment) (Scotland) Regulations 2011 (SSI 2011 No 139) reg 6(1).
122. Ibid. reg 6(6).
123. Ibid. reg 7(1).
124. Ibid. reg 7(4).
125. Ibid. reg 5(7).
126. *R. (Bateman) v South Cambridgeshire DC* [2011] EWCA Civ 157 per Moore-Bick at para [21]. See (2011) 148 SPEL 139.
127. Town and Country Planning (Environmental Impact Assessment) (Scotland) Regulations 2011 (SSI 2011 No 139) reg 8.
128. Ibid. reg 2(1).
129. *Berkeley V SoS for the Environment, Transport and Regions* [2001] 2 AC 603 at 608 [per Lord Bingham].
130. S. Tromans (note 75) at 4.11.
131. Town and Country Planning (Environmental Impact Assessment) (Scotland) Regulations 2011 (SSI 2011 No 139) reg 2(1).
132. Sched 4 Part 1 para 4 and Sched 4 Part 2 para 5.
133. See Scottish Government website.
134. [2001] 2 AC 603.
135. Ibid. at 617.
136. [2010] Env LR 40.
137. [2004] Env LR 29 at [41].
138. [2005] Env LR 30.
139. See also the Court of Appeal case of *R. (Jones) v Mansfield DC* [2004 Env LR 21 and *R. (Marton-cum-Grafton Parish Council) v North Yorkshire CC* [2014] Env LR 10. Tromans observes that many challengers of planning authority deci-

sions in EIA cases have a tendency to overlook this point; S. Tromans, 'EIA, SEA and energy projects: better decision-making or a game of snakes and ladders' (2014) 26 ELM 83 at 84.

140. Town and Country Planning (Environmental Impact Assessment) (Scotland) Regulations 2011 (SSI 2011 No 139) reg 9(1).
141. Ibid. reg 9(3).
142. Ibid. reg 9(4).
143. Ibid. reg 9(5).
144. Ibid. reg 10. The relevant information is specified in reg 7(3)-(5).
145. Ibid. reg 11.
146. Ibid. reg 11(1)(2).
147. Ibid. reg 11(3).
148. Ibid. reg 11(4).
149. Ibid. reg 11(5).
150. Town and Country Planning (Scotland) Act 1997, s 43A(8).
151. Town and Country Planning (Environmental Impact Assessment)(Scotland) Regulations 2011 (SSI 2011 No 139) reg 13(1).
152. Ibid. reg 13(2).
153. Ibid. reg 13(3).
154. Ibid. reg 13(4).
155. Ibid. reg 14(1).
156. Ibid. reg 2(1).
157. Ibid. reg 14(4).
158. Ibid. reg 14(7).
159. Ibid. reg 19(1). The appropriate authority is either the Health and Safety Executive or the Office for Nuclear Regulation when these bodies require to be consulted under the Regulations. The consultation bodies include the Scottish Government, Scottish Natural Heritage, and SEPA; ibid. reg 2(1).
160. Ibid. reg 22.
161. Ibid. reg 23.
162. See, e.g., *Tesco Stores Ltd v SoS* [1994] JPL 919.
163. S. Tromans (note 138) at 83.
164. S. Tromans (note 75) at 8.7.
165. Directive 2001/42/EU. Preamble.
166. Ibid. Art 1.
167. Ibid. Art 3
168. *Ashdown Forest Economic* Development *LLP v SSLG* [2014] EWHC 406 (per Sales J) at para [102].
169. European Commission's First Report on the SEA Directive, COM (2009) 469 final para 4.1.

170. *R. (Buckinghamshire CC) v Secretary of State for Transport* [2014] 1 WLR 324 at 338 (per Lord Carnwath).
171. Directive 2001/42/EU, Art 3. Directive 92/43/ EEC (Habitats Directive).
172. Directive 2001/42/EU, Art 4.
173. Ibid. Art 2.
174. Case C-567/10; [2012] Env LR 30.
175. [2010] EWHC 2866. At para [62].
176. [2011] NICA 17.
177. [2011] EWHC 97.
178. 2012 SC (UKSC) 67. For a discussion of *Walton* see M. McKay, 'Supreme Court refuses AWPR appeal' (2012) 154 SPEL 131.
179. Roads (Scotland) Act 1984.
180. 2012 SC (UKSC) 67 at [99].
181. [2014] 1 WLR 324.
182. Cmnd. 8247.
183. Ibid. at 334.
184. Ibid. at 338.
185. Ibid at 360.
186. Ibid. at 361.
187. Ibid. Art 5.
188. See Scottish Government, Planning Advice Note 1/2010. See (2010) 139 SPEL 67.
189. Environmental Assessment (Scotland) Act 2005 s 1(1).
190. Ibid. s 4(1)(2).
191. Ibid. s 5(2).
192. Ibid. s 5(3).
193. Ibid. s 5(4).
194. Ibid. s 6(1).
195. Ibid. s 6(3).
196. Ibid. s 7(1).
197. Ibid. s 7(2).
198. Ibid. s 7(3).
199. Ibid. s 8(1).
200. Ibid. s 8(3).
201. Ibid. s 8(2).
202. Ibid. s 9(1).
203. Ibid. s 9(2).
204. Ibid. s 9(3).
205. Ibid. s 9(4)(5).
206. Ibid. s 9(6).
207. Ibid. s 9(7).

208. Ibid. s 10(1).
209. Ibid. s 10(2).
210. Ibid. s 14(1).
211. Ibid. s 14(2).
212. Ibid. s 15(1).
213. Ibid. s 15(2).
214. Ibid. s 16.
215. Ibid. s 17.
216. Ibid. s 18(1).
217. Ibid. s 19.

CHAPTER 11

Nature Conservation

The law relating to nature conservation is fragmented. This approach evolves from the various reasons why we wish to conserve nature. The Wildlife and Countryside Act 1981 is the most important statute dealing with nature conservation. The Act makes provision for the protection of wild animals, plants, sites of special scientific interest nature reserves and Ramsar sites.

The Nature Conservation (Scotland) Act 2004 places a duty on every public authority and every public office holder to further the conservation of biodiversity.

In order to secure the survival of flora and fauna, it is important that habitats are protected. Both the Habitats Directive and the Birds Directive are implemented in Scotland by the Conservation (Natural Habitats) Regulations 1994.

Introduction

In this chapter we turn our attention to the subject of nature conservation.[1] We have already observed[2] that modern environmental law owes its origins to the popular belief that cholera was caused by miasms (or odours) which emanated largely from various forms of pollution in the built environment. In general terms, the legislation which was put in place by the government to deal with the cholera threat was, in effect, to regulate the physical environment in order to protect human health. Environmental policy was, therefore, anthropocentric. Since the nineteenth century such an approach has continued with a medley of legislation, the purpose of which is to protect humans from various forms of pollution. In this chapter we look at how the natural environment is protected. However, we may wish to protect or conserve nature for a variety of reasons. We may wish to conserve watercourses which yield fish, not simply for its own end, but rather, in order to ensure a suitable source of food and also in order to protect recreational angling.

The desire to protect the habitats of game birds may have the same rationale. However, certain forms of wildlife, for example, rats, may be regarded as posing a direct threat to human health. Such pests can also interfere with certain activities such as farming. Indeed, Reid, in commenting on the legislation of the Scottish Parliament, observes that the law actively encouraged action against pest species which are now the subject of considerable conservation effort.[3] The learned author notes that an Act of 1458 ordered the destruction of all birds of prey. Wolves were to be hunted and rooks were to be persecuted, with any trees where they were allowed to nest being forfeit. There is also a growing general appreciation of how the countryside provides us with valuable services.

Enough has been said to indicate that such a variety of objectives must, perforce, require different legislative approaches. We now discuss the relevant law, which is fragmented. Indeed, in this respect, the law resembles that relating to noise.[4]

Protection of wild animals

The Wildlife and Countryside Act 1981 ('the Act') is the most important statute governing nature conservation in the United Kingdom. The Act has been substantially amended since 1981. The Act makes provision for the protection of wild animals, plants, sites of special scientific interest, nature reserves and Ramsar sites.[5] The Act makes special provision for the protection of birds and their eggs.

Protection of birds and eggs

Part 1 of the Act makes provision for the protection of wildlife. It is made an offence for any person to intentionally or recklessly to:

(i)   kill, injure or take any wild bird,[6]
(ii)   take, damage or destroy, or otherwise interfere with any nest which is either in use, or is being built, or,
(iii) at any other time, take, damage or destroy or otherwise interfere with any nest which is habitually used by any bird which is included in the Act,[7]
(iv)   obstruct any wild bird from using its nest,
(v)   take or destroy an egg of any wild bird.[8]

Furthermore, if any person has in his possession or control any live or dead wild bird, or anything which is derived from such a bird, or an egg of a wild bird, or any part of such a bird, that person is guilty of an offence.[9] In *Robinson v Everett*[10] it was held that a stuffed bird constituted a dead bird for the purposes of the Act. Liability under the Act is strict. That is to say, it is not necessary to prove that the accused knew that the bird which he had in his possession fell within the scope of the Act.[11]

The Act makes provision for defences. A person is not guilty of an offence if he shows that:

(1) the bird or egg had not been taken or killed, or had been killed or taken, at or from a place in Scotland, otherwise than in contravention of the relevant provisions,[12]

(2) the bird, egg or other thing in his possession or control, has been sold at a place in Scotland (whether to him or to any other person) otherwise in contravention of those provisions, or

(3) the bird or other thing in his possession or control, had been killed at, taken or sold at a place outwith Scotland, and:

    (a) that the act of killing taking or sale, would not, if it had been committed in Scotland, have been in contravention of the relevant provisions, or

    (b) the bird egg or other thing had been brought from the place where it was killed taken or sold in accordance with the relevant regulations.[13]

It is also made an offence for any person to intentionally or recklessly, either disturb any wild bird which is included in Sched 1[14] to the Act, while the bird is either building a nest or is in, on or near a nest which contains eggs or young, or for any person to disturb the dependent young of such a bird.[15] Furthermore, it is made an offence for any person who intentionally or recklessly disturbs any wild bird which is included in Sched 1 which leks,[16] while it is so doing.[17] It is also an offence for any person who intentionally or recklessly harasses any wild bird which is included in Sched 1A.[18] Furthermore, any person who knowingly causes, or permits to be done, an act which is made unlawful by any of the provisions of s 1, commits an offence.[19]

For the purposes of s 1, a wild bird does not include any bird which has been bred in captivity, unless it has been lawfully released or allowed to escape from captivity as part of a re-population or re-introduction programme, or it is a mallard, grey or red-legged partridge, common pheasant or red grouse which is no longer in captivity and is not in a place where it was reared.[20]

The Act makes exceptions to liability under s 1 in relation to the taking or killing of certain birds[21] outside the close season.[22] The exception extends to injuring such a bird outside the close season, in an attempt to kill the bird. However, the exception only applies if the person who kills or injures the bird had a legal right to kill or injure the bird, or the person had permission from a person who had the right to give permission to kill such a bird.[23] A similar exception is made in relation to the taking of such a bird. However, the exceptions, to either taking or killing a wild bird, do not apply in Scotland on a Sunday or Christmas day, in relation to certain birds.[24] Furthermore, an exception to liability under s 1 is made in relation to the taking for, the purpose of breeding, a partridge or pheasant, or the egg of such a bird, provided either the person who takes the bird had the legal right to do so or had the requisite permission.[25] Again, an exception is made in relation to liability under s 1 to the taking of red grouse for the purpose of preventing the spread of disease or with the intention of releasing it from captivity within twelve hours, provided that the relevant person had the legal right to do so or he has the requisite permission.[26]

The Act makes further provision for exemptions from liability in terms of s 1, for example, if the taking or killing of any bird is required for preventing damage to crops in terms of the Agriculture Act 1947, or as a result of any action which is taken under the Animal Health Act 1981 or (subject to certain exceptions) as a result of any action which is necessary for the preservation of public health or preventing the spread of disease.[27] The Act also exempts from liability under s 1 (subject to certain conditions) anything done under a licence which has been granted by the Scottish Ministers (or any person to whom licensing power has been delegated).[28] Such a licence may be either general or specific in nature and may be granted either to persons of a class or to a particular person.[29]

In order to further protect birds, the Act prohibits a variety of methods of killing or taking wild birds including the poisoning of such birds.[30] Indeed, the recent publicity which has been given to the poisoning of raptors illustrates the fact that the problem is widespread.

The Act also makes provision for the sale of live or dead wild birds and eggs.[31]

The Act provides for the registration and marking scheme of certain captive birds.[32] As far as such birds are concerned, it is made an offence to either keep or confine any bird in a cage or other receptacle of insufficient height, length or breadth to allow the bird to stretch its wings freely.[33]

Protection of other wild animals
The Act makes it an offence for any person to intentionally or recklessly kill, injure or take certain wild animals.[34] Furthermore, it is also made an offence for any person to have in his possession or control any live or dead, or any part of or anything which is derived from, a wild animal which

falls within the scope of the Act.[35] However, the Act makes provision for a number of defences.[36]

It is not an offence if the accused can prove that the animal had not been killed or taken, or that the animals had been killed or taken at or from a place in Scotland, otherwise than in contravention of the relevant provisions.[37] It is also a defence to prove that the animal or other thing in his possession in his control had been sold at a place in Scotland, whether to him or to any other person, otherwise in contravention of those provisions. Furthermore, it is also a defence to prove that the animal or other thing in his possession or control had been killed at, taken from, or sold at a place outwith Scotland and that the act of killing, taking or sale would not, if it had been committed in Scotland, have been in contravention of the relevant provisions, or that the animal or other thing had been brought from the place where it was killed, taken or sold in accordance with the relevant regulations.[38]

It is also an offence for anyone to either intentionally or recklessly damage or destroy or obstruct access to any structure or place which any animal which is included in Schedule 5 to the Act, uses for shelter or protection, or for anyone to disturb any such animal while it is occupying such a structure or place which it uses for such a purpose.[39] Additional protection is given to dolphins, whales, porpoises and basking sharks. It is made an offence for any person to intentionally or recklessly disturb or harass any such wild animals.[40]

At this juncture brief mention should be made of separate legislation which protects wild animals. The Wild Mammals (Protection) Act 1996 makes it an offence for any person to mutilate, kick, beat, impale, stab, burn, stone, crush, drown, drag or asphyxiate any wild mammal with intent to inflict unnecessary suffering.[41] Whereas badgers are protected against being killed or taken by certain means under the Wildlife and Countryside Act 1981,[42] additional protection is given under the Protection of Badgers Act 1992. The Marine (Scotland) Act 2010 makes it an offence (subject to certain exceptions) for any person to kill, injure or take a live seal, whether intentionally or recklessly.[43] The Deer (Scotland) Act 1996 makes provision for the unlawful injuring or killing of deer.[44]

The Wildlife and Countryside Act 1981 provides further protection to the exploitation of wild animals. It is made an offence for any person to either, sell, offer or expose for sale, or have in his possession for the purposes of sale, any live or dead wild animal (or anything which is derived from such an animal) which is included in Schedule 5.[45] It is also an offence for anyone to either publish, or cause to be published, any advertisement which is likely to be understood that he either buys or sells, or intends to buy or sell, any of these things. Furthermore, it is an offence for any person to knowingly cause or permit any of the offences which fall within the scope of s 9 of the Act.[46] In any proceedings for an offence which falls within the scope of s 9, there is a presumption that the animal is wild, unless the contrary is shown.[47]

The Act provides for certain exceptions to liability under s 9.[48] For example, any act which is covered by an order which is made in terms of the Animals Act 1981 for the prevention of the spread of disease is exempt from liability.[49] Also the taking or killing of disabled wild animals, in certain circumstances, is exempt.[50] Furthermore, an exception is made in relation to anything which is done under a licence which has been granted by an appropriate authority.[51]

Brief mention should be made of the Conservation (Natural Habitats etc.) Regulations 1994[52] which make provision for the protection of animals which fall within the scope of the Habitats Directive.[53]

Protection of wild hares

The Wildlife and Countryside Act 1981 makes special provision for the protection of wild hares. It is made an offence for any person to intentionally or recklessly kill, injure or take any wild mountain hare or brown hare in the close season.[54] The close season for hares can be varied by an order of the Scottish Ministers.[55] Furthermore, the Scottish Ministers are given power to declare by order, that wild hares be protected outwith the close season if the Scottish Ministers consider it expedient to do so.[56] However, the period (a 'special protection period') which is so declared must not exceed fourteen days. Before making any order the Scottish Ministers must consult such persons who appear to them as being representative of persons who are interested in the killing or taking of wild hares.[57] The making of such an order confers the same protection to hares as if the period of special protection which is declared by the order was part of the close season.[58] Any order which either varies the closing season or declares a period of special protection for hares may apply either to the whole or part of Scotland which is specified in the relevant order.[59] In any proceedings for an offence which falls within the scope of s 10A, there is a presumption that the hare in question is wild unless the contrary is shown.[60]

The Act makes several exceptions to liability under s 10A. For example, no offence is committed if it is shown that the relevant animal had been so seriously disabled (otherwise by his unlawful act) that there was no reasonable chance of its recovering.[61] Additionally, a person is not guilty of an offence under s 10A by reason of his taking any hare if he shows that he had a legal right to take the animal or permission from a person who had a right to give such permission to take the animal which had been disabled otherwise than by his unlawful act and that it was taken solely for the purposes of tending the animal and releasing it when no longer disabled.[62] A further defence is provided to a person who is authorised[63] in terms of the Act. An authorised person is not guilty of an offence under s 10A(1) by reason of the killing of a wild hare if he shows that his action was necessary for the purpose of preventing serious damage to livestock, crops, vegetables, fruit, growing timber or any further form of property or to fisheries.[64] However, the defence cannot be relied on in certain circumstances. The defence cannot be relied on if it had become apparent before the action was taken, that the relevant action was necessary, and either a licence had not been applied for as soon as reasonably practicable after the fact had become apparent, or that an application for such a licence had not been determined.[65] Furthermore, an authorised person is not entitled to rely on the defence (in relation to any action which is taken by him) unless he notifies the appropriate authority (namely, the Scottish Ministers or persons to whom such power has been delegated) as soon as practicable after the action was taken that he had taken it.[66] Finally, a person does not commit an offence in terms of s 10A if the action which he took was carried out as a consequence of a notice which was served by the Scottish Ministers in terms of the Agriculture (Scotland) Act 1948[67] or anything which was done under or in pursuance of an order which was made under the Animal Health Act 1981.[68]

Prevention of poaching of wild hares and rabbits etc.
The Act also makes special provision for the prevention of poaching of wild hares and rabbits. It is made an offence for any person to intentionally or recklessly kill, injure or take any wild hare or rabbit.[69] In any proceedings for an offence, there is a presumption that an animal is wild, unless the contrary is shown.[70] However, a person is not guilty of such an offence if either he had the legal right to do so, or he had permission from a person who had the right to give permission to carry out the act in question.[71] Furthermore, a person is not guilty of an offence which comprises of the killing of a wild hare or rabbit, if he shows that the animal had been so seriously disabled otherwise than by his unlawful act, and that there was no reasonable chance of recovering.[72] Finally, a person does not commit an offence under s 11G if the action which he took was carried out as a consequence of a notice which was served by the Scottish Ministers in terms of the Agriculture (Scotland) Act 1948, or anything which was done under or in pursuance of an order which was made under the Animal Health Act 1981.[73]

The Wildlife and Countryside Act 1981 also makes it an offence for any person:

(i)   to have in his possession or control any live or dead wild animal which has been killed or taken in contravention of s 10A or s 11G, or any part of anything which is derived from such an animal,

(ii) to sell, offer or expose for sale or have in his possession or transport for the purposes of sale, any such animal or any part of anything which is derived from such an animal, or

(iii) to publish or causes to be published any advertisement which is likely to be understood as conveying that he buys or sells or intends to buy or sell any of those things.[74]

However, it is a defence for the accused to show that he carried out the activity concerned with reasonable excuse.[75] In any proceedings for an offence under s 11I the animal in question is to be presumed to have been a wild animal unless the contrary is shown.[76]

Prohibition of certain methods of killing wild animals
The Act makes provision for the prohibition of certain methods of killing or taking of wild animals. Essentially, the Act is striking at poaching. However, only a brief overview can be given of such provisions here. For example, the Act prohibits the use of certain snares, the use of crossbows, ammunition and decoys.[77] The Act makes detailed provision for the training and identification of persons who use snares.[78] A duty is placed on those who set snares to regularly inspect them.[79] The person who uses a snare is required to obtain the permission of the owner or occupier of the relevant land.[80] The person who has an identity number in relation to the use of snares is required to keep certain records which relate to the use of snares.[81] The Scottish Ministers are required either by themselves, or by another person, to carry out a review of the operation and effect of the provisions of the Act relating to the prohibition of certain methods of taking and killing of wild animals.[82] The first review is required to be carried out no later than 31 December 2016 and every five years thereafter.[83] After the review is carried out, a report on the review must be submitted to the Scottish Parliament.[84]

Brief mention should be also be made, at this juncture, of certain legislation, the object of which is to protect particular species.

Badgers
Whereas the badger is protected from being killed or taken by certain methods under the Wildlife and Countryside Act 1981,[85] additional protection

is provided under the Protection of Badgers Act 1992. The latter Act makes it an offence, subject to certain exceptions, for any person to wilfully kill, injure or take a badger.[86] It is also an offence under that Act for any person to cruelly ill-treat a badger.[87] Additionally, it is made an offence, subject to certain exceptions, for any person to interfere with a badger sett by certain means.[88] The Act makes it an offence, subject to certain exceptions, for any person to sell or offer for sale a live badger which is in his possession or under his control.[89] Furthermore, it is an offence, subject to certain exceptions, for anyone to cause or knowingly permit such an act to be committed.[90] Finally, the Act makes it an offence, subject to certain exceptions, for any person to mark, ring etc. any badger.[91]

Seals

Seals are protected under the Conservation (Natural Habitats) Regulations 1994.[92] Further protection is given to seals under the Marine (Scotland) Act 2010. It is made an offence, subject to certain exceptions, to kill, injure or take a live seal, whether intentionally or recklessly.[93] The Act also makes provision for the licensing of the slaughter of seals for certain purposes.[94]

Deer

The control and management of deer is in the responsibility of Scottish Natural Heritage (SNH).[95] The Scottish Ministers are under a duty to prescribe a close season in relation to every species of female deer, and also have the power to prescribe a close season in relation to the male species of deer.[96] It is made an offence, subject to certain exceptions, for any person without a legal right, to take or wilfully kill or injure deer, without permission of the person who has such a right.[97] The Act also makes provision for offences which relate to poaching.[98]

Protection of wild plants

The Act makes provision for the protection of wild plants. It is made an offence for any person to intentionally or recklessly uproot or destroy any wild plant or any seed which is attached to a wild plant which is specified in the Act.[99] Furthermore, it is made an offence for any unauthorised person to intentionally uproot any wild plant which is not specified in the Act. It is also made an offence to sell, offer or expose for sale, or have in one's possession or transport for the purposes of sale, any live or dead wild plant, or anything which is derived from such a plant.[100] It is also an offence to either publish or cause to be published, any advertisement which is likely to be understood as conveying that the person concerned buys or sells, or intends to buy or sell, any of those things. However, the Act provides for certain defences. It is a defence for the accused to show:

(i)   that the relevant act 'the unlawful act' was the incidental result of a lawful operation or other activity,

(ii) that the person who carried out the lawful operation or other activity either took reasonable precautions for the purpose of avoiding carrying out the unlawful act, or did not foresee and could not have reasonably foreseen, that the unlawful act would be an incidental result of the carrying-out of the lawful operation or other activity, and

(iii) that the person who carried out the unlawful act took, immediately upon the consequences of the act being apparent, such steps as were reasonably practicable in the circumstances to minimise the damage to the wild plant in relation to which the unlawful act was carried out.[101]

It is also an offence for any person to knowingly cause or permit to be done any act which is made unlawful by any of the aforementioned offences.[102] In relation to any proceedings for an offence which relates to the selling, offering for sale of any plant etc., or for knowingly causing or permitting an unlawful act, the relevant plant is presumed to have been a wild plant unless the contrary is shown.[103]

The Conservation (Natural Habitats etc.) Regulations 1994[104] make provision for the protection in relation to the European Protected Species of plants, that is to say, plants which fall within the scope of the Habitats Directive.

Habitat protection

In order to secure the survival of flora and fauna it is imperative that their habitats are protected. As far as the protection of the latter is concerned, it the loss of habitat, rather than any form of direct attack on fauna, which poses the greatest threat to most species today.[105]

European Sites

The Council Directive on the conservation of natural habitats and wild fauna and flora[106] ('the Habitats Directive') requires a European ecological network of special areas of conservation (SAC) to be set up under the title Natura 2000.[107] The network comprises sites which host the natural habitat types and species which are listed in the Directive. The purpose of the network is to enable the natural habitat types and the species habitats to be maintained or, where appropriate, restored, and also to protect the most seriously threatened habitats in Europe. The Natura 2000 network also includes special protection areas (SPAs) which are classified by Member States under the Birds Directive.[108] Both the Habitats and the Birds Directives are implemented in Scotland by the Conservation (Natural Habitats) Regulations 1994.[109] The Scottish Ministers are placed under a duty to propose a list of sites on the basis of criteria which are specified in the Habitats Directive.[110] The list was required to be submitted to the European Commission by 5 June 1995.[111] After the list is adopted, the Scottish Ministers are placed under a duty to designate the relevant site as a SAC as soon as possible and at least within six years.[112] The Scottish Ministers are also placed under a duty to classify such sites as SPAs in order to meet the objectives which are contained in the Birds Directive.[113] The Secretary of State is placed under a duty to compile a register of European Sites in Great Britain.[114] The Secretary of State has a duty to notify the appropriate conservation body.[115] As far as Scotland is concerned, the appropriate conservation body is Scottish Natural Heritage (SNH).[116] After SNH receives such notification, it is required to notify every owner and occupier of land within the site, as well as every planning authority in whose area the site or part of the site is situated.[117] The relevant planning authority is required to maintain a register which requires to be made available for inspection free of charge to the public.[118] SNH may enter into a management agreement with the owner, lessee or occupier of land which forms part of a European Site for the management, conservation or restoration of the site or any part of it.[119]

It is made an offence for any person to intentionally or recklessly damage any natural feature by reason of which the land is a European Site.[120] SNH is given the power to make byelaws for the protection of a European Site.[121]

Mention should also be made of the requirement that a competent authority (an expression which is not defined in the Habitats Directive, but would include a planning authority) before it decides to either undertake, or give consent to any plan or project which is likely to have a significant effect on a European Site, and is not directly connected with, or necessary to, the management of the site, is required is required to make an appropriate assessment of the implications for the site in view of the site's conservation objectives.[122] The terms 'plan' and 'project' are not defined in the Regulations. However, in *R. (Friends of the Earth) v Environment Agency*[123] it was held that 'plan' and 'project' should be given a wide meaning.[124] It is important to observe that the concept of plan or project is not restricted to that which requires planning permission.[125]

The competent authority must only agree to the plan or project if it is satisfied that it will not adversely affect the integrity of a European Site or a European offshore marine site.[126] The authority is required to address its mind to the effect of the plan or project on the particular site, in contrast to any particular species.[127] In the European Court of Justice case of *Landelijke Verening tot Hehoud van de Waddenzee, Nederlandse Vereniging tot Bescherming van Vogels v Staatssecretaris van Landbouw, Natuurbeheer en Visserij*[128] it was held that any authority which authorised a plan or project could only lawfully do so if there was no reasonable scientific doubt of the adverse effect of the plan or project on the site in question. Thus, a precautionary approach requires to be taken by the authority.[129] Furthermore, the relevant risk which is posed to the site by the plan or project must be real, rather than hypothetical.[130]

However, approval can be given for the plan or project if there are no alternative solutions and the plan or programme must be carried out for imperative reasons of overriding public interest.[131] The regulations do not prescribe the form which the relevant assessment must take. However, in the Inner House case of *Cairngorms Campaign v Cairngorms National Parks Authority*[132] it was held that the relevant competent authority had wide discretion as to the form and content of the relevant assessment it undertakes.[133]

By way of conclusion, one can endorse the view of Reid pertinently observes that in practice the need to protect European sites has led to the refusal of development proposals which have included windfarms and other renewable energy projects.[134]

Sites of special scientific interest

The Nature Conservation (Scotland) Act 2004 places a duty on Scottish Natural Heritage (SNH) to notify certain persons if SNH considers that land is of special interest by reason of any of its natural features, that is to say, its flora, fauna, geological or geomorphological features.[135] The notification of the site of special scientific interest (SSSI) must be accompanied by certain information which includes a map of the relevant site including details of acts which, in the opinion of SNH, are likely to damage a natural feature (that is, operations requiring consent).[136] The notification takes effect on the date on which it is given.[137] The relevant persons to whom notification requires to be given include the relevant owner and occupier, the Scottish Ministers and the local authority in whose land any part of the SSSI is situated.[138] Notification must also be given to members of the public.[139] The notification must be accompanied by a site management statement.[140] A site management statement is prepared by SNH and provides guidance to owners and occupiers of land within a SSSI on how that land is to be conserved and enhanced.[141] SNH is required to review the operations which require consent which are specified in a SSSI notification if SNH either if is requested to do so by the owner or occupier of land within a site of SSSI or if SNH thinks fit.[142] However, no review may be carried out within six years of the date on which notification was given of the SSSI, or within six years of the previous review or if SNH considers it fit to do so, it has the agreement of every owner and occupier of land within the SSSI.[143] SNH has the power to de-notify a SSSI.[144]

The Act makes provision for operations which affect SSSIs. Public bodies are placed under a duty not to conduct any activities which are likely to damage any natural feature which is specified in a SSSI notification except, subject to certain exceptions, with the written consent of SNH.[145] The Act also makes provision in relation to operations which require the consent of regulatory authorities before they can proceed.[146] The Scottish Ministers and local authorities *inter alia* have been designated regulatory authorities for the purposes of the Act.[147] The relevant authority is required to notify SNH before granting permission for any operation which is likely to damage any natural feature which is specified in a SSSI notification.[148] The regulatory authority is required to have regard to any advice which is given by SNH.[149] Owners and occupiers of land within a SSSI must not carry out or cause or permit to be carried out any operation requiring consent except with the written consent of SNH.[150] The Act also provides that the consent of SNH is not required in certain other circumstances, for example, where the operation is authorised by planning permission.[151] The Act allows relevant owners and occupiers of land to appeal to the Scottish Land Court in relation to *inter alia* the refusal of SNH to grant consent to any operation or in relation to any condition which is attached to consent.[152]

Offences

It is made an offence for any person to intentionally or recklessly damage any natural feature which is specified in a SSSI notification.[153] However, no offence is committed if it is shown that the act was the incidental result of a lawful operation and the person who carried out the operation took reasonable precautions for the purposes of carrying out the act, or did not foresee, and he could not reasonably have foreseen, that the act would have been an incidental result of carrying out that lawful operation, and furthermore, that he took all steps that were practicable in the circumstances to minimise the damage caused.[154] It is also made an offence for a public body or owner or occupier of land within a SSSI to carry out any operation within a SSSI without the consent of SNH.[155] It is also made an offence for a public authority which has carried out an operation on a SSSI to fail to restore the land in accordance with advice which has been given by SNH, or for the owner or occupier of land to fail to restore the land to its former condition in accordance with any advice given by SNH, in relation to operations which do not require the consent of SNH. SNH may serve a restoration notice on the responsible person in relation to these offences.[156] The purpose of this is to require the relevant person to execute works which are specified in the notice to restore, as far as reasonably practicable, the feature which has been damaged, to its former condition.

Finally, the Keeper of Registers is required to keep a register which contains certain information relating to SSSIs.[157] The register is required to be made available for public inspection.[158]

In 2014 there were 1,425 SSSIs in Scotland which covered an area of 1,022,260 hectares which represents about 13 per cent of the land in Scotland.[159]

Nature conservation orders

The Nature Conservation (Scotland) Act 2004 makes provision for nature conservation orders (NCOs). Power is given to the Scottish Ministers to make an NCO in respect of land for the purpose of conserving any natural feature of the land concerned (irrespective of whether the land is an SSSI), or the land is considered to be of special interest, or in order to comply with an international obligation.[160] The relevant NCO may prohibit (or partly prohibit) the carrying-out of a specified operation and the circumstances (if any) in which the carrying-out of the activity is not prohibited, and prohibiting any person from carrying out the operation other than in those circumstances. An NCO may be made in relation to land which either is a SSSI, or forms part of a SSSI; or land which is not or does not form part of a SSSI but, nonetheless, is considered by the Scottish Ministers to be of special interest by reason of any of its natural features; or land which is contiguous to, or which the Scottish Ministers consider to be otherwise associated with, land which is an SSSI, or is of special interest by virtue of its natural features; or any combination of types of aforementioned land.[161] The circumstances which may be specified in an NCO include, for example, the carrying-out of an operation at a particular time, or in accordance with particular conditions.[162] An NCO has effect on being made.[163] However, the NCO ceases to have effect unless the NCO is confirmed within twelve months or such longer period as is agreed with every relevant owner or occupier of land.[164] An NCO may be amended or revoked by the Scottish Ministers.[165] Any person who either carries out or causes or permits to be carried out a prohibited operation on any land to which an NCO relates commits an offence.[166]

It has been observed that NCOs (which are restricted to Scotland) do not play a major part in the conservation of habitat.[167] Indeed, at the time of writing,[168] there are only 9 NCOs which are operational in Scotland.[169]

Land management orders

The Act makes further provision in relation to land which either is an SSSI, or forms part of an SSSI, or land which is contiguous with, or land which SNH considers to be otherwise associated with, an SSSI, or any combination of such descriptions of land.[170] SNH is given the power to propose to the Scottish Ministers that a land management order (LMO) be made in relation to such land.[171] SNH must be of the opinion that an LMO is necessary or expedient for the purpose of conserving, restoring or otherwise enhancing any natural feature which is specified in a SSSI notification. However, such a proposal can only be made where SNH has offered to enter into a land management agreement in relation to the relevant land, and the offer has been unsuccessful, or where a person has failed to comply with a management agreement.[172] Any proposal which SNH makes must *inter alia* describe the relevant land in relation to which an LMO is sought, the relevant natural feature and also any operations which should be carried out for the purposes of restoring or otherwise enhancing the natural feature.[173] The Scottish Ministers have three months in which to respond to the proposal of SNH.[174] The Scottish Ministers may either make an LMO in the manner which has been proposed, or make such other LMO as they think fit in relation to the relevant land or any part of the land to which the proposal relates, or they may refuse to make an LMO. The LMO must, *inter alia*, be accompanied by a map, describe the natural feature which is to be conserved, and also specify the operations which are to be carried out on the land for the purpose of conserving, restoring or otherwise enhancing the relevant natural feature.[175] The LMO must also specify the persons who are to carry out the operations and how and when they are to be carried out. The LMO must also specify any operations (that is, an 'excluded operation') which must not be carried out on the land. Finally, the LMO must specify the date on which the order comes into effect and the period for which it is to have effect.

Any owner or occupier of land to which the LMO relates who is aggrieved by a decision of the Scottish Ministers to make an LMO or its terms or conditions may appeal to the Scottish Land Court within twenty-eight days.[176]

The Scottish Ministers have the power to review an LMO in order to decide whether it should be amended or revoked.[177] However, a review must take place within six years of the date on which the land management order was made.[178] Any subsequent review requires to be made within six years of the previous review. On completion of the review the Scottish Ministers may make an order which amends or revokes the LMO.[179]

It is an offence for any person without reasonable excuse, to fail to carry out an operation in the manner which is required by an LMO.[180] Furthermore, it is made an offence for any person to carry out an excluded operation on the land to which the LMO relates.[181]

In the event of any operation which is required by an LMO not being carried out within the specified period, or being carried out otherwise than in the manner which is specified, SNH is absolved from the obligation to make any payment in respect of the LMO and, furthermore, may recover any payments which have been made.[182] SNH may also carry out the relevant work and recover costs from the person who was required to carry out the operation.

Ramsar sites

Wetlands are among the most diverse and productive ecosystems.[183] However, they continue to be degraded and converted to other uses. The Act makes special provision for the protection of wetlands which are designated under the Ramsar Convention[184] The Convention gives the expression 'wetlands' a broad meaning, and includes areas of marsh, fen, peatland, or water, whether natural or artificial, permanent or temporary, with water which is flowing, fresh or brackish or salt, including areas of marine water the depth of which at low tide does not exceed six metres.[185] Each contracting party to the Convention is required to designate suitable wetlands within its territory for inclusion in a List of Wetlands of International Importance which is maintained by a bureau which is established under the Convention.[186] Contracting parties are required to promote the conservation of such wetlands.[187] Where a wetland is designated under the Convention for inclusion in the List, the Scottish Ministers must give SNH notice of that designation.[188] In turn, SNH must give notice of such a designation to the following:

(i)   the owner and occupier of the wetland or any part of it,
(ii)   the planning authority for the district in which the wetland, or any part of it, is situated,
(iii) the relevant National Park authority,
(iv)   statutory undertakers which SNH believes may carry out operations which may affect the wetland or any part of it, and

(v) every relevant regulatory authority which SNH considers likely to have functions which relate to any wetland or part of it.[189]

Perhaps, in practical terms, the main significance of Ramsar sites lies simply in the fact of their existence being brought to the attention of relevant bodies. In numerical terms, in 2014 there were fifty-one Ramsar sites in Scotland.[190]

Environmental Liability Directive

The Environmental Liability Directive[191] ('the ELD') establishes a framework of environmental liability which is based on the polluter pays principle to prevent and remedy environmental damage.[192] The phrase 'environmental damage' is a term of art, and includes damage to protected species and natural habitats.[193] In order to fall within the scope of the ELD, the damage must be caused by (a) operations which now fall within the scope of the Industrial Emissions Directive[194] (IED) or (b) damage which has been caused to protected species and natural habitats which is caused by 'occupational activities' other than those which are covered by the IED.[195] As far as (a) is concerned, liability in terms of the ELD Directive is strict. However, as far as (b) is concerned, liability only lies if the operator of the relevant plant is at fault or has been negligent. The ELD makes exceptions to liability.[196] For example, damage which is caused by an act of armed conflict or hostilities, civil war or insurrection is exempt as is damage which is caused by a natural phenomenon of exceptional inevitable and irresistible character. Where environmental damage has not occurred but there is an imminent threat of such damage occurring, the relevant occupier is placed under a duty to take, without delay, the necessary preventative measures.[197] In the case where environmental damage has occurred, the operator is required, without delay, to inform the relevant competent authority of all relevant aspects of the situation and to take all practical steps in order to immediately control, contain or otherwise manage the relevant contaminants and/or any other damage factors in order to limit or prevent further environmental damage and adverse effect on human health or the impairment of services.[198] Operators are required to identify appropriate remedial measures and submit them to the relevant competent authority for its approval.[199] The competent authority is required to decide which remedial measures require to be implemented in accordance with the ELD.[200] Finally, the operator is required to bear the costs for the relevant remedial and preventative action.

The ELD is implemented in Scotland by the Environmental Liability (Scotland) Regulations 2009.[201] The relevant competent authority in relation to environmental damage or an imminent threat of such damage is the Scottish Ministers as far as damage to either protected species or natural habitats in coastal waters is concerned.[202] As far as damage which is caused to protected species or natural habitats in any other place is concerned, the competent authority is SNH. Finally, as far as damage to waters or land is concerned, the competent authority is the Scottish Environment Protection Agency (SEPA).

Biodiversity

The concept of biodiversity owes its origins to the United Nations Environment Programme Convention on Biological Biodiversity 1992.[203] As far as domestic law is concerned, the Nature Conservation (Scotland) Act 2004 places a duty on every public body and office holder to further the conservation of biodiversity so far as is consistent with the proper exercise of such functions.[204] The expression 'biological diversity' is given[205] the same meaning as that in Art 2 of the Convention and means:

> the variability among living organisms from all sources including *inter alia* terrestrial, marine and other aquatic ecosystems and the ecological complexes of which they are part; this includes diversity between species and of ecosystems.

Reid argues that the power in this definition is that it covers several different but interconnected forms of diversity, all of which must considered if the natural heritage of the earth is to be passed down to future generations.[206] The Scottish Ministers are under a duty to prepare and publish a Scottish Biodiversity Strategy (SBS).[207] The Scottish Ministers are required within either three years of the date on which they first designate a SBS, or three years of the date when a report was last laid before the Scottish Parliament, to lay a report to the Scottish Parliament regarding the implementation of the SBS.[208] Public bodies are also required to prepare and publish a biodiversity report within three years from 1 January 2012, or within three years of the date on which the last report was published.[209] If a public body is established after that date, that body is required to prepare and publish a report within three years of the date on which it was established.[210]

Nature reserves

Nature reserves were established by the National Parks and Access to the Countryside Act 1949. A nature reserve is land which is managed for the purpose of providing opportunities for the study of and research which relates to flora and fauna.[211] The management of nature reserves is the responsibility of Scottish Natural Heritage (SNH).[212] SNH is empowered to enter into a management agreement with the owner, lessee and occupier of any land, where it is considered expedient to do so in the national interest, that the relevant land should be managed by SNH.[213] SNH is empowered to make byelaws for the protection of any nature reserve which it manages.[214] The byelaws may contain provisions which relate *inter alia* to restricting entry into and the restriction of movement within a nature reserve of persons, vehicles, boats and animals.[215] The byelaws may also prohibit or restrict the killing, taking, molesting or disturbance of any wild creature in a nature reserve.

A local authority may also establish a nature reserve in its area.[216] The powers which a local authority can exercise in relation to its nature reserve are similar to those possessed by SNH in relation to its nature reserve.[217] A local authority is required to exercise its functions in relation to its nature reserves in consultation with SNH.[218]

Invasive non-native species of animals and plants

The Wildlife and Countryside Act 1981 makes special provision in relation to the introduction of new species and plants into the environment.

It is made an offence for any person to release, or allow to escape from captivity, any animal to a place which is outwith its native range, or he allows to escape any animal which is of a type which is specified by order by the Scottish Ministers, or to cause any animal which is outwith the control of any person to be at a place outwith its native range.[219] An exception is made in relation to the common pheasant and the red-legged partridge which are allowed to escape from captivity for the purposes of being killed by shooting.[220] The Act makes similar provision in relation to plants. Any person who either plants or causes to grow any plant in the wild which is outwith its native range commits an offence.[221] However, in relation to both other animals and plants, the Scottish Ministers can exclude the animals and plants from the scope of the Act.[222] Furthermore, the Scottish Ministers may, by order, exclude any person from the scope of the Act.[223]

Finally, brief mention should be made of the recent EU regulation on the prevention and management of invasive species.[224] The principal aim of the regulation, which of course has direct effect, is to prevent, minimise and mitigate the adverse effects on biodiversity of the introduction and spread within the EU of alien species.[225]

National Parks

In international terms, national parks were introduced relatively recently. The National Parks (Scotland) Act 2000 ('the Act') makes provision for the establishment of national parks in Scotland. The Scottish Ministers are empowered to designate an area in Scotland as a national park.[226] However, a national park may be established only if certain conditions are satisfied.[227] These conditions are that the relevant area is important by virtue of its natural heritage, or is important by a combination of both natural and cultural heritage; that the designation of an area as national park would meet the special needs of the area; and that such designation would be the best means of ensuring that the national park aims are collectively achieved in relation to that area in a coordinated way. The Act specifically defines these aims as including conserving and enhancing the natural and cultural heritage of the area and promoting the sustainable use and natural resources of the area.[228] The Scottish Ministers have the power to require Scottish Natural Heritage (SNH), or any other body which appears to them to possess expertise which is relevant to the national parks aims, to consider a national parks proposal and then report to the ministers by a certain date on certain matters.[229] These matters include whether such an area should be designated a national park and also the desirability of designating the area as a national park.[230] In preparing the report, the views of local authorities and community councils require to be taken into account, as well as those of the local business community and others which the reporter thinks fit.[231] After the publication of such a report (or any statement which the Scottish Ministers make to the effect that such a report is not required), the Scottish Ministers may hold a public inquiry.[232] Thereafter, the Scottish Ministers are empowered to make a designation order, either in terms of the national park proposal or with such modifications as the Scottish Ministers think fit.[233] In considering whether to make a designation order, the Scottish Ministers are required to take into consideration the relevant report or statement.[234] Before laying a draft designation order before the Scottish Parliament, the Scottish Ministers are required, *inter alia*, to consult any local authority and community council whose area is included in the order for designation as a national park, and also give the order general publicity.[235] The Scottish Ministers are required to take into account any views which have been expressed by those who have been consulted.[236] A national park authority is required to prepare a national park plan, the main objective of which is to set out how the national park is to be managed.[237] The national park authority is required to periodically review the plan.[238]

Summary

- The Wildlife and Countryside Act 1981 makes provision for the protection of wild animals, plants, sites of special scientific interest, nature reserves and Ramsar sites.
- The Act makes provision for the protection of birds and eggs.
- The Act makes it an offence to intentionally or recklessly kill, injure or take certain wild animals.
- The Act makes special provision for the protection of wild hares and rabbits.
- The Act makes provision for the protection of wild plants.
- The Conservation (Scotland) Act 2004 places a duty on public bodies to further the conservation of biodiversity.
- The Act makes provision for nature conservation orders, and land management orders.
- The Act makes special provision for Ramsar sites.
- The Habitats and Birds Directives are implemented by the Conservation (Natural Habitats) Regulations 1994.

Notes

1. For a comprehensive coverage of the law which relates to nature conservation, see C. Reid, 'Nature conservation', in F. McManus (ed.), *Environmental Law in Scotland* (W. Green/SULI) ch 12. See also C. Reid, *Nature Conservation Law*, 3rd edn (W. Green, 2009).
2. See p. 4-5 incl.
3. C. Reid, 'Environmental legislation in the Scottish Parliament', in volume no. 54, *Miscellany* V1 (Stair Memorial Society: Edinburgh, 2009) 63 at 67.
4. See Chapter 4.
5. The Act also makes provision for limestone pavements.
6. 'Wild bird' means any bird of a species which is ordinarily resident in or is a visitor to any Member State or the European territory of any Member State in a wild state but does not include poultry; ibid. s 27(1).
7. The Wildlife and Countryside Act 1981 Sched A1.
8. Ibid. s 1(1).
9. Ibid. s 1(2).
10. [1988] Crim LR 699.
11. *Kirkland v Robinson* [1987] Crim LR 643.
12. 'Relevant provisions' means such of the provisions of the Protection of Birds Act 1954 to 1967 and any orders made under those Acts, and any provisions

of Part 1 of the Wildlife and Countryside Act 1981 which were in force when the bird or egg was killed or taken, or, as the case may be, the bird, egg, or other thing was sold; ibid s 1(3A).

13. 'Relevant regulations' means Council Regulation 338/97 on the protection of species or wild fauna and flora by regulating trade; and Commission Regulation 1808/2001/EC on the implementation of that Council Regulation, as amended from time to time, or any EU instrument replacing either of them; ibid s 1(3A).

14. In relation to Part 1 of the Act any reference to a bird is a reference to a bird which is included in Part 1 to the schedule, and during the close season to a bird which is included in Part II to the schedule; ibid s 1(7).

15. Ibid. s 1(5).

16. I.e., gather and display.

17. Ibid. s 1(5A).

18. Ibid. s 1(5B).

19. Ibid. s 1(5C).

20. Ibid. s 1(6).

21. The birds to which the exception applies are listed in Part 1 of Sched 2.

22. Ibid. s 2(1). The close season for each bird is defined in s 2(4) of the Act. The close season can be varied by order of the Secretary of State for the whole or a part of Great Britain; ibid. s 2(5).

23. Ibid. s 2(1)(A).

24. Ibid. s 2(3). The birds to which the exception is dis-applied are listed in Part 1A of Sched 2.

25. Ibid. s 2(3A)(3B).

26. Ibid. s 2(3C).

27. Ibid. s 4.

28. Ibid. s 16(1).

29. Ibid. s 16(5).

30. Ibid. s 5(1).

31. Ibid. s 6.

32. Ibid. s 7.

33. Ibid. s 8(1).

34. Ibid. s 9(1). The relevant wild animals are listed in Sched 5 to the Act.

35. Ibid. s 9(2).

36. Ibid. s 9(3).

37. The 'relevant provisions' means such of the provisions of the Conservation of Wild Creatures and Wild Plants Act 1975 and Part 1 of the Wild Life and Conservation Act 1981 as were in force at the time when the animal was killed or taken, or, as the case may be, when the animal or other thing was sold; ibid. s 9(3A).

38. The 'relevant regulations' means Council Regulation 338/97/EC on the protection of species of wild fauna and flora by regulating trade, and Commission Regulation 1808/2001/EC on the implementation of that Council Regulation, as amended from time to time, or any EU instrument which replaces either of them; ibid s 9(3A).
39. Ibid. s 9(4).
40. Ibid. s 9(4A).
41. The Wild Mammals (Protection) Act 1996 s 1.
42. Wildlife and Countryside Act 1981 Sched 6.
43. Marine (Scotland) Act 2010 s 1.
44. Deer (Scotland) Act 1996 s 1.
45. Ibid. s 9(5).
46. Ibid. s 9(5A).
47. Ibid. s 9(6).
48. Ibid. s 10.
49. Ibid. s 10(1).
50. Ibid. s 10(3).
51. Ibid. s 16(3).
52. SI 1994 No 2716, regs 38-41B.
53. Directive 92/43/EEC.
54. Ibid. s 10A(1). 'Close season' means, in relation to a mountain hare, the period in any year beginning with 1 March and ending with 31 July. In relation to a brown hare, 'close season' means the period in any year beginning with 1 February and ending with 30 September; ibid. s 10A(2).
55. Ibid. s 10A(3).
56. Ibid. s 10A(4).
57. Ibid. s 10A(5).
58. Ibid. s 10A(6).
59. Ibid. s 10A(7).
60. Ibid. s 10A(8).
61. Ibid. s 10B(1).
62. Ibid. s 10B(2).
63. An authorised person includes the owner and occupier of the land on which the action is taken and anyone who is authorised by such a person; any person who is authorised in writing by the relevant local authority; and anyone who is authorised by a conservation body; ibid. s 27(1).
64. Ibid. s 10B(3).
65. Ibid. s 10B(4).
66. Ibid. s 10B(5).
67. Agriculture (Scotland) Act 1948, s 39.
68. Wildlife and Countryside Act 1981 s 10B(7).

69. Ibid. s 11G(1).
70. Ibid. s 11G(2).
71. Ibid. s 11H(1).
72. Ibid. s 11H(2).
73. Ibid. s 11H(3).
74. Ibid. s 11I(1).
75. Ibid. s 11(2).
76. Ibid. s 11(3).
77. Ibid. s 11(1).
78. Ibid. s 11A. See the Snares (Training) (Scotland)(No 2) Order 2012 (SSI 2012 No 161) and the Snares (Identification and Tags) (Scotland) Order 2012 (SSI 2012 No 282).
79. Ibid. s 11B.
80. Ibid. s 11C.
81. Ibid. s 11E.
82. Ibid. s 11F(1).
83. Ibid. s 11F(2).
84. Ibid. s 11F(5).
85. Ibid. Sched 6.
86. Protection of Badgers Act 1992 s 1(1).
87. Ibid. s 2.
88. Ibid. s 3(1).
89. Ibid. s 4(1).
90. Ibid. s 4(2).
91. Ibid. s 5.
92. SI 1994 No 2716, Sched 3. See p. 314-15 incl.
93. Marine (Scotland) Act 2010 s 107.
94. Ibid. s 110(1).
95. Deer (Scotland) Act 1996 s 1(1).
96. Ibid. s 5(1). See the Deer (Close seasons) (Scotland) Order 2011 (SSI 2011 No 417).
97. Deer (Scotland) Act 1996 s 17(1).
98. Ibid. ss 18-24.
99. Ibid. s 13(1). The relevant wild plants are listed in Sched 8 to the Act.
100. Ibid. s 13(2).
101. Ibid. s 13(3).
102. Ibid. s 13(3A).
103. Ibid. s 13(4).
104. SI 1994 No 2716 regs 42-3.
105. C. Reid, *Nature Conservation*, 3rd edn (W. Green, 2009) at 5.1.1.
106. Directive 92/43/EEC. For a detailed analysis of the Habitats Directive, see

C. H. Born et al., *The Habitats Directive in its EU Environmental Law Context: European Nature's Best Hope?* (Routledge, 2014).

107. Directive 92/43/EEC Art 3.

108. Directive 79/409/EEC (Revised by Directive 2009/147/EU). In *R. v Secretary of State for the Environment ex p RSPB* [1997] QB 206 the European Court of Justice held that when a Member State was determining whether to designate a particular area an SPA in terms of the Birds Directive, no account could be taken of economic factors. Furthermore, in the Outer House case of *WWF-UK Ltd v Secretary of State for Scotland* [1999] Env LR 632 it was held *inter alia* that the boundary of a SPA fell to be determined by ornithological criteria alone.

109. 1994 SI 2716.

110. Ibid. reg 7(1) In *R. v Secretary of State for the Environment, Transport and the Regions ex p First Corporation Shipping Ltd* (C-371/98) the European Court of Justice held that when a Member State was selecting and determining the boundaries of a site, no account could be taken of economic, social and cultural factors.

111. Ibid. reg 7(4).

112. Ibid. reg 8(1).

113. Ibid. reg 9A(1)(2).

114. Ibid. reg 11(1).

115. Ibid. reg 12(1).

116. Ibid. reg 4(1).

117. Ibid. reg 13(1).

118. Ibid. reg 15(1).

119. Ibid. reg 16(1).

120. Ibid. reg 18(1).

121. Ibid. reg 28(1).

122. Ibid. reg 48(1).

123. [2004] Env LR 31.

124. See also *R. (Akester) v DEFRA and Wightlink Ltd* [2010] EWHC 232. For a useful analysis of this case see (2010) SPEL 93.

125. In *Akester* above, it was held that the introduction of new vessels amounted to a plan or project within the meaning of the Habitats Directive.

126. Ibid. reg 48(5).

127. *Royal Society for the Protection of Birds v Secretary of State for Scotland* [2000] SCT 1272.

128. [2004] ECR 1-7405.

129. See also *Bagmoor Wind Ltd v The Scottish Ministers* [2012] CSIH 93.

130. *R. (on the application of Boggis) v Natural England* [2010] Env LR 13 at 249. See also *Shadwell Estates Ltd v Breckland DC* [2013] Env LR D2.

131. Ibid. reg 49(1).
132. 2014 SC 37.
133. For an analysis of this case see J. Watchman, 'Local plan: appropriate assessment' (2013) 158 SPEL 87. See also *R. (Champion) v North Norfolk DC* [2015] 1 WLR 3710.
134. C. Reid (note 105) at 5.2.29.
135. Nature Conservation (Scotland) Act 2004 s 3(1)(2).
136. Ibid. s 3(4).
137. Ibid. s 3(6).
138. Ibid. s 48(2).
139. Ibid. Sched 1.
140. Ibid. s 4(1).
141. Ibid. s 4(2).
142. Ibid. s 6(1).
143. Ibid. s 6(2).
144. Ibid. s 9.
145. Ibid. s 13(1).
146. Ibid. s 15(1).
147. Ibid. s 15(2); The Nature Conservation (Designation of Relevant Regulatory Authorities) Order 2004 (SSI 2004 No 474).
148. Nature Conservation (Scotland) Act 2004 s 15(3).
149. Ibid. s 15(6).
150. Ibid. s 16(1)
151. Ibid. s 17(1).
152. Ibid. s 18(1)
153. Ibid. s 19(1).
154. Ibid. s 19(2).
155. Ibid. s 19(3).
156. Ibid. s 20A.
157. Ibid. s 22(1). See also the Sites of Special Scientific Interest (Scotland) Regulations 2008 (SSI 2008 No 221).
158. The Nature Conservation (Scotland) Act 2004 s 22(2).
159. Scottish Government official website www.gov.scot.publications/2014/08/8973/21.
160. Ibid. s 23(1)(2).
161. Ibid. s 23(3).
162. Ibid. s 23(4).
163. Ibid. s 23(6).
164. Ibid. s 23(7)
165. Ibid. s 24.
166. Ibid. s 27(1).

167. C. Reid, *Nature Conservation Law*, 3rd edn (W. Green, 2009) at 5.6.5.
168. May 2015.
169. SNH official website www.snh.gov.uk/protecting-scotlands-nature/protected-areas/orders/nature/ (last accessed 15 May 2015).
170. Ibid. s 29(1).
171. Ibid. s 29(2).
172. Ibid. s 29(3)(4).
173. Ibid. s 29(7).
174. Ibid. s 30(1).
175. Ibid. s 31(1)
176. Ibid. s 34(1)(2).
177. Ibid. s 32(1).
178. Ibid. s 32(2).
179. Ibid. s 32(3).
180. Ibid. s 36(1).
181. Ibid. s 36(2).
182. Ibid. s 37(1)(2).
183. Ramsar official site www.ramsar.org (last accessed 22 April 2015).
184. The Ramsar Convention is the Convention on Wetlands of International Importance especially as Wildfowl Habitat, signed at Ramsar on 2 February 1971 (as amended).
185. Ibid. Art 1.
186. Ibid. Art 2.
187. Ibid. Art 3.
188. Nature Conservation (Scotland) Act 2004 s 38(1).
189. Ibid. s 38(2).
190. Scottish Government official website, www.gov.scot/Publications/2014/08/8973/21.
191. Directive 2004/35/EC.
192. Ibid. Art 1.
193. Ibid. Art 2. 'Protected species and habitats' are defined in the Article as species which are mentioned in Art 4(2) of the Birds Directive or those which are listed in the Habitats Directive (see p. 313).
194. Directive 2010/75/ EU (Recast).
195. Directive 2004/35/EC Art 3.
196. Ibid. Art 4.
197. Ibid. Art 5.
198. Ibid. Art 6.
199. Ibid. Art 7.
200. Ibid. Annex 2.
201. SSI 2009 No 266.

202. Ibid. reg 7(1).
203. United Nations Programme on Biodiversity of 5 June 1992
204. Nature Conservation (Scotland) Act s 1(1).
205. Ibid. s 1(2).
206. C. Reid (note 167) at 1.2.2.
207. Nature Conservation (Scotland) Act 2004, s 2(1)(2).
208. Ibid. s 2(7).
209. Ibid. s 2A(1).
210. Ibid. s 2A(3).
211. National Parks and Access to the Countryside Act 1949 s 15.
212. Ibid. s 15A(1).
213. Ibid. s 16(1).
214. Ibid. s 20(1).
215. Ibid. s 20(2).
216. Ibid. s 21(1).
217. Ibid. s 21(4).
218. Ibid. s 21(6).
219. Wildlife and Countryside Act 1981 s 14(1).
220. Ibid. s 14(2A).
221. Ibid. s 14(2).
222. Ibid. s 14(2B).
223. Ibid. s 14(2C).
224. Reg 1143/2014/EU.
225. Ibid. Art 1.
226. The National Parks (Scotland) Act 2000 s 2(1).
227. Ibid. s 2(2).
228. Ibid. s 1.
229. Ibid. s 3(1).
230. Ibid. s 3(2).
231. Ibid. s 3(5).
232. Ibid. s 5(1).
233. Ibid. s 6(1).
234. Ibid. s 6(2).
235. Ibid. s 6(3).
236. Ibid. s 6(5).
237. Ibid. s 11.
238. Ibid. s 13(1).

Index